Expectant Peoples

EXPECTANT PEOPLES

Nationalism and Development

by

THE AMERICAN UNIVERSITIES FIELD STAFF

Edward A. Bayne · Frank Bonilla
Louis Dupree · Charles F. Gallagher
Willard A. Hanna · Selig S. Harrison
Edwin S. Munger · Richard H. Nolte
Lawrence Olson · Richard W. Patch
Albert Ravenholt · K. H. Silvert

UNDER THE EDITORSHIP OF

K. H. SILVERT

With a preface by Kenneth W. Thompson

RANDOM HOUSE · NEW YORK

To the People of the New Nations

Preface

□□□□□□□□□□□

For a world in the throes of multiple revolutions involving rapid social, political, and technological change, nationalism is a common force of organic power and compelling dynamism. It should be obvious throughout "the presently underdeveloped and intermediately developed worlds" that nationalism shows little sign of yielding to the logic of early regional or global union, despite pressures for military security and economic viability. Ironically, the imperatives of national unity and self-conscious national loyalties in Asia and Africa find expression at a moment in history when in important respects the nation-state has, for all practical purposes, become obsolete. Yet for the present in the emerging new nations long pent-up aspirations for self-determination and economic growth are linked with the achievement of national identity. Social justice and a place in the sun are goals men stubbornly pursue within the framework of revolutionary nationalism.

Yet nationalism for the emergent state is far more than a carbon copy of classical European nationalism. The new nationalism is unique. This fact escapes those who associate the new nations of the present with the Western industrialized nationhood of fifty or one hundred and fifty years ago. The drive to include all social groups within new societies is distinct from nation-building by a slowly developing middle class, even though a social class at the center may still be essential to a free and independent constitutional state. Having refuted the Marxist claim that free societies were predestined to fractionate into sharply separated rich and poor peoples, the developed countries are called on to join in partnership with the new nations to reduce the gap separating rich and poor nations. In this common objective, men of good will are caught up in a race against time and forces of chaos and disruption that threaten to engulf broad areas of the world.

The hope and faith of the civilized world that man providentially can be master of his fate persists in the developing nations. This faith coexists with circumstances that hem in and restrict those who strive for national unity: limited resources, leadership in short supply, soaring expectations and minimal cohesiveness. If nationalism is often irrational and emotional against the background of the burdens it must bear, those who study it must be steadfast in the search for reason, clarity, and understanding. They must apply the calipers of clear-headed analysis and penetrating definition to the new and to the old nationalism. They must relate nationalism to modernization, the development process, social justice, and the messianic claims of revolutionary political movements. They must answer the questions "What?", "Why?", "How?", and "To what end?".

Expectant Peoples: Nationalism and Development is a bold and daring attempt to explain and evaluate contemporary nationalism. The editor, Professor K. H. Silvert, who stands in the forefront of a new generation of political theorists, joins with an outstanding group of imaginative colleagues from the pioneering American Universities Field Staff in imposing an intellectual framework on their subject. Thus while they explore the diversity of nationalism "from Manila to La Paz," they do so in terms of an ordered conceptual picture of a sprawling landscape. They derive and employ "a working concept which would not violate European experience, be fitting to today's emergent nations, and contribute . . . by virtue of its possibly universal application." In so doing, they follow a functional approach that seeks to do justice to the varieties of patterns and institutions of nationalism. They see nationalism as involving "the acceptance of the state as the impersonal and ultimate arbiter of human affairs." They measure a succession of cases against this mold. For them, praising or blaming nationalism is not enough; they strive to lay bare the essentials of its present-day forms.

The role of the nation in arbitrating social disputes and providing for choice within a relatively impersonal secular order is for the authors the core and model of nationalism. It assumes the acceptance of civil authority in the realm of "intermediate and relative truth." The editor concedes that the underdeveloped world abounds with examples of uneven growth and maladjustment in the achievement and acceptance of an impartial secular order. He notes the problem of "elite groups faced with the problem of sharing their power if eventually they are to lead true nations, and the possibility of losing their near monopoly of power should they decide to share it." He acknowledges that authority may be arbitrary as often as it is impartial. The concept and model of nationalism employed raises problems, as do all other competing definitions, but the authors do not shrink from examining cases adverse to their thesis.

There are causative factors extraneous to nationalism that shape divergent political systems, for while nationalism is "necessary to democracy but insufficient to assure it . . . it is necessary in turn to totalitarianism, but also insufficient to guarantee its emergence." Both the flowering of healthy national development and the pitfalls of a corrupted super-nationalism rest on factors of class, ideology, values, bureaucracy, and international relations that intertwine with an unfolding nationalism. "The political party structure is . . . almost always under great strain, driven by the growing social need for impersonalism, and hampered by the continuing great importance of charisma."

As this sampling of the authors' trend of thought may suggest, the great merit of *Expectant Peoples* derives from its intellectual rigor, its honesty in the face of facts, and its marriage of the concrete and the general. Its studies of distinct nationalism in developed and less-developed states, its examination of both traditional and modern forms, its inquiries into culture, ideology, class, and race combine to form a rich and encyclopedic treatise on nationalism. No one who seeks his bearings in this complex and vital realm can for the future with easy conscience overlook this important contribution. A remarkable group of men possessing extraordinary overseas experience, who combine the philosopher's instincts with the practical grasp of men of affairs, have cut a fresh swath in thinking about nationalism. Everyone profiting from this book will hope for other full-scale studies by the American Universities Field Staff in the future.

KENNETH W. THOMPSON

Foreword

□□□□□□□□□□□

Perhaps it is for the best that in the Western developed countries the word "state" and all of its relatives should emit a partially unappetizing aroma. Such words and phrases as "statism," the commonly used French *étatisme*, interventionism, government, politics, politicians, leaders, ideologists, intellectuals, representatives of the people, and civil servants all connote potential if not actual oppression, the possibility that public power may be used to the detriment of individual freedom and democratic institutions. This suspicion is long-standing; the West, after all, is the site of the cultural invention of the nation-state, the most powerful form of social organization yet devised. There is nothing casual, then, about a deep-rooted fear of a creation without which we cannot maintain our life style, but which nonetheless constantly threatens to backlash against that very manner of life. In the developing lands, however, the independent state is usually seen only as the keystone of future progress, freedom, and dignity. This preoccupation with nation in the emergent countries is a profound revelation of their involvement with the explosion of Western culture, even though the developed lands themselves may fail to appreciate fully this re-creation of their own image, forgetting the fundamentally affirmative aspects of their own pattern of the secular nation-state. This misunderstanding is being ever widened by the increasingly obvious need of the industrial states for greater international confidence and commitment.

The justification for yet another book on nationalism is the attempt to re-examine conventional and stereotyped views and offer some theoretical suggestions and fresh data. Thus our first task was that of stripping bare the concept of nation, treating it as an artifact of social organization with a given relationship to industrial development and modernism. A value judgment at that stage was implied only as a reflection of a general acceptance or rejection of the entire constellation of effects called "modern" or "developed" or "Western" civilization. To be in favor of development is, we think, also to accept the kind of state organization necessary for it. Judgments, however, came easily to the several authors at other levels of the matter: in the decisions of leaders, the development of ideology, the borrowing of concepts and administrative practices from other lands—in all those areas which are the product of man's choice and which may make of the development process an exciting and optimistic adventure, or a desperately grisly exercise in violence, repression, and misery. We offer examples of both kinds of human experience.

Our concern with nationalism in the American Universities Field Staff is natural, for we are corporatively involved with the emergent nations where no intellectual question more urgently presses than a controlled knowledge of what the nation-state is all about. Indeed, the decision to work together on this matter was made when the AUFS was only two or three years old by the then-executive director, Phillips Talbot, now on leave as an Assistant Secretary of State. Because this venture is the first in cooperative book-writing undertaken by the AUFS, a word about the institution itself and about the techniques used to hinge the country studies together is in order.

The American Universities Field Staff is in its twelfth year, an autonomous corporate creature of a combination of American universities—Dartmouth College, the Harvard Graduate School of Business Administration, Brown University, Michigan State University, Indiana University and other affiliated Indiana colleges and universities, the University of Kansas, the University of Alabama, Tulane University, Carleton College, the California Institute of Technology, and the University of Hawaii. Our function is to inform our academic constituency concerning as wide a spectrum as our time and intellectual abilities allow of social and humanistic happenings in the developing countries which thus far are our almost exclusive area of interest. Naturally we seek to make ourselves as useful to others outside academic life as our resources permit and interest demands. We normally spend a year and a half or two years resident in our area of study, then return for visits to the campuses of the supporting institutions for an academic year; the cycle then begins anew after a period dedicated to writing or whatever else may restore the spirit and enthusiasm. We are but fourteen persons in all. The only contributor to this volume not at one time a regular member of the AUFS is Mr. Selig S. Harrison, New Delhi correspondent of *The Washington Post*, who has admirably filled in India for us in the absence of Mr. Talbot. Mr. Edwin S. Munger has left the AUFS for the California Institute of Technology, and Mr. Richard H. Nolte is now Director of the Institute of Current World Affairs.

AUFS associates not only work from Manila to La Paz, but they have also been very variously trained. Our common denominators are long tenure in foreign lands, a comfortable adjustment to foreign cultures, and a good knowledge of a wide spread of American academic requirements, especially in the social sciences. A firm rule of the organization is that each man be free to define his work as his professional judgment may indicate; participation in any such cooperative venture as this book is a voluntary matter. Under these conditions the coordination of our efforts and the agreement to centralize our thoughts about one single theoretical approach depended entirely on the conviction of each person involved. The procedure followed—and its spelling out is necessary, to indicate how we have arrived at comparability of materials—is that the editor prepared an initial analytically descriptive statement of the breadth of the subject, which was sent to all members of the AUFS. Then, in all but one case, one or sometimes many personal discussions between editor and contributor took place in order to determine what part of the total subject each person would emphasize because of the nature of his case. Then, in collaboration with Frank Bonilla, the editor prepared a theoretical statement sent out to reinforce the first descriptive analysis. This scheme, listing definitions, hypotheses, and propositions, is included as an appendix; it was distributed twenty months before the preparation of the final manuscript. And then normal procedure was followed: contributors mailed their chapters to the editor, letters flowed back and forth, new drafts were written, the final organization decided upon, and the concluding considerations weighed. The process of actual preparation of the book, from the initial descriptive statement to this foreword, has taken three years; the first formal discussions between the executive director and the editor on this matter date back to early 1955.

The most difficult problem we faced was comparability, of course. We had no intention of preparing yet another collection of articles about strange lands, their only connection a hard binding. We needed a conceptual cover broad enough to allow everyone—from anthropologists to political scientists working from Afghanistan to Japan—to be comfortable, and yet not so broad as to make our subject floppily embrace everything political, social, economic, educational, and familial. Because we presumed that each case would be used to accent one specific facet of the subject, the remainder merely to be sketched in, we also had to become mutually convinced that at one level we were all indeed speaking of a single common human occurrence. How well we have succeeded in blending personalities, theory, data, and cases is not for us to say.

The first chapter offers a survey of some major ideas out of the literature of nationalism and a discussion of the theoretical stand taken in common by the authors of this book. The first three cases treat of countries whose populations cover the spread from nomads to sophisticated nationalist intellectuals; the second two concern themselves with crises of political leadership and national consolidation in the early stages of independent nationhood; the next pair treat the relationship between culture and ideology; there follow two cases of race and caste inhibitions to national identification, and three examples of class and value impediments to full national participation and self-sustaining development. Although it was not consciously so planned, this order also roughly follows the level of development of the countries studied—from most underdeveloped Afghanistan and Saudi Arabia to most complex and industrial Argentina and Japan. These chapters were not difficult to organize on three dimensions: the manner of treatment by individual author, the type of national problem, and the country's general level of development. This organizational fact is one of the most heartening indications of the ease of adjustment of our collaboration, if not necessarily of the validity of the theoretical approach.

We owe thanks to the Rockefeller Foundation for assistance to the AUFS in the accomplishment of this study; perhaps more important, we are grateful for their concrete demonstration of confidence in this subject and this manner of approaching cross-cultural analysis. The Carnegie Corporation, too, should be thanked for making it possible for the editor and Frank Bonilla to devote a long and uninterrupted period to work on social development and national identification in Latin America, an empirical and theoretical study still in preparation, but one whose working out cast light on much of the thinking underlying this volume.

There can be no individual acknowledgments to the many persons in many lands who have aided in this undertaking. Instead, we have dedicated this volume to them, with our hopes for their success in strengthening the best of their traditions in accommodation with the best of modern life toward a more fruitful existence for all.

K. H. S.

Contents

□□□□□□□□□□

Contents : *xxi*

Contents

Expectant Peoples

Introduction

The Strategy of the Study of Nationalism

K. H. SILVERT

Clio is a fickle and seductive Muse. She tempts us to pride ourselves on our uniqueness and yet to solace ourselves with our necessarily helpless submission to preordained repetition, to our "being swept into the future by irresistible forces."[1] Philosophers succumb to her wiles by building systems of guesses about the future based on intuitions about the past, and good citizens respond to politicians who exhort the living to action in the name of the spirits of the dead. But if History betrays, she is also betrayed. There are those who use her shabbily and carelessly for the polemical pleasure of the moment, and those who mystify the past in order to lead us into a greater irrationality of the future. But the commonest of all despoilers of History is the little man of great smugness tranquilizing himself with "there's nothing new under the sun."

Rapid change and dazzling variety are today's dialectic.

[1] This phrase is used by Karl R. Popper in his highly controversial book, *The Poverty of Historicism*, Boston: 1957, p. 160.

In confounding array there spread before us bushmen and Englishmen, shamans and astrophysicists, tribal gerontocracies and supranational organizations. That some countries can be tabbed "affluent" and "overdeveloped" while others labor along at subsistence is not alone a matter for moral judgment, but also a challenge thrown down for our fresh vision by a disparity unique in human events. If history can aid us to understand our world, in turn the wealth of variety about us might better enable us to understand history. The discrimination of the historically unique from the humanly universal is an unavoidable obligation of those who pretend to discover the dynamics of contemporary change.

Our purpose in this volume is to explore the transformations in the presently underdeveloped and intermediately developed worlds, the powerful movements leading to an end of classical colonialism and the establishment of new constellations of nations, or at least of political states invested with formal sovereignty. We shall hobble ourselves in this task if we succumb unthinkingly to historical parallelism or the easy notion that we are treating of societies "fifty (or a hundred and fifty) years behind the United States." That there can be no neat temporal relationship must be clear to everyone, of course, for certainly the United States was never in its past equivalent to contemporary India, nor was any other portion of the present industrialized world. More subtle functional comparisons do suggest themselves, however. If we carefully and exclusively use loose chronologically lineal comparisons to mean that India is still largely a traditional society, in great part pre-industrial and so forth, then of course we are justified in making certain cautious comparisons with European phenomena. And should we wish to add that at some future date world societies may grow closer together as technology and aspirations and social circumstances come into equivalence, then we may be pardoned our desire to peer ahead. "Historical chronology, in other words, is not always scientific chronology."[2]

Whatever the process of development, however, we should be explicit in defining the core of what we mean by "modernism." Certainly all modern societies have created attitudes, social

[2] Leonard Reissman, "Class, the City, and Social Cohesion," *International Review of Community Development*, No. 7, 1961, p. 41.

devices, and traditions which permit orderly institutionalized change; they also all assume, in one or another degree, that public decisions must be secular, pragmatically derived, and subject to empirical test. The self-sustaining nature of change, supported by appropriate values and by other social institutions as well as by the state, is probably the most important single characteristic of modern society.

To return to the problem of historical comparison, then, it is clearly incorrect to imply that Indians or any other pre-industrial peoples must follow the same route to "modernism" as Europe, at the very least because the starting places are different. In addition, contemporary thought now offers various competing ideologies of development such as Western liberal gradualism, Soviet forced mobilization of resources, or the Indian mixed program. But even more important, the new technological practices and scientific attitudes in currency to-day make the development process intrinsically different in certain respects from that of the past. Not only does the present level of technology force very rapid and large-scale industrialization, but mass communications also permit cultural penetration and change to proceed extremely quickly, demonstrating "human nature" to be very malleable indeed. These two factors combine to induce a velocity linking economic to social and political development in manners substantively different from the experiences of the past. The mixture of the traditional with the modern occurs so rapidly as to produce immediate impacts throughout all levels of the affected societies.

The ideas of the national world are another factor new to history playing on the prenational world; not only the new techniques but the baggage of values and norms they carry with them are unique. When England was going through the process of the slow emergence of a strong and self-conscious middle class there was no hortatory body of doctrine or concrete messianic example urging that no groups should be left outside the social pale, that society should be "classless." Underdeveloped nations now have the economic model of the Western industrialized countries to demonstrate that class differences can effectively be blunted, and the communist ideological teaching that they should be erased in some Utopian future. The modernization process now tempts to total revolution instead of only partial adjustment, to learning how to walk and run and fly at the same time. We can no longer take comfortable refuge in explaining today's violence by arguing that "they are going through their own French Revolution." Revolutions of development now have for their purpose not only the "liberating" of a middle class, but also the extension of participation to a lower class which is not a proletariat in the sense of being helplessly alienated, a permanently marginal company of "sub-humans." The politicians of development must now answer to immediate demands for permitting lower economic groups to be identified with the total society, and provided with more than a mystical hope of climbing upward. The ideological acceptance of anything less in the way of social openness now dooms any developing country to warped and interminably repressive politics and faltering economic advance.

The classical manner of charting the process of social "growth" describes an inevitable progression from feudalism to mercantilism to capitalism. Many schools of thought debate the motor force behind such change, and worry about such theses as whether human development ineluctably stretches ever onward and upward, or whether the affairs of men are cyclical in nature. The various teachings of the Liberal-Utilitarian, Hegelian-Marxist, and Spenglerian schools—among many others—are sufficiently well-known and accessible to need no elaboration here. Although this book concerns a specific aspect of social change, it does not pretend to venture into areas of either ultimate causation or Utopian projection. We do have a most immediate interest in cause and effect relationships, but at the level of intermediate rather than universal theory. That is to say, we hope to indicate what influences play upon certain groups of persons at specific times to produce given consequences, but it is not our intention to say that these events had to occur in this fashion or that the patterns we may discover are applicable everywhere through all time. This disavowal does not stem from modesty, but merely from the definition of our task. Moreover, a willingness to discard some of the traditional ways of defining social "stages" would appear to be necessary if our view of the combined effects of speed of change and contemporary ideology is to be molded by evidence and not by prejudgment alone.

The high velocity impact of events in the underdeveloped world telescopes "stages" and even permits some to be by-passed. This fact has been unendingly commented upon with reference to ox-carts and airplanes, but rarely organized for policy use. If underdeveloped nations are "skipping stages," then they are also proceeding in necessarily unique manners. To view the events of our times in this fashion also implies that men are rather more the masters of their destiny than ever before, or that at least the theater of their decision-making has been enlarged. No longer must we wait only on the slow grinding of economic mills or the accidental appearance of great men to erect the "bases" upon which other social changes build themselves. The political and social functions of man, instead of being dependent upon other presumably more basic circumstances, assume importance as engines of fundamental choice in themselves. Franz Neumann, in commenting upon the shifts that take place in developed societies, has stated:

> It now [in the bureaucratic and mass society] appears as if political power has begun to emancipate itself from its economic roots and, indeed, tends to become a base for the acquisition of economic power . . . .
>
> The Soviet Union presents a clear-cut marginal case where political power not only has made itself supreme but has become the fount of whatever economic power positions exist. Nazi Germany . . . exhibited a transitional case.[3]

Even if the patterns of power and the designs for its use may be different, the same statement is also true of much of the underdeveloped world, and not only of the mass society. Although this similarity suggests that entirely descriptive comparisons drawn from the historical European processes of change are suspect, it does not follow that a cavalier rejection of a careful functional examination of the purposes and operations of the past and present solutions found by the modern world is at all justified. If the forms of change are different, the elemental content may remain similar in some vital ways and at some common level of social happenings.

To view the processes of total development through the lens of the formation of the nation-state imposes the obligation of

[3] *The Democratic and the Authoritarian State*, Glencoe: 1957, pp. 14-15.

painstakingly discriminating new forms and powers from old forms and powers. It requires also a careful appreciation of historical nationalism in order to isolate those quintessential features which in themselves are a significant portion of the concept of modernism anywhere. Our presumption in this study, then, is that the function of national organization is fundamentally the same everywhere; we assume certain universal characteristics of the nation-state that bind it irrevocably to social modernism as thus far experienced in the world. But we also assume that the uniqueness of each culture group will cause the patterns of development of the nation-state to differ from case to case, and that the changing technology and ideologies abroad in the world will also cause special characteristics in the emergent lands, depending on when each begins to change and how long the process takes. Our primary task in this introduction, then, is to derive a definition of nationalism in terms of its basic functions, discriminating among those other levels of generalization which vary with time, place, and culture within the case studies themselves.

Although the more rational procedure might seem to be to start immediately with the matter of definition, this obligation will be easier to discharge once we first attempt to recognize clearly and put under control the many emotional biases surrounding the subject.

Nationalism—Curse or Blessing?

All economically underdeveloped lands caught up in the whirlwind of the revolution of modernization sooner or later breed some kind of nationalistic sentiment. But simple universality of occurrence is not sufficient in itself to justify the selection of nationalism as a crucial area of study, for all developing countries also change their institutions, their economies, the nature of their cities, their daily schedule of the round of human activities, the content of their religious beliefs, and their clothing styles and slang. Our responsibility, if this study is to be more than merely descriptive, involves making at least a reasonable case for the argument that nationalism is intrinsic to the development process, that it discharges a strategic function in a particular kind and phase of change, and that, as has been said, part of its nature remains structurally as well as functionally unchanged everywhere it appears. This obligation must be satisfied not only to justify our choice of this subject rather than any one of the other universal aspects of development, but also to discriminate the area within which facts must be separated from legitimate differences of opinion.

Most definitions of nationalism which implicitly contain tones of approval or disapproval are but partial statements of the total subject. Especially difficult to manage are those seemingly neutral treatments which spill from objectivity to judgment without pausing to warn the reader. The first type of difficulty, the overly narrow definition with negative tones, is all too usual. The commonest version views all of nationalism as merely "economic nationalism," implying autarchy, expropriations, isolating tariff barriers, and statism. Thus we hear that "nationalism is the enemy of private enterprise," or that "nationalistic policies hinder the flow of capital." And yet, of course, the nation-state system of the West is itself the source of most of the world's investment capital, and the nationals of those nation-states are themselves the most important entrepreneurs.

Similar tones of reprobation resulting from the use of only a piece of the total concept flow from narrowly political and social statements of the subject. The disquieting xenophobia of many nationalists is a common subject for attack, as are the political excesses and the susceptibility to ingenuous blindness of those following "nationalistic"—or in this case exclusivistic and messianic—policies. These judgments concern the ideologies and styles of nationalism. Were nationalism only ideology and style there could be no reason for quarrel.

On the other hand, most undiscriminating supporters of nationalistic sentiment are from today's transitional underdeveloped regions. The simplest approach of the advocates of nationalism is that of ordinary legalism—the belief that nationalism is equivalent to political independence from colonial or more covert forms of alien domination, and therefore good. A much more subtle form of approval bases itself on the notion of a *mystique*, of a national consciousness waiting to spring into liberated being with the mere erection of the institutional vessels necessary for its transportation into a glowing present and an ever more glorious future. Metaphysical constructs of this type are by no means alien to the already developed nations, of course, not only as a historical manifestation but also as a source of present emotional reinforcement. Whether these well-springs of the national being are deemed to flow from God or merely from the souls of men appears to make little difference to the intensity of such mystical views. These opinions derive from a combination of ideological, religious, and formally political symbolic concepts which for all their complexity also neglect certain vital functional aspects of nationalism.

Rupert Emerson has succinctly laid the ghost of nationalism as the overt expression of the implicit "soul" of the people:

> Everywhere the nationalists are by definition in the forefront of the national movements and are assumed to have a more acute awareness of its existence than the ordinary man, but it is also assumed that their role is not that of creating the nation but of rousing it to consciousness. The nation is something which is there as a great historical fact; it requires only the appropriate circumstances and the appeal of the leaders to swing it into political action. The task of the men of mid-nineteenth century Germany, Meiji Japan, or early twentieth century Egypt was not to forge disparate elements into a hitherto non-existent entity but to give full expression to the deep underlying sense of national community which generations of living together had produced.
>
> In Africa this approach to the national issue is in great part an illusion. It might, indeed, be argued with only slight exaggeration that the nations so far exist only in the persons of the nationalists themselves since they are the only people who have moved beyond the tribal horizons and have come to a broader sense of the society in which they live. The mass of the population in whose name they continue to speak continues to be divided into tribes which are bound together by little, if anything, in the way of language, religion, culture, or shared historical experience. The one common aspect of their lives has been the brief

subjection to European rule, and this, for the bulk of them, has often meant virtually nothing in the way of a common life. . . .[4]

But not only the avowedly pro- and anti-nationalists confuse us. All of the more sophisticated scholars writing on nationalism naturally assume that the subject can be treated with objectivity, and many of them have managed admirable results. When these same authors, however, even cautiously allow themselves to express value judgments, very often they overlook some vital aspects of their own definitions in arriving at their normative conclusions. The result is that they judge all of the many different manifestations of nationalism at only one level of criticism. Hans Kohn, for example, has had substantially the same thing to say of nationalism in several different contexts, offering very valid judgments concerning fragments of the phenomenon which, however, should not be extended to the entire subject.

> Nationalism is in itself neither good nor bad, as little as capitalism, socialism, or imperialism are. It would be disastrous to rational thought and individual liberty to regard a rethinking of nationalism or capitalism as a prelude to a sophisticated justification of exploitation or domination . . .

Nevertheless, Professor Kohn, in attempting to distinguish historically among nationalisms at several stages of development, stated earlier in the same article:

> Thus nationalism has become a powerful political threat not only to international peace but also to human freedom, perhaps the most powerful threat because nationalism in our time far excels other appeals to human emotions—social or religious appeals—by its impact on masses and individuals alike. Communist Marxism, originally an a-national and anti-national movement, had to take this into account and has lately developed a new kind of national socialism. Nationalism today unleashes forces which deepen antagonisms and hallow them by appeals to an idealized and over-sentimentalized past. Thus nationalism has tended to be-

[4] "Nationalism and Political Development," *Journal of Politics*, Vol. 22, February 1960, p. 27.

come what it originally had not been, a threat to individual liberty and to the universality of human culture.[5]

Professor Kohn's historical discrimination is matched by the work of Carlton H. J. Hayes, also a distinguished contributor to the history of the subject, and also severely troubled by nationalism's negative implications. He has written, "Whether nationalism *as a process* is a curse or blessing, we have no stomach to declare. We have read enough history to make us timid, if not humble, about passing moral judgment . . . on great and long continued historic processes." Professor Hayes then permitted himself to add:

> But nationalism as a belief belongs to another category. To every thoughtful person, save only the unqualified fatalist, it is as fitting to criticize nationalism of this kind as to criticize any other popular creed, say Christianity or Socialism or Liberalism. . . . It is nationalism as a popular contemporary belief concerning which we would put the question, is it curse or is it blessing? And . . . we would unhesitatingly affirm that, judged by its fruitage of intolerance, militarism, and war, nationalism as the belief which we have indicated is evil, and should be cursed— and cured.[6]

As Professors Kohn and Hayes make clear, the control of value judgments depends upon the rigor with which nationalism is defined in its constituent parts, and on the various ways in which those parts are combined into a whole. Yet even their refinement of analysis accommodates an overwhelming tone of condemnation which belies their own protestations and violates our common sense. It is now bromidic to say that nationalistic revolutions cannot be contained forever and that therefore they may just as well be supported and guided, if possible. Are we to assume that the drive toward national organization in the underdeveloped world is some kind of manifestation of original sin, uncontainable and inevitable, but undesirable? If, indeed, the growing nationalism of the underdeveloped peoples is in-

[5] "A New Look at Nationalism," as quoted in Urban G. Whitaker, Jr., comp. and ed., *Nationalism and International Progress*, San Francisco: 1960, pp. 21-22.
[6] *Essays on Nationalism*, New York: 1926, p. 245.

trinsically evil, then humanity everywhere would seem to be hastening its own destruction, the developed nations with their new weaponry and the underdeveloped ones simply because they seek to become nations. It is quite another matter to say, however, that value judgments concerning nationalism should be based on very explicit criteria of "goodness" and "badness," most exacting considerations of time, place, and other special circumstances, and a very precise indication of the many dimensions of the subject. To condemn nationalism as a whole in its contemporary manifestations is to render the developed nations impotent in their dealing with the emergent lands: to support their nationalistic urges is by definition to be retrograde; to combat them is to engage in barbarous violence not foreign to our century, but still less and less acceptable. Algeria, Hungary, and other examples reveal that violence and civil repression are obviously not impossible to our world, but they are increasingly difficult to justify and to maintain as long-range governmental policy.

Taken in their entirety, the attitudes of scholars toward nationalism are seemingly colored by each scholar's area of study. Those persons who work in the underdeveloped countries tend to underline the affirmative aspects of nationalism in building social cohesion. Others who dedicate themselves to the industrialized countries and to the history of nationalism lean toward emphasizing the divisive influences of the nation within a context of growing necessity for international cooperation.

Toward a Definition of Nationalism

The task of definition is rejected by some persons as conducive merely to fruitless disagreement; they argue that it is preferable merely to take for granted an unexpressed area of common conceptual agreement, thus not running the risk of losing momentum in argument over abstract ideas instead of moving ahead in the analysis of concrete data. Certainly there can be no denying that social theorizing sometimes dedicates itself to little but the dream construction of personal ways of looking at the world. Nevertheless, the task of definition is imposed upon us precisely because in this volume we have made factual studies of so many differing culture areas in light of the same problem that if the organizing ideas are not made clear, then synthesis will become in turn a labor of instinct and not of reason.

Another motive for reaching for definition is that nationalism does not lend itself easily to "common conceptual agreement," as the previous discussion of opinions concerning nationalism clearly reveals. And even if theoretical judgments are put to one side and "factual" statements alone are considered, exactly what a nation is does not reveal itself with sufficient precision to satisfy the comparative demands of this work, let alone the requirements of policy makers who at times must arrive at very sensitive decisions concerning the relationship among the activities of nationalists, the prevalence of nationalistic sentiments, and the existence of a social nation.

> There is no real agreement as to what a nation is. No one has succeeded in devising a definition which is watertight in the sense that . . . it enumerates the constituent elements of the nations we know in such fashion as to distinguish them satisfactorily from other types of communities in which men have intensely lived their lives through the ages. By rule of thumb we can usually count on knowing a nation when we see one, but if we face up to the limitations of our knowledge it must be recognized that all too frequently the determination that a nation exists can be made only after the fact when the nation has emerged full-blown and leaves little reasonable doubt that it is there and must be reckoned with. . . .[7]

Despite the difficulties and confusions, however, there are many definitional conventions in use. One of the most usual ways out of the terminological impasse is to say that nationalism is a sentiment, an idea, an attitude, an emotional stance, a way of thinking, or some other such expression to indicate the all-embracing nature of the subject without being forced into greater specification of its intricacies as a dynamic element in certain types of social organization. A relatively straightforward expression of this view is found in such a statement

[7] Rupert Emerson, *From Empire to Nation: The Rise to Self-Assertion of Asian and African Peoples*, Cambridge: 1960, p. 90.

as "Nationalism is more a sentiment than a system of thought,"[8] for example. But this view will not do for our purposes. To state that something exists as a feeling or idea and then hazily to add that this ideational commitment leads to overt political action leaves out the proof of the relationship. To find out how nationalism grows as idea and action, where it stands in the ordering of social events, and what its complex components and types of manifestations may be demands a different kind of definition. Even when nationalism as idea is delineated in the anatomical complexity of the following quotation, it does not answer to the requirements of functional analysis:

> A legal and political nation is a group of particular persons locatable in the public space-time of nature, each with a nominalistic proper name, who have trapped in the hierarchically ordered reverberating circuits of their brains persisting impulses or their formal, analytic, physiological equivalents which are the concept by postulation epistemic correlates of the elementary concepts and propositions or postulates of a consciously or covertly held common philosophy to which they have committed themselves and of which they may or may not be introspectively conscious. In order, therefore, to know what a particular nation is, the descriptive method of philosophical anthropology must determine, in a manner that is empirically confirmable by anyone, its particular high-frequency common philosophy.[9]

A step toward useful complication is afforded by those authors who depart from the premise of nationalism as idea, and then proceed to treat of the complexity of the concept itself instead of turning immediately to its presumed overt manifestations. Hayes, for example, states:

> Nationality has always existed. Patriotism has long existed, either as applied to a loyalty or as extended to an empire. But the fusion of patriotism with nationality and

[8] C. Kerr, J. T. Dunlop, F. Harbison, and C. A. Myers, "Industrialism and World Society," *Harvard Business Review*, January-February 1961, p. 119.
[9] F. S. C. Northrop, *Philosophical Anthropology and Practical Politics: A Prelude to War or to Just Law*, New York: 1960, p. 79.

the predominance of natural patriotism over all other human loyalties . . . is nationalism. . . .[10]

Another example, now extending the notion of idea into the realm of action, is offered by Rupert Emerson, who says, "Reduced to its bare bones, nationalism is no more than the assertion that this particular community is arrayed against the rest of mankind."[11] This type of postulate begins to be useful for our particular purposes, for it is an example of the functional tying of attitudes to action with which we are concerned, so that we may then be able to push on into the question of the institutional mechanisms for ordering the attitude-action relationship we are studying.

Some authors have attempted to handle this relationship by listing a set of national characteristics and then indicating their institutional expression. One such writer[12] lists ten basic characteristics, adding that the list is not final. The nation, in this definition, involves "a certain defined unit of territory"; such common cultural characteristics as language, customs, etc.; "some common dominant social . . . and economic . . . institutions; a sovereign government or at least the desire for one"; "a belief in a common history" and "a love or esteem for fellow nations"; "a devotion to the entity called the nation" and a common pride in its achievement, as well as a feeling of exclusiveness and a common hope for the future. This construction is difficult to handle, for it does not indicate order of importance, and the categories are uneven in terms of their level of generality.

A major difficulty with all such abstracts from descriptive national characteristics is that they tempt to the conclusion that "nationalism is what the nationalists have made it." Either this statement is so narrowly circular as to be useless for studies of social change or else it implies that a nation exists if nationalists say it is there. To accept the latter equivalence between the nationalists and the nation is an abdication of responsibility by the researcher, for indeed nationalists may exist in the absence of a nation. And further, we must not succumb

[10] Hayes, *op. cit.*, p. 26.
[11] "Nationalism and Political Development," *op. cit.*, p. 20.
[12] Boyd C. Shafer, *Nationalism: Myth and Reality*, as quoted in Urban G. Whitaker, *op. cit.*, pp. 4-5.

to the convenience of assuming that self-definition is absolute definition. What a nationalist says is a nation may also be but a collection of mud huts. Analysis and predictions must come from penetrations inside the subject under observation, of course taking into account self-appreciations; but definition originates from reason as a conceptual superimposition, an exercise in science.

Whatever may be the merits of individual contributions to the subject, the general agreement is that nationalism concerns certain kinds of common characteristics, common feelings, and to a more limited extent, common action, almost always with relation to the state. Some authors, such as Hayes, identified nationalism as correlative to the emergence of a middle class, and E. H. Carr in his tiny but monumental *Nationalism and After*[13] developed a mature schema of the relationship between nationalism and class structure. More recent writings have attempted to link power to class to institutions to attitudes in order to describe nationalism as function and social artifact instead of mystical idea or mere set of epidermic characteristics. One of the more important and apt of these statements is, once again, that of Emerson:

> The nation today is the largest community which, when the chips are down, effectively commands men's loyalty, overriding the claims both of the lesser communities within it and those which cut across it or potentially enfold it within a still greater society, reaching ultimately to mankind as a whole. In this sense, the nation can be called a "terminal community," with the implication that it is for present purposes the effective end of the road for man as a social animal, the end point of working solidarity between men. . . . Within it there is the assumption of peaceful settlement of disagreement, based on the supreme value of national unity. . . .[14]

Favored with a rich body of literature, and pushed by the areas under study to concern ourselves with the subject of nationalism as related to the general problem of development,

---

[13] London: 1945.
[14] *From Empire to Nation, op. cit.*, p. 95.

we have sought a working concept which would not violate European experience, would be fitting to today's emergent nations, and would contribute to the study of comparative politics by virtue of its possibly universal application. We also needed a concept which could be adjusted to the various manners in which nationalism has been functionally treated in order not to lose the full benefit of the large amount of fruitful research already done. All studies of nationalism seem to lend themselves to being fitted into one or more of the following four general categories:

1. *Nationalism as a formal juridical concept*, referring to the legal relationships between individuals and the state (citizenship, nationality, legally imposed ethnic and religious discrimination, political proscription, etc.), and among states internationally (involving juridical questions of sovereignty, irredentist claims, and so forth). This category will be of only marginal interest to this study, although certain aspects of it necessarily appear in connection with such matters as border disputes, as in the case of Afghanistan and the question of defining the physical limits of the nation-state, or in matters of race, as exemplified in the problems of the Republic of South Africa.

2. *Nationalism as a symbolic concept*, that stock of patriotic symbols enveloping such common cultural characteristics as language, dress and food habits, and the expression of respect for familiar surroundings, the flag, the anthem, and so on. Patriotism as love of the familiar and known is not nationalism, of course, but the symbols of a common heritage and the affective element they carry infuse nationalism with much of its emotive content.

3. *Nationalism as ideology*, those express bodies of political thought concerning what the nation was, is, and ought to be, and the means to be employed for seeking national goals and for discriminating between state power and individual rights.

4. *Nationalism as social value*, that norm defining the loyalty due to fellow citizens and to the mandates of the state, the tacit consent extended to the activities of the state within the national society, and the internalized "feeling" of national community. This basic social value is normally very deeply held among

citizens of established nation-states, reinforced as it is by family teaching, public education, and the day-to-day expectations of one's peers.

The reduction of these four components leads us to the central statement of nationalism which we have employed as hypothesis and organizing concept in all of our individual studies: *Nationalism is the acceptance of the state as the impersonal and ultimate arbiter of human affairs.* This statement at first blush must certainly appear overly simple, and perhaps totalitarian in suggestion. What we are pointing out, however, is the core of nationalism: the establishment of a fully secular area of life regulated by a social institution before which all men are at least in certain public senses equal. This aspect of the nation-state is what makes national systems unique, what differentiates them from all other societies. As bald as this definition may at first appear, then, its implications are fulsome. The statement describes a function—the settlement of dispute. It names the state as the institutionalized means of bringing power to bear to satisfy that function. The necessity for the loyal participation of a citizenry within an explicit community which creates the consensual power necessary to the primary function of the state is indicated in the word "acceptance." And the definition states that the function must be exercised "impersonally"—over an appreciable territorial extension and across broad class lines, in ultimate cases overriding primary loyalties to intermediate family, religious, or other competing areas of identification. Nationality, patriotism, ideology, and social values all may be reflective of this national situation, of this willingness to permit a political institution to settle certain kinds of dispute, and to accept the settlements as though they were ultimate—that is, until such time as they may be changed *within* the polity itself, without institutional break.

This definition of nationalism is not in conflict with much of what has already been cited; it differs, however, in its level of generality, and in the explicitness of its applicability to the processes of social and political development. The originality of the suggestion, then, resides only in the manner of organizing otherwise quite conventional views, and in the ascription of

different orders of functionality to the various implicit elements
and implications of the statement.

All the cases discussed in the body of this book involve human
cultures in one or another degree of emergence into full national
existence. We are observing what is indubitably a major event
in the lives of people, a profound revolution involving not merely
flags and constitutions but basic reorientations of attitudes,
behavior, and ethical norms. The crossing of the frontier from
tribal or feudal organization—and sometimes both together—
into national polities signals a fundamental change in the human
condition, a reordering of social classes and the addition of new
meanings to class position, and new attitudes concerning one's
place in the social world and one's possibilities therein as well
as new hierarchies of values and loyalties. This Great Transformation is poignantly felt in its awesome magnitude by the
people experiencing it; the observer can do no less than to create
explanatory concepts which will allow the capturing on paper
of some of the sweeping excitement of this metamorphosis
in the lives of societies and human beings.

The development of modern society has been examined most
frequently by economists, by others within a religious and at-
titudinal framework, and sometimes even in magical terms.
We have chosen to shift the subject on its axis, and to examine
the changes introducing modernism in light of the relationships
between the attitudes, values, ideologies, and public behavior
of individuals, and the social institutions to which they both
cede and concede power by extending to them and investing in
them their loyalties, expectations, and obedience. The positive
function of nationalism is to order this set of relationships, thus
building reasonable expectations and security patterns into the
greater complexity which is social modernism. But the negative
aspects of nationalism, the increased dangers stemming from
heightened public power, sometimes obscure its basic reason
for existence not only for the scholar, but more importantly for
those political leaders who may destroy the very cohesion of
national societies in the name of falsely nationalistic ideologies
at the service of warped special interest.

But the matter of judgment should be allowed to emerge
from the discussion of the workings of nationalism as we view
it here, as in the case of the definitions of others cited above.

The most important aspects of the subject of nationalism for our purposes are the questions of social values and ideologies. We shall presume the symbolic content to be dependent on the other two factors, the means for their overt expression in daily life, while nationality remains their expression in specifically legal terms. Let us then examine national values and ideologies in some detail to explain further the organizing concepts running throughout this entire book.

Nationalism as Social Value

The heart of the matter beats here, in the way in which a people sees its world. The reason that nationalism has so far been an inevitable accompaniment of full modernism is our subject at this point. The ability, and the willingness, to accept civil authority in the ultimate settlement of secular dispute is a necessary attribute of any extended group of persons who pretend to the complications of industrialization, high consumption levels, and—in short—all the other hallmarks of what the world calls development. Just as magic cannot be invoked in empirical minds to explain the meanderings of a rainfall chart, tribal and traditional value orientations are useless in helping man to thread his way through the predictions necessary to living in lands in which it takes twenty-five years to produce a physician, and where a breakdown in the electrical distribution system can signify literal death. The acceptance of the belief that a human institution must proclaim "intermediate and relative truth" in order to assure the continuance of a daily round of interdependent and roundabout human activities must mark the entire spread of the individual's social life, from family affairs to religion to occupation to class identifications. An effort of will and imagination is involved which is not invoked by the demands of traditional society, and indeed which is viewed as the devil's work by many traditionalists.

The primary criterion used here for distinguishing among tribal, traditional, and national organization concerns the patterns of identification linking the individual to his entire human context. We are talking about what people "see," how they view their individual role in the collectivity and what they understand as that complete society. Tribal man does not usually

go beyond face-to-face relationships except in certain limited
economic spheres. Then he jumps to supernatural concepts,
tending to mingle the mundane and the religious in intimate
fashion. Although these statements are not completely and
universally true of all tribal systems, they constitute a fairly
reliable working ideal-type. The traditional man goes far beyond these narrow horizons, especially in seeing a more rational
division between the particular and the universal. He is able to
think in terms of physically extended human groupings, and to
see a highly ordered series of human events merging into the
supernatural in accordance with sometimes extremely speculative
philosophical postulates. It will be remembered that the school
of universalistic thought flowered during the period of the
Roman Empire and persisted throughout the age of European
feudalism, finally broken only by the familiar procession of city-
states, Renaissance and Reformation, Machiavelli, mercantilism,
and the emergence of the European nation-state system. The
traditional person does not "see" either utility or ethical justification in accepting relative truth, especially as prescribed by
an impersonal social institution. He continues to give his primary
worldly loyalty to himself, his family, his immediate peers, and
possibly to certain occupational and class segments. His social
views are universalistic and thus absolutistic appreciations of
man and his earthly condition, whether or not he is formally
religious. Social position is thus an ordained phenomenon; public
discord must then also necessarily be religious controversy. For
this reason church-state conflict was an inevitable concomitant
of the growth of the secular nation-state in Europe.

The modern man, on the other hand, is expected to "see"
across class boundaries and to identify in a real working sense
with the total complex of his national culture, demonstrating
his "loyalty" to others by his willingness to accept interim,
eclectic solutions to problems without imposing universally
absolute measures. So he invents the idea of "the rule of law."
This kind of person, then, must necessarily accept the notion
that working truth is only an approximation, and that empiricism
and pragmatism are a necessary part of living in a highly stratified modern society.

A person enmeshed in the transition from folk and traditional to modern society must undergo profound changes in attitude if he as an individual—and not only the group—is to survive in changed form. Robert Redfield, in *The Primitive World and Its Transformations*, discussing what is universal in the world views of all peoples, states, ". . . it is probably safe to say that among the groupings of people in every society are always some that distinguish people who are my people, or are more my people, from people who are not so much my people. The We-They difference, in some form, arranges the human elements on the universal stage."[15] This "in-group" versus "out-group" feeling suffers a fundamental transformation in the process of modernization; even though the sentiment persists, its qualitative nature is changed by the inclusion of entire collectivities of persons never to be seen by the individual, never to be conversed with, never to be physically touched. The citizen of the nation-state becomes aware of his fellow-citizens as part of his personal world, sadly or bravely prepared to defend them with his life if need be, willing to depend on their continued performance for the satisfaction of his own needs and at least tacitly knowing that they in turn depend on his continued compliance with a bargain he had nothing to do with making, and of which he may be only most dimly aware.

This social-psychological change has been quite clearly described in a recent study happily entitled *The Passing of Traditional Society*.

Empathy [is] . . . the inner mechanism which enables newly mobile persons to *operate efficiently* in a changing world. Empathy, to simplify the matter, is the capacity to see oneself in the other fellow's situation. This is an indispensable skill for people moving out of traditional settings. . . .

High empathic capacity is the predominant personal style only in modern society, which is distinctively industrial, urban, literate and *participant*. Traditional society is nonparticipant—it deploys people by kinship into communities isolated from each other and from a center . . . it de-

[15] Robert Redfield, *The Primitive World and Its Transformations*, Ithaca: 1953, p. 92.

velops few needs requiring economic interdependence; lacking the bonds of interdependence, people's horizons are limited by locale and their decisions involve only other *known* people in *known* situations. Hence, there is no need for a transpersonal common doctrine formulated in terms of shared secondary symbols—a national "ideology" which enables persons unknown to each other to engage in political controversy or to achieve "consensus" by comparing their opinions. . . .[16]

Nationalism is more than "empathy" or "in-group versus out-group" feelings, of course. Depending upon both, nationalism also describes the manner in which these attitudes serve to enlarge the power of given social institutions. And in turn, the empowered institutions require that the very same attitudes be held—or at least that action should flow as though they were held—so that the continuity of the national community may be assured. In other words, empathy extends the size of the "We" group, the enlarged social relationships being regulated in the last analysis by the state, whose expanded power to order and enforce compliance derives from the very strength of the enlarged patterns of social identification themselves. Nationalism, in a certain sense, is the institutionalized power reflection of "empathy," both constituting requirements of the ability to follow a modern style of life. This primary function of nationalism is an unavoidable aspect of development, and indeed may in itself be used as an operational definition of social and political development.

Nationalism, Class, and Development

The strategy of choosing nationalism for study at this particular period of human change is indicated by the ways in which economic development, class, and social cohesion are related. The processes of development necessarily involve class consequences, of course. Although we chose to base our definitions of tribal, feudal, and modern society upon the degree of social identification involved in each, the classical mode of analysis

[16] Daniel Lerner, *The Passing of Traditional Society: Modernizing the Middle East*, Glencoe: 1958, pp. 49-51 *passim*.

would have been to argue out of the differing class structures. Tribal societies are normally seen as occupationally stratified, but of essentially one social class. Feudal societies are always said to be characterized by an essentially bi-class structure, while modern society involves an equally conventionally accepted tri-class system. Whatever may be the concept of class one may use—short of denying its existence, of course—certainly no one will dispute the conclusion that modernism implies a different social structure from traditionalism.

Class is a generally divisive factor in society, an effect not in contradiction with the lower orders of cohesion it also produces.[17] Division implies differing sectors of interest, and thus disagreement and conflict. But it is an empirical fact that, despite the existence of class schisms, societies do not often shake themselves to pieces over the resulting differences. Logically, then, one must conclude that there are certain values and goals held in

[17] Our definition of class is based on neo-Weberian postulates. We have accepted from Weber the insight that class position is an expression of power—the real or potential ability to make others do one's will—and of the "life chances" of an individual, or the probability of his exercising effective freedom of choice during his life course with respect to his starting point, or his "social trampoline," in a manner of speaking. We also accept from Weber the postulate that social position is, for all practical working purposes, a composite of *economic power* (occupation, income, place in the economic institution), *social power* (prestige, status), and *political power* (from voting to leading opinion making to top policy decision, both within and without the formal political institution). This view is *neo*-Weberian because, among other reasons, we choose not to employ his terminology of "class," "status," and "power" for the three elements, and most explicitly use the power concept as the common denominator underlying the three. We also depart from Weber in his assumption that the economic power factor is basic to the others in defining individual class position. We neither deny nor affirm the proposition for long-range analysis, asserting merely that at the level at which we are working the presumption is not only moot, but may also serve as a hindrance. The point was made earlier in the text, buttressed by the quotation from Neumann, that at least in the short and intermediate runs power may have roots in political and status factors, and then spread over to economic manifestations. This statement also appears to hold for general societal happenings, in which ideological change and political manifestations serve as primary stimuli of economic change during the short and intermediate runs at which we are directing our questions. For a more detailed statement of class and economic and social development, see K. H. Silvert and Frank Bonilla, *Education and the Social Meaning of Development: A Preliminary Statement*, New York: 1961, mimeographed.

common which glue societies together despite the clash of interest. The more interdependent and extended a society, the more will the cohesive elements tend to be under human control, secular in nature, rational and empirical. We can follow the progression from the magical nature of tribal lore, to vertically hierarchical mingling of the moral and the public of the traditional, to the pluralistic complex and discrete secular and ethical relationships of modern society. Each set of class systems will demand its apposite set of cohesive values; there can be lags in the adjustment of values to class, but wherever such warping occurs, societies will be troubled and unstable, prone to irrationalities and violence.

What we are suggesting, of course, is that nationalism as a social value has been the major cohesive force to date within each separate modern society, and that its existence in underdeveloped areas is a necessary part of the process of development, very often anticipatory of the social class structure which is its only real support and its only ultimately legitimate social reason for being.

But maladjustments among value systems, ideologies, and social institutions must always exist, especially in developing societies, for underdevelopment is also invariably uneven development. Asynchronous growth creates special problems of political stability, social mobility, economic growth, and ideological interpretation. In the body of this book, we shall find cases in which economic development has far outstripped social development or the creation of a coherent set of values for coordination and integration of the society as a whole. There are many examples in which national integration is at a very low level, while the ideologies of nationalism flourish in wild and uninhibited profusion. We shall see yet other instances of lands in which the economic process and the formation of occupationally modern class structures have proceeded far, while the survival of tenacious traditional ideologies and value systems block any further movement. In a time span of fifty or even a hundred years, there can no longer be any doubt that the pulling and hauling accompanying development can lead to a rich variety of differing adjustments to change, some of them sterile and self-defeating, others seedbeds of future growth.

In the theory of economic development, all too often the social is approached by way of sad headshaking over the resistance of persons to occupational change. Studies have been proliferating of the stubbornness of individuals in accepting attitudes conducive to growth, of recalcitrant entrepreneurs who do not wish to take the risks of capitalistic business enterprise, and of ignorant tribesmen who object to smallpox injections. All too few of these investigations have also asked whether the society as it expresses itself through reigning ideologies and ruling elites is also ready to admit persons into the national play of power if they should manage to germinate the emotional stance of modernism. A society truly poised for change must be willing to admit into an even limited partnership all those persons whose horizons, aspirations, and powers have been broadened by the anticipation or the actuality of change. Class exclusiveness, "class interest," or "class consciousness" cannot be allowed to prevail over more general interclass interest in the long run if the necessary flexibility for relatively untwisted and eventually self-sustaining growth is to permit an avoidance of recurrent violence. If class is the first large sub-category analytically and actually carved out of a people as a whole, then it follows that a society which pretends to wholeness over a fairly broad range of human activities must invoke and enforce supraclass identifications at the level of the entire society itself. The invention of nationalism ascribes this enforcement function to the state in the name of the nation. The organized settlement of interclass dispute is thus a primary role of nationalism in development, permitting the building of extended market mechanisms and the predictions necessary to them, making real the social and political promise of occupational mobility, and increasing the objective power of the civil mechanism to impose and regulate secular order.

The extension of national identification often becomes arrested, however, and converts itself into what is essentially a class phenomenon, instead of a supraclass mechanism. Selective and limited nationalisms characterized the incomplete European nation-states of the early part of the last century, for example, a fact which strongly suggests that we should seek similar contemporary patterns of incompleteness and the unequal incidence of the pleasures and pains of national organization. In the early years of the European nations, nationalism was used to integrate upper and middle groups; lower social elements were consistently excluded from active participation in public affairs, from chances to ascend, and from wider economic horizons.

The ruling middle classes who were the bearers of the nineteenth century nationalism entertained almost everywhere throughout the middle years of the century a lively fear of revolution from below. The rights of property were scarcely less sacrosanct than the rights of man and the functions of the *bourgeois* democratic state—the "nightwatchman state" in Lassalle's sarcastic phrase—were largely concerned with its protection. Property . . . was a condition of political right and—it might be said without much exaggeration—of full membership of the nation: the worker had, in this sense, no fatherland. . . . In their [the propertied classes of Western Europe] competent hands the democratized nation was still proof for many years to come against the disruptive turbulence of popular nationalism.[18]

In what now seems the spaciousness of a century, Western European societies saw the gradual expansion of the social nation to include all class levels. There was no help for it. The commitment to industrialization, the growth of industrial urbanization, and technological developments—especially those in the area of communications—led to what Carr calls the "socialization" of the nation, in contrast with its earlier "democratization" under the tutelary rule of the middle and upper groups. Henceforth the lower classes, too, were to have their home, and no longer were revolutionary movements to presume on an alleged "internationalism" of the dispossessed. In Carr's words, "The socialization of the nation has as its natural corollary the nationalization of socialism."[19] The tasks of the nation now became involved with social security, free access to the polls, mass politics, and a broadening of the area of effective debate and legitimately recognized interest to include trade unions and an organized sense of "populism."

[18] Carr, *op. cit.*, pp. 10-11.
[19] *Ibid.*, pp. 18-19.

Developing countries no longer wait for the process to follow the above described "natural" path. Laborers working in copper mines and living in semitribal conditions, burdened by the pressures of very extended kinship systems, with a vivid belief in witchcraft organize themselves into trade unions, dream of controlling the mine themselves, and become aware—however dimly and even romantically—that at least one effective way to economic power is through seizure of the political mechanism and its ancillary means of coercion. The "popular nationalism" which the presently developed nations hesitatingly and unwillingly embraced over the course of more than a century is bursting upon the new nations as an immediate ideal, an urgent political imperative sharpened by the actions of leaders whose ambitions derive from the examples of the developed world. These avowed hopes do not define in practice the real situations and possibilities of many emergent nations or of those arrested in a state of incomplete national integration. The "national" citizens of developing countries are invariably persons of training and of middle and upper social position. The "massification" of national identification is fomented by the characteristics of new industrial procedures, communications systems, and ideological constellations, but the power structure directing the entire revolutionary complex necessarily remains not "massified," the property of the tutelary innovators.

The breaking of colonial ties, the destruction of traditionalism, and the establishment of "socially incomplete nations" involve a set of impressive and often gaudy crises. But these climaxes do not cover the complete trajectory of national development, and we may expect to see ever more crises of a second nature, those involving the emergence of "popular" nationalism. The failure to find adequate means for the complete extension of the rights and duties of national life is a major problem in all those older independent states which have not achieved self-sustaining economic structures or a solution to the harshest effects of class difference. This phenomenon is notorious in Latin America, whose republics have been independent of colonial control for 150 years, but where political crises still revolve about many problems characteristic of traditional authoritarianism. Tribal, feudal, and contemporary modern groups continue to coexist in

Latin America, a division further complicated by ethnic disparity in most of the republics.

> It seems to be abundantly clear that once industrializa-
> tion begins, when there is an industrial "take-off" in
> Rostow's sense of that term, urban growth, a class system,
> and a nationalistic political philosophy also are evident part-
> ners in that process . . . In effect, cohesion, class, and the
> city are all aspects of the same social complex.[20]

But when the partnership is unequal, or the value of one partner is denied, the results are unhappy. The rash of military governments and *coups* recently seen in Asia and the Middle East, often justifiably compared with Latin American practice, is in all cases related to the emergence of elite groups faced with the problem of sharing their power if eventually they are to lead true nations, and the possibility of losing their near-monopoly of power should they decide to share it. How to maintain a sufficient velocity of national development to satisfy the require- ments of social and economic development and still not fall into suicidal demagoguery and insupportable anticipatory "populism" is a major problem in some countries. In others, the question is how to prevent industrialization from increasing the power of certain groups to such an extent that they may be emboldened to strive with all their might and main to prevent continued eco- nomic development from leading to more popular social and political participation in the fruits of the new world.

The "socialization of nationalism" has its dangers. As in the times of the Mills, Montesquieu, Tocqueville, and the other thinkers of the earlier days of the restricted nation-state, the prob- lem remains how to control a state swollen with the power flowing from the involvement of ever more persons. For the worriers of the past, the question was how to civilize the *bour- geoisie*, how to make them accept the responsibilities of their new powers. Now the knot to be undone in the developed world is the civilization of so-called "mass man." But the problem for developing countries is the simultaneous creation of the *polis* and the integration of almost everyone within it. The new elites, the new middles, and the new lowers all need to go through the process at once, by no means a pleasant task, especially when

[20] Reissman, *op. cit.*, p. 51.

the literature of the social sciences offers them so little understanding in a plight which could be lightened merely by knowing what the trouble is all about.

Nationalism as Ideology

"Nationalism" is a base epithet in many parts of the world, made so by persons who elect themselves the representatives of the nation and attempt to bend others to their often manic will. In this sense nationalism is often synonymous with fascism. Despicable as these uses of the nation are, they are not the only ones which must be considered as the ideologies of nationalism. But it would indeed be blind to pretend that the sick national society does not lend itself to making possible totalitarianism, an authoritarianism whose rigor and generality of application are possible only in a modern situation in which the supremacy of the state is such that all intervening buffer institutions which may protect the individual have shrunk in power and normative significance.

Nationalism as a social value is necessary to modernism; it is also necessary to democracy but insufficient to assure it, as it is necessary in turn to totalitarianism, but also insufficient to guarantee its emergence. And yet there would seem to be some more positive correlation between freedom and the nation than the previous statements may indicate. Hans Kohn, in his most recent book concerning the growth of what he calls "pan-nationalism," has written:

> The complexity and ambivalence of all history may be seen in the fact that this broadening of the bases for a more dignified human life occurred in Europe after 1789 under the over-all concept of an age of nationalism, and occurs outside Europe in the twentieth century under similar guiding stars . . . nationalism, in Europe as elsewhere, has carried not only a hope and a promise but also a grave threat to the growing unity of mankind and to the rational freedom of man. The garb of nationalism clothes on the one hand the human aspirations for equality and dignity and on the other the passion for power over others. . . .[21]

[21] *The Age of Nationalism: The First Era of Global History*, New York: 1962, p. xvi.

Perhaps it is that a denial of those aspects of the nation-state which imply the rule of law—the carving out of a secular marketplace in which all men are publicly equal—weakens the value of national cohesion and hinders further general development. We address ourselves specifically to this question of the relationship between the nation and freedom as we progress through our case analyses to such countries as Japan, Israel, and Argentina, the closest to modernism among the examples chosen. A tentative conclusion may be advanced here, however, indicating that indeed there does appear a relationship between an inability to continue the developmental process and a use of the *ideologies* of nationalism to restrict substantive freedom, thus preventing a full acceptance of the *values* of national identification.

Ideology as it refers to the meaning and ends of the nation-state will be of great assistance in determining whether partially national organization will lead to greater freedom or more expertly managed slavery. But ideology by itself cannot provide the entire basis for judging where any society is going, and even in conjunction with national values as a twofold analytical device it remains insufficient, for the processes producing modern society do not mesh automatically.

A major pitfall in the prediction of social events stems from the belief that the total developmental process is unilinear, and that all that is needed is one good, strategic push in the right place to ensure that the whole historical ball of twine will unravel itself. This convenient dream is a favorite of economists, many of whom assume that a "take-off" guarantees a subsequent smooth flight. But anyone even superficially informed about air travel will recognize the fallacy. National development, as we have insisted throughout this introduction, is a total phenomenon involving industrialization, classes, values, economic and political organization, bureaucracy, ideology systems, and international relations.[22] When the patterns of change become snarled because of extremely stubborn resistance, or misguided leadership, foreign intervention, or whatever else may cause the paraly-

[22] This view of the totality of development is being approached from many different academic disciplines. We have cited Lerner and Reissman, for example. See also a very interesting article by Karl W. Deutsch, entitled, "Social Mobilization and Political Development," *American Political Science Review*, Vol. LV, No. 3, September 1961, pp. 493-514.

sis of one or another area crucial to the entire configuration, then it often happens that explanations become irrational and violent, and concomitantly violent and irrational actions follow. The danger of building the nation-state is, naturally, that the new power to coerce will be badly used in the name of destructive ideologies either to force change before the structure can easily support the new weight or to attempt to prevent change, implying a redistribution of power and of the fruits of economic growth.

The recent histories of many European countries and the daily newspapers demonstrate that there are dangers inherent in national development throughout the process from the earliest days of the nation to what some now consider its last fling before a flaming sunset. Afghanistan and Bolivia illustrate some of the kinds of costs of the attempt to blend tribalism into the nation, in place of the much easier task of governing tribalism through the traditional paternalism of colonialism. Argentina and Japan offer other examples of an intermediate set of troubles, the inability to make a definitive choice between traditionalism and modernism, and the consequent employment of some of the tools of modernism to maintain a stubborn traditionalism. At the other end of the scale of development we find the example of Nazi Germany and the emergence of what it used to be fashionable to call "supernationalism." The Nazi experience is often ascribed to a failure to achieve a sufficient degree of interclass cohesion to guarantee the continued harmony of a highly industrialized society. The resulting emergence of supernationalism was the verbal excuse for the cannibalization of dissident and scapegoat elements, devoured by a *déclassé* middle class abetted by a shortsighted and criminally irresponsible and selfish upper class. When the social value of nationalism is weak, very often ruling groups attempt the invocation of strong ideological appeals backed up by charismatic leaders to overcome the failure to order class and institutional conflict at a more fundamental and functional level. This substitution of overt ideology for implicit value is also characteristic of retarded as well as advanced stages of national development. The violently exhortative ideology of the present Indonesian political leadership is no less a case in point than the lunatic ideology of Nazi Germany. These examples suggest that a set of rough expectations concerning the principal earmarks of nationalistic ideologies can reasonably be developed in correlation with the degree of national development forming the framework for the ideology.

Two principal and divergent patterns appear in lands at the threshold of national organization. If the drive toward nationalism is confounded with anti-colonialism and anti-imperialism, then the ideology may be most xenophobic and violent, even though heavily imitative of foreign example and quite vague in matters concerning the steps to be taken for immediate internal social change. When the country has for long had nominal independence, as is the case in most of the following country studies, then the reigning ideologies tend to be much softer on the question of exclusivism, but still imitative and unsure concerning rigorous internal change. The development and use of the slogans and ideologies of nationalism in this stage of development are always limited to the upper and the rudimentary middle groups, with little really substantive sense of national identification, for as yet there are few institutions to which to be loyal. Politics almost invariably tends to be crude, either nakedly authoritarian or noisily but somewhat ineffectively revolutionary, while personalism is of great importance in organizing the budding political party systems as well as the limited public opinion. At this stage it is most important for future growth that ideologies should be as permissive as possible in the expression of ideals, for of course ideological belief will have a highly predictive value. The future will in important measure be governed by the general stance taken in this early period toward the proper use of the organs of the growing nation-state.

In this first emergence of nationalism, and especially in newly freed colonial lands, ideological alliances tend to be very broad—all those persons in favor of national development range themselves against all those opposed. For this reason far left political groups are often taken into nationalist coalitions whose general politico-economic ambitions may well be much more moderate than those of their leftist partners. These marriages of convenience, often most sincerely entered into, are explainable not only in terms of the grand objective of national organization held at least temporarily in common, but also by the nature of the

opposition, which often lumps all modernizing movements together as the common enemy. This view is current in Latin
America, where traditionalists often see American liberalism
and Soviet Marxism as fundamentally similar. Because the Soviet Union and the United States must appear more similar than
dissimilar to the eye of a fifteenth century man, this identification
is not unnatural, even though it is a mere confusion in any less
general terms of reference.

During the intermediate stages of the development of the
nation, the slogans and symbols of national ideologies become
widely distributed through the agency of the citizen armies, the
public school systems, and the newly developed interest associations. Ideologies are now addressed to the economically solidly
entrenched middle groups and also affect intimately the "new"
upper groups and striving members of the upper-lower elements.
Although the ideological content is usually still strongly anti-
imperialist, in practice the new security and the necessity for
external markets tend to soften xenophobia. But the ideology
must now express strong equalitarian desires on the part of
highly mobile elements in the new society, as well as the resound-
ing echoes of interinstitutional struggle as the state seeks to
affirm its full sovereignty. Economic and religious issues are
often in the forefront of this interinstitutional strife, but many
other complex questions also arise, such as the position of
political parties, the role of labor unions, and the accommodation
to be sought among social classes which are almost invariably
very sharply differentiated at this stage of national economic
development. The political party structure also is almost always
under great strain, driven by a growing social need for impersonalism and hampered by the continuing importance of charisma.
The parties must face up to the difficult transition away from
the comfortable cloak covering the representation of otherwise
naked interest to take up the modern garb of a generalized ideological and national commitment which must at least pretend to
supraclass and supra-interest group objectives. The grand division between traditionalists and modernists also breaks down,
leading the parties to assume their familiar configuration of left,
center, and right. This stage of development is very risky, for
during it either structures and practices emerge leading to an

ultimately balanced consolidation making unnecessary the repressive use of state power, or else the probabilities fall on the side of employment of the new institutional artifacts for authoritarian ends.

This intermediate level of national emergence also usually gives rise to economic demands and debates concerning economic policy which are often allowed to override other elements in the total analysis of national ideologies. The leaders of underdeveloped lands tend to see the state as the only agency of sufficient strength to mobilize large amounts of capital and to enforce the protectionism necessary for their growing industries. And the consumer in such countries has been prodded by the stimuli of modernism to such an extent that his expectations are high and his necessary disappointments all the keener. What is often forgotten, however, is that a rapid rate of national development in itself creates an excitement and an anticipation which often permit a most conscious and rational deferment of present consumption for the sake of future consumption.

The developed lands look askance at the economic policies of the growing nations as they tend to autarchy, blanket protectionism, and state control of investments. But given the rigidities in the world market, the protectionism exercised by the industrial states themselves, and the mixed economic practices of the staunchest advocates of free markets, there can be little surprise at the economic advocacies of the underdeveloped lands. The widespread belief in the intimate relationship between industrialization and modernism is not totally false, of course, for the continued production of raw materials coupled with low power on the marketplace do indeed make economic development difficult. In any event, the widespread tendency to equate state power with economic development is a very understandable dimension of nationalistic ideologies of the intermediate period of national integration.

If the process of national development completes itself in a reasonably accommodated fashion, we should expect to find ideological division evened out and simplified, and the values of national identification very widespread and almost beyond discussion. It now becomes possible to degenerate into a "super-patriot," a denigration invariably connoting a throwback to what was considered necessary and desirable in the earlier days of struggle. The state is unequivocally triumphant over other institutional forces in the event of ultimate conflict. Government becomes centralized in power, whether or not it is so in organization. The parties tend toward full professionalization, with the ideological function becoming muted. To a certain extent internal dispute is smothered, while external complications increase and what overtly nationalistic ideology remains concentrates itself on relations among nations. The countries at this stage of development mingle their local with their international questions. Whether failure or success will mark the resolution of these questions we cannot know, for that is the problem of today and tomorrow, of how the nation-states of the developed world will adjust themselves to the broader requirements of their new situation.

Nationalism and the Future

We have seen some of the fashions in which the nationalism emerging now in the underdeveloped and intermediately developed worlds departs from the content and practices of the nationalism of the last century in Western Europe—skipping stages, using new devices, and finding many differing paths to modern social organization. Whether this broad range of choices will be made wider yet depends not only upon the inventiveness of the leaders of the emergent states but also upon the solutions to their own problems found by the existing mature nation-states.

Nationalism both as value and as ideology is undergoing profound challenge in the developed world. If our propositions are correct, nationalism emerged as an ordering device for a degree of interdependence much higher than antecedent feudal and mercantile society had demanded. But new requirements continue to be forced on all parts of the world—developed and underdeveloped alike—by interrelationships contemptuous of man-made cultural and geographical boundaries. For example, the new bombs and their vehicles have made war a qualitatively different act from what it was before; they have thus also contributed to changing the very nature of diplomacy, and to developing a set of mutual dependencies in which internal politics of necessity also become foreign relations. No one anywhere in the world can any longer fail to have a vital concern in the course of domestic events within any country which has the wherewithal to poison the globe.

As in the early days of the nation some centuries ago, there exists a vested interest in adjusting to the new situation, but there are no institutional devices and no settled bodies of doctrine to control the daily aspects of the necessary change and to supply the rudder of prediction. But the concrete necessity for an ordering of control remains with us, and if we manage to conserve the time there can be no doubt that institutions, values, and ideologies will emerge to express the new supranational identifications man has forced on himself by exercising his restless mind.

Warfare is not the only example of the growing pattern of supranational relations. International cultural contacts are growing ever closer, economic systems ever more clearly need rationalization at regional and continental levels, science is becoming ever more universal with the spread of industrialization and a worldwide proliferation of demands for higher education, and governments meet these needs by reaching hesitantly for international organizations and regional arrangements. In response Western Europe has already spawned some fifty supranational bodies.

A slowly growing awareness of the new sets of mutual responsibilities is clearly spreading, binding all lands together even if most evanescently, and leading to the erection of experimental institutions and the fabrication of explanatory ideologies, pallid and flaccid as they still may be. As yet an underlying value structure on which to build even partial identifications seems to be lacking. The task of developing these values is the work of the century for the developed countries. The emergent nations will continue to have to cope with the problems of moving through all the complications of human development of which we have been writing. Whether they will be able to choose also from among supranational as well as merely national solutions is the primary responsibility of those who pride themselves on their power and maturity.

The Historical Distance
from
Tribe to Nation

"We live . . . lives based upon selected fictions. Our view of reality is conditioned by our position in space and time—not by our personalities as we like to think. Thus every interpretation of reality is based upon a unique position. Two paces east or west and the whole picture is changed."

LAWRENCE DURRELL
Balthazar

Chapter

1

Tribalism, Regionalism, and National Oligarchy:

Afghanistan

❧

LOUIS DUPREE

Colonialism often provides a convenient stone for the whetting of nationalism. An educated, middle-level colonial administrative class can be the rock of dissension around which nationalists may rally their complaints of economic and political exploitation; the colonial administrators and their local servants also create the ideological rock upon which the founders of nationalism can build their church. When there is no colonialism from which such a unifying and centralizing administrative group can come, the extreme stubbornness of tribal and regional interests cannot easily be broken with the tools of xenophobia or with techniques of centralizing power learned from abroad. Even the nationalist movement itself has a difficult development, for although the

existence of ideological and material aspirations borrowed from
the colonial power does not necessarily eliminate tribal or regional vested interest, these desires do serve to broaden the base
of a nationally oriented class whose elements often integrate the
positive goals of a nationalist movement.

Without the integrating effects of colonialism, therefore,
what are the patterns of the creation of nationalism within a
prevailing atmosphere of tribalism in which tribal and regional
power elites dominate most public loyalties? Afghanistan, a
landlocked and long semi-isolated monarchy, never became a
colony, even though it is surrounded by countries with varied
colonial backgrounds, and thus offers an excellent case for the
study of the question posed above. But this land did not succeed
entirely in escaping the immediate presence of European colonial
powers which, by investing surrounding areas and using the en-
capsulated territory as a buffer state, in effect defined the
boundaries of what we now call Afghanistan.

The Age of Imperialism made possible by the Age of Sail
led to the virtual isolation of Afghanistan from the mainstream
of human events. Czarist Russian ambitions in central and south
Asia and British expansionism in northwest India resulted in the
neutralization of Afghanistan, its enforced creation as a buffer
state. The British, concerned with protecting their Indian possessions, twice invaded Afghanistan, in 1838-1842 and 1878-1880.[1]
Both times the British suffered military disasters before their
eventually successful occupation of southern Afghanistan, and
both times they withdrew. This uncertainty ended in 1880 after
the Second Anglo-Afghan War, when Abdur Rahman Khan
became amir of Kabul with both British and Russian consent.

Before 1880 Afghanistan was but a collection of ethnic tribal
kingdoms, often with separate Pushtun[2] amirates in Kabul,

---

[1] For further details see Archibald Forbes, *The Afghan Wars 1839-42
and 1878-80*, New York: 1892, a good analysis; Sir Kerr Fraser-Tytler,
Afghanistan: A Study of Political Development in Central Asia, 2nd ed.,
London: 1958, for the British point of view; Sayyid Mohammad Qasim
Rishtiya, *Afghanistan in the Nineteenth Century*, Kabul: 1958, written
in Persian, for the Afghan point of view; and Dilip Kumar Ghosh,
England and Afghanistan: A Phase in Their Relations, Calcutta: 1960,
a new analysis which utilizes Lord Lytton's private papers.

[2] Pushtun, Pashtun, Pakhtun, Pukhtun, and Pathan are English
transliterations which refer to the ethnic group; Pashto, Pukhtu, Paktu,

Qandahar, and Herat which were periodically rent by fratricidal power struggles. Scores of minor tribal kingdoms straddled the present national boundaries: Uzbek, Turkoman, Tajik, and Kirghiz khanates spilled over into modern Soviet Central Asia; minor Pushtun kingdoms indiscriminately wandered over the modern Durand Line, which separates Afghanistan from West Pakistan; and independent mountain states flourished in Kafiristan,[3] the Hazarajat,[4] and other isolated ethnic and tribal areas.

Abdur Rahman attempted the first centralization of the country. The limits of modern Afghanistan had been included for brief periods in such native empires as that of Ahmad Shah Durani in the eighteenth century,[5] but at best these temporary liaisons were loose confederations. Meanwhile, Great Britain, Czarist Russia, and Qajar Persia combined to define the external boundaries of the land. Thus two acts of definition occurred simultaneously: while Afghan boundaries were being drawn by imperial powers to create a no-man's land—an act which split cultural and geographic areas for only political reasons—internal conquest by domestic power was also occurring, creating a sort of intramural imperialism. Abdur Rahman succeeded in subduing even such previously impregnable areas as Kafiristan. Although he did not destroy tribalism, he did manage by force to extend a centralizing political influence, if not a decisive control. At the same time, the very necessity for the employment of massive force served to make even deeper the existing intertribal schisms.

Overt Russo-British rivalry in Afghanistan theoretically ended with the Treaty of 1873, under whose provisions—as they were reaffirmed in the Convention of 1907—the British gained control over Afghan foreign affairs, but agreed not to interfere in domestic matters or to annex any part of the country. Other

---

and Pushtu refer to the language and its dialects. Pathan, usually used in British sources, is a Hindi bastardization of Pukhtun. Pushtun is the term generally used in Afghanistan.

[3] "Kafiristan" means "Land of the Heathens," now called "Nuristan," or "Land of Those Who Have Seen the Light," for its inhabitants were forcibly converted to Islam in the 1890s.

[4] The Hazarajat, the central mountain core of Afghanistan, is inhabited by the Hazara, a physically Mongoloid, Persian-speaking people.

[5] Laurence Lockhart, *The Fall of the Safavi Dynasty and the Afghan Occupation of Persia*, New York: 1958.

articles of the Convention concerned the division of Persia into two zones of British and Russian influence and recognized Chinese hegemony over Tibet. A joint Anglo-Persian Commission settled the western boundary of Afghanistan in 1895, while several Russian-British boundary commissions established the northern and northeastern frontiers between 1880 and 1895.

The Durand Line of 1893[6] is the most important single boundary for this discussion of prenational Afghan integration. A British delegation led by Sir Mortimer Durand visited Kabul and literally forced the amir to accept a line dividing British India from Afghan Durani[7] influence and responsibility. The line also split the Pushtun tribes almost equally between Afghanistan and British India. Sections of the same tribe often lived on opposite sides of the meandering, and in places unrealistic, border. This artificial political boundary still poses a major problem in southern Asia, halving a cultural area as it does and thus offering a constant invitation to fish in easily troubled waters.

The First Attempt at Modernization: 1901 to 1929

Abdur Rahman was succeeded as amir in 1901 by his son, Habibullah, without an internal dynastic struggle, an event almost unique in Afghan history. Domestically, Habibullah continued his father's efforts to spread a unifying governmental influence and control; externally, Afghanistan remained isolated with its foreign affairs determined by Great Britain. The amir attempted to demonstrate characteristic Afghan independence by a unilateral rejection of the Anglo-Russian Convention of 1907, but the two powers declared the Convention binding in any event. Until World War I Afghanistan continued to let the world pass by; few Afghans knew or were able to know what went on beyond their mountain valleys, as few do still today. In spite of the activities of able German agents[8] and the desires

---

[6] For a British account see Sir Percy M. Sykes, *The Right Honourable Sir Mortimer Durand*, London: 1926.

[7] The current Durani dynasty was established in 1880; one branch ruled until 1929, in which year another took over.

[8] See Oskar von Niedermayer, *Unter der Glutsonne Irans. Kriegserlebnisse der deutschen Expedition nach Persien und Afghanistan*, Dachau/Munich: 1925.

of some Afghan religious and tribal leaders to join the Ottoman Turks in an active holy war against the infidel British, Habibullah maintained Afghanistan's traditional neutrality throughout World War I.

With the assassination of Habibullah in 1919, dynastic strife returned to Afghanistan. Amanullah, Habibullah's third son, managed to fight his way to the amirship. In order to gain solidarity among the Afghan Pushtuns and to prevent the spread of internal civil violence, Amanullah in May of 1919 launched the month-long Third Anglo-Afghan War. Although the military results were inconclusive, the British, fresh from four bloody years of European trench warfare, happily agreed to cease hostilities and negotiate peace with the Afghans. Under the terms of the Peace Treaty of Rawalpindi concluded in 1919, the Afghans won the major victory of regaining the right to conduct their own foreign affairs. Afghan intellectuals thus consider 1919 as the year of their country's national independence.

Except for the ubiquitous tribal uprisings, Amanullah's reign was relatively uneventful until his extended eight months' tour in 1928 of India, Egypt, Europe, the Soviet Union, Turkey, and Iran. The remarkable strides toward modernization of Turkey, Iran, and the U.S.S.R. impressed the king (he had adopted the title in 1926), and he determined to lead Afghanistan down the same road. But Amanullah's advanced dreams of social and political reform became a personal nightmare. His attempts to remove the veil from women, introduce Western dress, establish coeducational instruction, separate church and state, and institute economic development programs with the aid of Soviet technicians brought opposition from all sides—the British, the Afghan religious leaders, the army, the royal family, and practically all other vested groups.

Revolts broke out among the Pushtuns of the south; the army, long neglected by Amanullah, deserted him, and he fled when an illiterate Tajik folk hero-bandit, one Bacha-i-Saqqao,[9] entered Kabul from the north and crowned himself Habibullah Ghazi, King of Afghanistan. Amanullah, in his zeal to reform, had

[9] Bacha-i-Saqqao means "son of a water carrier." For a fascinating though far from accurate account of this hectic period see Amir Habibullah, *My Life from Brigand to King*, London: n.d.

failed to realize that organized power is essential to effective reform. He died in European exile in 1960.

Nadir Shah and the Constitution: 1929 to 1933

General Mohammad Nadir Khan returned from exile to overthrow Bacha-i-Saqqao, whose reign lasted but nine months. Nadir Khan, formerly commander-in-chief of the Afghan army, had opposed Amanullah's attempts at revolutionary reform, preferring slower evolutionary methods, and paying with exile in France from 1924 to 1929. The bandit was no more to his liking. Despite warnings from the British, Nadir Khan and the four brothers with whom he mounted his enterprise succeeded in raising an army from both sides of the Durand Line, promising local tribal leaders freedom from central governmental interference in the event of victory, and thus encouraging a continuation of the tribal regionalism still plaguing Afghanistan. Much disagreement exists among Afghan intellectuals concerning the exact role of the British in the Amanullah–Bacha-i-Saqqao–Nadir Shah succession. Whatever the exact part may have been, the delicate light of British interest shines throughout this period of revolt and counterrevolt. After being declared king, Mohammad Nadir Shah reaffirmed all prior Anglo-Afghan treaties and agreements.

One of Nadir Shah's most important legacies is the Afghan constitution of 1931, which at least in theory made Afghanistan a constitutional monarchy. But in a land in which about 95 per cent of the population is illiterate, a constitution cannot be very effective as a guide to public conduct. Even today some Afghan students learn their country has a constitution only after they arrive in the United States for study. The constitution incorporates some of the most crisis-inspiring features of the pre-de Gaulle French constitution, modified by elements of Ataturk's Turkish constitution and the Iranian constitution of Reza Shah; it attempts to combine a *mélange* of Western economic, social, and political reform within a framework of Islamic law, tribal customs, and religious mandates. But an Afghan constitution still exists, ready to serve as a potential rallying point for the liberal, literate Afghan. Because the 1931 constitution does not separate church and state and offers only an illusion of popular participation in the affairs of state, a new organic law will probably be necessary before any type of substantively representative government can become a reality.

Nadir Shah also restored traditional Afghan neutrality, dismissed the Russians hired by the previous monarch, and refused a Soviet request for permission to establish commercial offices in Afghanistan. He and his successor son instead hired Germans, Italians, Japanese, and Indians as advisers, teachers, and technicians, pointedly ignoring both the bordering British and Russians.

This short but significant reign ended in March of 1933. A member of a rival group assassinated Nadir Shah—another incident in a continuing blood feud. His brother, Mohammad Azziz, also was assassinated in the same year in Berlin, victim of the same feud.

Slow Steps Forward: 1933 to 1953

Upon the death of Nadir Shah an unusual event occurred— his son, Mohammad Zahir, then 19 years of age, became king and occupies the throne today. Nadir Shah's surviving brothers realized that survival of the dynasty depended on a solid fraternal front, which they have managed to maintain against all subsequent temptations. In the first part of this period, spanning world depression, world war, and Cold War intrigue and rivalry, Afghanistan began to build at least a few of the elements of a modern social superstructure, particularly in the area of economic endeavor.

The policies of the state were generally conservative, based on a laissez-faire view of the role of private ownership and the establishment of a few government-chartered monopolies in banking and external trade.

The *Bank-i-Milli*, a private corporation, was licensed to control most import-export monopolies. With most of the important families represented as stockholders, the bank returned substantial profits. Although a large portion of such moneys stayed outside the country or was spent on luxury imports, some internal investments of significance were made, such as the cotton growing-textile plant complex in northern Afghanistan, the textile mill-power station complex in the central mountains, and sugar cane mills in the east. In 1938 the State Bank of Afghanistan was founded, opening up financial windows in British India, Munich, Paris, and London and controlling also the Afghan-American Trading Corporation of New York. The bank offered mineral concessions to foreign companies and encouraged foreign investments in general. Many German, Italian, Japanese, and Indian companies responded and some still have offices in Kabul.[10]

During the thirties and forties modern ideas penetrated very slowly. Any general trends toward modernization occurred only as by-products of the Afghan power elite's desire for economic development, an appetite made more effective after the conclusion of World War II. Like all countries supplying raw materials, Afghanistan could sell but not buy during the conflict. Much of Afghanistan's agricultural surplus flowed to the Allied armies in India, and the major caracul market shifted from London to New York. By employing the large dollar and sterling surplus which accumulated, Afghanistan immediately after the war launched a huge, ambitious irrigation, land reclamation, and power project in the south along the Helmand River watershed, which drains 40 per cent of the country. Misunderstandings existed from the very start between the Afghan government and the American engineering company building the installations; by 1949 most of Afghanistan's war-accumulated foreign exchange had disappeared and Import-Export Bank loans become necessary to insure completion of the project.[11]

A major political problem also dates from this period, with economic as well as international political repercussions of importance to the path of Afghan national integration. Briefly, the so-called "Pushtunistan" problem involves the status of several million Pushtuns living in West Pakistan along the Afghan frontier. Several times since 1950 Afghan agitation along the frontier has caused the Pakistanis to slow down or, in effect,

[10] E. F. Fox, *Travels in Afghanistan*, New York: 1943.
[11] See Aloys Arthur Michel, *The Kabul, Kanduz, and Helmand Valleys and the National Economy of Afghanistan*, National Academy of Sciences, National Research Council, Washington: 1959. Michel includes a complete bibliography on this problem.

to blockade goods in transit to and from Afghanistan. During the 1950 blockade the Afghan government asked the United States to help it develop an alternate in-transit route through Iran in order to bypass West Pakistan. The United States refused,[12] thus encouraging the Afghans to sign a barter agreement with the Soviet Union for the exchange of Afghan wool and raw cotton for Soviet petroleum products, cement, textiles, sugar, and other commodities. In addition to this barter, the Soviet Union began economic assistance programs, modestly at first with the construction of several large gasoline storage tanks, but increasing in scope as the 1950s slipped by. (See Table I.)

Slow as these developments were, and ripe with difficulties for the future as they turned out to be, during this period Afghanistan laid the first solid institutional pillars for whatever degree of modernization and national development has since come about. The external stabilization of boundaries and the internal growth of unification continued to be reflected in the molding of an Afghan nation.

Mohammad Daud and Statism: The Big Gamble

A major political change began in Afghanistan in 1953 when General Sardar (Prince) Mohammad Daud Khan, first cousin of the king and nephew of the prime minister whom he deposed, seized power. Four interrelated elements motivated the coup: first, discontent caused by the governmental policy of emphasizing returns to stockholders from the state-chartered monopolies, with relatively little forced reinvestment to assist in the creation of either an economic or a social middle class; second, misunderstandings between Afghans and Americans over the costly Helmand Valley project; third, the slowness of previous prime ministers in pushing large-scale economic development and social reform; and last, simply the personal desire of Prince Daud

---

[12] The major reasons for the American refusal may have been a belief that the Russians could not deliver, for only five years had passed since the end of World War II, in which the Russians had suffered more than the other Allies; Soviet Central Asia, too, is underdeveloped and the Soviets were working there. In addition, the Korean war was shaping up, and the project appeared too expensive at the time.

TABLE I

AFGHANISTAN'S EXPORTS AND IMPORTS BY TEN MAJOR TRADING COUNTRIES IN SELECTED FISCAL YEARS

(In thousands of afghanis. The official rate of exchange in the Spring of 1959 was 21 afghanis per U.S. $1.00.*)

EXPORTS Country	1951-1952	IMPORTS Country	1951-1952
India	215,054	India	255,995
U.S.A.	194,100	Pakistan	104,778
U.S.S.R.	133,963	U.S.S.R.	100,113
Pakistan	95,336	Japan	58,687
United Kingdom	59,315	U.S.A.	57,502
W. Germany	21,916	United Kingdom	30,562
Saudi Arabia	1,729	W. Germany	10,891
Netherlands	1,316	Italy	4,347
Japan	612	Czechoslovakia	120
Italy	50	Others (not specified)	23,048
Country	1957-1958	Country	1957-1958
India	580,252	U.S.S.R.	606,679
U.S.S.R.	455,818	Pakistan	406,171
U.S.A.	336,123	Japan	353,827
United Kingdom	254,783	India	214,924
W. Germany	117,750	U.S.A.	150,972
Czechoslovakia	111,939	West Germany	69,312
Pakistan	96,536	United Kingdom	53,032
Netherlands	8,329	Czechoslovakia	20,631
Lebanon	7,587	Italy	20,179
Poland	5,319	Red China	10,080
Country	1958-1959	Country	1958-1959
India	614,589	U.S.S.R.	685,445
U.S.A.	367,452	Japan	493,244
U.S.S.R.	294,467	U.S.A.	477,040
United Kingdom	202,046	India	313,010
Pakistan	100,884	Pakistan	208,789
West Germany	90,068	West Germany	107,490
Czechoslovakia	11,768	United Kingdom	72,775
Switzerland	10,631	Czechoslovakia	62,525
Lebanon	9,682	Italy	33,554
Austria	4,269	Red China	23,672

*A more realistic open market rate for this same period would be approximately 40 afghanis per U.S. $1.00.
Note: The fluctuating patterns of 1957 to 1959 are probably in response to Afghanistan's attempts to remain neutral in trade as well as in political relations.
Source: *Surveys of Progress: 1958, 1959, 1960,* Ministry of Planning, Royal Government of Afghanistan, Kabul.

for power. The movement was assisted by support from the army and the royal family and was so handily consolidated that no executions followed. In fact, Shah Mahmud, the deposed prime minister, died peacefully of old age in 1959.

The constant themes which run through Daud's policies are *étatisme*—state control of economic activities—the desire for increased U.S. and U.S.S.R. assistance programs, five-year development plans, social reforms, and the broadening of the bases of political power. These aims are, of course, within the now classical tradition of the nationalistic policies of underdeveloped areas. A summary examination of these policies, then, serves as an inventory of the present status of official nationalist aspirations in Afghanistan, against which can be measured the various impediments to and factors favoring national integration and development.

Statism was demonstrated early in the new prime minister's regime when the privately owned *Bank-i-Milli* was forced to sell most of its interests to the national government, including the various cotton combine investments, electric power projects, cement plants, and so forth. Two new branches of the State Bank were created, the Agricultural and Cottage Industries Bank (*Bank Zerati*) to assist small landowners, artisans, and home industries, and the Afghan Commercial Bank (*Pushtun Terjarati*) to service import-export merchants in order to break the *Bank-i-Milli* monopolies. The latter continues to operate, but its activities are kept under close surveillance in order to prevent continued tax evasion and to insure accurate reporting of foreign currency transactions.

Recently the Afghan government began to encourage the investment of foreign capital once again, reviving the concept of *étatisme* plus private enterprise with governmental coordination "to provide maximum benefit to all sections of the population."[13] The ideal that the nation's public and private economic sectors should be guided for the public welfare is still far from reality, however. Corruption continues to exist in many places, but administrative efficiency and the percentage of total capital outlay properly utilized in developmental programs increase each year

---

[13] Afghanistan Mission to the United Nations, *The Five Year Plan of Afghanistan*, New York: 1956, p. 1.

as the prime minister's special investigative branches ferret out corrupt officials.

Assistance programs for Afghanistan from the Soviet Union and the United States date from 1954, after the accession of Daud Khan, when the Soviets extended their first loan. Since then both American and Soviet assistance have increased, with the Afghan government integrating these loans and grants into the First Five Year Plan of 1956-61. (See Tables II-A and II-B.)

TABLE II-A

U.S.S.R. ASSISTANCE LOANS TO AFGHANISTAN

Purpose of Loan	Date Authorized	Amount (in millions of dollars)
1. Grain silos, bakery, flour mill	Jan. 1954	$ 3.5
2. Gasoline storage tanks, pipelines	July 1954	1.2
3. Road building equipment	Aug. 1954	2.0
4. Cement and other industrial plants (from Czechoslovakia)	Aug. 1954	5.0
5. Asphalt plant, paving machines, etc.	May 1955	2.1
6. Industrial, power, irrigation, road and airport projects	Dec. 1955	100.0
7. Arms and ammunition (Soviet bloc)	July 1956	32.4
8. Oil drilling, exploration, and transportation equipment	Aug. 1957	15.0
9. Highway construction	May 1959	80.0
10. Port development and wheat	May 1959	5.0
TOTAL		$246.2

Source: After Peter G. Franck, *Afghanistan Between East and West,* Washington: National Planning Association, 1960.

Military assistance, however, also constitutes an important part of Soviet aid to Afghanistan. The Afghans, as has been their invariable custom, turned first to the United States for arms after Pakistan signed arms aid agreements with the United States in 1954. Pakistan then subsequently joined SEATO and CENTO. The American government refused the request because of Pakistani objections and the fact that Afghan officials refused to sign the required mutual security agreements. Since 1956 a steady flow of Soviet bloc arms including small arms, tanks, MIGs, Ilyushin jet bombers, and helicopters has bolstered the Afghan

TABLE II-B

U.S.A. ASSISTANCE PROGRAMS TO AFGHANISTAN

Obligations Contracted, 1950 through September 1959

Purpose of Credit	Amount (in millions of dollars)
1. Transportation (including airline development)	$ 51.9
2. Helmand Valley Project	49.4
3. Wheat	22.7
4. Education	7.6
5. Industry (primarily surveys)	4.2
6. Agriculture (experimental stations, etc.)	3.8
7. Public administration (surveys and training)	1.9
8. Others	4.3
TOTAL	$145.8

Note: Included in these figures are loans of almost $52,000,000, divided as follows: $8.4 million for transportation, $41 million for the Helmand Valley Project, $1.4 million for wheat, and $800,000 for industry.
Sources: United States Agency for International Development, United States Operations Mission/Afghanistan, and publications of pertinent Afghan ministries.

army's efficiency and morale, and thus strengthened the government in its centralizing efforts.

Afghanistan's five-year development plans have had no smoother going than the ill-fated Helmand Valley project. The first, the 1956-1961 plan, achieved few of its original objectives; the second is dedicated to completion of the first and the initiation of small-scale regional industrialization. The present plan represents a departure from the thinking of the first undertaking, which emphasized agriculture, improved transport and communications facilities related to increased agricultural output, mining and power, and education. On careful examination the five-year plans appear to move in the two mutually supporting though initially divergent directions of regional economic development and national political cohesion. The plans revolve about efforts to substitute national production for such imports as petroleum products, cement, textiles, and sugar, which have been consuming large amounts of foreign exchange. The continued improvement of the roads and the internal air transport system will facilitate the nationwide marketing of these products. In turn, an improvement in communications should help tighten and extend central governmental control, a tendency which is of course abhorrent to the tribes. The government also hopes to promote mobility and eventually to create national unity through compulsory education at the village level. The accent on regional economic development, then, tends to emphasize region over nation only in the short run.

Economic development and social reform are, of course, directly related. As Galbraith has written: "There can be no effective advance if the masses of the people do not participate; man is not so constituted that he will bend his best energies for the enrichment of someone else. As literacy is economically efficient, so is social justice."[14]

This subject will be discussed much more exhaustively later in this chapter when we turn to the fundamental cohesive and divisive elements in Afghan society. A preliminary mention here is necessary, however, to indicate that the incumbent government of Afghanistan recognizes—even if only intuitively—the relationship between social reform and economic development; this is evidenced by their gradual secularization of law, land reform, and the very slow movement toward a centralized representative government. The voluntary removal of the veil from women is another profoundly difficult reform which can also create a massive enlargement of the labor force.

The power base imposing these economic, political, and social policies has also been readjusting itself. For the first time since he came to the throne in 1933, King Mohammad Zahir Shah has a prime minister of his own age. The two previous incumbents, both uncles of the king, ruled as the patriarchs of a patriarchal society, seldom consulting the younger king. The situation roughly resembled a gerontocratic oligarchy having only a very loose connection with the nominal monarch, where the important social, economic, and political positions were all held in the same aged hands. Even though much closer liaison now exists between the king and all the major power elements, with a leveling out of the nature of the peer groups in power, government is still in very large measure a family and patriarchal matter. For example, the foreign minister, who

[14] John Kenneth Galbraith, *Economic Development in Perspective*, Cambridge: 1962, p. 13.

is also a deputy prime minister, is a brother of the prime minister himself and a first cousin of the king.

The prime minister, king, and foreign minister form a staggered power triangle, having influence in the order given. Because the prime minister is supported by the army, he holds the ultimate decision-making power. He is also maintained by a very broad consensus of agreement, a product of the fact that at this point in history almost all literate Afghans agree with his goals, if not with his means of attaining them. And despite the continuing importance of kinship, the situation has become sufficiently complicated so that the cabinet and the country's corps of influential persons now include many individuals outside the royal family. The power distribution at the topmost level has thus been broadened, and the number of individuals who, with varying degrees of intensity and diverse motivations, are interested in the national welfare of Afghanistan continues to expand with increased educational opportunities.

The historical course of the centralizing events of Afghan political life thus has moved the country closer to the possibilities of national development, but the crucial events of the passage from tribalism to modernism have yet to occur. It is to the more internal parts of social life, the questions of values and organization, of inhibition of growth and promotion of change, that we now turn.

Internal Divisive Factors

Out of the ashes of World War II arose many new nations. The process of development goes on in all of them, but the case of each nation presents a unique combination of circumstances, of factors inhibiting and promoting development. Various divisive and cohesive factors, each with built-in contradictions, affect the concept of nationalism in Afghanistan in ways unlike those familiar from better known cases. A discussion of the divisive factors follows.

1. *The tribe.* Throughout Afghanistan the basic organization is a tribal system with all the ingroup loyalties and outgroup antagonisms this structure implies. Afghan social organization can be described as patriarchal, patrilineal, and patrilocal (that

is, the bride moves to the village of the groom). The preferred marriage is with the father's brother's daughter (parallel cousin), which tends to reinforce group solidarity and facilitate the maintenance of patrilocal residence.

Traditionally, a man owes first loyalty to his extended family, usually limited to the three generations of grandparents through grandchildren. The middle generation fulfills its role as economic provider, while early child socialization often rests almost exclusively with grandparents. A man's further loyalties, in descending order of importance, are to lineage (all kin on father's side of family), sub-tribe, tribe, tribal confederation or ethnic group, and nation, but he is related to the last-named mainly in the role of taxpayer and conscript. The sub-tribe and tribe are essentially territorial designations strengthened by mythical or assumed kinship ties.

Blood feuds still exist, especially in the Pushtun areas of southern and eastern Afghanistan. Feuds seldom include major tribal units; "limited wars" are the pattern. Pushtun lineages in the same sub-tribe will fight one another, for example, but will unite to fight non-Pushtuns.

A man's basic political loyalty focuses on an individual leader within his own tribal or ethnic group, and is generally unrelated to issues or national symbols, essential features of evolving nationalism. The villager or tribesman supports his leaders against all outsiders, even engaging when necessary in sporadic warfare with the central government. Reciprocally the local leaders serve as buffers between their people and the central government, especially in matters of taxation and conscription.

The nomads and seminomadic groups, still relatively large in number in Afghanistan, contribute little to the nation-building processes. Recent attempts to settle small numbers of nomads in the Helmand Valley have succeeded only in part. The government plans eventually to include nomads in the educational programs and to force them to pay more taxes and serve in the armed forces, obligations which most groups now evade. By settling farmers on marginal grasslands normally used by nomads as pasturage the government graphically encourages nomadic groups to adopt seminomadism and become part-time farmers. In Afghanistan, unlike Iran, nomads seldom own pasturelands, but simply have grazing rights. The Afghan government owns all uncultivated land. The government, therefore, backs farmers who convert grasslands to cropland; as a result of this policy several nomadic groups have successfully converted to a transitional seminomadic existence in which part of the group remains behind in the winter grazing lands to farm, while the majority travels to the alpine summer pastures. Such changing settlement patterns continue to reduce the political power of the tribes.

2. *Religion.* Many observers believe religion to be a cohesive force in Islamic countries, but strong religious belief and organization imply also the retention of the *status quo*. In a peasant society without a constitutionally separated church and state, religious leaders have powerful vested political interests and, at times, economic interests such as major landholdings. The religious groups realize that modernization includes increased educational opportunities with accompanying secularizing effects, and that increased secularization means a diminution of their political power. In such a situation, religious leaders preach against any and all reform programs. Religious resistance helped bring on the downfall of King Amanullah in 1929.

Approximately 99 per cent of all Afghans are Muslims, mostly *Hanafi Sunni. Hanafi* refers to a *Shari'ah* or school of law and means roughly "denomination"; *Sunni* is one of the two major divisions of Islam. *Shi'i* (the second major Islamic grouping of breakaway sects) comprise about 10 per cent of the population, but many *Shi'i* try to pass for *Sunni* because the constitution of Afghanistan states that the law of the land will be the *Hanafi Shari'ah* of *Sunni* Islam (Article I of the 1931 Constitution). Some *Shi'i* practice *taqiya* (denying that one is *Shi'i* under duress or for advantage, but remaining pure in belief) in order to obtain government jobs or to escape public and private ridicule.

Religion, especially among non-literate peoples, serves to identify members of an ingroup from everyone else—Muslim from Christian, Muslim from Hindu, Muslim from communist. The more sophisticated, literate Afghans make no such distinctions privately, but many do so publicly. The Afghan clergy, however, especially the untutored, illiterate folk *mullahs* of the villages and nomadic camps, fight all such modern infringements

on the social, economic, and political order as the removal of
the veil, secularization of the school system, cadastral surveys,
and land taxes, and even the most feeble attempts to separate
church and state. Four factors have recently kept the religious
leaders in check: loyalty of the army to the person of Prime
Minister Daud, quick arrest and subsequent reorientation of the
mullahs when they voice opposition to reform policies, increased
mobility of the law-enforcing branches of government and the
army brought about by improved telecommunications and road
networks, and increasing literacy.

Although the urban religious leaders and the folk *mullahs*
have lost political power, they are far from impotent. The
present regime cleverly uses the concepts of Islam to combat
the religious leaders, although the ideology of modern nationalism—including the separation of church and state—runs counter
to religious doctrine as interpreted by the priestly class. The
central government wishes to destroy the political power of the
religious groups without impairing their role in spiritual guidance.

To true believers, Islam is the only nation on earth; Muslim
rulers serve as Allah's representatives. In Muslim countries the
king rules by divine sanction, not divine right. The religio-
political theory holds that if a ruler should break the law of
Islam, Allah withdraws sanction and ultimately the ruler will
be overthrown. This concept can justify pragmatic politics in
such a manner as partly to account for the continuing process
of political fission and fusion in the Islamic world.

The present social reforms and modernization programs in
Afghanistan strike at many key customs which have the aura
of religious sanction, although in reality no formalized religious
justification may exist. Prime Minister Daud operates within
this framework of the adjustment of political practice to religious
precept and custom. His chief legal advisers, trained religious
leaders with Western legal educations as well, carefully examine
each modernization step to insure against violation of Muslim
law. The prime minister institutes the program; he issues no
firmans (royal decrees), but rather presents the country with a
fait accompli.

Let us examine such a reform, the previously mentioned successful removal of the veil in 1959. This is perhaps the most important social, political, and economic event of this century, for all institutional dynamics have been affected by this one major move. For centuries the custom of *purdah* (isolation of women) and wearing the *burqa* or *choudry* (veil) was justified by an assumed religious sanction. A careful examination of the *Quran*, the *Hadiths* (Sayings of the Prophet), and the *Hanafi Shari'ah* of *Sunni* Islam (the religious law practiced in Afghanistan) reveals no definite, unqualified sanction. Early Islam in truth did not consider women inferior, and they played important, active roles in political as well as social and economic matters. During the process of urban adaptation, however, most Muslims adopted *purdah*, a relic of the property-conscious, then decadent Byzantine Empire which the virile, nomadic Arabs conquered in the seventh century.

Having determined that *purdah* and the veil could not be absolutely justified in Islamic law, the prime minister and his advisers acted dramatically but unofficially. During the 1959 independence holidays the king, prime minister, cabinet members, army commanders and other influential persons stood on the reviewing stand accompanied by their wives and daughters, who appeared with their faces bared. The large crowd of spectators stared in stunned disbelief, encouraged by the fact that many of the ladies were lovely.

The inevitable happened. A delegation of religious leaders requested and received an audience with the prime minister. The *mullahs* accused him of being anti-Islamic, of permitting atheistic communists and Christian Westerners to pervert the nation. The prime minister informed the delegation that if they could find total, undeniable justification for *purdah* and the veil in Islamic law he would be the first to return his wife and daughters to *purdah*. This sporting proposition did not appeal to the religious leaders, several of whom were illiterate folk *mullahs*. Mere logic cannot destroy overnight the aura of religious sanction hanging over a custom for longer than anyone can remember, as witness the cries of some southern American crossroads preachers (Christian folk *mullahs*) who insist the Bible condones racial segregation as the will of God.

Immediately after leaving the prime minister's office the

religious leaders began to preach against the present regime. Prince Daud's very efficient secret police arrested and jailed about fifty of the ringleaders. No popular revolts followed the arrests, as had been predicted by some Afghans and many foreigners. The government did not fall, but rather became stronger. Within the context of Islamic law the logic is irrefutable, for the concept of divine sanction makes the *mullahs* guilty both of treason and heresy. In attacking the state and failing to destroy it, the *mullahs* actually attacked Islam as well as the Afghan state.

The prime minister released the *mullahs* after about a week's incarceration and indoctrination. Government spokesmen informed the religious leaders that the removal of the veil was voluntary; this was only partly true because the government forced officials to attend public functions with unveiled wives in order to set examples for the masses. For the bulk of the population, however, unveiling is an elective act, and many women still wear the *burqa*, either by their own or their husbands' choice.

The prime minister plans to continue this policy of first instituting reforms and then waiting for the religious leaders to attack him and the ruling group. Earlier King Amanullah had moved first against the Muslim clergy, thus hardening resistance against him and his reform programs. Whenever the religious leaders attack the central government and lose, they also lose prestige and power in the eyes of the Afghan people, who become even more convinced that Allah does indeed support the government programs. But the political power of the conservative religious groups is far from smashed, for, in fact, most of the population continues to listen to local religious leaders for political guidance. On the whole the religious men protest increased education, land reform, and other such proposals as anti-Islamic. The high-level fights between church and state can have little immediate effect as yet on the rural peasants and wandering nomads. Islam, therefore, functions as a cohesive but anti-nationalist force at the village and nomad camp level.

3. *Discrimination among ethnic groups.* A pecking order exists among Afghan ethnic groups in the following progression from

top to bottom: Pushtun-Tajik-Uzbek-Turkoman-Hazara. Most of the other groups usually stay in their respective geographic homes, thus avoiding the daily measure of the status hierarchy. As previously mentioned, religious discrimination also plays a role, as in the case of the Tajik, many of whom are *Shi'i* Muslim. Although the basic Afghan physical type is an Iranian Plateau variant of the great Mediterranean white racial stock, much Mongoloid admixture occurred among northern and central peoples. The non-Mongoloid Afghans believe the dominantly Mongoloid-appearing groups, especially the Hazara, to be the descendants of the thirteenth century Mongols who, under Chinggis Khan, devastated the Middle East. Some Afghans therefore consider discrimination a justifiable revenge for historic wrongs. Small dark-skinned groups persist also, probably genetic remnants of ancient Dravidian speakers now to be found principally in southern India. As an aside, it may be added that Afghans prefer light-skinned mates.

Discrimination manifests itself in two primary fashions— in an ethnocentrism almost racist in its intensity in the minds of some Pushtuns, and in the lack of equal job and educational opportunities. Non-Pushtun peoples usually believe that Pushtuns get all the good jobs, just as all commoner Pushtuns believe that all good government jobs go to the royal family. Few Pushtuns work as servants, and Mongoloid-looking Hazara serve almost exclusively as a coolie class when they leave their mountain homes for urban centers. Discrimination is breaking down at the highest levels, however, and many non-Pushtuns hold important administrative and military positions. Strong discriminatory outgroup feelings continue to exist among the illiterate urban, village, and nomadic groups, of course.

4. *Suppression of political opposition by the central government.* The present regime permits no opposition parties. The one short period of political permissiveness occurred during Shah Mahmud's prime-ministership in 1950. Student groups, at times covertly encouraged by their foreign teachers, produced opposition plays often derogatory to Islam and the royal family. After a hectic period of unorganized, non-directed opposition, the government quieted the students. The lack of a positive program helped kill this nascent opposition movement. Today, however,

several of the 1950 student leaders hold high positions in government, working on positive programs. In Afghanistan, "opposition" has always meant only one thing—preparation to overthrow the government. The present prime minister, for example, seized power from his uncle, an extra-constitutional pattern of succession common throughout Afro-Asia and parts of Latin America. Complicating Afghan political procedures is the fact that most presently influential persons received their advanced education in France during the 1930s, and became contaminated with the cynical *incivisme* of the French intellectual class who, along with most Frenchmen, traditionally love France the Nation and hate the Government in the broadest sense. A long tradition of mutual mistrust between government and governed flowers in both Afghanistan and France, and the coexistence of graft and love of country does not seem incongruous.

When young men return with Western education and talk of responsible opposition, then the ruling clique views them with suspicion. Most of these young men do in fact favor the ends desired by Prince Daud, including the eventual growth of representative government, but would like to participate in the decision-making as well as the decision-implementing processes of government. A Western education usually trains them for such functions, but the government makes little or no use of these talents. A man is assigned a job and told exactly how to do it. The rulers not only find it difficult to believe that opposition to methods and policies can be a loyal opposition in the Western sense, but also cling to the logic of the patriarchal social structure in which age serves as one of the key prerequisites for knowledge and authority; the young should obey and learn while doing.

Whatever his motives, Prime Minister Daud encourages the student population with such statements as this:

> The one dream of the Royal Family is someday to give the country of Afghanistan to the Afghans, and let the people select the type of government they want. It will take more than the four or five people in power to do this, however. It will take the education of the majority of our people. This is a slow process. We would not for a minute

hesitate to give up the throne if this would advance true freedom in Afghanistan. This I say very sincerely and frankly.[15]

If, however, the prime minister does nothing to satisfy these aspirations after dangling them before students, he will lay the foundation for the possible downfall of his clique, because student groups almost always lead truly revolutionary factions in underdeveloped countries. The danger is especially great in this case, for Afghan students studying in the West often adopt extremist attitudes and feel revulsion toward the Afghan scene when they return home. They lack understanding of their own culture, a common phenomenon among any people in any given society. The returning students are blind to the total directional patterns which, when viewed within the context of the Afghan cultural and historical background, are probably valid for this moment of socio-political time. The students might best work within the existing system if they consider the government's announced and publicized ends to be good for the nation. Anti-government attitudes and actions may well lead to suppression and defeat, hinder long-range roals, and render trained hands and minds impotent.

5. *Illiteracy.* The problem of illiteracy obviously is directly related to the creation of a responsible opposition. Although Islamic civilization is literate and highly sophisticated and some of the finest Persian poetry was written in Afghanistan, approximately 95 per cent of the Afghans are illiterate. To foster nationalist feeling, the appropriate symbolism, and the dissemination of ideas a nation needs a literate population. Also, with an emergent literate class, there can be more prestige jobs for minorities and the trappings of ultra-conservative Islam will be weakened.

6. *Nepotism in the power elite.* Theoretically a constitutional monarchy, Afghanistan is actually ruled by an oligarchy consisting of controlling elements of the Musahiban family (the extended royal family) of the Yahya Khel lineage of the Mohammadzai sub-tribe of the Durani tribe of the Pushtun ethnic

[15] Louis Dupree, "An Informal Talk with Prime Minister Daud," American Universities Field Staff Reports Service, Vol. III, No. 3, 1959.

group. This system relates to the Afghan kin-political structure which reinforces group and individual loyalties.

Most Afghans believe that all good government jobs go to the Mohammadzai, an attitude which robs the regime of much loyalty. Every Afghan can cite specific examples. Since 1953, however, the present prime minister's attempt to weed out members of the royal family holding sinecures in the government and to appoint qualified non-Pushtuns to important jobs has gained some support from ethnically subordinate groups, and at the same time naturally has created personal antagonisms and opposition within his own group.

7. *Improper utilization of educated manpower.* Mismanagement in manpower assignments usually results because of a misunderstanding of the function of Western education. Afghan young men with Western college degrees often receive jobs inconsistent with their training. Men trained in medicine, for example, have worked for the government press department while others trained in economics teach law, the theory being that a college-educated man can handle any job. Such maladministration creates personal and group antagonisms among those affected. The misassigned individual seldom does a productive job, and often becomes bitter and either adapts to the lassitude and graft of the accepted way of life or becomes a rebel fighting the system. The government interprets such opposition as disloyalty, and the individual involved may lose his job or be otherwise punished. This currently unorganized, wronged group—a so-called "intellectual proletariat"—may develop into an organized opposition.

Although the present regime is consciously trying to rectify the misuse of manpower, this major problem still plagues governmental efficiency.

External Divisive Factors: The Problem of "Pushtunistan"

The mid-twentieth century presents us with a volatile phenomenon on the political landscape, the artificial political boundary cutting through cultural and geographic entities. If we carry this concept to its logical—or illogical—extreme, *all* boundaries are artificial. But the ones of particular interest to us in this discussion are the end results of the imperialist land grabs, primarily by European powers, during the eighteenth and nineteenth centuries. Border disputes are an important bitter fruit of colonialism, coming into greater prominence everywhere with the recession of imperialism itself.

As has been noted earlier, the Durand Line of 1893 divided the Pushtuns into two areas of political influence, British India and the Durani kingdom of Afghanistan. The British, for reasons which they felt were justified, considered the Durand Line a boundary; the Afghans always took the line as delimiting zones of responsibility and subject to negotiation. In several diplomatic documents, however, the Afghans accepted reference to the Durand Line as a "frontier," a word which, depending on various interpretations, may refer either to a specific line or a zone. This chapter is not the place to argue the niceties of international law, but the Afghan demand for a plebiscite in the Pushtun areas of West Pakistan has led to a Pakistani counterdemand for a plebiscite in the Pushtun areas of Afghanistan.

Since the first mention of a separate Pushtun state just after World War II, the situation has steadily deteriorated, with occasional bloodshed punctuating the war of words. As stated earlier, the problem of "Pushtunistan" led directly to the partial blockade of Afghan in-transit goods through West Pakistan in 1950, 1955, and 1960, and the subsequent appearance of extensive Soviet aid to Afghanistan. The military alignment of Pakistan with the West accentuated this process, of course, and also gave rise to Russian support of Afghanistan's demand for a "Pushtunistan" plebiscite. Many Afghans admit privately they would like to see the Pakistani Pushtun areas incorporated into Afghanistan, although the official line pleads for independence of the region. Because of this not-so-hidden desire, Pakistan, in turn, demands that the Afghan Pushtuns also be permitted to vote on independence. The issue remains hazy, and even the areas delineated by Kabul as "Pushtunistan" vary, at times including almost all West Pakistan west of the Indus River down to the Arabian Sea, and embracing many non-Pushtun peoples.

Whatever the merits of the two cases, the "Pushtunistan" issue channels much energy away from internal nation-building and functions as an extremely divisive force because the Pakistanis beam propaganda at Afghanistan's Pushtuns as well as vice versa. In addition most non-Pushtun Afghans—about 50 per cent of the total population—consider the issue none of their business and resent the present ruling group's emphasis on "Pushtunistan."

Soviet Penetration

Both Afghan and Soviet officials insist that Soviet aid is strictly economically oriented and that no Russian personnel proselytize. But some Soviet technicians do indeed preach dissidence.[16] Russians have told Afghans who work with them that the country's woes spring from a royal family that is "corrupt and keeps good men from advancing," and a religion which "provides paradise after death, but helps the royal family control the peasants and workers during life." Both statements, unfortunately, contain some elements of truth.

On the other hand, prior to 1950 official Soviet propaganda attacked "feudalistic Afghanistan," but today nothing but praises echo from Radio Tashkent and the Soviet embassy in Kabul. The Soviets no longer believe in the inevitability of social revolutions to overthrow the governments of neutral, underdeveloped countries. Economic penetration will do the trick. Mr. Khrushchev and his advisers realize that massively affecting one institution in a society affects all institutions. In the past century the Afghans became masters at gambling for political survival, but their current economic gambles are still inconclusive. Overtly, however, the Soviets make no move to disturb the political status quo—yet. Instead the Soviets prefer to keep the Pakistan-Afghan pot boiling over the "Pushtunistan" issue. The United States, caught in a familiar post-World War II posture, has been straddling the shaky fence of nondecision, trying to remain neutral in the area, while Russian support for the Afghan position feeds emotional fuel to an already volatile situation.

[16] For more details on Soviet methods and motives see Henry Byroade, "The Changing Position of Afghanistan in Asia," Department of State Bulletin, January 23, 1961, pp. 125-134.

The Soviets constantly propagandize among the northern minority groups in Afghanistan, especially those with counterpart Soviet Socialist Republics in Central Asia—the Turkomans, Uzbeks, Tajiks, and Kirghiz. In most cases the propaganda is unheeded because the Afghan northerners are either refugees or the descendants of refugees who fled Czarist or Bolshevik oppression. If the rulers of Afghanistan fail to give these minority groups and the educated young men of all ethnic groups a more active role in government, however, Soviet siren calls may have a potential audience.

An important element of Soviet penetration revolves about Soviet arms assistance to Afghanistan. The Afghan army, pampered by Prince Daud, remains loyal, but young colonels and some older generals seem to be susceptible to political ambition in countries from Argentina to Korea where barracks revolts are acceptable patterns of political behavior. But although the Soviets totally arm the Afghans, many officers still come to the United States for training. Some pilots, for example, learn to fly American military jets and then return to Afghanistan to fly MIGs.

Cohesive Factors

1. *History and legend.* Most Afghans, regardless of ethnic origin, share the myth of the invincibility of Afghan arms. Old men often recount half-legendary accounts of Afghan victories over Alexander the Great, Chinggis Khan, Tamerlane, Nadir Shah of Safavid Persia, the Indians, the British and the Russians. These stories and the *Pushtunwali* ("code of the hills") breed the generalized, idealized basic personality structure of the Afghan, who is seen as a man of personal honor, valor, and independence, a great lover and great warrior. This epitome of masculine egotism insists that the most glorious feat in a man's life is to kill or be killed in a feud or war. The warrior-poet remains the ideal folk hero of the Afghan.

The dissonant note is struck by ethnocentrism. Pushtuns are proud of Pushtun glory, Uzbeks of their once great Central Asian khanates, Tajiks of their brief glory under Bacha-i-Saqqao in 1929. But all are proud of their military heritage.

2. *The army.* The military, power base of the present prime minister, serve nationalism by maintaining order while reform programs roll roughshod over local customs, and by integrating draftees into units indiscriminately, try to infuse minority elements with feelings of belonging.

3. *The schools.* The high rate of illiteracy of Afghanistan makes national unity difficult. Few reliable statistics exist for the country; no one knows even the total population figure because a simple nose count has never been taken. The usual estimates range from eight to twelve million persons. An ICA study developed the following educational estimates, based on the higher population figure. (See Table III.)

The Afghans have no consistent definition for literacy, but some officials estimate that in 1929 only one thousand Afghans were literate, and that by 1960 the figure had jumped to five hundred thousand; in other words, if twelve million is accepted as the total population figure, about 4 per cent of the total population is estimated to be literate. Recognizing illiteracy as a major deterrent to development, the Afghan government gives education a major role in its five-year plans. The First Five Year Plan (1956-1961) emphasized the establishment of teacher training institutes, with Columbia University Teachers College assisting under an ICA contract. The next five years will be spent primarily in building schools in towns and villages and sending teachers to staff them. American aid is also being extended to the Afghans in the construction of Kabul University, officially founded in 1946. Previously the university consisted of a series of colleges (Medicine, Science, Literature, Religion, Engineering and Agriculture, Economics, etc.) scattered about Kabul in separate buildings with a student body of about a thousand. The graduates of Kabul University numbered approximately one thousand at the end of 1960.

Many Afghan students must therefore still go overseas for college and university training. Some pay their own way, but the majority have government support. About five hundred students studied abroad on Afghan government scholarships during the decade of the 1950s, a figure which has undergone such a sharp increase since 1960 that it should easily be quad-

TABLE III

ESTIMATED SCHOOL-AGE POPULATION AND SCHOOL ENROLLMENTS IN AFGHANISTAN, 1959

Age Groups	Approximate Population	Percent of Total Population*	School Enrollment	Percent of Total School Enrollment	Percent of Age Group Enrolled in School
Elementary and rural school ages (7-12)	1,920,000	16.0	141,319	91.0	7.4
Middle school ages (13-15)	720,000	6.0	9,950†	6.4	1.4
High school ages (16-18)	672,000	5.6	2,450††	1.6	.4
University ages (19-22)	696,000	5.8	1,495	1.0	.2
Total	4,008,000	33.4	155,214	100.0	

* Estimated at 12,000,000.
† 80% in vocational schools.
†† 20% in vocational schools.
Source: Richard E. Spencer, "An Estimate of the Population of Afghanistan Enrolled in School," International Cooperation Agency, Kabul: October 21, 1959, mimeo. The study is an extrapolation from the study of one village to the country as a whole.

rupled during this decade. Some approximate figures comparing 1960 with 1962 are as follows:[17]

Table IV

AFGHAN STUDENTS OVERSEAS

Country	Number of Students 1960	1962
United States	172	250
West Germany	76	200
Lebanon (American University of Beirut)	35	25
France	32	20
Switzerland	29	5
United Arab Republic	8	5
U.S.S.R.	8	300
Italy	6	10
Czechoslovakia	—	80
Poland	—	5
Hungary	—	4
Japan	—	4
TOTALS	356	908

[17] These figures, gathered from Afghan sources, are approximate both in the numbers given and the roster of countries, for a few Afghan students are also found in India, Iran, Turkey, and the United Kingdom, but no adequate sources could be found for a reasonably reliable approximation of their numbers.

Both the United States and the U.S.S.R. offer scholarships. Most Afghan students receiving overseas educations on government scholarships win them honestly, but some nepotism does exist. Prominent Afghans can and do get preferential favors and grades changed for their sons, and qualified students sometimes remain in Afghanistan while sons of the privileged run around American or European universities. This situation, however, is constantly improving.

Examined in cultural context, Afghanistan's educational progress in the past five years has been phenomenal. As more young Afghans are exposed to various Western liberal and communist ideologies, the oligarchical basis of the present power elite will be undermined and a process of self-liquidation begun. Whereas nationalists in a colonial milieu can flex their newfound ideological muscles against imperialist nations, the emerging Afghan literate class can turn only against their own rulers.

4. *Internal migrations.* Forced migrations during modern times date back to the period of pacification and loose unification under Amir Abdur Rahman (1880-1901).[18] Abdur Rahman divided Afghanistan into provinces with little regard for existing tribal boundaries in an attempt to break down regional tribal loyalties. The new system split many tribes and ethnic groups between two or more provinces. Provincial governors, usually distinguished generals, had administrative *carte blanche* so long as they sent the allotted taxes and conscripts to Kabul. An internal spy system helped keep the officials honest. A manorial type of political organization grew out of this decentralization of authority,[19] creating a system of quasi-independent states.

The tribesmen and villagers, unused to recognizing any but tribal law and customs, knew little about the actions of the central government; for many, especially in zones of easy accessibility, the provincial governor and his private army replaced the old tribal authority. Any signs of discontent were immediately put down by the army.

Before 1880 the clan community existed as the dominant socio-economic-political unit in southern Afghanistan. Although the governors had the right and the obligation to collect taxes, they did not own the land. In southcentral and southwestern Afghanistan, however, the right to collect taxes became confused, either consciously or unconsciously, with *bona fide* ownership of land. Government officials sold land without regard for the traditional joint ownership of village lands by the clan. The landlord-tenant system which developed after 1880 gradually broke down the socio-economic and political functions of the clan and tribe, so that today no clan villages exist in this part of Afghanistan.[20] The family (either extended or nuclear) has

[18] For a detailed discussion of this process see Louis Dupree, "The Changing Character of South-Central Afghanistan Villages," *Human Organization,* Vol. XIV, No. 4, 1956, pp. 26-29.
[19] Louis Dupree, "Medieval European Feudalism and the Contemporary Middle East," *Report on Current Research,* Washington: Spring, 1957, pp. 47-55. The article also discusses the misuse of the term "feudalism" when referring to the modern Middle East.
[20] The 1880 ethnic distributions show up clearly in the maps by Lt. R. C. Temple, "Rough Notes on the Distribution of the Afghan Tribes about Kandahar," *Journal of the Asiatic Society of Bengal,* Vol. LXVII, Part 1:3, Calcutta: 1879, pp. 181-185.

emerged as the basic socio-economic unit. Peasants must sign tenancy agreements annually, and they can be shifted from village to village by landlords. Often a tenant farmer will live in one village and farm fields in another. This split farming system, as it may be called, keeps individual villages and groups of villages in a constant state of social upheaval.

From this social disorientation has arisen a sort of free enterprise. Rival landlords seek out a good farmer and compete for his services. The lack of roots makes it easier for a man to move his family to a new locality for economic gain, a favorable atmosphere for the creation of an urban labor force with the introduction of regional, small-scale industrialization. No one planned this labor mobility; it just happened as the result of normal human greed.

Post-World War II internal migrations have occasionally been forced, as, for example, in the case of the shift of large numbers of *Safi* Pushtuns from south to north after the *Safi* revolt of 1949. Many Afghans also migrate voluntarily to new lands reclaimed for agriculture. In both the major areas being settled, Qunduz in the north and the Helmand River basin in the south, the government closely links itself with the programs in an attempt to shift loyalty from tribal region to nation. External political as well as internal economic reasons motivate the current large-scale northward movement of Pushtuns to the Qunduz area, for the central government hopes to establish large Pushtun colonies among the more numerous Uzbek, Tajik, Turkoman, and Kirghiz groups, all with their counterpart Soviet Socialist Republics across the border. In some regions of northern Afghanistan Pushtuns now constitute a majority of the population. The policy of the present government appears to be to mix up the Pushtuns with other ethnic groups and to create a feeling that one is an Afghan first, and not just a Pushtun, Uzbek, Tajik, or Hazara.

In order to increase political loyalty to nation and replace the lost tribal orientation, the Afghan government shifted its pattern of provincial administrative appointments about five years ago. The emphasis on education constitutes a part of this plan. Previously many elderly civil servants about to retire served as lower grade governors, and few took any interest in their constituents outside of the usual tax collecting and conscription. Today educated young men replace the old "white beards" as men of authority, and actively work within the development programs. Naturally, effective implementation depends on effective individuals and these, unfortunately, are still rare. But the framework for future modernization now exists.

A clue to the future is offered by what happened to a group of Pushtuns moved north by Amir Abdur Rahman 75 years ago and settled in an Uzbek area. The Pushtun and the Uzbek villages are geographically adjacent, but separate. Their village councils, however, meet jointly to consider matters of mutual interest; the Pushtun village chief serves as head of the joint council. Many families in the two villages exchange daughters as brides, a practice which shocks recent Pushtun immigrants into the area. New settlers tend to isolate themselves from non-Pushtuns, just as the old settlers did 75 years ago.

Non-tribal integrative group feeling in Afghanistan, whether local or national, emerges slowly and painfully, but the new migrations related to land reclamation should accelerate the process.

5. *"Pushtunization."* Related to all cohesive factors (and several divisive ones), the government policy of "Pushtunization" attempts to "Pushtunize" all Afghans. There exists a one-to-one relationship between this factor and the "Pushtunistan" problem, for the government wants all the world to believe that Pushtuns are Afghans and vice versa. This policy involves making Pushtu the official language, although several in the royal family cannot speak Pushtu and many others by choice speak Persian, still the *lingua franca* for much of the country. For ten years the Afghan government encouraged and finally ordered officials to learn Pushtu. In the summer of 1960 a directive made Pushtu the official inter-office language, and letters in Persian began to be sent back to their originators for translation into Pushtu. Many Afghan bureaucrats still cannot read or write Pushtu, which often proves embarrassing for those high administrators who must ask lower ranking secretaries for help with translations.

6. *Improvement in transportation and communications systems.* Since World War II, and with great acceleration after

the $100 million Soviet loan of 1955, the road networks and telecommunications system in Afghanistan have been overhauled, improved, and extended. An Afghan airline connects Kabul with Teheran, Cairo, Frankfurt and other foreign cities as well as with all important Afghan centers. The Afghans themselves, taught by Americans and Russians, constantly improve roads in the interior, while the United States and the U.S.S.R. pave roads which will eventually connect all major Afghan cities with the outside world. The official government radio station in Kabul reaches every town bazaar, because many *chai khanehs* (tea houses) have portable radios, frequently powered by flashlight batteries. Government policies saturate the people quickly; so does the army when trouble arises. No longer do tribal revolts go unreported for days or weeks as they did in the past, for now even the lowest subprovincial governors have direct telephone communications with the capital.

Summary and Conclusions

At the top level of Afghan society two groups struggle to identify their land with an image of a national future. The first is the small and exclusive ruling oligarchy headed by a strong man with ultimate power. The second is the growing literate class, which might better be understood as a vested interest group rather than a self-conscious and clearly defined social class. The literate elements in general support the announced goals of the government but yearn for a more dynamic and active role in the decision-making processes of state. The only organized opposition to these two change-oriented groups is composed of religious and tribal leaders, committed to the maintenance of regional tribalism and ethnocentrism in order to preserve their political and economic power.

These three groups comprise only about 5 per cent of the total population of Afghanistan. Even though the remaining 95 per cent look to their tribal and religious leaders rather than to the heads of the national state for political guidance, the groups with vested traditional interests are slowly losing ground to the modernizing elements.

The emergence of a new literate and semiliterate economic

group since 1953 is a result of the advent of statism, the acceleration of foreign aid and development programs, and the opening of possibilities for internal competition with the licensed import-export monopolies. Though the ideal personality type of the warrior-poet persists, even Pushtuns among the urban Afghans no longer consider business an effeminate vocation and look to literacy as a future means for legal resistance against governmental intervention. Land reclamation, by creating new independent landowners, is also serving to change the social structure. Increased industrial vigor breeds miners, truck owners and truck drivers, and factory workers of both sexes. Unorganized but organizable labor groups have come into existence.

The challenge of this kind of change is breeding group pride and individual avarice. Under these conditions the socio-economic emphasis is shifting, albeit extremely slowly, to the nuclear family, while political loyalty moves painfully toward the favoring of mutually beneficial associational groups with articulate, literate leadership. Only the first steps have been taken up the slopes of the Everest of full modernization, but at least they have been taken. Despite the creation of new social layers, no real class struggle exists in Afghanistan, a situation reasonably close to that prevailing in pre-Soviet Muslim Central Asia. Instead we find widespread feelings of social equality, a most healthful result of centuries of development of mountaineer independence and generations of egalitarian Islamic law.

The relatively rapid steps taken by the incumbent government are moving the country closer to the reality of a truly national unit and the liquidation of one-man rule. But the strength and vigor of this process still depend largely on one man, as is true of many such innovating movements in the developing nations of the world today. If Prime Minister Daud should disappear from the scene, the modernization movement might be temporarily halted or deformed, for the forces ranged against his program are many and widespread throughout Afghan society.

Given the present explosive "Pushtunistan" issue with its many political and economic ramifications, the grand re-entrance of the U.S.S.R. into the Great Game in Central Asia and the other complications discussed in this chapter, the nagging question remains of how Afghanistan will go about creating the necessary positive emotions required for national unity without the convenience of the administrative benefits and unifying impetus of a century or so of colonial occupation. If the great powers permit Afghanistan to maintain neutrality, and if Pushtun fanatics do not drive the nation into an unwanted war with Pakistan over "Pushtunistan," Afghanistan may be able to continue without interruption her difficult voyage, begun in 1880, toward modern nationhood—which is still but a distantly seen objective.

Postscript

After this chapter was written, Prince Daud voluntarily left his position as prime minister in March 1963. King Mohammad Zahir Shah then appointed a commoner prime minister, the talented Minister of Mines and Industries in Daud's cabinet, Dr. Mohammad Yusuf. The king now rules, but with loose reins. The liberal forces discussed above have accelerated: a liberalized constitution is being written, press reforms are under way, most political prisoners have been released, and the new prime minister favors the formation of two political parties, government and opposition. In addition, greatly improved relations with Pakistan now exist. If the new government succeeds, Afghanistan will have taken a giant step forward.

Chapter

2

□□□□□□□□□□□□□

From Nomad Society to New Nation:
Saudi Arabia

RICHARD H. NOLTE

When the kingdom of Saudi Arabia was proclaimed in 1932, there had been no heavy background of foreign domination, or even of external pressure. Modern economic development certainly had not begun. Almost the entire population was illiterate, and the great majority were tribal nomads. There was nothing resembling a modern ideology of nationalism with its call for independence and unity, and yet formal unification had been achieved and independence was an acknowledged fact.

As new nations go these days, Saudi Arabia is thus in many ways something of an anomaly. But not wholly so. With the sudden stimulus and wealth provided by the new oil industry, it is now plunging headlong into twentieth century modernity.

Concomitants of this process have been an accelerating disruption of traditional social patterns and the emergence of new features typical of societies in rapid transition toward national integration, such as a fairly large number of transitional and even anomic individuals, and the growth of nationalism as an important social value.

Traditional Patterns

The population of Saudi Arabia is tripartite. Some 65 per cent —three or four million people (there has never been a census) — are Bedouin tribesmen with their flocks of camels, sheep, and goats. Ten or 15 per cent are date, grain, and vegetable raising villagers, and somewhat more than 20 per cent live and work in the fast-growing cities and towns.

The birth rate of this three-fold society, particularly among the Bedouins, is very high, but is still mainly offset by high rates of infant, child, and maternal mortality. Nevertheless, the bulk of the population is less than twenty years of age and, with the spread of medical care and royal handouts for the hungry, it seems clear that a population explosion is in progress.

Since ancient times there has been a certain homogeneity in the composite population of the peninsula. The common tongue is Arabic, the language of the Prophet and the holy Quran. The religion, with the exception of a Shi'ite (non-orthodox) minority, is orthodox Islam; the Shi'ites, concentrated in the oasis villages and new oil towns along the Persian Gulf are rather looked down on. There is a shared memory of past greatness and conquest, and a system of values in which family loyalty, hospitality, generosity, and valor rank high. An economic basis for cooperation lies in the exchange of animals and animal products for food, and of all three for the imports and manufactures of the towns. Without the firm hand of a Muhammad or an Ibn Saud, however, all these ties were never enough to maintain more than a suspicious coexistence underlined by feuds, raids, and mutual scorn.

Until the House of Saud imposed its strong control, the tribes, independent, arrogant, and ready to fight, existed in isolation; they moved on their well demarcated rounds in pursuit of forage, feuding with each other and trading with, exacting protection money from, and occasionally plundering the villages. There are over a hundred major tribes numbering a thousand or more persons, and some such as the Anaza counting more than fifty thousand. The present royal family proudly asserts relationship with the Anaza tribe.

The primary organizing principle is kinship, with each independently moving band (an extended family or group of families) claiming membership in and owing allegiance to the sheikhs of larger sub-tribal and tribal groupings on the basis of a commonly recognized ancestor. Control of the basic camping unit is exercised by a council of family heads and a sheikh who is chosen from a particular family and entitled by tradition to provide candidates. The sheikh in turn represents his unit in the larger sub-tribal councils, and the pattern repeats itself at each level right up to the paramount sheikh of the tribe, who nowadays owes allegiance only to the king. It is an equalitarian system based on consensus in which all adult males participate.

In tribal society status is conferred mainly by ancestry and, within this limitation, by age, reputation, ability, and wealth. Social classes in the broad Western sense are absent; the significant differences are vertical ones between noble camel-based tribes and less noble semi-sedentary sheep and goat satellite tribes and on down through the ignoble non-warrior tribes of blacksmiths and tinkers. Within the tribe, differences of status and authority imply no sense of personal inequality. Paramount loyalty is vested in the family and tribe; in the immemorial isolation of nearly a million square miles of desert and semi-desert, modern nationalism and concepts of the nation have not yet become significant factors.

Saudi villages are of two main types which shade into each other. Tribal villages, chiefly those in the interior uplands, may be settled by nomads who continue to be primarily pastoral, moving away from the fields with their flocks and returning to the villages for planting and harvesting; or, the villages may be more settled, although the tribal organization still continues. In non-tribal villages typical of the long-settled oases of the Persian Gulf area, kinship is no longer the collective tie and village defense, organization, and individual loyalty are based on the territorial unit instead. The influence of the desert remains strong, however; land is owned and a common dwelling inhabited by the extended family, and leading families are entitled by tradition to supply the elders and sheikhs. Only recently have the development of new water resources and the emergence of a new wealthy class produced the beginnings of individual land ownership and absentee landlordism. All villagers, high and low, share in the same agricultural way of life with little notion of class. The Western idea of class as an economically determined stratum of persons having approximately equal status does not apply. As in the tribe, status in Saudi villages is still conferred mainly by family membership, and thereafter by age, reputation, and wealth: a rich tinker still ranks below a poor farmer of noble lineage.

Paying tribute to the Bedouins and taxes to the towns, and being looked down on by both groups, the villagers with their food production and markets have played a vital if precarious middleman's role throughout the history of the peninsula. Now, with the impetus lent by the beginnings of modern economic development and by governmental encouragement of tribal settlement, the villages are rapidly increasing in numbers, size, and importance.

Since medieval times the towns in the Arabian peninsula have had even less in common with the villages than the villages with the tribes. Based on a year-round supply of fresh water and protected by fortress walls of mud, the towns have traditionally provided the meeting places of trade and the administrative seats of political control. They have had a monopoly on wealth, education, and culture, and have been the effective centers of power.

Only in the towns, in contrast to the casual semi-paganism of the Bedouins and the mindless ritual of the village, did Islam gain a theological dimension of learning, prestige, and law. Social stratification, all but absent elsewhere, was a fact in the towns, with a more or less hereditary elite of sheikhs' families, wealthy merchants, government officials, and professionals on top, and a much larger lower rank of vendors, lesser officials, craftsmen, beggars, and slaves. In the absence of intergroup organization for social, economic, or political purposes, town society was a stable mosaic of separate entities based on occupation, lineage, ethnic origin, religion, or level of income, and set apart by differences in dress, comportment, and manner of living. Frequently such groups lived each in its particular quarter of a town, and interquarter jealousies and blood feuds provided an occasional echo of the desert. Intergroup immobility and aloofness were the rule, setting limits to occupation, education, and marriage. Meanwhile paternal authority and loyalty to the extended family continued strong. Only slaves, the boisterous and not very numerous lowest rank of society, had an occasional chance at education, wealth, advancement, and even emancipation through the good will of an owner or patron sheikh.

The House of Saud

Isolated from the changing world outside and uneasily coexisting within, the shifting elements of peninsular society, now waxing, now waning, formed a pattern that endured essentially unchanged from medieval times well into the twentieth century. To the ancient equation, Ibn Saud (1881-1953) added the polarizing force of central power and control. Beginning in 1902 when he and his handful of exiles recaptured Riyadh from its Turkish-oriented governors, and completed in 1932 with the establishment of the kingdom of Saudi Arabia, the task was accomplished in three phases.

During the first decade—a swirling period of thrust and parry —Ibn Saud, supported by his tribal allies and the more disciplined yeomanry of the towns, gradually subdued his rivals and made himself master of the Nejd, the stony interior heartland of Arabia. This much, however, had been done over and over again with no lasting result. To be sure, in the eighteenth and early nineteenth centuries an earlier Ibn Saud and his son, after gaining control of the Nejd, had gone on to rule briefly from coast to coast, only to be smashed in 1818 by the Egyptian troops of Ibrahim Pasha acting in the name of the Porte, the Ottoman Turkish court and government. Had these early Sauds not run afoul of Ottoman policy, or had they been successful in their challenge, they might perhaps have had a more consequential and lasting rule. But the question is moot. Only the

Prophet and his immediate successors in the seventh century had been able to unify the peninsula, consolidate control, and establish an enduring state. How had they managed to neutralize and subject to the requirements of stability and order the fierce conflicting loyalties of towns and tribes? Like the Prophet before him, like his eighteenth century forebears, Ibn Saud in seeking an answer to this problem found an initial ally in religion.

For Muhammad and the caliphs, the religion was Islam. Their new community of Muslims was based on the tie of faith rather than kinship, which made it easier to keep order at home while focusing fighting energies abroad. For the eighteenth century Ibn Saud, the religion was a puritanical crusade of Islamic reform preached by Muhammad Ibn Abdul Wahhab and directed against the sins of the towns and the pagan laxity of the tribes. Taking up the cause, Ibn Saud set out, with a fanatic horde of Wahhabi Bedouins, on the double task of conquest and religious purification. The Sauds and Wahhabism have been linked ever since, the temporal ruler being at the same time *imam*, the leader of the faithful.

Gaining control of the Nejd, the twentieth century Ibn Saud set about proselytizing the unconverted, and tribesmen from all over the peninsula began to join the *Ikhwan*, the Wahhabi brotherhood of true believers. Settling in rapidly growing military cantonments as a new subsidized class of zealous warrior-peasants, they added a cutting edge of unparalleled ferocity and absolute loyalty to the forces of the Sauds during the second phase of conquest, 1912-25. In these years the Persian Gulf province, along with Hejaz and the holy cities in the west, was brought firmly under control.

The third phase, consolidation, was interrupted in 1929 by a revolt of the *Ikhwan*. Resentful under the new restraints of peace and incensed by Ibn Saud's dealings with infidels and his use of such sacrilegious modern devices as the telephone and automobile, the religious fanatics of the *Ikhwan* settlements and their Bedouin kinsmen rose up in Praetorian ire only to be defeated; they were no match for Ibn Saud's modern and increasingly effective professional military forces. Deprived of subsidies, prestige, and function, the *Ikhwan* declined and was eventually abolished; but the importance of religion as a pillar of rule has not been forgotten by the House of Saud.

Religion could be important and could supply a crusading intensity to the purposes of a strong leader, but the experience of Ibn Saud suggests equally that the sword of faith was two-edged, not to be neglected but not wholly to be relied upon, and that the hard core of zeal was subject to decay. Religion as the basis of an enduring state was not enough. That it was not enough even in the seventh century is indicated by the wholesale falling away of the tribes at Muhammad's death in the great "Apostasy," and by the frequent religiously inspired revolts that plagued his successors.

A far more vital basis of enduring rule was the vast increase of income the new state was able to secure. Initially (and traditionally), the new income took the form mainly of plunder won in battle, four-fifths of it being divided among the fighting men concerned. It is not without significance, incidentally, that the very first office of government established by the caliphate in the seventh century was the registry (*diwan*) of tribesmen and townsmen to whom warrior's shares were due. Almost at once, however, mushrooming revenues from the subject provinces and cities of the rapidly expanding Arab empire became a far more lucrative and stable source of income. Distributed in tribal subsidies, administrative and military salaries, public works, and charity, the profits of conquest supplied the Arabs of the caliphate with a powerful vested interest in the new status quo. Income was to prove no less effective as a means to unity and control in the organization of the present Saudi state.

In form the new state established by Ibn Saud was an absolute monarchy maintained by military force. In fact the degree of absoluteness and, indeed, the survival of the kingship itself in the turbulent context of Saudi society depended and still depends on public allegiance. Playing all the traditional leadership roles, utilizing every claim to legitimacy, Ibn Saud sought and won public allegiance as never before in the history of the peninsula, a vital support he did not cease to cultivate.

As sheikh of sheikhs, ostentatious (though a townsman) of his Bedouin lineage, he won the sheikhs by his democracy in council, his hospitable table, and the bounty of his purse. The tribal subsidies thus provided eliminated the economic basis of raiding, rendering enforceable the royal ban on these guerilla-like adventures. He was magnanimous to his erstwhile foes and married their daughters, utilizing his prodigious matrimonial powers to bind families with the tie of blood in his numerous offspring. In his single stately person he embodied all the virtues of the sheikh; the men of the tribes gave him their devotion and their indispensable military support.

As *imam* of the faithful, Ibn Saud maintained the austere piety demanded by the role, lavished funds on mosques, charities, and other objects of religious merit, and maintained a constant respect for the savants of religion. As *imam* he could appoint his son heir apparent and require an oath of allegiance to respect the succession even as he himself had been appointed and sworn to before his father's death. As ruler Ibn Saud upheld the Holy Law of Islam, which is still the official law of the land, and in every way he made the power of the faith his ally.

In his role as king, Ibn Saud became the secular leader of a sovereign territorial state, its representative and symbol abroad, the center of administration and bureaucracy at home, and commander of its small but growing regular military forces. He was the Amir of Nejd on a larger, more complicated scale. The kingship, least traditional of the leadership roles, has been least circumscribed by tradition in its rapid institutional devolopment, and it may prove for the same reason to be most susceptible in the future to constitutional or other non-traditional kinds of limitation.

At all events the modern apparatus of a state developed with great rapidity in the era of peace and order established by Ibn Saud and so far maintained by his successor (in 1953), King Saud Ibn Abdul Aziz. With the income and impetus provided by the new oil industry, the pace since 1945 has been jet-propelled. Governmental forms in the Saudi state, if still incomplete and rudimentary by Western standards, now cover the full range from cabinet ministries (Foreign Affairs, Interior, Finance and National Economy, Agriculture, Communications, Petroleum and Mineral Affairs, Education, Defense, and Health) and subsidiary departments (e.g., Monetary Agency, Labor Office, Locust Control Office, Government Railroad, Coast Guard, Saudi Arabian Airlines) to municipal councils and local police, radio, customs, health, education, poor relief, and public works services. Elsewhere a process of many centuries, the growth of government from undifferentiated one-man rule to nation-state modernity in Saudi Arabia has been compressed into the span of a single generation.

Oil is the key. In 1933, encouraged by indications of oil and by the Saudi era of security and order, an American oil company signed a sixty year concession agreement covering a vast area of eastern Arabia. In 1938 oil was discovered in commercial quantities. In that year government income was seven million dollars. In 1945 it was sixteen million dollars, a quarter of this sum from oil. From then on the rise has been swift indeed, the estimate for 1961-62 being four hundred twenty million dollars, 80 per cent from oil. Oil royalties have exceeded a million dollars a day since 1959.

In addition to providing a prodigious income to government, the new oil industry gives well-paid employment to 14,000 Saudis, and indirect employment to many times that figure. It has created and trained a whole new working class where none existed before, and has fostered the development of a middle class of entrepreneurs, contractors, traders, and professionals of all kinds. It has built schools in the oil province and elsewhere, provided scholarships, introduced Western notions of health and housing, and established model communities of privileged Western foreigners together with all the enviable paraphernalia of their affluent way of life. Responding to governmental demands, the industry has built roads, a railroad, port facilities, and a communications net. It has assisted in agricultural development and in the procurement of equipment for electric power, refrigeration, air conditioning, water supply, and a host of other proliferating needs. In sum, within the Saudi framework of order, the oil industry has provided not only the means but also the great stimulus for the rapid and profound transformation now evident in Saudi Arabia.

Dissolution and Change

Among the effects produced by the addition of oil to the Saudi equation has been an accelerating dissolution of traditional patterns of society. The bulk of the population continues to be composed of Bedouin tribesmen, proud and illiterate, but their

time-honored way of life is visibly in decline. Royal subsidies
have reduced the sheikhs to court retainers and introduced them
to the softer joys of town houses, night life, and regular meals.
The camel, mainstay of the elite tribes, cannot compete with the
motor vehicle and has all but lost its economic value. Forbidden
to raid and decreasingly able to live off their animals, the tribes
have become more and more dependent on government bounty.
Membership in the White Army (the Saudi national guard) or
in police forces has provided a way for many to live up to the
manly fighting tradition, but the trend is nonetheless unmistakably away from the old wild freedom toward slavish dependence
on the governmental dole.

Settled around government wells designed to consolidate support for the king, the cluster of tribes on the outskirts of Riyadh
illustrates the rule. Secure in their water supply, drawing their
daily free rations, they are becoming a sort of suburban proletariat, and all the while the spread of communications and new
ideas, exposure to attractive new commodities in the markets,
and the visible benefits of regular wages have weakened old
values to the point that many Bedouins, even of noble lineage,
have perforce wound up as daily laborers living in barracks or
shanty towns and working under the somewhat scornful direction of Shi'ites or other lowly persons. Tribal society, which
once afforded livelihood, status, and security for its members,
is increasingly unable to do so, leaving frustration, insecurity,
and social instability instead. As a pillar of Saudi rule, it becomes steadily less certain.

Change is even more a fact in the villages. The development
of truck and bus transportation, radio broadcasting, schools, and
newspapers has opened up the villages to new influences from
the towns. At the same time, private and government investments in wells, pumps, roads, and other facilities have made the
villages attractive to the new class of investors from the towns.
Growing distinctions of wealth in the villages along with the
new goods and ideas from outside have resulted in dissatisfac-
tions which many villagers, especially the young, have sought to
erase by taking up employment in the towns. The extended
family unit and kinship ties are thereby weakened as factors of
social stability in favor of the independent, nuclear family.

Change has been most drastic, however, in the towns, the first and major beneficiaries of the new wealth. Change is physically obvious in the proliferating clusters of new oil towns, in the razing of mud walls in older towns to make room for expansion, in the new double lane boulevards with streetlights and palm trees, in the booming construction of multistory concrete buildings for stores, showrooms, hotels, and government offices, and in the new suburbs of wealthy villas and royal palaces. Riyadh was a town of perhaps 80,000 persons in 1955 before it was made the seat of government; now it numbers over 300,000 and is the largest city in the kingdom. Other cities and towns, particularly in the oil region, have had growth rates almost as impressive.

Less tangible but more important has been the dissolution of the old stable mosaic of town society, leaving a situation of instability and flux. The old elite, the first to benefit from the new wealth, was quick to embrace the joys of foreign travel, imported luxuries, and Western ways. Made conspicuous by their un-puritan ostentation, they have become increasingly divorced from the rest of society. Their ranks have been swelled by a thousand princes of the Saudi family, each with his mansion, cars, servants, and royal allowance, each rarely performing a more useful function than to represent his mother's tribe in palace politics.

For the rest, old autonomous groupings by occupation, ethnic origin, and religion are crumbling away. Imports have tended to squeeze out old crafts, new occupations have overshadowed traditional ones, Western clothes and manners have blurred old identifying distinctions. New streets and buildings and urban expansion are breaking up the old residential quarter system.

Contributing to this fluidity has been the emergence of a new middle class of government officials, contractors, merchants, teachers, army and air force officers, office workers, technicians and professionals. An urban working class of semiskilled and unskilled laborers is constantly being augmented by new recruits from the villages and tribes. Comparatively rootless and finding themselves in a situation where old norms and ways no longer seem germane, this growing mass constitutes an explosive and still unorganized potential for the future.

Even religion, the traditional stiffener of the social fabric, is in retreat. True, the old religious court system based on the Holy Law continues to operate with relative efficiency. But some of the harsh penalties prescribed by the Law for certain crimes—chopping off the hand for theft, stoning to death for adultery—are modified in practice by more modern, and more moderate, notions of justice. Moreover, various secular administrative courts and agencies have emerged to deal with new kinds of disputes and abuses which the canonical system is increasingly inadequate to handle. Notable among these agencies is the Grievance Board, which provides a sort of "king's justice" outside the religious law system. One may expect, if the present pace of change continues, to see the progressive curtailment of Holy Law jurisdiction in Saudi Arabia and the substitution of criminal, commercial, and eventually civil codes and courts of modern type, as has been the case in more advanced Muslim countries.

In any event the decline of Wahhabi Islam goes on. The government continues to subsidize Committees for the Propagation of Virtue and the Condemnation of Vice as a sort of spiritual police, but their puritanical opposition to tobacco, music, luxury, photographs, TV, radio, and dealing with the infidel is already a lost cause. The comment of a scornful young nationalist about these committees suggests the trend: "Jobs for the unemployed and feeble minded!"[1] Once the second staunch pillar of Saudi rule, the conservative force of religion seems in the present context of change more and more a liability.

Nationalism Emergent

With the beginning of a decline in his massive leverage as sheikh of sheikhs and *imam*, the king must perforce rely more heavily on his role as secular chief of state—a state in which the burgeoning new middle class and proletariat of the cities and towns are ever more clearly looming as an important and perhaps decisive basis of political power. Can the king successfully shift his weight and win the support of these important new

---

[1] The remark above and those hereinafter quoted were made during the writer's visits to Saudi Arabia in 1957 and 1960 and at various other times and places, 1957-1960.

groups? Or to re-phrase the question, what kind of leadership would win their respect and support?

What do these new groups stand for? The doctrine or ethos or philosophy giving articulation, focus, and direction to the feelings and aspirations of the new groups in Saudi Arabia is the constellation of social values summed up in the concept of nationalism, as discussed in the Introduction to this book. But an immediately striking feature of nationalism in Saudi Arabia is that it is not specific to the Saudi state but rather to the broader concept of the Arab nation which embraces more or less closely all the Arab populations of the Middle East. It is Arab nationalism, not—or at least not yet—Saudi nationalism. The words themselves, *qawmiyyah* (folk nationalism), *wataniyyah* (patriotism), and above all *'uruba* (Arabism) are not specific to any country and evoke a special feeling in all nationalist Arabs, including Saudis. *'Uruba*, according to one Saudi, "embodies all our ideals of nationalism and all our cultural heritage. It is a magic word."

The Saudi flag evokes no great response, but the colors— green and white—are approved as being the colors of Arab nationalism. The numerous popular patriotic songs refer always to the larger nation; e.g., "From the Gulf to the Ocean": "Dear fatherland, my greater land/Day by day its glory grows/ Day by day it grows more free/ Its history now all victory." Treason is not defined by nationalists with reference to the Saudi state, but rather according to the canons of Arab nationalism. In this view the king and government themselves might be guilty of treason. The charismatic leader for Saudi nationalists has been of course the great nationalist hero, President Nasser of Egypt, not King Saud; and the Nasser charisma remains strong although somewhat tempered recently by criticism—in terms of Arab nationalist objectives—of various policies such as his disrupting slangfests with Iraq and Jordan, his misuse of press and radio, and his doctrinaire economics.

There are occasional hints, it is true, of a basis for a more specific Saudi nationalism based on a conception of past peninsular glory and on a feeling that the best people are not Egyptians, Palestinians, Lebanese, Westerners, or even local Shi'ites, but orthodox Saudi Muslims. The greater Arab nation tends to be thought of as a federation or even confederation in which the Saudi state would retain a separate identity. In general, however, Saudi nationalists, like Arab nationalists elsewhere, envisage themselves as part of the great Arab caravan (inevitable metaphor!) moving steadily forward toward a better life for its people. Leaders may emerge to guide and exhort, but if they falter or turn aside the caravan pushes inexorably forward nonetheless. Arab betterment as the great objective, while mainly self-centered, is not lacking in an altruism going beyond the Arab people themselves—a larger sense of mission is implicit. As they had in their days of glory, the Arabs would again have much to contribute to human civilization.

In the nationalist conception the task confronting Saudi Arabia as a part of the great caravan is to create a Saudi contingent that is stable, unified, and moving forward in good order. In the absence of the proper ordering and control, this is not now the case. Some parts of Saudi society are moving, some are not, with a resulting instability and unrest. The crash program for educating boys but not (until very recently) girls is one example; the squandering of resources on royal luxury at the expense of economic development and jobs for the poor is another. All this must be put right, in the nationalist view, if the people of Saudi Arabia are not to drop hopelessly behind in the onward march of the Arabs.

Nationalism in Saudi Arabia is relatively new, and has only begun to be significant within the past decade. It is true that the Arab revolt in 1916, led by the Hashemites of the Hejaz under the leadership of Husain, amir of Mecca, and his sons, was a war of liberation against the Turks with the objective of setting up an independent Arab state. For the more advanced Arabs of the Levant where Turkish rule lay more heavily, the beginnings of real nationalism, as Mr. Gallagher points out in Chapter 6, were very much involved in this struggle. But in retrospect it is difficult to see much difference, so far as the peninsular Arabs are concerned, between Husain and his sons and Ibn Saud and *his* sons in their rival campaigns for hegemony. In neither case was modern nationalism a factor. Present-day nationalists in Saudi Arabia, of course, in common with other Arab nationalists, now look back on the Arab revolt as a glorious opening chapter.

But in fact the development of nationalism on the peninsula is very recent indeed.

The Palestine War of 1948-1949 sent the first shock of awareness through Saudi Arabia; Israel and the Palestine issue have been a constant threat and stimulus ever since. But the rapid spread of nationalism in Saudi Arabi has been parallel to and a direct concomitant of the development of the oil industry. To the nationalists the causal relationship is amply clear. One of them phrased it succinctly: "Nationalist awareness derives from education and contact with the modern world. Education began slowly; the surge came with oil."

Education and contact with the modern world: but if one then suggests that nationalism is an imported ideology or an imitation of a foreign ideology, the denial is vehement. Communism, capitalism, and fascism would be imported ideologies, but not nationalism. For the nationalists, nationalism is a spontaneous awakening to the existence of pressing social, political, and economic needs, and who is to say they are wrong?

Products of "education and contact," the nationalists in Saudi Arabia are synonymous with the emerging urban middle class and working class groups who more and more have been exposed to and have absorbed modern political and social assumptions, conceptions, and values. Purveyed in any of a thousand subtle and unsubtle ways—by radio and newspaper, by the example of foreigners with their material wealth, by experience in the oil industry and the host of new urban occupations, by training and travel abroad, by the flood of imported artifacts—these new ideas have fallen on the thirsty ground of a society more and more alienated from its old social patterns and values. The consequence is a group looking at and around itself with critical modernized eyes, with a new awareness of dirt and poverty, ignorance, economic and military weakness, corruption, "feudalism"—all the stigmata of inferiority and backwardness. The resulting impulse is to reform and rebuild their society into modern civilized respectability. This is the major motivation behind nationalist feeling, the horsepower that makes the vehicle go.

As for the vehicle itself, its outlines are relatively broad and imprecise—a circumstance which in a way gives it the added strength of flexibility. Lacking any hard doctrine, a definition of methods or priorities, or even a generally accepted definition of itself, nationalism in Saudi Arabia can enlist as allies many who would be enemies in detail, and can modify its objectives and priorities in line with changing circumstances.

"Vehicle," however, may be the wrong metaphor. So far as is known, nationalism is not yet represented in Saudi Arabia by an organized movement. In the absence of elections or a parliament, there are no political parties to embrace a nationalist ideology. There have been none of the riots or demonstrations so noticeable elsewhere; the nearest approach was an oil industry strike in 1953 led by a handful of young men demanding privileges more nearly equal to those of the Americans. Implicit was an attack on the "feudal tyranny" of a government that did not allow labor unions. The government response was prompt and effective: dismissal and imprisonment, and, for the non-Saudis involved, deportation. The equally instructive sequel was the subsequent re-employment of the strike leaders by the oil industry or by the new Government Labor Office.

So far there has been no recurrence of a strike threat or evidence of a labor movement which might serve as a carrier of nationalist sentiment. Occasional articles on nationalist themes appear in Saudi newspapers, which are mostly privately owned, but the threat of censorship and the possibility of jail or unemployment imposes a certain restraint. The most that can be said is that nationalism in Saudi Arabia is an urban climate of opinion made articulate mainly abroad and propagated by foreign newspapers, journals, and radio broadcasts, notably by that Pied Piper of nationalism, Cairo's Voice of the Arabs.

But if formal expression is so far lacking, it has nonetheless made itself evident. When Nasser visited Saudi Arabia in 1956, popular enthusiasm was so overwhelming as to embarrass his royal host. In 1958, when King Saud was accused of having laid out $5,000,000 to have Nasser assassinated, he was forced in a family showdown involving some three dozen leading princes to relinquish plenary powers to his brother, Crown Prince Faisal. The motive, basically, was to preserve the House of Saud during a crisis of discontent. Some of the pressure came from the tribes, pinched in their subsidies by the shortage of funds. But a large part came from an urban public disgusted at the king's squander-

lust and openly incensed at the underhanded plot against its nationalist hero.

Basically, however, nationalism in Saudi Arabia remains comparatively moderate, and not only because of the existing hindrances to free expression and the lack of organization. Perhaps because there has been no history of "colonial oppression," Saudi nationalists in private tend to be less carried away and more practical than their Egyptian or Syrian or Iraqi counterparts, tempering their feeling with a more realistic appraisal of existing conditions. This moderation can be seen in their attitude toward corruption in high office, of which Saudi Arabia offers some impressive examples—evil and wrong surely, but the inevitable result of old feudal habits in the sudden presence of huge wealth. It has been ancient practice writ large, but it is temporary and a "passing phase."

Another example is the nationalists' attitude toward the king, who gives rise to a fury of invective among less moderate nationalists in other Arab countries. The Saudi nationalist argues that strong central control is necessary in his country lest the old centrifugal forces of factious clan pride and the tribal habit of war tear it apart, jeopardizing both the oil income and the chances of building their new society. "You see these?" said one young leader, dangling a string of prayer beads. "This is Saudi society. The only thing that holds them together is the string, the king. In a feudal society, the king is necessary. We need to strengthen the string and guide it, not get rid of it. When all the beads are fused together, then will be time to think about the future of the king."

Such moderation suggests that, in spite of the anti-royalist direction of nationalism in general, there may yet be a basis for cooperation between the king and the nationalists. The new groups in Saudi Arabia may yet develop into a sturdy alternative basis of support for the crown. There are recent indications that the king is thinking along these lines, seeking out nationalist support in his family quarrel with Crown Prince Faisal.

After acquiring plenary powers in 1958, Faisal proceeded to repair the breach with Nasser and set about replenishing the bankrupt treasury and reversing the steep decline in value of the *riyal*. Faisal cut down sharply on his royal brother's extravagance and the allowances to the princes, and substituted modern budgets for the king's unbridled whim. By the end of 1960, however, with the treasury restored, the defects of Faisal's austerity in terms of commercial stagnation and a government standstill on development projects had become all too apparent. The king, meanwhile, having learned the lesson of 1958, had been wooing nationalist support with a certain permissiveness about a constitution, a partially elected parliament, education for girls, and freedom of the press—all items dear to the nationalist heart but strongly opposed by Faisal.

By late 1960, the palace tide had turned, and Saud resumed control. He appointed his young brother, Prince Talal, as Minister of Finance and Economy; and the Texas-trained Galahad of Arab oil, Abdullah Tariki, as Minister of Mineral and Petroleum Affairs. Both men are strong and articulate nationalists, and although they themselves did not long survive in office, the results of the new direction were soon apparent. The U.S. was told in a gesture of nationalist orthodoxy that its lease on the Dhahran airbase would not be renewed in 1962, and a promise had been secured from President Nasser to visit the kingdom before the end of 1961. Construction projects dropped in 1958 were resumed, and a $45,000,000-a-year program of basic development drawn up by the World Bank is in the offing. A development board has been established, and there is talk of new water supplies, roads, diversification, and utilization of the 200 million cubic feet of gas daily going to waste in the oil fields. And girls are to go to school.

From a nationalist point of view all this change is heady progress indeed. Faisal and the conservatives may feel with good reason that the throne cannot long survive nationalist reform; but even should they briefly regain control, there will have been net progress in the direction of nationalist goals. As for the king, he may well feel a restored power and luster on the basis of his new support, but he has in measurable degree become its prisoner. It seems clear it will be the nationalists who will increasingly call the tune. The king has not imposed his will on them; it is they who have made an agent of the king.

Chapter

3

◼◻◼◻◼◻◼◻◼◻◼

Peasantry and National Revolution:

Bolivia

RICHARD W. PATCH

Bolivia is a country with a long history of ostensible nationhood. It was an independent republic before Germany or Italy became nation-states. Its revolution of independence lasted sixteen years, but even this long war did not stir truly nationalistic feelings, and indeed the country's first assembly seriously debated union with Peru, or even union with the United Provinces which were to become Argentina. The name chosen for the new country was that of a Colombian-Venezuelan, its first president and army were Gran Colombian, and its first native-born president fought a successful war to join Bolivia and Peru in a short-lived Confederacy of Peru. When the first assembly voted to form a new nation carrying the name of the Liberator, one delegate counseled independence as the best policy because, he said, if the experiment turned out a mistake it would be easier to vote for union with another country than to achieve independence again after union had been established. Such were the tentative, hardly nationalistic beginnings of Bolivia in 1825.

Nor did the spirit of nationalism prosper in the succeeding one hundred years under a variety of leaders from dictators through demagogues, and under conservative parties trying to repair the wreckage left by the War of the Pacific and "liberal" parties whose constitutionalism made Bolivia one of the more stable and respected republics of South America in the first quarter of the twentieth century. It was not until the decay of this "liberal" rule (which, however, left untouched the peonage of the Indians and the exploitation of the miners) that nationalism began to appear.

Nationalism arose in Bolivia in several stages. The fall of the Liberal Constitutionalists in 1920 marked the end of nearly a hundred years during which the state was an empty vessel, in which constitutional forms masked a government of and for the few; those few had so little regard for the state as nation that state territory was parceled out to neighboring countries by treaties. The mass of the population was systematically atomized; bound to feudal communities, exploited because their horizons of consciousness were limited to the local community, they were unmoved and uninspired by national pride or even hope of participation in a national society, economy, or polity.

The first evidence of approaching change was intellectual. The new political writers of the 1920s and 1930s expressed a revulsion against apparent slavishness to forms of law which in fact only imposed stability on unjust social institutions, on an economic system from which few benefited, and on a political structure perpetuating federal provinces rather than promoting a nation-state. Many of their ideas were imported. Marxism, socialism, even fascism impressed many as alternatives to the forms of law, as means of undertaking direct measures to cure the "vital," *national* problems. The new writing had three theses: the form of law must yield before direct action, including revolution; action should be aimed against the prevailing restrictive atomization of the inward-looking village and toward the establishment of new national institutions; social justice should be achieved by the destruction of social barriers and the growth of an integrated society conscious of and mobile within a nation. Paternalism was to be replaced by participation.

Events and accidents thrust Bolivia into the holocaust of the Chaco War from 1932 to 1935, when scores of thousands of Bolivians died in a futile conflict with Paraguay. The conduct of the war and the conscription of Indians demanded a new way of thinking, and the new nationalism appeared ready made. After Bolivia's defeat the hypernational socialism of Germany, also a defeated country, seemed especially congenial. Young officers, veterans of the Chaco and sympathetic to the ideas of national socialism, became part of the group which later formed the Nationalistic Revolutionary Movement (MNR), dedicated to an ideal of the nation and accepting revolution as a legitimate means of attaining it. They meant revolution in its true sense, not the peculiar North American sense which does not distinguish revolution from barracks revolt.

The MNR made revolution a reality in 1952. But World War II and the defeat of the Axis (after which a president of Bolivia supported by the MNR was hanged in the public square of La Paz) had destroyed the feasibility of fascist national socialism as an intellectual vehicle. The influence of the army group in the MNR was dimmed. The revolution had not been won by the regular army, which was one of the first casualties of the new regime. An estrangement took place between the civilian leaders of the MNR and the officers who had earlier cooperated with them. The search was on for new intellectual explanations of ongoing events to shore up the few basic tenets of national socialism which were retained to justify such actions as the confiscation of the major tin mines by the state.

The search goes on and will not be ended until the exponents of the MNR realize that the permanently significant part of their revolution is not such "nationalization" but the achievement of true national integration. The leaders of the MNR have not yet seen any necessary connection between democratic forms and the well-being of the greatest number. In the past the "demos" of democracy had been the wealthy, the urban dwellers, or the literate. With their own national history in mind the MNR leaders have allowed the ideal end to transcend the political means. Marxism, national socialism, and constitutional democracy have all been considered as means to the end of national integrity. But it has become obvious to many MNR leaders that Marxism is linked to communism and may be the antithesis of national sovereignty, and we have seen that fascistic national socialism became opprobrious after the defeat of the Axis.

In the spirit of experimentation, then, the MNR in 1952 turned once more to ideas of constitutional democracy, not as an end in itself, but as the means by which, and the context within which, the ultimate ideal of meaningful, respected, integrated, sovereign nationhood with justice and bread for all could be achieved. Therefore "democracy," "constitution," and "law" do not evoke in the Bolivian mind the same deep emotional commitment that they do for a North American. Conversely, "land," "nation," and "fatherland" have an importance to the Bolivian not generally appreciated by the North American.

But even without the deep commitment, the forms of constitutional and parliamentary democracy are being tested as a framework for revolution and nationalism. This experimentation has led to such apparent paradoxes as abuses of power by peasant leaders and their armed militia, regimented voting, banishment of an opposition group within the MNR party, imprisonment without trial of persons who are debtors of the government, and a general weakness of governmental structure. But as the forms are followed they may be strengthened through use. In 1960 a second consecutive constitutionally elected president finished his full term in office, and a third elected president was sworn in— for the first time in living memory.

This commitment to democratic nationalism is, then, the significance of the case of Bolivia in a comparative study of nationalism. The movement grew up independent of, and long after, release from colonial rule and the formation of the state. Its spirit is not reaction and aggression but emphasis on national integration and a solution to the problems raised by the destruction of an old, localistic and rural-oriented, anti-nationalistic regime. While a mixture of political philosophies contributed to the present experiment, the pervading thought is democratic, and the political processes which are being given as full a trial as may be possible in a burning revolutionary setting are within the forms of democracy. The eventual outcome may be in doubt, but the significance of the occurrence is not.

The Historical Background

A brief historical sketch may give the reader a fuller understanding of how these events came to pass in Bolivia, of all the countries of Latin America.

Union or independence? The territory known as Bolivia has a long history and even prehistory of existence as part of a larger whole. For over a century it was economically dominant within that whole, and boasted a city, Potosí, which ranked as one of the richest in the world in the sixteenth and early seventeenth centuries.

Many deeply felt traditions have their roots in the time when Bolivia was, roughly, the Audience of Charcas under the vice kingdom of Peru. At the apex of its power, the Audience of Charcas challenged even the power of the vice kingdom, and held sway over what are today Bolivia, Argentina, Paraguay, Uruguay, and parts of Brazil, Chile, and Peru. In 1778 the vice kingdom of Peru was split into two parts, with the territory of the Río de la Plata elevated to the status of a new vice kingdom. The formal administration of the Audience of Charcas was shifted from Lima to Buenos Aires. In actuality, however, the seat of government of Charcas at Chuquisaca (now Sucre) was so distant from both Lima and Buenos Aires that the Audience was nearly autonomous until the institution of reforms in 1782. The 219 years during which Charcas was associated with the vice kingdom of Peru have left an abiding sense of identification with that region. The common name for Charcas until independence was "Upper Peru."

Another strong factor binding Bolivia to other countries of the Andes is the concept of Tawantinsuyu, the geographical totality of the Inca empire. The Inca empire left more than an archaeological heritage. Among other legacies was a living language, Quechua, which is more a *lingua franca* in the Andes today than is Spanish. But even beyond language, Tawantinsuyu and the intellectual indigenous movement (*indigenismo*) which accompanies it provide a mystique giving a strong sense of communality to Bolivia—the ancient Kollasuyu, one of the four territorial quarters of Tawantinsuyu. For this reason the center of gravity of Bolivia's national consciousness is still precariously perched high in the mountains of the west. It centers on the *de facto* capital, La Paz, on the edge of a plateau, 12,000 feet high, which was the heart of Kollasuyu and where the people are still called "Kollas."

Tawantinsuyu has played its part in the political history of republican Bolivia. The nation's first native-born president, General Andrés de Santa Cruz y Calahumana, went to war with Peru to establish a Confederation of Peru in which both Peru and Bolivia became dependencies of an approximation of the old Tawantinsuyu. Although the political reality faded quickly and such a reincarnation has never again been attempted, the ideal remains, and an indigenous or "Indianist" movement is an important part of the intellectual scene in Bolivia as well as in Peru. *Indigenismo*, though its expression was muted for most of the nineteenth century, provided an ideational base and a constellation of symbols for the eventual acceptance of the Indian as more than a plodding peon forever destined to inferiority. *Indigenismo* was by no means the causal force in the emancipation of the Indians, but it kept alive an idea of the intrinsic dignity and past glories of the Indians which facilitated their move from village Indian to *campesino* while retaining some Indian cultural characteristics.[1] Today *indigenismo* remains important by furnishing unifying national symbols. The nation, in expressing its individuality, is constantly producing an idealized Indian who in fact is disappearing as "Indians" become peasants and mestizos.

The history and prehistory of submission to a larger whole, as well as certain practical considerations, were arguments voiced against the creation of a new nation when Charcas as well as Lower Peru and the United Provinces of the Río de La Plata became independent from Spain. Bolívar and others favored union with Peru while other factions favored union with the United Provinces, but romantic ideas and even eminently

---

[1] The word "Indian" as used here has, consistent with common Latin American understanding, a cultural and not a physically "racial" meaning.

rational considerations could not stand against the realities underlying the wars of independence. Generally the support for the
wars did not come from men fighting for principles of freedom
and self-government against an imposed monarchy. The fact
that a Bonaparte sat on the throne of Spain somewhat confused
the issues. The motive for the wars, however, resided in a
struggle between first-class and second-class Spaniards in the
New World. The first-class Spaniards were the *peninsulares*, the
Spaniards who had been born in Spain and had emigrated to
America and who as a matter of course occupied the positions
of privilege in the political and religious hierarchy. The second-
class Spaniards were the *criollos*, born in the New World of
Spanish parents but relegated to secondary positions because of
the stigma attached to their extra-peninsular birth. Normally the
peninsulares were royalists, the *criollos* revolutionaries.

When the *criollos* vanquished the *peninsulares*, it became
clear that a multiplication of the number of new republics also
multiplied the number of privileged positions open to *criollos*.
The political and economic difficulties attending the creation of
such new nations as Bolivia were overridden by men who had
fought for power and were determined to have it in full measure.
The first Bolivian assembly, in 1825, debated the merits of union
with Peru and with the United Provinces, then voted overwhelmingly to create a new "Republic of Bolívar."

The construction of a nation. Bolivia's debut was not auspi-
cious. The Colombian hero, Marshal Antonio José de Sucre,
was prevailed upon to become the nation's chief executive under
the absentee presidency of the liberator of most of Hispanic
South America, the Venezuelan Simón Bolívar. Sucre laid the
groundwork for order by establishing territorial departments
and provinces, naming departmental prefects and provincial
subprefects, taking a census as the basis for imposition of direct
taxes to replace the indirect colonial taxes, and establishing
schools and colleges. But the nation which owed its existence to
personal interests soon gave great difficulties to its forward-look-
ing chief. The Church was outraged that its property was taken
for the establishment of public education. The departmental
prefects who had the responsibility for collecting taxes preferred
to increase their popularity by making only token collections.

By 1826 Sucre wrote to Bolívar asking to be relieved of his office.

Presidential elections were held in October, 1826, and in December the constitution was adopted, making Sucre Bolivia's first "constitutional president." Sucre accepted the presidency only on condition that he be allowed to leave office after two years. Difficulties increased. Argentina suspended relations with Bolivia because of a territorial dispute. An officer of the Colombian army unit stationed in Cochabamba revolted. Bolívar was occupied in attempting to prevent his own country, Venezuela, from separating itself from Colombia. Peru, suffering from a reaction of anti-Bolivarianism, refused to establish relations with Bolivia "until [Bolivia] is free of foreign armed interventionists and has its own national government," and prepared troops to invade Bolivia. On Christmas Day, 1827, a battalion of Colombian troops in La Paz rose against Sucre. The barracks revolt was put down, but it was only the first of a series which was to demoralize the new republic. Another, in which Sucre was wounded, broke out four months later; Peruvian troops crossed the border. Sucre resigned even before his short term of office had ended, and Bolivia was embarked on its catastrophic nineteenth century history.

The fundamental lack of ideological motivation in the wars of independence and in the establishment of the republic was one of the factors inhibiting nationalism. A narrow regional self-interest also prevented the growth of nationalism in this period. Departmental and provincial officials took power in their own hands, rivalry grew between Sucre and La Paz and between La Paz and Cochabamba. Social prestige remained inseparable from the *latifundia*. Bolivia, instead of taking the road to nationalism and true nationhood, settled into a long night of revived feudalism and regional competition; the majority of the population was assiduously kept in ignorance of the idea of nation.

It is unnecessary to write about this period in detail. There were well-intentioned presidents such as Santa Cruz and Ballivián who left their mark on the republic. There were arrant demagogues like Belzu. There were civilian dictators, such as Córdova and Linares, and military dictators like Achá and the amazing Mariano Melgarejo, who traded off pieces of national territory as if the country were his personal property. Domestic upheaval prevented the growth of an effective national army. When Chile invaded Bolivia's Pacific coastal territory, Bolivia declared war and, in alliance with Peru, was defeated by Chile in the War of the Pacific, Bolivia thus losing its access to the sea. The end of the war was brought about by a party of men who called themselves first *pacifistas*, then "constitutionalists."

In this climate, which might be typified by the slogan of a military hero, Camacho—"Long live order, down with revolution"—Bolivia entered a new era of political consciousness. A wealthy industrialist, Gregorio Pacheco, won the election of 1884, inaugurating "The Age of Silver" or "The Reign of the Conservative Oligarchy," as it was variously called. Succeeding governments, elected in free but very limited contests, had in common the defense of "religion, the family, morality, and good customs," and they were strongly supported by the Church. Only one president of this period was not personally wealthy before taking office, but he also was vigorously supported by the Church and the urban elite, and even he identified the nation's interests with those of the upper class. Peace was made with Chile, exploration was encouraged, railroads were built, and industry prospered. The gains of prosperity and peace, however, materially benefited only the small class which participated in the government. The urban lower class derived little advantage, and the Indian half of the population continued to be ignored by the government, as the Indians themselves continued ignorant of "The Age of Silver" or the nationhood of Bolivia.

The year 1898 marks the end of "The Age of Silver" and the Conservative Oligarchy, and the beginning of the reign of the Liberals. The spark which ignited popular indignation against the former was a struggle between the Conservatives who wished to maintain the capital at Sucre, and a group who wished to move it to La Paz—the natural trade center of the country. One of the several groups which entered the revolt called for a new "federalism" to replace the centralized national government. The Liberals won municipal elections in 1897. Fighting broke out in 1898. The revolt was successful and the Liberals came to power under General Pando, a paradox for a party calling for civilian rule. The change is difficult to describe in conventional terms. Many former Conservatives joined the Liberals. The new government removed its offices to La Paz, but Sucre remained (and still remains) the legal capital. One Bolivian historian stresses the "imponderables,"[2] for the change from Conservative to Liberal was not the innovation which the party names imply. There was no contest of ideas, no break with tradition, no promise of change in the conditions of the governed, no breath—as yet—of nationalism.

The clearest spokesman of the Liberals was General Helidoro Camacho, who had expressed his views years before the party came to power. He believed liberty was threatened by two evils: the excess of power which pretends to protect it, and social acts which "dishonor" it on the pretext of serving it. His propositions are no different from the Conservatives' ideas: "[Liberalism] does not consist, as those who define it believe, in breaking with the traditions of the past; leaping into violent innovations; or adopting, without reason, all imaginable reforms. . . . A free people is a society of good men, and good men are those who believe in a bountiful God and a just God."[3] The Liberals were not about to revolutionize the political system or the existing society. The spirit of the times was more federalism than nationalism, as was appropriate in a feudal society with power and social participation reserved to the *latifundia* owners.

There were Liberal writers, however, who at least registered consciousness of the anachronistic and inhuman conditions of the Indians. José Carrasco, who in 1920 published a monumental comparative study of constitutions and who had many suggestions for the revision of Bolivia's oft-revised fundamental legal document, wrote that the unfortunate Indian who serves as a model for literary odes and a pawn for political discourses in reality demands independence, civil and political emancipation, and a recognition of his rights.

Time was growing short for the platitudes of Camacho and the ineffective indictments of Carrasco. The era of strong and stable governments, orderly elections, and constitutionalism had come to an end. Railroads had been built, and a new national resource, tin, developed—but no attack had been made

[2] Enrique Finot, *Nueva historia de Bolivia*, La Paz: 1954, p. 335.
[3] Quoted in Guillermo Francovich, *El pensamiento boliviano en el siglo XX*, México: 1956, pp. 11-12.

on the basic problem of the country. It remained half a nation fascinated with the possibilities of Western technology, and half a nation living much as it had in the sixteenth century. From the reaction against constitutionalism and order came nationalism, exploiting the gulf between the governors and the governed, and appearing one hundred years after independence and long after colonialism had become a misty memory.

Nationalism and Anti-Constitutionalism

One of the crucial factors in Latin American politics, seldom described because of its inherent lack of definition, is *cansancio* —a widespread public tiredness with an existing regime. This public state of mind is not necessarily the result of government ineffectiveness, but rather—in a country of massive poverty—the result of a deep suspicion that continued stability has in itself become a major government goal not because it provides the base for economic growth or increased political participation, but because it protects the property of those who have property, and maintains a class system permitting exploitation. In Bolivia the "tiredness," therefore, does not turn into apathy, as in some countries, but rather becomes a positive reason for attacking the government.

By 1920 the Tweedledum and Tweedledee Conservative and Liberal parties had maintained a regime of constitutionalism for thirty-six years. National problems such as the situation of the Indians, the state of the tin miners, and growing tension with Paraguay over the disputed Chaco territory all added impetus to the "tiredness." No single spark fired the tinder. Almost as a matter of course officers of the army rose against the government in July, and President Gutiérrez Guerra sought asylum in a foreign legation in La Paz. Traditions were broken from the outset. The Liberals had tried to keep the military out of politics, but the army played a decisive part in the 1920 revolt. The day of the old military *caudillos* was over, however, and the new army protested that it had no interest in permanent rule. It had become simply the guardian of public order. Some officers remained loyal to the Liberals, however, and in the resulting confusion an ambitious civilian, Bautista

Saavedra, seized the presidential office and held elections to justify his coup. Power had come to those who believed in direct action.

Groups never before active in politics began to make themselves felt. Intellectuals who had concerned themselves with literature during the reign of the Liberals began to think in political terms, some using Woodrow Wilson as their prototype. But the most attractive new political ideas came from Europe: Marxism, socialism, fascism—theories compatible with direct action towards national goals. This incipient nationalism remained but a pool of ideas until December, 1928, when a Paraguayan attack on Bolivia's Fort Vanguardia in the Chaco led to a tragic war in which Bolivia's initially confident defense of its sovereignty became a grim battle for survival which shook old social ideas and relationships to their foundations.

The significant fact of the Chaco War was neither the defeat of the army nor the loss of the Gran Chaco, virtually unpopulated then as now. As the war became desperate the elite army and enthusiastic volunteers were supplemented by conscripts from every social stratum. Tin miners fought beside university students, and thousands of Indians who had believed in a world coterminous with their communities were suddenly transported to the remote Chaco. There they learned about the nation of Bolivia and heard much about the fatherland, the obligations of citizens, and invidious ideas about equality—at least on the firing line. When the war was lost these ideas were not forgotten. The Chaco had introduced the idea of nation to the majority.

The loss of the war also produced a split between the older army officers and the younger ones who blamed their superiors for the debacle. The disaffection of the younger officers was to prove invaluable to a new kind of political party and fatal to the institution of the army. The junior officers were even more attracted in defeat to the ideas of national socialism then in the ascendancy in Germany and Italy. They formed secret lodges and called themselves the RADEPA, the *Razón de Patria*, or "Reason of the Fatherland." By 1940 they had joined ranks with the intellectuals, the visionaries, and the men of good family who had similar ideas of a new fatherland based on a planned economy and an integrated society. Together they formed the Nationalistic Revolutionary Movement (MNR) which succeeded in crystallizing the prevalent desires for nationalism and the direct measures of revolution into specific goals. Bolivia was approaching the point of no return.

At first the military faction was dominant. In May of 1936 the secret lodges of officers organized a coup which placed Colonel David Toro in the presidential chair. Toro gave expression to the growing nationalism by creating a state oil monopoly, the Y.P.F.B., which took over ownership and operation of the Standard Oil properties in Bolivia. He also attempted to organize local unions to support his government, bypassing normal administrative and party channels. He was not successful, however, and the army lodges allowed Lieutenant Colonel Germán Busch to assume the presidency. Busch, 33 years old when he captured the presidency in 1937, was the greatest of the popular heroes of the Chaco War. He proceeded with the national, Socialist program inaugurated by Toro by making the Central Bank of Bolivia an organ of the state.

After Busch became head of the government, elections were held which conferred on him the coveted label of "constitutional president." But by April 1939, public and government disorder had become so alarming that Busch proclaimed himself dictator. One of his last important acts was the eventually fruitless attempt to require the tin mine owners to turn over to the government their foreign exchange proceeds, clearly the first step toward seizure of the mines. In August Busch met a violent death under circumstances which leave it unclear whether he was assassinated or committed suicide.

The RADEPA disappeared from the national scene until 1943, when the lodges succeeded in ousting General Enrique Peñaranda, an old soldier, sympathetic to the Allies during the war, and replacing him with Lieutenant Colonel Gualberto Villarroel, more sympathetic to the Axis. The intellectual head of the MNR, Víctor Paz Estenssoro, became Minister of Finance. Villarroel attempted to continue with the program of national socialism but constant harassment by the opposition left him little opportunity to do much more than stay in power, permitting his partisans to reply to the harrying of the opposition with acts of violence in which some prominent political and military figures were assassinated.

But the military approach to nationalism was foredoomed by its ties to fascism. After the defeat of the Axis, Villarroel removed the civilian MNR members from his cabinet and tried to consolidate his position with an all-military council of ministers. On July 21, 1946, a popular revolt broke out in La Paz in which mobs stormed the presidential palace, shot Villarroel, and hanged his body in the Plaza Murillo. The MNR again went underground and into exile. The public's opinion of army officers, junior and senior, was epitomized in the spectacle of bodies being pulled through the streets with an army boot placed under one arm. The armed forces never fully recovered from this blow, and were destined for near destruction after the MNR revolution of 1952. Henceforth the civilian wing of the MNR was dominant. With the fall of Villarroel, the more militant and totalitarian aspects of the imported fascistic national socialism also died. The civilians were more interested in democracy and in nationalism as the means to an effective national integration.

During five years of makeshift governments the MNR remained in eclipse. Traditional governments attempted to restore the old order but failed to muster popular support. Two presidents in succession gave up their jobs in despair and went into voluntary exile. An election in 1951 gave a plurality to Paz Estenssoro and the MNR, but the election was annulled. A military junta governed briefly, then disintegrated.

It appeared by early 1952 that if Bolivia was not to have an MNR government it would have no government. The MNR had planned a revolution for later in the year but by April the nation was about to fall into literal anarchy. For this reason the revolution of April 1952 was not a dramatic struggle between strong partisans of the old regime and the revolutionaries. The conservatives had failed to govern and there were few to defend their further claims. The revolutionaries began fighting in the streets of La Paz headed by MNR leaders Hernán Siles Zuazo, rebel son of a former president, and Juan Lechín, labor leader and self-described Trotskyite. Civilian irregulars and a portion of the army quickly subdued the loyal army forces in fighting mostly contained in La Paz. The MNR was in power, but the party dedicated to direct action had only begun its real revolution. In spite of the lack of drama Bolivia had taken a long step toward a new society and a new political system, a step which could not be retraced.

1952

Nationalism as well as revolution had been vindicated. The turn which nationalism took may be the most significant point which the Bolivian case lends to our understanding of nationalism.

The new nationalism had nothing to do with reaction against colonialism or imperialism. It was a response to Western ideals of government, a consequence of technological aspirations which require a high degree of integration, a result of new ideas of justice which destroyed the existing class structure. This nationalism was internal, directed towards domestic goals of planning and integration, not a nationalism directed at the rest of the world. Its intellectual explanation drew on ideas which had grown slowly since 1920, suffered reverses, and had not yet combined into a system sufficient to account for the sweeping change.

The first formal step was seizure of the tin mines. The government decree, however, affected only the largest holdings, properties of two nationals and an Argentine who were popularly believed to have controlled previous governments. Smaller holdings were not affected, and even a large U.S. firm, W. R. Grace and Company, continues operations. The government-controlled mines did not become an economic success for many reasons, but their removal from private hands in 1952 was a political necessity. Tin is the country's symbol of national wealth. To proceed with the leveling of special interest groups would have been impossible while the three major owners received an income larger than the national budget.

Another part of the revolution was the dismemberment of the already discredited army. The methods exceeded democratic bounds—officers and men were imprisoned until they were proved subservient to the MNR, or they were politically neutral-ized and relegated to menial civilian employment. The army was replaced as an effective force and national symbol by civilian militia and armed tin miners and farmers. The transfer of the means of power to the latter solidified the interdependence of the MNR leaders and the masses, and made certain the eventual absorption of the miners and Indians into national society.

A third reform brought the miners and Indians into one more dimension of national life: a new electoral law enfranchised all citizens without regard to their literacy. The literacy requirement had previously limited the vote to the urban upper classes and the rural land owners. The rest of the population, mostly Aymará and Quechua speakers, had no written language and thus were doubly barred from the polls. Given the existing system of education there was little likelihood of their learning Spanish or writing in any language. The reform gave them the vote and, considering their numbers, the ultimate control of elections.

An educational reform gave promise of bringing Spanish and literacy to the younger Indians over a period of years. But the rapid pace of events leading to national integration and a self-conscious Bolivia of all Bolivians was not to await the amalgamation which education might bring in a generation.

Other basic changes centered, as might be expected, around a program of agrarian reform. Tempting as it may be to read into the reform the vision of a government determined to distribute land and meeting with a large measure of practical success in breaking up feudal estates and giving the Indians control over the countryside, it would be a mistake to overemphasize the government's intent or to minimize the role which the Indians themselves played in organizing and in precipitating the reform. In fact, the government part in reform consisted of providing the machinery for the resolution of disputes and the formalization of land redistribution. But it was the unexpected organization of the Indians, their warfare on the land owners, and their own expropriation of land which furnished the driving force of the reform. The formalities should not be mistaken for the fundamental motor force.

It was Indian participation in the Chaco War which made

possible the rapid growth of an autonomous Indian organization. During the war the Quechua speakers in particular were impressed by their sudden introduction to the idea of "Bolivia," the notions of citizenship and fatherland, and the inflammatory concept of their equality with Spanish speakers. If they were equal in their obligations to the nation, how could their privileges be less? The war was lost, the army disbanded, but the Indians who returned to the serfdom of semi-feudal estates did not forget their new ideas.

Indians, mainly veterans, formed groups for the purpose of renting land for cash payments to escape the onerous obligations of the *latifundia* system in which they were given usufruct of small plots in exchange for three to six days of unpaid labor each week for a *patrón*. These organizations were suppressed by the landowners, but the suppression increased the cohesion of the Indians, who for the first time felt persecuted as a group rather than exploited as individuals. The organizations, called "agrarian syndicates," turned to school construction and other group activities when their attempts to rent land were frustrated. The syndicates grew slowly, but came under firm Indian leadership in the 1940s. They took no direct part in the 1952 revolution, but with the breakdown of army and police authority in the provinces after April 1952 the organizations spread widely and rapidly among the Quechua speakers, mainly in the heavily Indian department of Cochabamba. The Aymarás were never recruited with the same success. Finally the syndicates were strong enough to challenge the landowners, many of whom resisted the full implications of the revolution for several months in 1952. When the challenge broke into open battle, the major landowners were driven into the cities or into exile. The Indians carried out their own land distribution, even taking houses, vehicles, and machinery. The government was still preoccupied with the army and the nationalization of the mines, but the threat of civil war between rural and urban populations precipitated quick action to establish a formal agrarian reform council and requisite procedures. Studies were made and a decree drafted and ceremonially signed by the president and his full cabinet at a gathering of some 500,000 Indians in the remote Indian village of Ucureña on August 2, 1953. The

"Indians"—actually so mixed that the racial appellation no longer applied—dropped the designation of *indio* and insisted they were *campesinos*, or "rural folk." Social change was outstripping economic change.

The foundation of national integration, the prerequisite of valid nationalism, had been laid. Full accomplishment of the task would await not only political stability and a workable economy, but also countless social and ideological adaptions to the new class structure and to the acculturating peasants.

The accomplishment of full integration is doubly difficult now because the drastic reforms undertaken in so short a time have seriously unbalanced the economy and upset longstanding political institutions. In this predicament the government can take nothing for granted but must attempt many different approaches at once, some in conflict with others. The results so far are not spectacular. The non-dramatic social advancement of the peasants is overshadowed in many minds by the crumbling economy and the destruction of the former elite. But many persons misunderstand the exclusiveness of alternatives in true revolution. The impressive fact is that the Bolivian government, in its state of perpetual crisis, has turned neither to communism nor to attacks on other nations as ways of distracting attention from the problems of moving in ten years from insularity to responsible and conscious nationhood.

Bolivian nationalism is an extraordinary thing. It is not the work of a man or group of men, or of a party. The success of the MNR in promoting nationalism came about not because it had originated the idea but because it seized on the themes of nationalism and revolution which had been imbedded in the public mind ever since they provided the rationale for reaction against the constitutional order of the few in 1920 and for the Chaco War. The internally directed nationalism of the 1950s corresponded closely to the long latent pressure of the Indians to become mestizos, and their potential for acculturation to the modes of the Spanish-speaking society. The MNR in giving voice and direction to strong currents of ideas became in part the creature of changes it had initiated itself. The study of nationalism becomes the study of the interplay of forces; of governed and governors, goals and economic realities, peasants and wage-earners—not the study of policy, intent, or party leaders.

Nationalism as Social Integration in the Emergent Nation

As we have seen, not all nationalism is reaction against empire. On the contrary, the nationalism we are examining is the product of the decay and collapse of internal institutions which supported merely a loosely affiliated state that focused on the political individual rather than structure, on the geographical community rather than the nation, on the social elite rather than the mass. Clearly this nationalism is not the same as the outwardly oriented nationalism of states recently freed from imposed dominion whose institutions, from social classes to political bureaucracy, remain virtually untouched in the transition from colony to nation.

Bolivian nationalism is representative of the new nationalism of underdeveloped countries which have long enjoyed statehood, but statehood that existed only for an elite which maintained its domination of the masses through feudal obligations and the maintenance of allegiances on a community level. The subjection of the great majority of the population *depended* on the nonexistence of the nation; the power of the elite *depended* on nonadaptation to the new forces tending toward democracy and mobility which modern technology, war, and mass communications made irresistible. The result was inability on the part of the elite either to control or to conform to the seemingly inevitable procession of collapse, revolution, democracy of a sort, nationhood, and a nationalism inwardly oriented toward rebuilding the shattered society, economy, and polity. Similar situations led to the Civil War in Spain and to the Russian revolution. It is an ominous truth that the Bolivian revolution of 1952 was only the second such breakdown and struggling reformation in Latin America.

Institutional breakdown and social reintegration. The most striking feature of the Bolivian case is the breakdown of the *latifundia* and the cultural accommodations or acculturation of the former Indian peons (*colonos, pegujaleros*, and the many other terms in use) to the encompassing mestizo culture.

Bolivia is an especially interesting example of mass emergence because 60 per cent of its population are speakers of Indian languages—Quechua and Aymará. It is true that not all of these persons lived as serfs on the large *latifundia*—a few were small landowners, some lived in theoretically communal communities, some were sharecroppers on small mestizo holdings. But the greater number were serfs on the large estates which date far back into colonial times and which formed the world for most of their residents. The obligations of the peon were truly feudal. He was assigned a small plot of land which he held at the pleasure of the landowner. In return he gave the landowner from three days of work each week (in the Cochabamba valley) to six days (on parts of the high plateau) with no recompense except a ration of coca. If the lands of the *patrón* did not suffice fully to occupy this supply of labor, the peon could be rented to another landowner or even sent out to domestic service for the profit of the lord. If the peon were for any reason unable to serve he had to provide a substitute. In addition the peon owed a certain period of service each year for such special offices as caring for the horses and mules (*mulero*); keeping the door of the estate house at night (*portero*), or feeding the fires of the great chimneys which open on the outside of the house and warm a brick shell extending into the sleeping quarters.

The wife of the peon was required to give a similar period of service (*pongüeaje*) in the house of the *patrón*, as cook, maid, maize sheller, *chuño* maker, or whatever other work was in season or desired. When the date was fixed for the marriage of a peon's daughter, she was required to spend a period, usually a month, in residence at the house of the parish priest. This practice was theoretically to receive religious instruction, but actually it was the priest's way of securing domestic service, and not infrequently of exercising a *droit du seigneur*. Children spent most of their time caring for the cattle and sheep of the landowner, taking them to the high and often dangerous pastures. If any livestock was lost the peon was responsible for its replacement. In addition to this immense levy of labor, the lord made levies in kind: spun wool, maize beer, and the like. And finally he exacted a cash tribute, the ancient *canon*. The system and even some of its nomenclature date back far beyond the time of the Spanish conquest. Parts of it were familiar to Charlemagne.

Most urban Bolivians were ignorant of the functioning of this system, thinking of it, if at all, as a benign paternalism in which the estate owner generously cared for the sick, stood godfather (*padrino*) for christenings, and gave money to bury the dead. They did not realize that nearly all landowners lived not on their estates but in the large cities or at best in neighboring mestizo towns. The estate house was visited only at long intervals, often in the spirit of a vacation. The day-to-day operations were left to a hired administrator whose proximity to *cholo* status bred a contempt and a brutality toward the Indians comprehensible to those in the United States who are familiar with the relations in the South between poor whites and Negroes. These institutions have disappeared in Bolivia and many would have us believe that they never existed. The doubter has only to visit the high sierra of Peru to see it still in full operation, and then to talk to a resident of Lima who will tell him that the abuses of the *latifundia* were legislated out of existence years ago.

A country atomized by *latifundia* is hardly a breeding ground for nationalism. It is in fact the opposite. A nationalistic state cannot maintain feudalism; a feudalistic state cannot support nationalism without destroying its own foundations. The latter is what happened in Bolivia. The immediate result need not be nationalism; it can be totalitarianism and a straining social reorganization bordering on chaos, as was the case for a generation in Mexico. Nationalism has emerged, somewhat tentatively, in Bolivia because the imported and manufactured ideas of the elite are paralleled by a remarkable integration of the formerly Indian population into an emergent national society and a true base for a nation-state.

The intellectual elite of all countries have a curiously distorted view of their own influence. Bolivia's is no exception. Few of its members are aware that they are providing a reservoir of ideas which the course of events may adopt and proclaim or reject and relegate to histories of forgotten parties and abandoned causes. The thinking and writing leaders of the

MNR claim the conversion of the Indians into peasants as their own accomplishment, the result of four much publicized reforms: the assumption of the large tin mines by the state, the agrarian reform, the educational reform, and the electoral reform. Actually the ideational underpinning of these reforms comes from writers of forty years ago. But neither the ideas nor the reforms, as carried out to this date, are the causal factors in a real shift of the Indians from caste to class. The actual process, and it is still continuing, is more complex and more interesting.

We must go back to the Viceroy Toledo for a part of the explanation of the rapidity and effectiveness of the change in the Indians' status. It was his decision in the late sixteenth century to press forward the Christianization of the recalcitrant Incas by resettling them. In the first fifty years after the conquest, the Spaniards had made little progress in this direction. The Incas by and large had remained in their original communities, administered by their own leaders, *caciques* and *curacas;* or they lived on *encomiendas*—fiefs given by the king to the *conquistadores* with a number of Incas whom they were obligated to convert to Christianity. The *encomenderos*, however, had small appetite for evangelism and a large appetite for the labor of those entrusted to them. *Encomiendas* became hereditary, while the religion of the Incas upon them remained untouched. Toledo wished to change this state of affairs by removing large numbers of Incas from their indigenous communities and from the *encomiendas* to new settlements which were given the name of *reducciones*. The *reducciones*, so called because they were reductions or concentrations of indigenous populations, were established in such a way that they would be dominated by and practically attached to Spanish towns. Where towns did not exist, new ones were founded for the specific purpose of extending a Catholic sway over the transferred and resettled Inca population.

Toledo met great opposition from the *encomenderos*. In the areas of the vice kingdom of greatest Spanish penetration, the *encomenderos* were nearly as powerful as the viceroy, so in large parts of his domain Toledo was unable to accomplish his project. He was more successful in the far reaches of the

Audience of Charcas, and apparently reservations and new
Spanish towns were effectively established in such regions as the
Cochabamba valley and surrounding territory. The reservations
were short-lived. Both they and the *encomiendas* were soon
replaced by the *latifundia*, but this development did not change
the settlement pattern of these areas nor alter the fact of a much
closer relationship of the Indian population with the Spaniards,
and particularly with the growing class of mestizos (persons
of both Indian and Spanish descent).

The result was not higher status for the Indians; in fact,
familiarity seemed to breed abuse. But the new settlement
pattern did lead to a greater knowledge among the Indians of
mestizo culture, even though they could not share it. They
were living in physical juxtaposition with mestizo society; thus
the preconditions for acculturation were laid down over three
and a half centuries ago. During this long period the *latifundia*
congealed the society in a revived and antiquated feudal mold.
Within it, mobility and acculturation were impossible. But
pressure was building—intellectual and diffuse with the collapse of the long Conservative-Liberal reign, direct and physical
in the catastrophe of the Chaco War.

The Chaco War was the beginning of a movement in Cochabamba which grew into the Agrarian Syndicate of Ucureña,
then into the Agrarian Syndicate of the Valley, and finally
became a well-armed militia of 500,000 men which dominated
the peasant movement of Bolivia. The salient fact is that the
movement grew up independent of, and at first antagonistic to,
the government; it was also virtually independent of political
parties. This growth was a natural and autochthonous one
which gave an ever firmer base for the conversion of "Indians"
to peasants and their eventual acculturation toward mestizo
norms.

Several factors explain the Indians' rapid assumption of the
role of peasant. The *latifundia* vanished almost overnight. As
we have seen, many landowners and administrators did not
take seriously the revolution of April 9, 1952. There were
still *pegujaleros* asking for the reinstatement of their usufruct
plots. The landowners refused, but soon both they and the
pegujaleros discovered there was no army or police force to

maintain old relationships. The peasants rose against the owners and their agents. Those who did not flee fast enough were killed. The estates were abandoned almost intact—furniture and pictures were left in the houses, livestock in the barns, seed in the granaries, trucks, tractors, and machinery in the out-buildings. But of the institution of *latifundium* nothing was left but the memory. The estate house of Ucureña became a barracks, others became hospitals and schools. The houses, granaries, and barns were looted, the property dispersed. The society was leveled. Mestizos of the towns were impoverished. The newly gained possessions of the more successful of the *campesino* looters rivaled the resources of the mestizos who had managed to survive economically. It was worth the life of a landowner to attempt to visit his former property.

The new rural society came alive on market day. The markets were traditionally held in the mestizo towns; the Sunday fair of Cliza was the best known. The fair was once the province of the mestizos and a few Indians who had grain or stock to sell, or who manufactured maize beer to slake the Sunday thirst. It had now become the province of the peasants and mestizos alike. A peasant was as likely as a mestizo to be the buyer of a small Swedish kerosene stove, or a bicycle, or a handmade guitar. But the new fraternity was most apparent in the *chicharías*. Here peasants and mestizos drank maize beer together where once the few Indians who could afford it were quietly served on benches placed apart near the rear entrance— humble but basic beginnings of a new status and a leveled, newly cohesive society.

The perceptible movement of the peasants toward mestizo culture closely resembles the anthropologists' model of acculturation. In many other situations, what has been described as acculturation is in fact a phenomenon of mobility: individuals who leave their native communities and seek a higher status in another society by rejecting the norms of their original culture and uncritically embracing the norms of their adopted culture. This process, which leaves both cultures unchanged, is not acculturation. But what is taking place in Bolivia *is* acculturation, and important changes are occurring in both Indian and mestizo cultures.

There is not the same kind of geographical mobility among Bolivian speakers of indigenous languages that is found in other parts of the Andes. In Peru the coastal haciendas and large cities are a powerful attraction for sierra Indians. Such opportunities do not exist in Bolivia. The mines, which might be comparable, are supplied by permanent communities of miners, and cannot offer enough work to utilize large numbers of Indians. There are few large cities and these are oversupplied with unskilled workers. Partly because of this labor situation, and partly because of a naturally strong attachment to the land, the peasant usually remains in his own community.

The *campesino* does not reject his own culture. Quechua remains a respected language in Cochabamba and Chuquisaca, and those peasants who have learned Spanish usually prefer to speak Quechua. (This is not true of Peru, where an Indian who has acquired Spanish will often pretend to be ignorant of Quechua.) Nor are the *campesinos* secretive about their practice of vestiges of the Inca religion, especially acts of propitiation of the Pachamama, the earth and fertility goddess whose hostility is much feared. Curing rites and witchcraft might be included here, but they are really of Spanish colonial origin and are practiced and believed as much by mestizos as by peasants. Coca chewing continues, as does the wearing of Indian sandals and distinctive hats by the women, and the eating of indigenous foods prepared in traditional ways.

But the peasant borrows freely from his mestizo neighbors. Spanish is becoming more and more common in the villages, especially among children of school age. The men have for the most part abandoned traditional homespuns for purchased manufactured clothing. (The more conservative women, however, still cling to the voluminous homemade *pollera*.) Sewing machines, bicycles, kerosene stoves and lanterns, guitars, Italian accordions, radios, metal eating utensils, beds, and shoes are becoming common. The interesting feature is that they are not considered marks of status—they are simply items desired, or not desired, by individuals. A peasant will wear shoes to Sunday market, but continue wearing sandals while working in the fields. It is rare for a single individual to attempt to acquire all the different characteristics of a mestizo when there is no reward for such status and no penalty for remaining a *campesino*.

The mestizos, too, have borrowed or retained many Indian traits. In Cochabamba most Spanish speakers also speak Quechua. This is not remarkable; it is also the case in the Peruvian sierra. But in Cochabamba the Spanish speakers are truly bilingual. Their Quechua is not a halting and rudimentary version learned from servants in the nursery, but a fluent and eloquent Quechua in which they take pride and which they use as much in singing and telling stories as in directing servants. The Cochabamba mestizos have enthusiastically adopted the native drink, *chicha*. Mestizo housewives themselves prepare the beer on special occasions and the quality of their product is a common topic of conversation.

Another large area of shared experience is the folk culture which grew up in early colonial times and consisted largely of importations from Spain, with some Indian elements and flavor. In this category fall the witchcraft and medical beliefs mentioned above, music, dances, stories, items of clothing, belief in "hot" and "cold" foods, house design, and the secular celebrations that accompany nearly all religious occasions.

This social movement has political significance. The large sector of the population speaking indigenous languages has grown from a restricted caste to a class within the national society. People who had previously considered themselves— and had been considered—merely Indians now thought of themselves as Bolivians. The electoral reforms gave immediate and practical meaning to this new status; with the abolition of the literacy restriction the great mass of illiterate peasants became the deciding factor in the election of candidates. The *campesinos* were not only granted this considerable power, but they also consolidated power in their own right. The agrarian syndicates originally formed to acquire land and build schools became political bodies which, after the revolution, spread rapidly through the Cochabamba valley and throughout the rural areas of Bolivia. The historic division between Quechua speakers and the Aymará speakers of the *altiplano* persisted, and the Quechua speakers were better organized. But even leaving the Aymará speakers out of consideration, the peasant power centered in the syndicate of Ucureña, able to mobilize 500,000 armed men at short notice, was and is a power to be reckoned with by the national government. This power has been used, with and without the advice of the government, to put down uprisings in Santa Cruz and to break miners' strikes. The peasants are not only Bolivians and citizens: they are the Bolivians on whom the future of the country depends. They are the broad base on which the new nationalism is founded.

Urban social leveling. Nationalism based on social integration is not confined to the rural areas. Before 1952 the social life of the cities was bound by a rigid class structure following the colonial model. At the top was an aristocracy priding itself on its blood and family tradition, the latter usually connected to ownership of land—of an historic *latifundium* or *latifundia*. Money was present as a matter of course, but was not in itself a criterion of status. Simón Patiño, owner of the largest tin mines and one of the wealthiest men in the world, was never socially acceptable in Bolivia.

Beneath the aristocracy were the "decent people" (*gente decente*): the doctors, lawyers, school teachers, smaller landowners, foreigners of some position, businessmen—people whose families were known or who had attained professional capacities. Below them were the people who spoke Spanish as a first language but who worked with their hands. The distance between the "decent people" and the working class was enormous. The workers lived in their own neighborhoods, drank in their own bars, and interacted with the *gente decente* only in the course of their work. At the bottom were the *cholos*—people supposedly Indian who had come to the cities as domestic servants, laborers, or vendors in the market. Since the social distance between the *gente decente* and the *cholos* was conceived of as reinforced by racial difference, there was more familiarity between the two classes than between the "decent people" and the Spanish-speaking workers.

The revolution of 1952 destroyed the aristocracy. It eliminated their principal symbol and source of revenue, the *latifundia*. The hyperinflation of 1952-1956, when the boliviano dropped from 190 to the dollar to 12,000 to the dollar, wiped out savings. The general decline in the economy made alternative employment impossible. The aristocracy coincidentally

acquired the epithet of *la rosca*. The basic meaning of *rosca*
is something resembling a spiral or screw, but in Bolivia it
came to mean a person who gains his livelihood at the expense
of the Indians or lower classes. Townhouses of the formerly
wealthy were daubed with the opprobrious word; some formerly
wealthy people were killed, many maltreated. The class as such
has disappeared. Many of its members emigrated to other countries, and those who remain are indistinguishable from the professional class. The night-painted signs which appear now in Cochabamba and La Paz are no longer "Death to the Rosca" but "Death
to the New Rich"—mainly corrupt politicians and businessmen
who have taken illegal advantage of United States assistance.

The *cholos* have moved upward. The racial distinction has
largely disappeared and they have coalesced with the working
class, becoming factory workers, truck drivers, and mechanics.
Paradoxically, they are no longer on such free and easy terms
with the "decent people," because they are now more mobile
and therefore a status threat.

The gap between the workers and the "decent people" still
exists, but the economic decline has inhibited its material expression. The result of the leveling is a two-class society of
workers and *gente decente*. The workers have as much or more
political power than the "decent people" because of their unions.
Industrial and craft unions have flourished and many are organized on a national level. The tin miners' union, particularly,
exerts powerful pressure on the government. In fact the situation is out of hand, and illegal work stoppages by the unions
are one of the government's prime economic problems.

All classes now participate in the nation's social life and
very directly in its political affairs. The natural result is a
growth in national feeling—a nationalism directed toward national problems.

Decay of government paternalism. One of the props of the
old regime was government as a father figure. A government
dispensed as it pleased, could be approached with unusual and
even illegal requests, granted benefices to individuals, and "gave"
roads, hospitals, power plants, schools, and potable water
plants to deserving communities. Workers were "given" pay
increases by decrees. But in return the government demanded

the personal allegiance, the obedience, the lack of questioning inherent in a paternalistic system. Government personnel were the representatives of the system.

The revolution of 1952 changed this pattern, partly through the growth of unions, partly through the economic shrinkage which reduced the means for largesse, and partly through the people's sense of participation in the government. Paternalism is not dead. Public figures still like to make the handsome gesture and would like to enjoy the unquestioning loyalties of other times but, except for a few officials such as Víctor Paz and Juan Lechín, the focus is away from individuals and to- ward the nation—one more factor in the new nationalism.

Increased mobility. One of the consequences of the kind of institutional breakdown discussed above is a greater opportunity for mobility of several types—social, political, and geographical. The importance of social mobility for nationalism has already been considered. The possibility of movement within the na- tional society leads to increased identification with that society and with the nation which gives it shape.

As yet the social movement is only nascent. Some *campesinos*, particularly Aymará speakers from the *altiplano*, are leaving the countryside for the towns and cities, either permanently or at frequent intervals. In most cases this movement signifies their leaving the *campesino* class for the lower echelons of the *cholo*- working class; some persons think of them as the new *cholos*. The line between the working class and the "decent people" is more difficult to cross for the same reason that transference from peasant to worker is usually incomplete and ends in the limbo of *cholo*-hood: the main mobility route has become edu- cation, now that peasant status is a reality. Money in itself is not a means of mobility, nor are the material things which money can buy. Even today there are wealthy smugglers and rich peasant leaders who cannot move into the class of *gente decente*. Money is useful in securing an education, but those who have money are usually past the age when they can secure it for themselves. The emphasis, then, is on education for one's children, primary and often secondary among the *campesinos*, secondary and university among the workers. The prospect is for massive movement in the future, but on the basis of generations. The present school generation of peasants, as they acquire facility in Spanish and are exposed to mass communications, can easily pass to mestizo-worker status. Their children, and the present workers' children, can become *gente decente* through secondary education and enough further specialization or university training to gain professional status. In the process, a further growth of national consciousness is inevitable. The Bolivian school system, as elsewhere in Latin America, is not based on state or county divisions but is an integrated national system depending directly from the Ministry of Education. In it there is intense interest in national history, institutions, and problems.

A product of interest in education and the generally increasing national awareness is a larger exposure to mass communications. Radio ownership has grown rapidly, especially with the introduction of cheap, battery-powered transistor sets which are well adapted to the many areas of Bolivia where electric power is unavailable or uncertain. There are now several regularly scheduled broadcasts in Quechua and Aymará—one originating in Moscow. Newspapers have a wide circulation. The number distributed is not so impressive as the number of readers of each copy. A traveler in the more remote areas is constantly stopped by road repair gangs, police, militia, and even field workers, all asking for a newspaper. And once placed in the countryside it is passed from hand to hand until it is limp and torn. The implications for nationalism are obvious.

Political mobility is not new in Bolivia, where an unlettered peasant from Tarata could seize the presidency as did Melgarejo, but the movement possible since 1952 is of a different sort. Previously the movement from humble beginnings had usually been through the military hierarchy and the capture of high political office was possible only after consolidation of military power. Now the influence of the military is small, but mobility is possible through the political hierarchy. Peasants are sub-prefects and alcaldes. One became Minister of Rural Affairs. A small landowner can become successively sub-prefect, mayor, and national deputy. With the road open to political power, if not necessarily social recognition, there is still another stimulus to awareness of and identification with the nation and its government.

A final impetus to this awareness through mobility patterns is given by simple geographical movement. Someone who has lived all his life in the colonial insularity of Sucre, or in the bleak altitude of La Paz, or in the misery of *campesino* villages of the *altiplano* or Cochabamba, can hardly imagine the diversity and richness of Bolivia as a whole. Any escape from the horizons of the villages or the confines of the cities may be a revelation. And now more than ever a peasant has the chance to travel. The first recourse of the less wealthy is the truck, usually a relatively light, stake-sided vehicle used primarily for freight atop which passengers may clamber for a small price. It performs wonders in navigating deeply rutted roads, fording rivers, and penetrating to the farthest reaches of poorly maintained roads and beyond. Standard buses and popular microbuses also perform remarkable feats for a modest fee. They are replacing the passenger service of the railroads, which are suffering near-collapse after being abandoned to the state by a private company. Bolivia also enjoys a national airline which covers most of the country and is eagerly used by peasants and "decent people" alike.

The connecting road between Cochabamba and Santa Cruz, and the penetration road into the Alto Beni are important innovations. Both have made travel common into areas known but a few years ago only to forest Indians and the most intrepid explorers and settlers. The Yungas road has introduced Aymará speakers of the *altiplano* to the hot lands of the valleys, and the Santa Cruz road has brought highland Quechua speakers and even *chicha* drinking to the eastern lowlands. Peasant leaders and union delegates attend congresses in many parts of the country. *Campesino*, *cholo*, and working class small-time dealers in contraband make frequent trips to the Peruvian, Brazilian, Argentine, and Chilean borders (and beyond, to Puno in Peru, Porto Velho in Brazil, and Arica and Antofagasta on the Pacific coast of Chile) where they acquire a small stock of goods to take back to the interior. The increased volume of travel has made thousands more knowledgeable about their country, if not quite cosmopolitan. Such knowledge brings another affirmation of their belief in the nation.

Conclusion

Nationalism and social revolution have been the two vital processes in this underdeveloped country's movement from local particularism to national integration. They are also the product of strain toward technological change and of new ideas of social justice and of a war which made use of these ideas. The interplay of forces is complex, but it is indisputable that nationalism made effective by revolution has transformed Bolivia from a country divided between urban and rural sectors—the urban sector interested in technological change but hampered by its dependence on social and political forms which restrained the rural elements, bound by the forms of feudalism to anti-nationalism and to non-adaptation.

It may be that this route must be traveled by other nations of Latin America. Aside from Bolivia, only Mexico and Cuba have experienced the deep dislocation of revolution and painful rebuilding under a banner of nationalism which may be inevitable for countries in which the mass of population is exploited by a restriction of its horizon to the infra-national. There is, then, particular significance in the Bolivian case.

Bolivia has accomplished a greater social revolution than Mexico and in a fifth of the time. Yet it has done so under a nationalism that, unlike Cuba's, has preserved the forms of democracy. In a way the nationalism is pure—unaffected by anti-colonialism, anti-imperialism, anti-communism, communism, or recent independence. It is a nationalism concerned with the social, economic, and political integration of the people and with the national problems which this integration raises. A country which can move so far in so short a time, maintaining the single-mindedness of its nationalism and continuing the experiment with democratic forms, must be of interest to any comparative study of nationalism.

{ PART }
II

Leadership
and the New States

"Oh, call them not, the well-known swarms
That streaming spread throughout the murky air;
In every quarter they prepare
A danger for mankind in a thousand forms,
Sharp spirit-fangs press from the north
Upon you here with arrow-pointed tongues;
And from the east, now parching, they come forth
And feast themselves upon your lungs;
And when the south wind from the desert drives
Those that heap glow on glow upon your brain,
The west wind brings the swarm that first revives,
Then drowns you and the field and plain.
They like to hear, on mischief gaily bent,
They like to hearken, for they like to try
To fool us, pose as if from Heaven sent,
And lisp like angels when they lie."

GOETHE
Faust

Chapter

4

□□□□□□□□□□□

Nationalist Revolution and Revolutionary Nationalism:

Indonesia

WILLARD A. HANNA

• I tell you frankly: I belong to the group of people who are bound in spiritual longing by the romanticism of revolution.

I am inspired by it, I am fascinated by it, I am completely absorbed by it, I am crazed, I am obsessed by the romanticism of revolution. And for this I utter thanks to God Who Commands All Nature!

There are people who do not understand revolutionary logic. . . . This is revolutionary logic: once we start off a revolution we must continue that revolution until all its ideals have been implemented.

This constitutes an absolute law of revolution, which can be denied no longer, this can be debated no further!

Therefore do not say, "The revolution is already over," whilst revolution is on the march; and do not attempt to dam up or to oppose or slow down a particular phase of revolution which is but a consequence of prior phases of the revolution!

There are also people who, oh yes, understand and agree about all the phases, but they ask: "Do we need to be always inflaming the spirit of revolution?"

"Is it necessary for everything to be done in a revolutionary way? Could it not be done by means of '*Alon-alon asal kelakon*'—'slow but sure'!"

Good heavens! "Slow but sure!" That is not possible. That is not possible, unless we want to be crushed by the people! . . .

This world today is a revolutionary ammunition dump. This world today holds revolutionary electric power. This world today is "loaded with revolution."

Three-quarters of the whole of mankind on the face of this earth . . . are in a revolutionary spirit.

It has never before happened that the history of man has gone through such a revolution as this at present—so strong and so tremendous, so widesweeping and universal—a Revolution of Humanity which at the same time surges, flashes, thunders, in almost every corner of the earth. . . .

We see the red glow of fires reflected in the Eastern skies, the red glow of fires reflected in the Northern skies. . . . We see that all the skies around us are glowing with the fire of revolution. . . . [So] it is forbidden to us to go "slow but sure," forbidden to us to creep like snails, to crawl like tortoises . . . forbidden to us to nurture revolution-phobia!

Look and take heed! A state which does not grow in a revolutionary way will not only be crushed by its own people, but also will soon be swept aside by the typhoon of universal revolution which is the most important phenomenon in the world at the present time. . . .

The states and nations which are already old, and the states and nations which feel that they are already "settled," will also eventually be shaken up by that typhoon of universal revolution, if they do not adjust themselves to the changes and upheavals leading toward the formation of a new world, free from colonialism, free from *exploitation de l'homme par l'homme*, free from oppression, free from exploitation, free from color discrimination, free from spying upon one another with atomic bombs and thermonuclear weapons in their hands.

This is why I, who have been given the topmost leadership of the struggle of the Indonesian nation, never tire of appealing and exhorting: solve our national problems in a revolutionary way, make the revolutionary spirit surge on, see to it that the fire in our revolution does not die or grow dim, not even for a single moment.

Now, come on, *keep fanning the flames of the leaping fire of the revolution. Let us become logs to feed the flames of revolution.*[1] [Italics added.] •

This extract from his two hour Independence Day oration of August 17, 1960, epitomizes the message, at once incendiary and chilling, with which President Sukarno has been seeking to perpetuate the Indonesian revolution. To many Indonesian auditors, as well as to most Westerners, it seems a message not of revolution *gratia* evolution but of revolution *gratia* revolution itself, a formula not of progress and prosperity but of fervor and ferment.

Among those Indonesians for whom the message lacks validity, in reply to whose counsels it was explicity directed, is ex-Vice President Mohammad Hatta. Just before retiring on December 1, 1956, dismayed by the course of Indonesian politics in recent years, Hatta analyzed the situation as follows:

When one looks at recent developments in our country and society, one gets the impression that after the independence of Indonesia had been achieved, with no small sacrifice, our idealistic leaders and freedom fighters were pushed back, while political and economic profiteers came to the foreground. They have used the national movement and its slogans for their own ends and have ridden on the backs of the political parties for these same private ends.

[1] *Times of Indonesia*, Djakarta, Vol. 23, No. 99, August 20, 1960, p. 4.

This has inevitably resulted in political and economic anarchy, followed in its wake by a reign of corruption and demoralization. [Italics added.]

This is the face Indonesia presents today, after having been independent for a number of years. It is clear that it was not this kind of Indonesia that was visualized by our freedom fighters of earlier days.[2]

He continues:

A thoroughgoing social analysis would show that *all our rebellions and our splits, our political anarchy and adventurism, and all the steps taken in the economic field which have created chaos* are the result of the fact that our national revolution was not dammed up at the appropriate time. *Those who say that our national revolution is not yet completed are wrong indeed.* A revolution is a sudden explosion of society which brings with it an *"Unwertung aller Werte"* [upsetting of all values]. A revolution shakes the floor and the foundation, it loosens all hinges and boards. Therefore, a revolution should not last too long, not more than a few weeks or a few months. It should then be checked; the time will then have arrived for a consolidation which will realize the results produced by the revolution. *What is left unfinished is not the revolution itself, but the efforts to carry its ideals into effect* over a period of time after the foundations have been laid. The revolution itself takes only a short time. The revolutionary period of consolidation may take quite a long time, even up to several decades. . . .

. . . if [the Revolution] is not checked in time, all the hinges and boards that have come loose will become a jumble and in the end the entire structure will tumble down. In the meantime, new elements will come in and take advantage of the chaotic situation. *It will no longer be clear where freedom ends and anarchy begins.*

[2] "Past and Future," an address delivered by Mohammad Hatta upon receiving the degree of *doctor honoris causa* from Gadjah Mada University at Jogjakarta on November 27, 1958, in *Translation Series, Modern Indonesian Project*, Ithaca: 1960, p. 13.

In point of fact our national revolution, having continued for several years, ought to be checked. Its energies should be guided in an orderly fashion so as to teach the mass of the people to become conscious of their responsibilities in democracy. Democracy cannot possibly live without a sense of responsibility. Therefore, our people who have never known democracy at the level of the state must first be trained in democracy.[3] [All italics added.]

Democracy, yes, declares President Sukarno—not, however, "liberal, Western style democracy," which "we must hurl as far from us as possible," but rather "Guided Democracy," which means "complete retooling" of the nation, its leaders, and its ideology. And not "free enterprise," he says, the "free-for-all" economy of "vulture capitalists," but a "Guided Economy," which means swiftly increasing state ownership and control. And "Indonesian identity," too, the return to Indonesia's own "pure soul and spirit," which means rejection of alien, especially Western, values, and of all that makes for "text-book thinking," "revolution-phobia," and "communist-phobia." Every aspect of national life must be "guided," but along "dynamic" revolutionary lines so that the "old house," with its creaky boards and hinges, is not merely renovated but razed, regardless of the wishes of the tenants.

> We can . . . hear squeals and convulsions from the inhabitants of the old house. [They] still want to preserve that old building: the unofficial councils . . . this League, that League, this newspaper, that newspaper, this document, that document. They squeal in consternation!
>
> Yes, without hiding anything, I certainly admit it: we make radical changes but also we construct! We construct, and for that we make radical changes. We break down, we pull out, we uproot.
>
> All in order to construct. Revolution is uprooting and constructing. Constructing and uprooting. Revolution is to "build tomorrow" and to "reject yesterday." Revolution is to "construct tomorrow, pull down yesterday."[4]

[3]*Ibid.*, p. 15.
[4] Sukarno, *op. cit.*, p. 4.

The Sukarno-Hatta dichotomy, signaled by an open personal break between the two in 1956 and by sharply contrasting statements of ideology then and since, symbolizes the basic conflict within the Indonesian nationalist revolution itself. It is the dichotomy which is inherent within any nationalist or revolutionary movement—between those forces which "pull down yesterday" and those which "build tomorrow."

Sukarno's affinity is for demolition, Hatta's for development. The balance between the two men and the forces which they typify, after being precariously maintained from 1927 to 1956, has now completely broken down. Sukarno and his group have established themselves in the ascendancy, but seem incompetent to construct as much as they destroy. Hatta and his adherents have passed into eclipse, and seem impotent to regenerate either their own energies or those of the nation. The emergence of a third force more effectively constructive than Hatta's and less dangerously destructive than Sukarno's seems not at all imminent. The tragedy of Indonesia today is that its present leaders are channeling the nation's tremendous resources and abilities away from national reconstruction into nationalist agitation.

Given even reasonably favorable circumstances, Indonesia would seem destined for reincarnation as one of the world's truly great nations. Until half a millennium ago, it was the seat of the vast Hindu-Buddhist Sriwidjaja and Modjapahit Empires (seventh to fourteenth centuries) which dominated much of Southeast Asia. Then, after an interval in which Islam came to prevail, it became for nearly 350 years a rich colonial domain of the Netherlands. On August 17, 1945, after three and a half years of wartime Japanese occupation, it became independent by declaration of its own leaders, Sukarno and Hatta, who for twenty years had been heading a nationalist movement and for the next four and a half years successfully resisted reimposition of Dutch control. On December 27, 1949, Indonesia achieved international recognition of its independence. With a land area one-quarter that of the United States and immensely rich in oil, rubber, tin, copra, and other raw materials, with a population of 92 million industrious people of extraordinary cultural accomplishment, with 3,000 superbly beautiful islands stretching strategically 3,000 miles along the equator, Indonesia should rate today as the hopeful giant of Southeast Asia.

The nation's problems, unfortunately, are at least as formidable as its potential. It suffers from an acute shortage of qualified or experienced personnel, a predilection for political intrigue rather than administration, and an intense resentment of any outside counsels of moderation. Fragmented into many geographic and cultural entities, hampered by bad communications and regional animosities, Indonesia's task of unification seems almost impossibly difficult. The country has been beset with official incompetence, opportunism, and corruption, public ignorance and excitability, and economic dislocation intensified by bureaucratic muddle and malice. It has dissipated upon an anti-colonial, anti-capitalist campaign at home and abroad the energies and resources which might far better have been expended upon critical domestic problems which remain not merely unresolved but unanalyzed. Indonesia is the very prototype of the underdeveloped, overly suspicious new nation which has endured much under colonialism, but declines to concede that it has benefited as well, or that mere prudence dictates the consolidation of postcolonial gains rather than the perpetuation of colonial grievances.

Indonesia, in consequence, has lived since 1950—indeed, since 1942—in a constant state of crisis. That in spite of immense difficulties it has actually achieved and maintained independence as a single nation must command the great admiration of any observer. That it has not yet made very impressive progress, however, in converting independence into national strength and stability is an unhappy fact which it would be naive to deny or gloss over. Nor would it be particularly illuminating to attribute this failure, as do Indonesia's present leaders themselves, to the inherited evils of colonialism, the interference of imperialist and capitalist nations, the unnatural tensions of the Cold War, and the inevitable "growing pains" of a new nation. All of these factors have a very important bearing upon Indonesia's troubles. What needs to be clearly pointed out, however, even at the cost of giving offense to many Indonesians, is that Indonesia's national leaders have vastly compounded their nation's difficulties by their own policies and lack of policies.

Conjecture concerning what Indonesia might have accomplished under happier circumstances would be unproductively hypothetical. The measurement of her leaders against ideal standards of political behavior would be unrealistic. The sustaining of certain judgments on the Indonesian leaders and the Indonesian problem nevertheless would seem worthwhile, for the light which such judgments may throw upon the still very imperfectly understood experiences of Indonesia and similar nations in their emergence into the modern world.

First, then, the Indonesian revolution was the work of relatively few national leaders of very great personal accomplishment who achieved success in revolution against a designated national enemy, the Dutch, but have failed as national administrators. Second, the revolution was conditioned by an intensely emotional ideology of nationalism which became more rather than less intensely emotional once independence was actually achieved and which grew gradually destructive of its own objectives. Third, the transformation of Indonesian nationalism into an obsession and many of Indonesia's top national leaders into zealots constitutes both a domestic and an international tragedy for which, even with the greatest of good-will and hope for Indonesia, it is reckless to assume a fortunate outcome. Fourth, the manifestations of Indonesian nationalism over the last few years show a profound shift away from the original ideas of nationalism, which inspired the revolution of independence, toward a new ideology of mere revolutionary conflagration described and promoted today by Sukarno and his followers as "revolutionary nationalism."

Indonesian nationalism may fairly be defined as the self-conscious determination on the part of the national leaders, especially the Westernized elite, to achieve national identity and all else that identity implies in the way of national sovereignty, territorial cohesion, government organization, economic autonomy, social and cultural integration, and international recognition and prestige. The Indonesian revolution was the successful attempt to achieve independence by arousing national enthusiasm for nationalist objectives and resistance against Dutch colonialism. "Revolutionary nationalism," on the other hand, is the attempt on the part of the present clique of revolutionary leaders to resolve the immensely difficult post-independence problems of the nation by deliberately destroying old forms and values, especially those regarded as "Western," in order to experiment with new forms and values not yet clearly defined in theory but authoritarian in practice. Indonesian revolutionary nationalists knowingly risk national disaster on the chance that Indonesia, like the phoenix, will emerge revitalized from the fires of revolutionary nationalistic immolation.

These distinctions among nationalism, nationalist revolution, and revolutionary nationalism are not, to be sure, a theoretically unassailable formulation, but they are nonetheless useful in distinguishing between the nationalism of advance and idealistic confidence which on the whole characterized the earlier period, and the nationalism of frustration and desperation which is that of Indonesia today. As the nationalist revolution aimed at the liberation of the country, so revolutionary nationalism strives to confine it in a straitjacket which is only now in the process of being tailored.

The reasons for the emergence of Indonesian revolutionary nationalism and the prospects that it may yet evolve into a form better calculated to achieve national viability may be seen through an appraisal of the events of the last few decades.

The Eclectic Pre-1942 Period of Marhaenism

The early decades of the Indonesian nationalist revolution were marked by the convergence of influences, the emergence of leaders, the contrivance of techniques, the definition of conflicts, and accommodation to the obstacles which—with certain exceptions and shifting emphasis—have persisted to this day.

The quickening influences came from all over Europe, Asia, and the Americas. The decisive leaders identified themselves as Sukarno, Tan Malaka (d. 1948), Hadji Agus Salim (d. 1954), Mohammad Hatta, and Sutan Sjahrir. The techniques were: (1) the creation of the illusion of a relatively harmonious coexistence of diverse personalities and ideologies; (2) the concentration of effort upon anti-colonialism, anti-imperialism, and anti-capitalism; and (3) the formulation of a packaged rationale and a catchy slogan on the basis of which the intellectual elite assumed the leadership of an inchoate mass movement. The conflicts were: (1) the discord which, despite the appearance of a united front, developed among persons, ideologies, and cultural groups as disparate as Tan Malaka's communism and Hadji Agus Salim's liberal Muslimism, and between the Western and the indigenously educated; and (2) the clash among Eastern, Western, and indigenous political, economic, and social systems. The major obstacles, which paradoxically at times also constituted major advantages, were: (1) Dutch efforts at suppression, which only inflamed the politicians; (2) the intricate feuding of leaders, which taught survival tactics; (3) public apathy, which cushioned the shocks of defeat; and (4) geographical remoteness, which both obscured and romanticized what was happening.

The most distinctive single characteristic of the period was the catholic eclecticism of the top echelon of leaders. These men—the few hundred, or at most the few thousand, who had achieved high school or university level education, most of them in the Western, some in the Muslim tradition—constituted an intellectual elite of extraordinary versatility. By racial and cultural inheritance they were preconditioned to a universalistic outlook and to the study and synthesis of the most diverse alien systems. They had been brought up in the Indonesian tradition, which was at base animist and feudalist, but had been profoundly transformed in the course of two millennia by Hindu and Buddhist civilization, Muslim faith and European domination. They frequently had at their command not only various Indonesian languages but also Dutch, English, French, German, and Arabic. They deliberately exposed themselves to the impact of the Japanese resurgence, the Philippine insurrection, the Chinese revolution, the Muslim revival, the Indian national awakening, the twentieth century liberalism and radicalism of Western Europe, and the Russian communist experiment. They selected and combined intellectual influences in widely varying proportions and disguised dissident views in acceptance of a single dogma, the necessity for the creation of a great, composite, and independent Indonesian nation.

From the very beginning, the ideal and to a remarkable extent the practice of the Indonesian nationalist movement has been the One Happy Political Family which includes all types and degrees of nationalists and allows for quarrels in anticipation of eventual reconciliation. The original One Happy Political Family was born in 1911 in the home of one H. O. S. Tjokroaminoto, a Surabaja businessman-theologian, the founder of the Serikat Islam, a trade league with religious overtones which became the nation's first political party. In Tjokroaminoto's home, the adherents of the Serikat Islam, who spanned the political spectrum from Muslim theocrats to Marxist theorists, studied and discussed Marx, Renan, Voltaire, Hegel, Jefferson, Sun Yat-sen, and Ataturk, as well as the Koran, the Bible, the Mahabharata and its Indonesian equivalents, and the modern commentaries upon each. They exhibited marked differences in outlook, but were unanimous in their desire to learn and to fuse their views and actions.

The first serious breach in the Happy Family came over the issue of growing doctrinaire arrogance on the part of the communists, who attempted in 1923 to usurp control and were themselves expelled from the inner clique, although not from the outer fringe. Significantly, the members of the Happy Family did not really begin to split until they had collaborated in training up a youthful protégé who admired and emulated them all. This most engaging and impressionable foster son of the household, whose school-teacher father had consigned him to Tjokroaminoto's care and support, then went by his boyhood name of Kusnososro. He is better known today by his adult name of Sukarno.

Sukarno was the ideological heir of Tjokroaminoto. He was trained in political dialectics by Tjokroaminoto and his group; his formal education in a Dutch-style secondary school and then in the engineering college was paid for by Tjokroaminoto, and for a brief period he was married to Tjokroaminoto's daughter. He grew up with many mentors, many languages, many philosophies. Sukarno later broke personally with Tjokroaminoto, divorced his daughter, and formulated a political philosophy of his own, one in which he exhibited a marked preference for Marxist over other ideological sources. By 1927 he had emerged as Indonesia's top political leader, the founder and spokesman of the nation's most powerful political organization, the *Perserikatan Nasional Indonesia*, the first of many successor groups to bear the initials of PNI now attached to the Indonesian Nationalist Party. Ideologically and politically Sukarno nevertheless remained within the mainstream of the widely, indeed wildly, inclusive Tjokroaminoto eclecticism. He has tolerated deviations which amounted almost to secession from his own nationalist movement and endeavored always—but most persistently since the mid-1950s—to restore the original One Happy Political Family by sweeping aside all differences.

Handsome, facile, magnetic in personality, a mellifluous orator, agile in adjustment, pampered by his mentors, doted on by his followers, the consummate master of political maneuver, Sukarno quickly assumed the role of the charismatic leader. Although he has seemed to falter occasionally in his conviction that he is the chosen instrument of fate, he has seen it demonstrated again and again that the other national leaders cannot hold the nation together without him. Early and late, he has conceived of his mission as that of reconciling apparently irreconcilable men and ideas, of constituting himself the mind and the voice through which the destiny of the Indonesian people projects itself upon Indonesia and upon the world, guiding the Indonesian nation toward a national greatness whose exact shape and structure will reveal itself with the passage of time.

Sukarno in the late 1920s coined for the Indonesian nationalist movement both the slogan and the mystique of *Marhaenism.* To the word "Marhaen," the name of a philosophical peasant with whom he had fraternized in his youth, he assigned the meaning of "The People." To the Europeanized abstract noun "Marhaenism" he assigned—much later, not originally—the definition "Indonesian Marxism."

Marhaenism, as officially defined, is "the formulation and reflection of the ideals, ideas, thoughts and emotions as to State and Society that potentially slumber in the minds and hearts of the Marhaen masses, which are unable to express these things for themselves."[5] Marhaenism, therefore, as Sukarno then expounded it in fiery orations, was directed not toward the Marhaen themselves but toward the intellectual elite. It was their role, with him as leader, to guide the Marhaen to *Merdeka,* liberation from Dutch colonialism.

Sukarno, as the prophet of Marhaenism, has alternately informed the Marhaen of the movement's irrepressible demands and the world of his inflexible determination to achieve them. For a period of decades he made the demands inclusive enough

[5] Partai Nasimal Indonesia, *Manifesto of Marhaenism,* Djakarta: n. d., p. 4.

to satisfy almost any nationalist leader. He managed to allow for enough compromise to placate the moderates and enough repudiation of compromise to placate the extremists. His campaign for Merdeka was geared to anti-colonialism, anti-imperialism, and anti-capitalism. It was vaguely enough directed against "certain powers" to suggest to the Western-oriented that perhaps it was not inclusively anti-Western, and specifically enough pro-proletariat to suggest to the Marxist-oriented that it was distinctly pro-communistic. Marhaenism was always accompanied by protestations of its religious base, so that it could offend no Muslim or Christian. In theory, it involved championship of a program of mass action to achieve nationalist goals, but until well within the fighting period of the revolution it seemed in practice to favor non-violent methods. Sukarno, who had learned in the Tjokroaminoto household to compartmentalize ideas and to commingle personalities, managed by exercise of personal magnetism and political opportunism to maintain himself over the decades as the commanding central figure of an inherently amorphous movement.

Marxism was a major element of Sukarno's philosophy and of Indonesian nationalist thought in general. The Indonesian Marxists were at once Sukarno's allies and his competitors. The Indonesian Communists—members of Asia's first Communist party, founded shortly after World War I by Dutch converts —provided a second nationalist organization, a cause, and another figure of tremendous appeal. Their most prominent leader, Tan Malaka, epitomizes in his personal history the communist brand of Indonesian eclecticism, rivaling in importance that of Sukarno himself and, indeed, threatening at times to displace it.

Tan Malaka, a Sumatran sent to Holland for education by Dutch sponsors, turned Communist in Holland at the end of World War I during a period of bitter disillusionment induced by ill health, academic failure, racial and religious discrimination, and association with drifting young intellectuals as frustrated as himself. He returned to Indonesia to teach school on a Dutch plantation in Sumatra and to make himself the center of both social and political controversy. Accepting a cash settlement for termination of his teaching contract, he proceeded to Java and there, in the city of Semarang, where the Indonesian

Communist Party (PKI) had lately been established, he started his own school for the children of workers and peasants. Tan Malaka rose swiftly in the PKI hierarchy, and in 1922, after a brief period as head of the party which was just then involved in a series of abortive strikes, he was arrested and exiled by the Dutch colonial government. Given his choice of place of exile, he named Holland. Shortly after his return to Holland, he almost succeeded in getting himself elected to the Dutch Parliament on the Communist Party ticket. Eluding the Dutch police, he removed himself to Berlin, and from Berlin, eluding the German police, to Moscow. There he was lionized by the Russian leaders, and after careful indoctrination was named Comintern agent for Southeast Asia. Soon after being sent to join the Communist advisers assigned to the Chinese nationalist headquarters in Canton, he shared the opprobrium which fell upon all Moscow agents in China at that time and departed from Canton to fulfill his assignment elsewhere.

Tan Malaka's life from this point on was a serial thriller of international intrigue and escape. With the police usually close on his trail, he moved about with astounding agility through China, the Philippines, Hong Kong, the Straits Settlements and Malaya, Burma, Thailand, and possibly Japan, with several clandestine visits even to Indonesia. He assumed Chinese and Filipino disguises which deceived even Chinese and Filipinos, picked up languages like a tape recorder, founded little Communist cells wherever he went, and both lent and gained support wherever anti-colonial movements of any political description were stirring. On one visit to Indonesia he traveled on an American passport acquired under a Filipino alias with the aid of highly placed Filipino friends. On his various travels he was interrupted now and again—but much less frequently and much less protractedly than might have been expected—by arrest and imprisonment. In 1941, at the outbreak of the Pacific war, he was living in Singapore, posing as a Chinese, teaching English in a Chinese school, awaiting a chance to get back to Indonesia again. He promptly followed the Japanese to Indonesia, crossing the Straits of Malacca in a leaky old junk. Upon arrival in Indonesia he went underground, persuaded—with reason—that his saga was much too well known to the Japanese, and awaited the day when he could re-emerge with greater hope for survival.

The Tan Malaka legend is that of the romantic fugitive, the ideological Pimpernel, the internationally renowned apostle of Indonesian revolution, nationalism, and communism. He is the symbol of early Russian communist sympathy and intermittent support for a movement which the Western world branded as dangerously subversive. He is also the author of much of Indonesia's revolutionary philosophy, and the first clearly to formulate the concept of *Indonesia Merdeka*, doing so in a brochure surreptitiously published in Singapore in 1927 and smuggled into Indonesia to serve as text for Sukarno and the other nationalists. He also formulated the concept of *Massa Aksi* (Mass Action) as a means of achieving Merdeka, a concept which in part complements, in part contradicts, the Sukarno thesis of Marhaenism.

Whether Tan Malaka was a Communist first and a nationalist second, or vice versa, has been the subject of much argument both within and without Indonesia. The question has agitated some of his most intimate personal followers, including PKI members who came to brand him as a traitor and a Trotskyite, as well as Sukarno associates who at times acclaimed him, rather than Sukarno, as the true Indonesian national hero. Tan Malaka himself insisted from the first that communism was not a dogma but a guide to action, and on that same basis many of the members of the PKI have maintained from the outset, whatever their feuds and splits and deviations, that theirs is the genuine, indeed, the one constant base of the nationalist movement.

The Sukarno nationalist and the Tan Malaka Marxist streams of Indonesian political eclecticism, at times converging, at times diverging, are less readily distinguishable from each other than from the third important stream, that of Muslim religious revival. A single person, Hadji Agus Salim, while himself far too much an individualist to be as representative of his disparate group as Sukarno and Tan Malaka were of theirs, reveals much of the spirit of the more liberal element. Hadji Agus Salim was at various points in his career a businessman in Indonesia, an official in the Dutch foreign service, a religious scholar in Mecca, a magazine editor, a radio commentator, and a philosopher and statesman who gathered about him a devoted coterie of young disciples. He was an early convert to the Serikat Islam, the gadfly of that body during the period when the Communists were seeking to gain control, the gadfly later of the Dutch colonial *Volksraad* during the period when the Dutch, by conferring a little autonomy, were seeking to forestall demands for independence. He attempted ceaselessly to bring liberal religious principles to bear upon political and social problems, welcoming the new Muslim modernism which spread from Cairo and Istanbul, as well as the influences of Christian Socialism from Europe.

The Hadji did not create a movement or a party, but he did typify the vitalizing effect within Indonesia of the twentieth century Muslim religious reawakening, which brought with it sharpened political and social awareness as well. In contrast to Hadji Agus Salim there arose at the same time in Indonesia other religious leaders whose response to the Muslim revival was retreat into intolerant orthodoxy and reaction against Western and Christian influences. The religious stream of Indonesian political eclecticism, consequently, was never as clear, united, or vital as those generally distinguished as nationalist or Marxist.

Still a fourth stream of Indonesian political eclecticism involved Indonesian students studying in Holland in the 1920s. Among them the most powerful conditioning factor at first was Western European political liberalism, but by the mid-1920s the influence of Marxism was almost as great; always, the effect of differences of race, religion, and social tradition was considerable. These students in the mid-1920s organized a "radical revolutionary" body dedicated to the anti-colonial struggle, known as the *Perhimpoenan Indonesia* (Indonesian Union). The P.I., like the Serikat Islam before it, was torn by conflict over Communist efforts to usurp control. Afterwards, despite the encouragement lent it by ill-advised Dutch efforts at suppression, it never regained its earlier drive or influence. Most of its more prominent members, in any event, returned to Indonesia in the late 1920s and there joined other Indonesian independence movements.

The most significant figure of the *Perhimpoenan Indonesia* was Mohammad Hatta. One of his closest associates was Sutan Sjahrir. Hatta and Sjahrir, to a greater extent than any other long-time Indonesian national leaders, retained their commitment to Western-style liberalism. Both joined forces with Sukarno, Hatta being a more intimate personal associate than Sjahrir. The latter, paradoxically, was himself close to the Marxist stream of political thought; Hatta was close to the religious. Both experienced personal betrayal by the Communists, Hatta at the time of the attempted Communist takeover of the P.I., and Sjahrir years later during the fighting period of the revolution. Both also underwent repudiation by Sukarno, Sjahrir first, again during the fighting period of the revolution, and Hatta almost a decade later.

Hatta and Sjahrir have come to represent the revolutionary right wing, and are branded by extremists as counter-revolutionaries. Both of them, while dedicated to Indonesian independence and the anti-colonial struggle, have proved themselves to be men of intellectual discipline and emotional moderation. The two were also associated on terms of high mutual esteem with Hadji Agus Salim. It is tempting to speculate what might have been the course of the Indonesian revolution had Hatta, rather than Sukarno, gained ascendancy among the nationalists, and Sjahrir rather than Tan Malaka among the Marxists, with Hadji Agus Salim heading a cooperating and unified Muslim religious group. Such a coalition would have been no more improbable than the one which actually emerged, with these three and other leaders as well rallying to Sukarno's call, inspired by Tan Malaka's example, and making uneasy common cause against the Dutch.

The Indonesian nationalist movement rose to a high pitch in the early 1930s. The Dutch, stirred to alarm and vigilance, packed Sukarno, Hatta, Sjahrir, and others off to prison or to exile. They filled the detention camps of Boven Digul in New Guinea with persons accused of implication in the Communist-inspired disorders that broke out in late 1926 and early 1927 and threatened to spread. They made overt political activity too dangerous to be widely attractive and too difficult to provoke more than a very few new martyrs. The Dutch then relapsed

into near-complacency as those members of the Indonesian intellectual elite who remained at large reconciled themselves to
a *modus vivendi* with alien rule, and as the Marhaen showed
little evidence of having grasped the implications of Marhaenism.
The Indonesian nationalist movement, which had threatened
for a time to turn into rebellion, began to look more like a
gradual and retarded national awakening. It seemed subject
to calculated Dutch controls, and to the uncalculated but even
more efficient control of the balance and counter-balance of the
complex elements within itself.

Suddenly in 1941 came war in the Pacific, the Japanese invasion of Indonesia, the defeat and humiliation of the Dutch,
and the release and reactivation of the top Indonesian leaders.

The Empirical Years of AAR and Pantjasila (1942 to mid-1945)

Three and a half years of Japanese occupation and their
immediate aftermath added to the theoretical eclecticism of the
Indonesian nationalist leaders the factor of practical experience
in affairs of state. The Japanese occupation brought an opportunity for Indonesians to replace Dutchmen, and a consequent
Indonesian determination to replace not only Dutchmen but
Japanese as well. It meant creation of an enlarged although
still far from extensive administrative group, as well as an
army, a youth corps, a business class, and even a new clique
of writers, artists, and actors. The occupation also meant the
offsetting of early gratitude for Japanese "liberation" by later
rancor over Japanese "exploitation" and "betrayal." The new
attitude led to Indonesian intrigue and sabotage on the one
hand and Japanese retaliation and brutality on the other. But
since the Japanese had no choice but to rely upon Indonesian
collaborators, to the Indonesian nationalists as a whole the
occupation meant the chance—opportunely offered and oppor-
tunistically seized—to achieve nationalist ends by devices generally far less idealistic than practical.

The years from 1942 to 1945, then, were a period of empiricism. The Indonesian nationalists learned that they could run
the nation, not as well, certainly, as the Dutch, and largely

on momentum, but well enough at least to get by. They discovered that they could operate the banks, the businesses, the estates, the transportation system, and even the government offices. They might have worked under the supervision of Japanese officials, but these officials either taught what they knew or obviously knew less than the Indonesians themselves. They learned, most of all, that what succeeded politically was collaboration, then pressure, then defiance, each as it proved appropriate to changing circumstances. Indonesian nationalist leaders and followers soon lost what little political innocence had survived feudalism, colonialism, and nationalist awakening.

The events of these years in Indonesia are still a matter of ill-documented dispute. So far as the activities of the top leaders were concerned—activities revealing not only of the men but of the period—it is safe to summarize as follows: Sukarno busily collaborated, and Sjahrir went underground, while Hatta served as intermediary between the two. Hadji Agus Salim alternately exposed himself to the blandishments of the Japanese and exposed the Japanese to the display of his erudition. Tan Malaka first hid out as a Marxist student and writer, then pseudonymously hired out as a clerk at the coal mines, and then, finally, hit out as a "youth representative" of mature years to join the activists at exactly the correct psychological moment. Other prominent leaders and followers made more or less anomalous adjustments and readjustments as best they could.

Meanwhile, a new generation of potential leaders, the young intellectuals, was arising. They marked time as teachers and students in the reorganized secondary schools or in the university, joined the new armed services or civil service training schools, or else served in government offices in junior positions. More frequently than not they also engaged in underground study groups. Their informal curriculum included the theory of Marxism, the history of democratic liberalism, and the actuality of wartime developments among the great powers as reported by clandestinely monitored radio broadcasts.

The events of the crucial summer of 1945 are a matter of better documented but even more disputatious record. Two specific episodes, however, were as consequential as they were contradictory. One was Sukarno's courageous reformulation of the nationalist demands and rationale; the other was his last-minute vacillation and sophistry.

Sukarno had earlier acclaimed Japan as the elder brother and liberator. He had crusaded for the Greater East Asia Co-Prosperity Sphere and solicited recruits for the Japanese labor corps, proclaiming all the while that Indonesia must receive its independence not as a gift but as a reward for cooperation in defeating the Western powers. As Japan's fortunes declined, he began to urge that the Japanese set a date for Indonesian independence. On June 21, 1945, he went before the Japanese-appointed Constitutional Consultative Body to give the keynote address, one intended to guide that body in its preparations for actual independence, now definitely and immediately in prospect. In his address he formulated the *Pantjasila*, or Five Principles of State, at once acclaimed as Indonesia's official philosophy.

Sukarno's Five Principles were defined as Nationalism, Internationalism, Democracy, Belief in God, and Social Justice. These principles, of course, are in themselves as unexceptionable as they are unoriginal; but to the presentation of them was added the Sukarno touch, combining rhetorical dash with ideological dilution, intellectual dazzle with political daring. Sukarno, a collaborator with the Japanese and still vulnerable to Japanese vindictiveness, an agitator against the Allies and presently to be vulnerable to Allied vengeance, delivered an oration which would at once please and offend both. It extolled all about-to-be-accepted virtues, specifically those of the postwar world in which Western forgiveness would presumably prevail and Western liberal democracy would presumably be paramount. It was a much more incisive condemnation of all vices, not only specifically Dutch but also Japanese, British and American colonialism, imperialism, and capitalism. As an exercise in Indonesian eclecticism—empirically adjusted, quasi-democratic, quasi-Marxist, and quasi-Indonesian, a Marhaenism updated as Marxism for the bourgeois Asian—it was a masterly performance.

On August 15, 1945, Sukarno faced the greatest crisis of his career to that moment. Japan had collapsed. Sjahrir and his underground agents had relayed the word and had urged the immediate declaration of Indonesia's independence. Sukarno and Hatta refused to believe the reports. They argued that they must adhere to the timetable already set up by Japan for Indonesia's independence, that they had to insure the legitimacy of the move by making it within the framework of constituted and accepted authority, that an attempt to defy the Japanese would result in a blood bath, and that an attempt to circumvent the Allies would result in their own trial as war criminals.

All arguments evaporated when youthful activists and radicals—university students and army officers who counted Tan Malaka (then incognito) among their confidantes—staged a midnight kidnapping. These young "hot-heads" carried off Sukarno and Hatta to an Indonesian military barracks outside Djakarta, devoted eighteen hours to persuading or intimidating them, and then restored them to the nationalist group in Djakarta on the promise that independence would be declared at once. That night (August 16), in the home of the Japanese Admiral Maeda, Sukarno, Hatta, and a miscellaneous gathering of others devised the 24-word Declaration of Independence which Sukarno duly promulgated the following morning. Pro-independence demonstrations, organized by the same forceful youths, went off under the apprehensive eyes of a badly demoralized Japanese garrison. City and nation-wide manifestations of nationalist zeal mounted. Bands of youthful activists roamed the land, occupying Japanese offices, seizing Japanese arms and equipment, installing Indonesian civil and military officials, and working themselves, the urban public, and the hesitant politicians into a state of enthusiasm and heroism. When British occupation forces arrived one month later, the Japanese had been thoroughly cowed and the Indonesian nationalist politicians were thoroughly committed. The newly independent Republic of Indonesia, made up of unorganized geographic, political, and ethnic elements thrown together by the accident of colonialism, was becoming adjusted—not without episodes of violence and incidents of backsliding—to the proposition that it was a single sovereign nation. Despite the misgivings of the British occupation forces and the protests of the Dutch who soon joined them, the Indonesian Republican government gained tacit Allied acceptance as a *de facto* state. Shaky and sketchy as it was, it had to be dealt with not by force of arms but by devices of diplomacy.

If any conclusive evidence regarding the successful technique of nationalist revolution in Indonesia was still necessary, the events of August 1945 provided it. The political leaders had long advocated independence, then at the last moment had hesitated to seize it. They had been bemused by considerations both of objectives and tactics, deterred by weighings of consequences, and, despite their experience of the last few years, blind to the simplifications of expediency. Mass action of a sort—the mass action of youthful enthusiasts rather than of the public—had achieved what intellectual nationalism had not. It superimposed on the sophisticated montage of ideologies the simple device of seizing and using power as opportunity offered, in accordance with a premise originally Tan Malaka's, rather than Sukarno's, but one which from that time onward gained increasing acceptance.

The Electric Period of Merdeka (mid-1945 to 1949)

Merdeka (independence) had been achieved more by accident and audacity than by calculation. The problem now was to maintain it in the face of the hostility of the Japanese—who were not for some months fully disarmed or repatriated—the misgivings of the slowly assembling British occupation troops, and the determination of the Dutch to restore colonial control. The early experiences with Merdeka brought death, destruction, and near-disintegration. The conviction grew, however, that as miraculously as Merdeka had been achieved, so it would be preserved.

The emotional spirit of Merdeka, like the philosophical and practical phenomena of the earlier period, manifested itself primarily among the intellectual elite. Now, however, the intellectual elite had been extended to include not only the hundreds of dialecticians of 1942 but also the thousands of activists of 1945.

Merdeka, bung! was the revolutionary password. *Merdeka!* to the accompaniment of a clenched fist salute became the revolutionary gesture. Bands of revolutionary youths chanted

"Merdeka" as they roamed the streets in demonstrations, waving red and white flags, singing the national anthem, *Indonesia Raja*, and painting slogans on walls and shop windows and tram cars. They converted Merdeka into a fiesta and, if they met with resistance, into a riot.

The spirit of Merdeka penetrated even to the upper layers of the urban Marhaen, who made up in volume and endurance what they lacked in comprehension. They did grasp the one basic concept that Indonesians were permanently replacing both Japanese and Dutchmen, and for that matter Chinese and other aliens, and that was good.

By a sort of spontaneous compulsion, self-designated political representatives converged upon Djakarta from all parts of the nation. Government bureaus filled with volunteer civil servants. A shadowy cabinet coalesced about Sukarno, now president by acclamation. Even an army of sorts materialized, formed of Japanese-trained troops, young vigilantes, and street and jungle guerrillas. The government exercised only the vaguest authority outside the capital city and not much more effective authority within it. Just as soon as a government began to organize, so did an opposition. Tan Malaka, for instance, instigated an abortive anti-Sukarno plot (September 1945) within weeks of pledging support. The government proved remarkably resilient in reacting or, more commonly, in accommodating itself to such phenomena.

The prospects of the new Republic flickered dangerously during the latter half of 1945, as swift developments demonstrated that neither theoretical projections nor outright commitments regarding the roles of the various forces could be relied upon. For a time the Japanese seemed disposed to surrender themselves to the Indonesians. They then decided, for the most part, to wait and surrender to the Allies and even, on Allied orders, to resume garrison and patrol duties. The British occupation forces seemed disposed at first to stage a mere token occupation after delaying their arrival for a month, a circumstance far from unfavorable to the Republican cause. Presently, finding that to cope with Republican armed resistance was difficult if not disastrous, they started unloading responsibility onto the eager and often belligerent Dutch. The return of the Dutch had been semi-surreptitious in the first place, since the Allies had deemed outright Dutch occupation forces would be psychologically inadvisable. The Dutch nevertheless set about strengthening their forces and consolidating their positions in defiance of spoken and unspoken Allied-Republican understandings, and as soon as they were capable of doing so, they reasserted themselves vigorously and violently.

A series of armed clashes, including street fighting between Indonesian and British forces in Surabaja, led to withdrawal of the Republican government and its main supporters from Djakarta to the Central Javanese city of Jogjakarta. The conflict also resulted in the virtual fragmentation of the archipelago into the Republic of Indonesia, centering on Jogjakarta but holding both big and little enclaves elsewhere, and the Dutch-controlled areas which were even more extensive and scattered.

The Republic thereafter was beset by an incessant series of crises. All were exacerbated by Dutch machinations, animosities among the Republican leaders themselves, suspicion between leaders of the Republic and Indonesian leaders of other areas, and always by Communist readiness to make a tense situation explosive. The crises were attended by conspiracies, kidnappings, insurrections, ultimata, attempted coups, cabinet upsets, insubordinations, and defections, plus the physical and psychological strains of Dutch blockade. Seen in retrospect, the crises revolved about four major events: the negotiation of the Linggadjati Agreement (November 15, 1946), the first Dutch "police action" (July 21, 1947), the Madiun Communist rebellion (September 18, 1948), and the second Dutch "police action" (December 18, 1948).

The Linggadjati Agreement took almost ten months to negotiate, almost six more months to ratify, and probably never stood a chance of success, so moderate were its terms and so eager were both Dutch reactionaries and Indonesian extremists to sabotage it. The Republic, under the terms of the agreement, was to retain control of the areas which it already held; the Dutch would likewise control their respective areas; both were to cooperate in the creation of a federated and independent Indonesia, a partner in a new Netherlands-Indonesian union under the Dutch Crown. The British, who had given impetus to the negotiations by announcement of their decision to withdraw by November 1946, expeditiously removed themselves on schedule, leaving hostile Indonesians and Dutch to make the agreement work.

Primary responsibility for negotiation of the agreement had rested on the Indonesian side with the then Prime Minister Sjahrir, on the Dutch with Lieutenant Governor-General van Mook. Van Mook was denounced in Holland as a traitor by "old colonial hands," who contrived to delay ratification of the agreement until March 25, 1947, and to create obstructions to its implementation. Sjahrir was denounced by Indonesian extremists for selling out to the colonists and the capitalists.

Indonesian extremist opposition to the Linggadjati Agreement reached a peak while negotiations were still in progress. Tan Malaka's followers organized formidable Republic-wide agitation against any compromise with the Dutch. On June 27, 1946, they kidnapped and threatened Sjahrir. On July 3, they presented Sukarno with an ultimatum that he grant them virtual plenipotentiary powers. Meanwhile, they prevailed upon major elements of the armed services to promise them support. By sheer chance, the extremists mistimed their moves, the critical army units switched loyalty again, and the plot collapsed. Sjahrir proceeded with negotiations, and the Linggadjati Agreement was concluded. Events had already demonstrated, however, the perils of compromise, the appeal of agitation, and the extremely precarious internal situation of the Republic. Dutch opponents of the agreement did not have to look long or hard to find Indonesian "provocation" which would justify a "firm stand," the provocation consisting of a continuing series of military disorders and failure on the part of the Republic to implement plans for cooperation.

When the Linggadjati Agreement proved unworkable, the Dutch colonial administration on July 21, 1947, launched its first "police action" to put down the Republic by force of arms. The Dutch, who held it easily within their power to achieve military victory, found themselves unable to defy the national and international outrage which the "police action" itself provoked. They were compelled to accept a United Nations ceasefire, mediation, and eventually the ambiguous Renville Agreement (January 17, 1948), reverting in effect to the terms of the Linggadjati Agreement which had already failed.

Before, during, and after the negotiation of the Renville Agreement, the Republic and the Dutch engaged in a spirited exchange of accusations and counter-accusations regarding armed violation of each other's territory—charges which were all too well justified in general if not always by the specified incidents. Negotiation and compromise achieved only a very temporary and uneasy suspension of open hostilities. During the lull, the Republican government vigorously pressed its case abroad, especially in India, the United States, and at the United Nations. The Dutch, meanwhile, set about creating a federal system of semi-autonomous states intended to rival the Republic in any new all-Indonesia union. Dutch success in actually building up a federated system provoked the indignation of the moderates as well as extremists within the Republic. Since economic conditions were becoming desperate as a result of continued Dutch blockade, indignation was easy to convert into violence.

The most serious violence was directed against the Republican government itself. Acting upon instructions precipitously relayed and belatedly rescinded from Moscow, the Indonesian Communists, beginning on September 18, 1948, staged a series of bloody insurrections at Madiun, Surakarta, and elsewhere in East Java. The Sukarno-Hatta government condemned the "Communist conspirators" and called upon the nation to oppose them. Major elements of the Republican army, after wavering in loyalty, obeyed orders to fight the rebel forces. In the course of confused and bloody campaigns during the next six weeks, the Communist insurrection was put down, but not without great loss of life and property and a great increase in animosity between pro- and anti-Communist factions. The Republican government, purged of major extremist elements, seemed on the whole sounder than before and again disposed to rational compromise.

On December 18, 1948, as suddenly as the Madiun coup, came the second Dutch "police action." The Dutch started with aerial bombings and paratroop landings at the Republican capital of Jogjakarta. They captured the city against token resistance, and also took the chief Republican leaders, hustling them off to Sumatra and then to Banka under armed detention. By early 1949 Dutch troops had virtually eliminated the Republican armed forces and destroyed the Republic's capacity for further overt resistance.

What looked like almost total Republican defeat soon transformed itself miraculously into almost total victory. Those Republican leaders and the scattered military forces remaining at large refused to surrender. The leaders who had been captured refused to negotiate. The heads of the federal states rallied to the Republic's cause. India, the United States, the United Nations and even important segments of the Dutch nation brought pressure to bear upon the colonial government to relinquish all that it had just won and more besides. The pressures were irresistible and the Dutch, by mid-1949, agreed to grant independence. On December 27, 1949, they made good their promise.

The successful assertion of Merdeka against all odds by men who risked property, livelihood and life itself for so fragile a hope inspired a justifiably high degree of national faith and pride. The period 1945-1949, accordingly, has come to represent the Golden Age of the Indonesian Revolution. It appears retrospectively as an age of idealism, conviction, and integrity, glowing in ever sharper contrast to the new era in which ideals have become tarnished, conviction falters, and the maintenance of integrity requires even more heroic effort than did fighting the revolution. Sukarno, seeking to restore to his regime the luster of the past, deliberately adopted as his new "policies" and slogans "Return to the Spirit of '45," "Return to the Generation of '45," and "Return to the Constitution of '45." Despite his explanation that the revolution has faltered and must now fulfill itself, he places himself in the position, both logically and emotionally precarious, of proposing to drive the revolution forward by turning it back.

Realistically appraised, the Golden Age of Merdeka was not, of course, a period of unmixed heroism and idealism or even of the One Happy Family style of political cooperation. The same leaders were in the ascendant as during the earlier period—Sukarno, Hatta, Tan Malaka, Sjahrir, and Hadji Agus Salim.

They were surrounded by a widely varied collection of others ranging from extreme right to extreme left, from responsibility to fanaticism. These leaders exhibited the same strengths and weaknesses as before and an even more pronounced tendency, now that the Happy Family was long since disbanded, toward feuding and intrigue.

In spite of serious friction Sukarno and Hatta managed to achieve the political miracle of the *Dwitunggal*, the joint headship of state. Sukarno provided, as before, the dazzle and the dramatics, Hatta the organization and the rationality. Tan Malaka flashed on and off the stage, sometimes conspiring, sometimes cooperating, eventually, and no doubt violently, vanishing. Sjahrir served for a period as prime minister and chief negotiator with the West. For a time he headed his own left-wing coalition in opposition to Tan Malaka's, later being betrayed by his friends as well as by his enemies. Amir Sjarifuddin, for instance, one of his closest associates and a belatedly self-announced Communist, masterminded the Madiun coup. Hadji Agus Salim, both as foreign minister and in other capacities, adroitly played the field. He dispatched emissaries to the Communist nations when there was a chance that their support could do the Republican cause some international good. He blocked the Communists at home when their strength seemed a menace.

Among the newcomers on the national scene were relays of members of Parliament, a heterogeneous collection of politicians appointed and removed by Sukarno on no one quite knew whose advice or according to what system. These politicians devoted themselves more to politicking than to parliamentary routine, as was natural, since legislating for a virtually hypothetical nation was more form than function.

Most significant of all the newcomers was a group of generals, colonels, and captains, recently promoted from lieutenancies in the Japanese-trained armed forces. As commanders of the revolutionary armies they deployed themselves and their forces not only against the Dutch but also, quite unpredictably, for or against various conspirators, especially the Communists. These men, many of them of outstanding physical and intellectual qualifications, were imbued with a paternalistic attitude toward their troops and a proprietary attitude toward government. More patriots and politicians and *bapak* (patriarchs) than soldiers, they added a new and uncertain dimension to Indonesian politics.

The army itself was a conglomeration of trained, semi-trained, and untrained troops, armed with anything from a sharpened bamboo spear to a captured Japanese or Allied machine gun. It was far more amenable to exhortation than to command, and almost as readily disposed at times to counter-revolution as to revolution. The navy was without ships, save for a few small smuggler craft, and virtually without officers or men on any other than a casual basis. The air force operated derelict Japanese planes salvaged from junk heaps, haphazardly reassembled, and manned by new crews and pilots who learned as they flew. Twice it was all but obliterated by the Dutch, only to fly again. The army, the navy, and the air force were not representative, only more visible than other national entities. Spirit, not matter—and certainly not organization—was what counted.

All of this improvisation, rather than inspiring a feeling of futility, induced a glow of accomplishment. The new Indonesian Republican government itself, a fabrication of chance and impulse, whether or not it actually governed, maintained the miracle or the mirage of existence. It thus achieved a major victory in the eyes not only of Indonesians but of outside observers, to whose reactions Indonesians were acutely sensitive.

"You are what you are," declared Dr. Frank P. Graham, the American representative on the United Nations Good Offices Commission, when he was pressed to define the indefinable legal and moral status of the Republic. Dr. Graham thus gained for himself among knowledgeable Indonesians a reputation for enormous sagacity and for mystical perception, almost Indonesian in quality, of the nuances which are more real than reality itself.

The true glory of Merdeka, however, was to be most clearly observed not among the high officials or the military commanders or the politicians, but among those of the people who comprehended Merdeka and sought to preserve it. University professors, for instance, set up a Republican university in the

outer pavilions of the sultan's palace at Jogjakarta, working
with practically no books and only such equipment as they had
been able to spirit away from Djakarta. One professor of medicine set up a little Pasteur Institute. First manufacturing his
own laboratory equipment, he produced vaccine in sufficient
quantities to have a surplus available for good-will export at
a time when an epidemic struck in Egypt. Secondary school
teachers wrote new texts, for the first time using the Indonesian
language as their primary medium. Primary school teachers
devised and carried out courses in adult literacy. University
and secondary school students doubled as teachers. They also
found additional time and energy to work as volunteer employees
in government offices and to serve as part-time guerrillas, cour-
iers, and propagandists.

Newspaper editors, to continue the recital of achievements,
produced miniature but informative one-sheet papers by can-
nibalizing press equipment, pirating international wire services,
and operating their own little workshops to produce coarse
brown paper from rice straw. Doctors continued to keep hospitals open, to treat patients, and even to perform delicate sur-
gery, despite the lack of drugs, bandages, and equipment. The
state employees managed somehow to keep the rudimentary
telephone and postal-telegraph systems functioning, water and
electricity adequately if not predictably flowing, a few decrepit
trains moving, and even a fleet of ancient automobiles in spas-
modic operation. They managed all despite desperate shortages
of repair and replacement materials which, like clothing, pharma-
ceuticals, and other essential goods, had to be smuggled through
the Dutch blockade.

The history of the Republic during this period was a series
of hair's-breadth escapes from disaster. Providence played a
major role, as did day-to-day improvisation of short-term amel-
iorations of long-term problems which no amount of organization
of available resources could have resolved. The common impression among Western observers and the Indonesians themselves was that if the nationalists could do so much with so
little under such disastrous circumstances, they would certainly
be able to accomplish national regeneration, once they had the
means at their disposal.

The electric 1945-1949 period of Merdeka added to the eclecticism of the pre-1942 years and the empiricism of the Japanese occupation period certain new elements, or perhaps reformulations of elements already present but obscured. All of them can be summarized in the single word "elasticity." The events of 1945-1949 seemed to demonstrate four important propositions. First, that political commitments, like policies, are tentative and experimental, subject to reconsideration and reversal at will, as all factions demonstrated repeatedly in violating or reconstruing their agreements. Second, apparently insurmountable crisis generally transmutes itself into a new crisis, thus placing the premium not upon resolution but upon resiliency. Third, that in a nationalist struggle against colonialism, histrionics are far more potent than logic. Fourth, assuming destiny is with you and you take the risks, just as likely as not out of apparent defeat will come victory.

This set of still half-formulated convictions conditioned the nationalist leaders in their final negotiations for independence from the Dutch in late 1948. At the Round Table Conference in The Hague, held under sponsorship of the United Nations, they launched themselves upon a bold new experiment, confident of their politics, their resourcefulness, and their destiny. They accepted some intrinsically unacceptable conditions attached by the Dutch to the transfer of sovereignty, providing, for instance, for membership in a Dutch-Indonesian union, postponement of negotiations over Western New Guinea, formation of a federal system of government, and preservation of Dutch economic and cultural interests. Neither the Indonesians nor the Dutch nor anyone else expected that the Round Table terms would be scrupulously observed. Very few persons, however, save perhaps for the most extreme left-wing Indonesian politicians, foresaw quite how soon or how totally they would be jettisoned.

The Indonesian leaders disdainfully dismissed the suggestion of a gradual transition and demanded full and immediate political responsibility over the immense Indonesian archipelago. They were aware that there were formidable problems of nation-building, but they were confident that, whatever the problems, Indonesian ingenuity would suffice to surmount or at least to circumvent them. They were inheriting the world's sixth most

populous nation and one of its most richly endowed, but a nation
that was littered with the debris of world war, colonialism, and
revolution, beset by every dilemma of underdevelopment, and
bedazzled by every promise of Merdeka. Intimations of im-
pending disaster were drowned out by the more insistent intimations of manifest destiny.

The Enigmatic Years of Politik Bebas (1950 to 1956)

"After Merdeka, what next?" The question had scarcely even
been asked, so obvious was the answer: "After Merdeka, more
Merdeka." The Merdeka of December 27, 1949, it was apparent,
was not that of the revolutionary ideal or even that of the first
joyous days after August 17, 1945. It was hedged about with
restrictions, the most galling of them being the reluctant concessions made to the Dutch and, by extension, to the Western
World. Alien "capitalists and colonists" still controlled Indonesia's wealth, and alien powers exercised tremendous pressure
upon Indonesia's government both in domestic and foreign
affairs. What was needed was a new formula by which, in the
common Indonesian phrase, "to perfect Merdeka."

The formula was soon devised. It was *Politik Bebas*, or independent policy, a nationalist fixation which to a degree superseded Marhaenism, the Pantjasila, and even Merdeka itself.
Politik Bebas was the natural outgrowth of the eclecticism,
empiricism, and enthusiasm of the earlier periods. It was also,
in half a dozen important respects, an enigma which served
to obscure both the short and the long-term policies of the new
government and thus to confound analysis or prediction at
home or abroad.

Politik Bebas, signifying determination not to be maneuvered
and at the same time to maintain complete freedom to maneuver,
was a policy of absolute independence such as is obviously
unworkable not only in any community of nations but in any
community of politicians. It was originally formulated by the
very men—Hatta and his associates—who realized that it might
well defeat their own purposes and prejudice the nation's freedom, but who held, nevertheless, that while it might be intellectually deplorable it was politically imperative. The policy

provided a justification both in domestic and foreign affairs less for action than for inaction, for any action was necessarily an unpopular compromise, whereas inaction was a demonstration of immunity to pressures. Hatta and the moderates used it as an expedient device to gain time and experience by which to determine what the most healthful policy for the new nation might be, while forestalling the reckless actions demanded by the extremists. It failed, of course, to satisfy anyone, and led to the stigmatizing of the Hatta group as "negative and reactionary" and to their ultimate replacement by "positive, revolutionary" leaders.

For more than half a decade, however, Politik Bebas did not result in a clearcut swing in the balance of power. Just as the radicals effectively blocked any real progress on the part of the moderates in the early years (1950-1953), so, too, the moderates managed with almost equal success to block the radicals later (1954-1956). Politik Bebas, which made in theory for unrestrained freedom of political action, resulted in fact in near stalemate, so complex and contradictory were the forces at work during the period.

The early years (1950-1953) of Politik Bebas, then, were the years of Hatta and his friends and associates of the *Masjumi* (liberal Muslim), the Socialist, and the liberal wing of the Nationalist Party, most of them increasingly subject to attack for caution and inaction. The later years (1954-1956) were those of Ali Sastroamidjojo and the left wing of the Nationalist Party, most of them increasingly subject to attack for recklessness and corruption. The months from mid-1955 to early 1956 were an interval of a reformist and short-lived Masjumi and Socialist-dominated government which seemed to combine action with moderation but was sabotaged by moderates and radicals alike.

During the whole period, Hatta as vice president was in effect the administrative head of state, but Sukarno was the behind-the-scenes manipulator who devoted himself to undermining Hatta's influence. Relations between the two deteriorated to the point where Hatta on December 1, 1956, resigned and retired. He was promptly exhorted by Sukarno, among many others, to reconsider and to restore the balance which the

Dwitunggal—the joint Sukarno-Hatta headship of state—had provided in other times almost equally as trying.

Politically, the whole period 1950 to 1956 was one of drift, conditioned at the outset to a very great extent by the historic circumstance of paramount Western influence, then by growing resentment of this influence, and finally in the latter part of the period by mounting determination to correct for the Western bias by exposure to communist world contacts. These years were marked by the intricate interplay of political factions, a few wishing to attach Indonesia somewhat more firmly to the West, most others wishing to detach it, but all determined to retain the fiction of complete impartiality. It became necessary, if one wished to gain support for a policy which would be favorably viewed by the Western world, to make it appear more than a little anti-Western; for a policy agreeable to the Communist bloc, to make it appear more than a little anti-communist; for a policy distinctively non-Western, non-communist, but exclusively Indonesian, to make it more than a little incomprehensible. Political operations came more and more to resemble mirror writing against a distortion glass.

The evolving Indonesian political system made politics an end as much as a means. As the president and the vice president increased their feuding, so did the leaders of the thirty-odd political parties. All cabinets were of necessity the products of coalition, to which the parties assigned and from which they withdrew representatives with little regard for individual competence or national welfare. The parliament, appointed by the president, deteriorated into a semicaptive audience for vague statements of policy by the government and for oratory by party politicians. At times Parliament found difficulty in mustering a quorum, since many members checked in only long enough to sign the roll and get credit for the session's pay. Others developed an insatiable taste for junkets at home or good-will visits abroad, always on a per diem allowance much more generous than their salaries.

The central administration, which started as the government of a loosely "federated" group of states, had arrogated to itself in mid-1950 the right of strong centralized authority over a "unitary" nation and, without a firm policy of its own, sought to impose firm control. It thus engendered bitter resentment among those regional leaders who did not migrate to the capital, and even among many who did. The administrative bureaucracy, which started out as a forced marriage of Republican and Federalist incumbents, was from the beginning overstaffed, underpaid, and far more concerned with prerogative than with administration. It has never achieved organization, direction, or a strong sense of public responsibility. The Indonesian nation as a whole exhibited near-heroism in tolerating an administration of spectacular incompetence, but it did not experience progress. The leaders who sought to make improvements found themselves involved in so much political controversy that they had time for very little else.

From the point of view at least of Western observers, the most significant political development of the period was the resurgence of the Communist Party. The PKI had been all but eliminated as a potent political force after the 1948 Madiun rebellion. After 1950, it restored itself slowly to respectability and influence. The party popularized the apologia that the Madiun rebellion had been the result of "intolerable provocation" on the part of the "Hatta government." In so doing, it capitalized upon and widened the Sukarno-Hatta breach, and represented itself as a truly nationalist party, sincerely disposed to join in a united front with all other "progressive" groups, and patriotically opposed to the "reactionary" Masjumi and Socialists. The PKI gained control over major segments of organized labor and made swift and massive impact upon the younger, newer group of the intellectual elite. It grew to a total of 150,000 members and candidate members by 1954, and from there took off on a tenfold increase in the next few years.

The PKI was at that time by far the best organized, the best financed, the best led, and the fastest growing of all Indonesian parties; but even its sudden resurgence in strength and influence did not clearly upset the political balance. The Communists themselves helped obscure matters by aligning at times with the far right-wing Muslims against some of the most extreme of the left-wing nationalists.

Economically, 1950-1956 were years of stagnation, disguised at first by an illusion of prosperity, in part the result of the sudden transfer to a relatively few Indonesians and to the Indonesian government of a large part of the wealth which had previously gone to the Dutch and to the Dutch colonial government. The new riches were not, however, the product of any systematic economic development or nationwide sharing in the profits. They flowed largely from inflated world market prices for rubber, tin, and other Indonesian products much in demand during the Korean war, an economic windfall widely assumed at the time to be the norm. Indonesian production for export, on which the nation's international solvency depends, was increasing in value and even in tonnage in the case of the two most important products, rubber and oil. It was not increasing in proportion either to worldwide production or to Indonesian population growth. Furthermore, there were already clear danger signals that production in most categories would soon drop off, that profits were being diverted more and more into nonproductive enterprise, and that significant new development was lagging.

The new Indonesia had inherited a dual economy, part colonial and part feudal. The first was the economy of raw materials production for export, the second that of rice and other foodstuffs for local consumption, both sectors being controlled by rigorous regulations and restraints. The new Indonesian government, conditioned by colonial, feudal, and Marxist economic practice, set itself far more vigorously about the task of nationalizing and regulating than of developing. It sought to transfer foreign holdings and profits to Indonesian official or private bodies, with resultant widespread inefficiency, deterioration, and corruption. The improvement of the condition of the ordinary citizen was the aim, but bureaucratic regulations proved so stifling that even textile and rice supplies, both inadequate unless supplemented heavily by subsidized imports, proved far from commensurate with the needs of a growing population. Living standards dropped below, rather than rising above, the level of colonial times. Government spending, meanwhile, spiraled upward, and budgetary deficits plunged ever deeper into the red. Established enterprises sought to salvage and to export capital. Wildcat operators parlayed political pull into paper profits. Inflation took over to the point where the Indonesian rupiah became by far the softest of all the currencies of South-east Asia. The badly controlled salary-wage-price system became a fantasy in which, for the urban population, special privilege regarding housing, transport, clothing, and food became the incentive for official and private maneuver.

A few persons made strenuous attempts at reform, but their efforts bogged down by reason of the sheer magnitude of the problem and the prevailing preference for a kind of economic Politik Bebas in which manipulation prevailed over rationalization. The government tried for over five years, for instance, to work out its first Five Year Plan, then allowed it to expire in parliamentary study. It operated, meanwhile, as though one dollar could be made by fiat to equal Rp. 3.40, or Rp. 11.40, or Rp. 30, or Rp. 100, or almost any intermediate figure; as though a minister of state could live on Rp. 1,500 per month, when an ordinary suit of clothing cost that much on the open market; and as though a laborer could live on Rp. 5 per day when for a family of five the daily rice supply cost more than twice that amount.

Economic nationalism was the popular economic theory and practice, based on the assumption that foreign capitalistic interests were deliberately engaging in sabotage and that national recovery depended upon preventing them by political means from accomplishing their purposes, rather than upon stimulating the population by economic incentive to work out its own salvation.

Militarily, the period was one of suspense. At first there was uncertainty over whether small regional military insurrections, which began within weeks of the transfer of sovereignty and were rarely quite put down, were going to erode the nation from the edges. Then, as headquarters feuds and coups grew so common as to become almost monotonous, the question was whether the military command was about to fall apart, creating chaos at the nation's center or in its major provincial capitals. Later, as the general situation deteriorated still further, apprehension grew as to whether the military was about to stage a major coup and impose a dictatorship.

A long succession of military "incidents" lent substance to both the fears and hopes that the military was readying itself in 1955 and 1956 for concerted action. The "October 17 Incident" of 1952, when a headquarters clique attempted to dissolve Parliament and dictate to the President, seemed to many persons to give the most significant clue. The incident was vividly recalled to memory when the officer who bore primary responsibility for it and had volunteered as scapegoat when it failed was recalled in October 1955 as chief of staff. In that post, Colonel (now General) Nasution seemed intent upon perpetuating, not resolving, the suspense. Other officers within his headquarters, practicing a military Politik Bebas, fomented such frequent insubordination that a major military move appeared to be the most likely of many alternatives facing the nation.

Socially, 1950-1956 was a period of impressive, if far from completely successful, effort at an exceedingly difficult national synthesis. Of all the undertakings of the new nation, its program of social change and enlightenment was the most clearly conceived and the most systematically conducted. Possibly, also, since economic and political developments were not brought into phase, the social program was the most dangerous. It attempted to transform a widely diversified assortment of regional cultures into a national culture, at once preserving distinctive regional features and developing a sense of national identity. The program intended to consolidate and to advance Muslim, Christian, Hindu, and pagan religions; Sumatran, Ambonese, Balinese, Javanese, Bornean and many other groups of both high and low degree of cultural attainment, but always of a high degree of local pride.

Total school enrollment, for instance, increased from 1,528,-000 in 1950 to 6,404,000 in 1958. University enrollment rose from about 1,000 in 1941 to about 30,000 in 1960. Daily newspaper circulation doubled—from 500,000 to 1,000,000 copies—in the decade of the 1950s. Other statistical gains were equally impressive, including those in the critical area of public health, particularly with regard to yaws inoculations, DDT sprayings, and the treatment of patients in newly-established rural clinics.

Inherent in the development of the consciousness of a new and common Indonesian identity was the growth of a sense of purpose and achievement. It was at this point that the greatest social problems appeared. Nationalist awakening was accompanied by realization on the part of the newly educated and semi-educated that opportunity for their own advancement was still severely limited and that the revolutionary leaders of the older generation had become cynical and corrupt. Latent regional antagonisms, which for a time seemed to be diminishing, became recrudescent because of the arrogance of the central government in dealing with the provinces. Conflicting forces of national unification and of fragmentation became conspicuous even within the schools, the very institutions which were the pride of the new nation. In Sumatra, for instance, both teachers and students became persuaded that Djakarta was starving them of funds, discriminating against them in the apportionment of facilities, stifling them in bureaucratic regulations, and demeaning their own regional cultural base before supplying a comprehensible new ideal. Social dissatisfaction with government policies, apparent everywhere in the schools, was matched by civil dissatisfaction visible in every regional government office, and by military dissatisfaction even more apparent in every barracks and command post. For lack of firm central government control or successful development of loyalty, persons in positions of responsibility, if they implemented their responsibilities at all, did so by means of policies and actions determined by themselves, and often wildly conflicting with those of others.

These and many other domestic problems were enough to occupy the full time and energy of the nation's leaders. International problems, however, crowded in upon them with equal or greater urgency. These latter seemed to the Indonesian leaders to be all too commonly the gratuitous intrusion of a chaotic modern world, which was none of their making, upon a new Indonesia which they had hoped to fashion at leisure according to their hearts' desire. The Japanese Peace Treaty, the emergence of Communist China, the status of Taiwan, the overtures of the Soviet Union, the Korean war, the war in Indo-China, all the dilemmas of the Cold War, the question of whether to accept aid from the United States, whether to respond to the importunities of the Soviet Union, what role to play in the United Nations—these and many other problems presented themselves in rapid succession before the nation had the machinery or even the personnel with which to deal with them. All grew more and not less complex with the passage of time and with the adoption of certain half-decisions, most of them presently half-rescinded. The Hatta group, for instance, decided to accept American aid but then, after the collapse of one cabinet (1952) when word leaked out that there had been a secret agreement pledging support to "free world objectives," the government backed and filled in a manner which kept the immediate and future status of any aid program highly uncertain. The Ali group sought to establish close relations with Moscow and Peking (1954), but so great was the uproar over communist bloc orientation that Indonesia experienced for the first time since 1948 a build-up of overt, self-declared anti-communist factions.

By the end of 1955 it had become clear that Indonesia's Politik Bebas, as extended from the area of international relations in which it originally applied to all areas of national life, had brought the nation close to foundering. It was not yet clear, however, whether the nation would seek regeneration through the counsels of the moderates or of the radicals. Two major events of the year 1955, leading to apparently contradictory interpretations at the time, in fact gave the clue. The first was the Bandung Afro-Asian Conference, competently staged by Indonesia. The other was a series of national and local elections for a parliament, a constituent assembly, and regional councils, which were peacefully and on the whole honestly conducted.

The Afro-Asian Conference seemed in advance to many Western observers virtually an invitation to Communist-inspired harangue and manipulation. It seemed in immediate retrospect to have been on the whole salutary in demonstrating Communist infiltration tactics, Western restraint, and the critical differences as well as the similarities among the Afro-Asian nations themselves, whose spokesmen, in assuming the world stage, frequently displayed a high sense of responsibility. In longer retrospect, it now appears to have persuaded many Afro-Asian leaders, including especially the Indonesians, that national prestige and power are contingent far less upon developing internal strength than upon an international display of forensics.

The balloting in the 1955 general elections seemed at first to justify the hope that democratic processes were really beginning to work in Indonesia. Then, when the vote was counted, the four major parties proved to be running almost neck and neck, while the PKI proved not only to have made a spectacular showing but to have improved its position even in the interval between ballotings. The immediate prospect seemed to be a continuation of unstable, ineffectual coalition government, with further acceleration of the Communist rate of gain. The long-term prospect seemed to be some sort of authoritarian coup.

The Escapist Years of the Djalan Keluar, the Konsepsi, and MANIPOL-USDEK (1956 to 1961)

The year 1956 was the most crucial in Indonesian nationalist history since 1945. It was one of swiftly spreading realization that, as Sukarno himself admitted, the nation was "deteriorating in every respect" and was approaching the "abyss of annihilation." It was a year of nationwide preoccupation with marathon crisis and search for the *djalan keluar,* or "way out." As crisis crowded upon crisis, each seemingly more critical than the last and less susceptible to resolution, so the formulations for the "way out" seemed each more controversial and inconclusive. With everyone proclaiming the necessity for a "way out" and everyone blocking the exits, the need, obviously, was for a prophet with a message. There then came forward, after waiting to let the necessity for change become indisputable, the one paramount prophet of the nation—President Sukarno. On February 21, 1957, he announced his historic *konsepsi* (concept) and, after encountering and overcoming violent opposition, re-formulated it in mid-1959 as *MANIPOL-USDEK.* Under whatever name, it is his old nationalist message recast in escapist terms with the embellishment of new slogans.

The sense of desperation which infected the Indonesian nation in 1956 and made it susceptible to the new Sukarno formula becomes apparent from even a brief recital of events. The moderate Harahap cabinet (mid-1955 to early 1956) collapsed; the radical second Ali cabinet took its place on March 24, 1956, but cabinet crisis remained endemic throughout the year and the Ali cabinet survived only because no one could imagine what would happen if it were allowed to fall. Thanks to the indefatigable efforts of a muckraking press, headed by the editor of *Indonesia Raja*, Mochtar Lubis, who was arrested December 21, 1956 and held without charges, one government agency after another was revealed as a morass of incompetence, intrigue, and corruption. Scandals involving misuse of huge government funds advanced to businessmen and officials were exposed so incessantly as to become almost tedious. Embezzlement, misappropriation, and mere fiscal irresponsibility competed with revelations of evasion of government controls such as those which netted the military commands in Sumatra and Sulawesi many millions of dollars in clear profits from export smuggling of rubber and copra. Within military headquarters there occurred a series of mysterious attempts at coup and counter-coup. From the provinces came undeniable accounts of neglect and exploitation on the part of Djakarta-appointed officials who acquired notoriety as "Javanese colonialists" or "brown Dutchmen." At the end of the year the three military commands of Sumatra openly defied the central government, gaining support not only at home but in Djakarta and throughout the nation.

Indonesia was cracking up politically, economically, militarily, and psychologically. President Sukarno, meanwhile, in preparation for the resumption of his role as prophet, spent a good part of 1956 abroad. He paid state visits to the United States, the U.S.S.R., and Communist China. Everywhere he carried the message of nationalism as the irresistible force of the Afro-Asian world and of Indonesian nationalism in particular in its endless struggle against colonialism, imperialism, and capitalism, as a drive which must not only be accepted but also accelerated. Everywhere he exercised the dazzling Sukarno charm and the mellifluous Sukarno oratory and everywhere he met with heady applause—from audiences of mere hundreds or thousands in the United States, but of a hundred thousand or more at each important stop in the U.S.S.R. and China.

Sukarno's world travels, it would appear on the basis of his own extended and repeated public statements, convinced him of the following important propositions:

(1) He, Sukarno, and the huge Indonesian nation which he

symbolized, were the object of the most solicitous attention on the part of every important nation, East and West; competition for his and for Indonesia's friendship could be turned politically, economically, and militarily to Indonesia's very great advantage.

(2) The Western world exhibited most impressive evidence of material prosperity but little evidence of planned and coordinated programming for achieving predetermined objectives; it also exhibited marked misgivings regarding Afro-Asian nationalism and considerable panic regarding communist world expansion.

(3) The communist world exhibited most impressive evidences of recent and planned material advance, and also of an effectively coordinated and controlled national system calculated to achieve clearly defined objectives; it displayed unbounded enthusiasm for Afro-Asian nationalism and confidence that the rest of the world, led by the communists, would soon overtake Western material achievement.

(4) The example of the communist world, recently liberated from imperialism, colonialism, and capitalism, was much more appropriate and congenial as a pattern to Indonesia than that of the Western world, still itself imperialistic, colonialistic, capitalistic, and basically anti-Afro-Asian.

Sukarno's by no means superficially considered travel impressions were fortified by a lifetime of political experience. He proceeded to convey these conclusions to the nation and indeed to impose them upon it. His sense of mission was compounded by a sense of desperate urgency, induced by incontrovertible evidence that the Indonesian nation, modeled largely on Western liberal precedent, was at the point of disintegration. His first major move was the formulation of his *konsepsi* in which, quite explicitly, he rejected the Western-style democratic experiment in favor of a return to the Marxist ideological base, the revolutionary activism, and the One Happy Political Family coexistence of his youth.

The feuding political parties, Sukarno announced, were the cause of most of the trouble—the parties, that is, and Indonesian and foreign agents of colonialist and capitalist influences. The Indonesian nationalist leaders, whatever their previous party affiliation, should now repent and reassemble amicably about the "national board" over which he, Sukarno, would preside. The Communists, long excluded from their "due share" of office and influence, should be accepted by the others as loyal, cooperating partners. All problems would be resolved by a distinctively Indonesian device, *gotong-rojong* (mutual aid) after *musjawarah* (consultative consensus) among non-voting representatives of all "regional and functional groups." The nation would thus return to the spirit, the goals, and the methods of the "true revolutionaries," renouncing the false doctrines and the false prophets of the last few years, and stepping up the campaign against the Dutch and all others who imposed limitations upon "complete independence" and "fulfillment of the revolution."

Sukarno's *konsepsi* was equivocally received by most of the nation's politicians; the Communists, however, applauded loudly. The policy was ambiguously supported by the military headquarters, but the regional commanders openly protested. It was publicly propagandized by youthful activists who painted up pro-*konsepsi* and anti-opposition slogans over most of the available wall space in Djakarta, especially the walls of foreign "capitalists," and mounted vigilante patrol over suspected dissidents, especially the leaders of the Masjumi and Socialist Parties.

The *konsepsi* shook the nation and all but shook it apart. It immediately intensified all of the long-smouldering animosities within the nation, especially those between pro-communist and anti-communist forces and between regional and central authorities. The most important provincial leaders, both military and civil, began almost immediately after February 21, 1957, to declare that the new Sukarno policy was even more ruinous to the national polity and economy than the old official ineptitude. Furthermore, they declared, it was calculated to destroy regional prerogative and to bring the nation as a whole submissively within the orbit of world communism. Even prior to the announcement of the *konsepsi*, the Sumatran provinces on December 20, 1956, began an open rebellion which soon spread to Sulawesi and threatened to extend to Kalimantan and other areas.

To the amazement of many local and most foreign observers, the Sukarno government in early 1958 rallied its forces to put down the regional insurrections by force of arms. By mid-1958 central government military and civil authorities had reoccupied most of the insurrectionist areas and had restored a central administration at least as effective as that which had existed before. It did so, however, at a great cost in life and property, and in the perpetuation of political animosities. Indonesia had moved visibly closer to the communist bloc, which offered aid and support, and farther away from the Western world, which openly but ineffectually sympathized with the rebels. The government relegated to near oblivion whole relays of one-time national leaders: Hatta and Sjahrir, who had remained aloof from the rebellions but even more pointedly aloof from those who sought to put them down; Sjafruddin, Natsir, and Sumitro —the nation's foremost banker, religious leader, and economist respectively—who had openly joined the rebels; Kawilarang, Hussein, Sumual, and others of the nation's most competent military leaders, who had commanded the rebel troops and had been routed.

Determination to win support for his *konsepsi* and to destroy those who opposed it has thrown Sukarno himself into the almost exclusive company of three factions which feud with each other but profess total loyalty to him and his policies. First is the "palace clique," which supports Sukarno for its own power and profit. It is a group of old-time politicians and younger activists hailed by Sukarno as the "Generation of '45" and the "true revolutionaries." Conspicuous among them is Chaerul Saleh, Sukarno's kidnapper in 1945, his scornful critic in prison and exile between 1946 and 1954, then his Minister of National Reconstruction and Development. Second is the central military command, which supports Sukarno in order to revenge itself upon insubordinate regional officers and to protect itself from Communist challenge to its own authority. The chief military figure is General Abdul Haris Nasution, a diligent student of all the Sukarno techniques of political action, but an insecure tenant among the rival cliques within his own headquarters. Third is the PKI whose chairman, Comrade Dipa Nusantara Aidit, divides his loyalties—no one quite knows how—among Khrushchev, Chou, and Sukarno, and is likely to be nominated as Communist scapegoat any time the party itself makes a clearcut choice. The new Sukarno coalition seeks to maintain itself by constantly accelerating the pace of what Sukarno terms "revolutionary nationalism."

The major manifestations of the new "revolutionary nationalism" have involved great intensification of the policies slowly formulated and mildly applied during the latter period of Politik Bebas. In foreign and military affairs, for example, the government stepped up its campaign for the acquisition of Irian Barat (Netherlands New Guinea). It shifted from diplomatic representations at many world capitals and in the United Nations to military preparations and the threat of the imminent attack by armed forces now fully equipped by the Soviet Union. The intensified campaign for Irian Barat came, in fact, to dominate every aspect of Indonesian policy, domestic and foreign; the government decided that all else, excluding only preparations for the Asian Games, had to await a successful resolution of the problem on uncompromisingly Indonesian terms. In foreign affairs more generally, Indonesia has stepped up its effort to take the lead in developing greater cooperation on the part of "neutral" and "unaligned" nations in the achievement of immediate and worldwide "liquidation" of colonialism. Meanwhile it has continued its promotion of Afro-Asian solidarity on all world issues, and its exchange of state visits.

In domestic civil and military affairs, the government has worked for a "normalization" of the chaotic situation created by regional and military insurrections. It has achieved a major degree of success in bringing both the local civilian administrations and the one-time military rebels back under the jurisdiction of the central government. The national government itself has been reshaped in accordance with Sukarno's concept of "Guided Democracy," involving the dissolution and replacement of elected bodies of state, the appointment of consultative councils, the proscription of most political parties and related activities, and governance largely by emergency decree.

In economic affairs the government has moved far and fast toward state ownership and operation of—or at least constant state intervention in—all important productive enterprise. It has redistributed among favored entities and individuals vast private properties once held by the Dutch, the Chinese, and those Indonesians who have passed from political favor. It has adopted economic policies involving such extravagant state spending and such endless state interference that the economic system has come close to foundering, the currency has become sensationally weak, essential goods have disappeared from the market, and hoarding, speculation, and corruption have become more flagrant than ever. Whether from sheer economic bungling, deliberate political design, or a combination of the two, the whole economic base of the state is being revolutionized.

President Sukarno's *konsepsi*, as modified and applied in the years following the initial announcement, achieved its fullest and to date most authoritative formulation in his August 17, 1959, Independence Day address. In a somewhat condensed and revised form, this address is now called the Political Manifesto, or MANIPOL. The major points of MANIPOL are arranged under five slogans whose initial letters form in the Indonesian language the acronym USDEK: (1) The 1945 Constitution; (2) Indonesian Socialism; (3) Guided Democracy; (4) Guided Economy; and (5) Indonesian Identity. The controlling concept of MANIPOL-USDEK, today Indonesia's official political philosophy, is that the country must reject "liberal," "Western" political and economic principles along with "communist-phobia" and "revolution-phobia," that it must adopt instead "revolutionary nationalism" in every aspect of life and find to every problem a solution which is at once dynamically revolutionary and distinctively "Indonesian." As yet, MANIPOL-USDEK provides fewer solutions to problems than diversions of attention to domestic witch-hunting and international irredentist causes.

Conclusion: The Nationalist Mystique of Charisma and Acronym

For Indonesia, the half century from 1911 to 1961 brought successively self-generating, self-realizing, and self-defeating phases of nationalism. These correspond to the periods of nationalist renascence (1908-1942), revolution (1942-1950), and reappraisal (1950-1961), the latter substituting for a genuine nationalist revolution a spurious revolutionary nationalism. The

Indonesian record is that of a potentially great people and nation enmeshing rather than liberating itself in a nationalist mystique.

The two primary elements of the mystique are neither new nor unique to Indonesia. They have now assumed, however, an all-engrossing importance which makes review and interpretation imperative for any understanding of Indonesian nationalism today. Element number one is the paramount position of the charismatic leader—President Sukarno—whose emergence and re-emergence as self-designated *deus ex machina* has already been stressed. The second is a national intoxication, Sukarno-stimulated, with the symbol, the slogan, and the shibboleth. Today the two elements are almost interchangeable. Sukarno, once the living, vital symbol of the Indonesian nation in its nationalist aspiration, has become so enamored of his own slogans and has so bewitched the nation by them that for the new revolutionary nationalism, slogan is spliced to slogan and both the new Sukarno and his adherents transfix themselves in incantation of the Sukarno acronym, MANIPOL-USDEK.

For decades now the Sukarno symbol and slogan have been a national shibboleth, but the Sukarno image today is badly tarnished and the Sukarno word coinages are becoming tinny. The nation still looks to Sukarno as its leader, the elite more because there is no one else to take his place than out of the old sense of personal and nationalist loyalty. Even though they still accept, or at least tolerate, new slogans, they do so as a sort of distracting exercise, in much the way Westerners concentrate on double crostics: more for the sake of verbal dexterity than for intellectual content, and often taking pleasure in cynical parodies. Others, elite and non-elite alike, accept and follow Sukarno and his slogans because they know no alternatives.

The most alarming factor in Indonesia today may in fact be not the immediate threat of chaos, collapse, or communism, all of which have proved repeatedly deferrable. Rather, it may be the revolutionary nationalism which makes revolution its own justification, nationalism its own criterion, and USDEK a self-perpetuating process of generating new and equally futile USDEKs to succeed the old. The symbol and the slogan are being enshrined as eternal verities; the old become the test of the new. In Indonesia today under the Sukarno government

USDEK is publicly unassailable because it conforms to the Pantjasila, and whatever is undertaken in the name of USDEK is a sacred national mission, to be questioned only by traitors. Sukarno, who created the slogans in the first place, now acclaims them as a divine revelation of Indonesian destiny to which he himself is bound by indissoluble ties.

By such circular logic have other nationalist mystiques been contrived, but seldom for the benefit of the believer, and never for the security of the nonbeliever. Despite all indications to the contrary, the Indonesian sense of national rationality is still widespread and resilient. The practitioners of rationality, however, are having a bad time. They are likely to have a still worse time in the immediate future. It is not yet by any means clear that they can or will take measures adequate to save themselves or to restore to the concept and practice of nationalism the constructive devices which, along with such of their advocates as Hatta and Sjahrir, have fallen into official disrepute.

Chapter

5

□□□□□□□□□□

The Spoils of Nationalism: *The Philippines*

ALBERT RAVENHOLT

Should José Rizal, Filipino martyr and among the first of the great modern Asian nationalists, have returned on the centenary (in 1961) of his birth, the probabilities are that he would have disowned much that is being done in the name of a cause he championed. For the struggle that he led with such utter dedication and disregard of personal sacrifice is increasingly being distorted to serve the narrow purposes of privileged individuals and special interests. The indications are that unless new and more exacting criteria are employed to measure the human worth of the numerous enterprises justified in the name of nationalism, the emerging nations of Southeast Asia will be crippled in their evolution by the very forces that contributed to their creation. It is relevant to ask whether nationalism as now defined by its most ardent practitioners in these lands actually meets the aspirations felt by most of their fellow citizens. Can it be reinterpreted to guide the molding of these societies in a manner that enhances the well-being of the individual and contributes to a solution of those problems that concern him? Has the nationalism being practiced outlived its past historical usefulness, and must it be replaced by a larger and more creative concept if development and democracy are to grow together?

It has become customary in both Asia and the West since World War II to deify nationalism as the omnipotent and sacrosanct force before which all must bow without a critical look behind the political façade. The "American myth" is in part responsible. It assumes that because the thirteen colonies on the eastern seaboard declared, seized, and managed their independence in 1776 and made democracy relatively viable, so all other peoples now must be equal to doing likewise. The fundamental justification—the enhancement of individual liberty—is often ignored, as are the propitious circumstances of time and place. Far too little attention is focused upon the related question of the requisite "social ingredients" and the caliber of leadership available. Rarely has the issue been raised of how independence is to yield the national performance that fits the aspirations of the majority of citizens concerned. Nor has there been an adequate examination of the suitability of "elementary" independence as a vehicle for enabling all countries, and particularly the less developed lands, to share creatively in an emerging and increasingly integrated world economy and society. The challenge of safeguarding indigenous institutions and cultures against the onrush of a standardizing way of life, let alone making these values known elsewhere, has yet to be met.

The unpalatable fact is that in the name of nationalism abuses are being committed today upon peoples in some regions of Asia that compare to those justified in the name of Christianity during the period of the religious wars in Europe. The average citizen in much of Southeast Asia is worse off now than he was twenty five years ago—and war and burgeoning populations are not the only causes. He knows it and sometimes says so, although anyone who speaks out bluntly soon may be rapped down and charged with being unpatriotic. In several countries there is an evident loss of faith in some nationalist leaders who nevertheless continue to speak loudly in world councils. Most of these leaders won their political spurs by demanding the ouster of colonial powers, and now prefer to coast with old slogans rather than accept the creative debate of present problems. The loss of public trust may be traced in part to the anti-democratic nature of post-independence nationalism, and its frequent inclination to restore ancient autocracies in modern guise. Perhaps no more disturbing feature of nationalism has emerged in recent years than the tendency for it to become a justification for intensifying race hatred; some self-styled Asian nationalists lend substance to Goethe's denunciation of their cause as the passion of a culturally backward people. Meanwhile, nationalism also is often becoming an excuse for the abdication of responsibility by the more fortunate and economically advanced peoples of Western Europe and North America. While awarding military and economic assistance to developing countries, Washington, London, and other Western capitals are employing shibboleths of nationalism to justify ignoring the human consequences of their actions abroad.

Leadership in Revolution and in Governance

How is it that nationalism has become so distorted since the efforts of Rizal and his near contemporaries of the late nineteenth and early twentieth centuries? Southeast Asia affords particularly illuminating examples of how actions and propaganda in an entirely ideological pursuit of this goal can run counter to needs for internal and international survival. Because the impact of Red China as both a major power and a revolutionary force is here felt so strongly, a failure of development in these neighboring lands is most dangerous. This region saw the first postwar emergence of a large number of new states struggling to achieve their own identity in juxtaposition with each other; it may thus afford valuable guides to what can be expected elsewhere, as in Africa.

The portents of the future are not altogether dark, however. Statesmen are beginning to appear who call the attentions of their people to the limitations of the former assumptions. In Malaya and elsewhere there are leaders who argue that more can be accomplished by united action than by following the path to the petty nationalisms that produced for several centuries "Europe's civil wars." Over a period of three and a half centuries the Philippines experienced the "most intensive Christian missionary effort in the Orient," and was subjected to both Spanish and American colonialism. This first Asian postwar republic went through a presidential election in 1961 that brought to power a new generation of political leaders who insist upon dealing rationally with the problems at hand; an older generation of leadership that cloaked its designs with arguments of "Filipino First" was rejected at the polls throughout the Islands. Here in the "Balkans of Asia" there are modest but encouraging signs of the new type of diplomacy and domestic policy this "historical landslide toward independence" demands.

In order to appreciate the positive character of early Asian nationalism as typified by Rizal, we must look to its origins. Rizal even as a youth became convinced that the "misfortunes of his people were the business of his life." It was a time when Spanish Christianization in the Philippines had lost its creative quality. Instead, most of the religious orders had turned increasingly to supporting their organizations by managing huge landed estates and collecting ever larger portions of the crops from the primary cultivators. The Spanish empire was in a period of decay; the energy and concern that once infused Iberian colonization had given way to colonial tyranny under officials out of sympathy with more modern trends at home in Spain. This oppression was felt intimately in the community of Calamba on the shores of the large lake, Laguna de Bay, east of Manila, which was home to Rizal's family. His mother, a kindly and gentle woman, was unjustly imprisoned for two years after his father had dared to argue with the local commander of the civil guards. His relatives suffered as the religious orders that claimed the land demanded still higher rentals and in time many members of his family were driven from the fields they had long tilled. Justice seemed nowhere to be found within the structure of the then existing order.

Spurred by such experiences Rizal became convinced that knowledge offered the only available avenue to setting the world right. He enrolled in the *Ateneo de Manila* and became one of the most brilliant students the Jesuits ever schooled in the Philippines. But even within the academic sanctuary his personality and ideas proved too revolutionary to be welcome to the authorities. After graduation, Rizal went on to Madrid to study medicine, completing his work in 1885. Spain then was feeling the impact of nineteenth century European enlightenment. Struggling continuously against the obstacles of poverty, Rizal still had the will and the heart to be fired by the ideas of liberty and personal dignity for all which were then being heard. In the libraries of Europe he dug deeply to discover the character of the Filipinos when they first came into contact with the West; like some others among his contemporaries, he wanted to confirm the belief that his people did indeed possess the qualities needed to make them the equals of the technologically more advanced Europeans. Once he had satisfied himself on this count, Rizal sought the reasons for the state of affairs in his home islands. The nature of Spanish colonialism, he became convinced, was the immediate cause. But Filipinos, he concluded, must also remake themselves in a larger image in order to be equal to managing their birthright.

These insights were distilled into Rizal's writings. His first novel, *Noli Me Tangere*, published in 1887, had been suggested in part by Harriet Beecher Stowe's *Uncle Tom's Cabin*. Like his later novel, *El filibusterismo*, it was a work of passionate social protest. The two books differed, however, in that the first was more humorous and friendly to the Spanish administration of the Archipelago, while the latter, published four years later after a trip home, revealed his disillusionment. Rizal, more a thinker than a man of action, did not entirely foresee the revolutionary movements his writings would help set in motion, although he did anticipate that he himself would suffer for his role. When he was unjustly accused and executed for his alleged part in the unsuccessful revolt of 1896, the Filipino people gained a martyr who is still a model for many an idealistic young man and woman.

If Rizal did not see clearly the immediate course of political events, he did succeed in seeing far beyond them. With a human insight that recalls Mahatma Gandhi's teachings of a more recent day, Rizal believed that it was not enough for his people to free themselves of foreign rulers. In his second novel one of his protagonists says:

> The school of suffering tempers, the arena of combat strengthens the soul. I do not mean to say that our liberty will be secured at the sword's point, for the sword plays but little part in modern affairs, but that we must secure it by making ourselves worthy of it, by exalting the intelligence and the dignity of the individual, by loving justice, right, and greatness, even to the extent of dying for them, —and when a people reaches that height God will provide a weapon, the idols will be shattered, the tyranny will crumble like a house of cards and liberty will shine out like the first dawn. Our ills we owe to ourselves alone, so let us blame no one . . . while we see our countrymen in private life ashamed within themselves, hear the voice of conscience roar in rebellion and protest, yet in public life keep silence or even echo the words of him who abuses them in order to mock the abused; while we see them wrap themselves up in their egotism and with a forced smile praise the most iniquitous actions, begging with their eyes a portion of the booty—why grant them liberty? With Spain or without Spain they would always be the same, and perhaps worse! Why independence, if the slaves of today will be the tyrants of tomorrow?[1]

This view reveals the essential quality that distinguished Rizal; he saw the nationalist cause of which he was such an ardent proponent chiefly as a means to enhancing individual liberty and the capacity of his people so to mold themselves as to be equal to this responsibility. He and a significant number of near contemporaries, such as Dr. Trinidad H. Pardo de Tavera, were "renaissance men." Like Thomas Jefferson and many of his fellow framers of the Declaration of Independence, they labored within a given national context, but still saw themselves as citizens of the world. This breadth of concern was reflected in their personal lives. While they occupied themselves with political action, they also cultivated the arts, studied sci-

[1] José Rizal y Alonso, *The Reign of Greed* (*El filibusterismo*), tr. by Charles E. Derbyshire, Manila: 1939, p. 360.

ence, and delved deeply into the mysteries of man's nature. Life had a unity for them, and they were determined that political emancipation should be matched by comparable human advancement.

Such were many of the men who led in establishing the idea of Asian national identity and independence. The quality of their character and thought commanded a devoted following at home and sympathy abroad. They contributed mightily to that creative by-product of colonial imperialism defined by Salvador de Madariaga as the "process of universalization." The distinguished Spanish scholar described it in a lecture delivered at Manila in December 1961 for the Rizal Centenary:

> Under this universalism which is the mark of our era, there works a humanistic spirit in which I venture to detect two typically European traditions: the Christian tradition which emphasizes the value of the individual as an end in itself; and the Socratic tradition which requires freedom of thought and thirsts after truth. I am not saying that love and respect for our neighbor and a free mind bent on truth are exclusively European. I am fully aware of what both the mind and the heart of Europe owe to Asia; and I also believe that both the Christian and the Socratic attitudes are in one way or another inherent in all men. What I am saying is that these two attitudes are peculiarly strong in the European, and that they have given rise to two traditional currents which inspire nearly every form of European life. The Socratic tradition has acted as the liberator of the European mind; and the Christian as the purifying influence on the European heart. Taken together, they constitute that humanism which in our day has eliminated colonialism by attaining universality.

At least in Asia there appears to be a cycle that governs the evolution of new states. Once independence is won and nationalism becomes profitable both politically and financially, a new type of leadership appears composed of persons completely new to the scene as well as transmuted "independence" leaders. Idealists of broad vision and heroic action are supplanted by administrators whose skill lies in harnessing the motives that gave birth to independence. These men see themselves compelled to become manipulators. As a rule independence was held up as a panacea for all the ills felt by the society. Now the men in office must accept responsibility for performance—not an easy task, particularly when complicated by the atomization of the internal pressure groups which previously were preoccupied with the common goal of achieving independence. The monumental problems of restoring production and expanding it to meet the needs of an ever growing population with rising expectations, of rebuilding governmental administration, and of offering a new sense of national direction would challenge the capacities of the ablest men anywhere. And all this profound modernization must be done amidst the authoritarian and paternalistic tradition so deeply imbedded in Asia's heritage, and despite the often fanatically held traditions of conservative religious persuasions.

The Costs of Economic Nationalism

It is at this juncture that contemporary nationalism in Southeast Asia frequently wanders into blind alleys. The actual ventures differ from one new country to the next, but they all have a common quality: they tend to substitute grossly crude nationalistic apologias for a critical and objective examination of the suitability of chosen official courses of action for meeting the felt needs of their people. In six of the seven new countries of Southeast Asia, the most pervasive recent manifestations of this substitution of ideology for reason have been the numerous efforts at economic nationalism. Wherever such autarchy has been attempted, it has crippled the material progress so urgently needed and encouraged a distortion of the internal economies that has made the products of these countries less competitive in world markets. There has been a concentration of wealth and power in the hands of the few—either officials or private businessmen whose principal capital often consists only of influence —at the expense of the mass of consumers. Government administration has been burdened with chores it is neither designed for nor equal to managing. The result is a corrupting of the political process that undermines the prospects for encouraging democratic institutions.

The Philippines over more than a decade has offered numerous examples of how costly such an adventure can be. When controls on the acquisition and use of foreign exchange were imposed late in 1949, the justification was the conservation for purchases and payments abroad of dollars, the supply of which was proving inadequate. But soon many private interests discovered that these controls could be manipulated for their personal advantage. To acquire dollars and an import license was a guarantee of quick and easy profits. The individual or firm that secured this dispensation frequently did not actually bring in any goods. Instead, the allocation might be sold to an established trading firm that needed the funds to continue in business. But it added substantially to the prices paid for goods by Filipino consumers. In the beginning those persons granted allocations paid the government entities two pesos for every dollar and sometimes sold the same allocation to an actual importer for three to four pesos per dollar. In time a privileged group grew up that thrived upon this traffic; substantial allocations were parceled out among some four thousand individuals, families, and firms of whom 80 per cent were in Greater Manila. The favored few who profited from this practice built fancy houses, sent their children to private schools, and joined country clubs, but made scant contribution to the progress of the economy.

When Filipinos, foreign observers, and international banking institutions began questioning such practices, those who benefited donned the cloak of nationalism. "Filipino First" became their slogan. The justification was advanced that these measures were necessary in order to insure that Chinese and other aliens were ousted from their role in the economy. In time, as the competition for foreign exchange allocations became more keen, Philippine government agencies, including the Central Bank, began curtailing the trading activities of foreign and Filipino firms without political influence. During 1959, five European firms that had been in business in the Islands for more than a century were virtually excluded from importing the products in which they had long dealt. The next target was the naturalized Chinese, who are among the more aggressive and successful businessmen. Increasingly, in the administrative decisions of governmental agencies, they were treated as "second-class citizens." And the process did not end there. Filipinos known to be unfriendly to the administration found it increasingly difficult to engage in business that required any importations, even when their needs were as simple and essential as machinery parts and raw cotton for textile mills contributing both to employment and production.

Official regulations governing this system of controls became increasingly cumbersome, and a class of "fixers" appeared who for a consideration would secure approval of documents covering shipments. Filipinos with modest resources, particularly in the provinces, who lacked influential connections, were inhibited from importing the simplest requirements for managing their farms and businesses. Tempted by tax exemption during the initial years and a protected market guaranteed by denial of licenses for importers of similar commodities, entrepreneurs launched "necessary new industries." A few were genuine and did contribute to modernizing the economy. But most of them were either paper organizations for the securing of special favors, or packaging plants importing commodities in bulk and preparing them for sale. Even some of the more responsible new industries made profits of 100 to 140 per cent the first year, and many with still less regard for legitimate enterprise were even more lucrative—at the expense of product quality and, of course, of the consumer. While the profiteers usually justified their enterprises as a great venture in Filipino nationalism, their actions have borne bitter social fruit. In a society already suffering from great disparities between the favored few and the impoverished many, they fostered a further concentration of wealth.

Since official influence had become a matter of such consequence commercially, those who benefited from this arrangement turned increasingly to financing politics. The cost of winning election to public office, and particularly to the national congress, became so great that usually only the rich or those supported by them could hope to win. When the public conscience of Filipinos began to rebel at this spectacle, the first critics were frequently denounced as opposed to the nationalist cause. Some who were friendly with the communists joined with the profiteers to provide intellectual justifications. The great majority of the Filipino people, however, became increasingly disenchanted with this system. Fortunately for them, theirs is still an open society with a free press and radio. It is also a new country with comparatively strong private colleges and universities where ideas can and do germinate. Since independence it has elevated to public attention a generation of able young leaders, schooled in the values of a free society and intimately concerned with the public welfare. Such men in recent years have undertaken to mobilize the political opposition; regardless of party most of the older leaders who won their place with the cry for independence during the decades of American rule joined the administration in office which best protected their financial interests.

Among Filipinos in the rural *barrios* these younger opposition leaders campaigned for a new quality of management in government. They had the courage to expose "Filipino First" for what it was, despite the financial power their attacks mobilized against their cause. When Filipinos went to the polls in November of 1961, the majority throughout the Islands voted for a new kind of leadership that argued for dealing rationally with problems and proclaimed "Faith in the Filipino." During his campaign the subsequently victorious presidential candidate, Diosdado Macapagal, had promised to abolish the system of exchange control and "open up" the economy to clear the way for progress. Within three weeks of assuming office he proceeded to do so. The dire predictions of economic disaster that had repeatedly been marshalled to justify retention of the controls proved unfounded. In fact the peso strengthened substantially in the world money markets, while credit was curtailed and tariffs were employed to protect domestic industry. After a long and costly experiment with economic nationalism for its own sake, Filipinos found that they were better served by relying for development upon a criterion of usefulness rather than upon xenophobic slogans.

Other forms of Philippine economic nationalism have fostered practices that more stubbornly resist reform. When the constitution was framed in 1935, it stipulated that agricultural land and other natural resources could be acquired and used only by

Filipinos or by corporations in which they controlled 60 per cent of the capital; by subsequent amendment Americans were exempted from this provision until 1974. According to leading members of the Constitutional Convention, their intent was to prevent the development of an alien landowning class that would inhibit the emergence of independent, propertied farmers. Following inauguration of the independent Republic of the Philippines in 1946, however, the Supreme Court interpreted this provision also to deny foreigners the ownership of commercial real estate. Now that the Philippines is seeking foreign investment to speed development, the inability to own the land on which to place factories and other installations discourages European and other firms which could otherwise make a significant contribution to the progress of the country.

Over the past fifteen years the Philippine Congress has enacted successive laws to "nationalize" selected segments of the economy and certain professions—or conversely, to deny them to non-Filipinos. This legislation has aimed chiefly at curtailing the role of Chinese merchants who comprise a large proportion of the commercial middle class. It has also attempted to create greater career opportunities for Filipinos. In order to implement these moves further, Congress created an "Anti-Dummy Board" to seek out and punish Filipinos who served as "fronts" for alien merchants. But this attempt to exclude aliens and legislate Filipinos into business has produced rather different results from those stipulated. The "Anti-Dummy Board" proved an utter failure and is now officially so recognized; enforcement was impossible. Attempts to set up individuals in business on the basis of nationalism usually ended with the government's having to write off many of the loans concerned as bad debts. The Retail Trade Nationalization Law has served primarily to make the Chinese merchants more vulnerable to being plucked financially by politicians.

Meanwhile, Filipino businessmen have come into their own in an entirely different way without a significant assist from Congress. Often, after serving an apprenticeship in larger foreign firms in the Islands and abroad, they have mastered management skills. On their own initiative they are organizing banks, mining enterprises, manufacturing corporations, mutual funds for the sale of stock, and other modern businesses. With their more intimate understanding of the local scene which affords a quick perception of opportunity, they are able to outwit many foreign firms, including large American corporations. However, this new generation of Filipino entrepreneurs is finding that frequently it is mutually beneficial to enter into partnership with commercial and industrial interests abroad that have valuable technical know-how, equipment, and markets. Once they had set themselves to mastering the skills that production and trade demand, Filipinos found they were fully able to compete and thus to assume an ever greater role in managing economic affairs at home and even in expanding abroad.

Throughout much of Southeast Asia, however, this lesson of competent performance as the essential criterion for commercial success has yet to be learned. And appeals to nationalism are still the touchstones for determining much of economic policy in a number of new countries. In Burma allocations of foreign exchange and import licenses have been managed so as to curtail trade by Indian and Pakistani merchants who once occupied a dominant and aggressive role. In Indonesia, the twin causes of nationalism and socialism have served to oust Chinese, Dutch, and other foreigners from substantial sectors of the economy. In the truncated, troubled land of Laos, nationalism is the principal argument for trying to build a separate economy despite the absence of a viable base, an experiment the cost of which the American taxpayer helps to bear. Throughout Southeast Asia today stand a number of factories—often government enterprises—that have absorbed scarce foreign exchange and other valuable resources but are unable to operate economically. They are symbols of the universal desire of new countries to possess their own industries, but unfortunately the criteria of national pride rather than of economic suitability have often weighed heavily in their design.

Several new and frequently lucrative types of careers are developing in this region that reveal the extent to which these economies are out of harmony with world commerce. Smuggling has become large-scale business in several countries. During the years when exchange controls were in effect, entire shiploads of copra were smuggled out of the Philippines and contraband cargoes of watches, transistor radios, and cigarettes were carried in and discharged at remote ports. The smuggling of copra, rubber, and spices is continuing out of Indonesia. Like the Filipinos, some citizens of other lands have made profitable professions out of serving as "fronts" for foreign business firms, particularly Chinese, and negotiating with the government for licenses to import and export. A new type of "national capitalist" is appearing whose principal assets are his passport, influential connections in official circles, and a highly flexible set of business ethics. Such individuals, who are often highly vocal nationalists, are developing a vested interest in the maintenance of uneconomic government policies. Usually they retard the recognition and facilitation of the emergence of regional economic arrangements wherein larger markets and complementary production can contribute to growth. The consequences can be appreciated by comparing the prosperity and progress of Malaya, which has maintained a relatively free economy, with the economic doldrums experienced by some of her neighbors.

The Costs of Cultural Nationalism

Although it is less obvious, cultural nationalism is also in hibiting progress in some of these lands; the consequences can be critical for the future. Each of the new nations in Southeast Asia is possessed of a richly diverse heritage of arts and customs often submerged during the era of European colonial rule. This was a reflection of the then prevailing ignorance or prejudice of foreign administrators regarding the indigenous institutions. Few among them learned to know the literature or appreciate the painting and sculpture of the people among whom they lived. Such innovations as the celluloid products of Hollywood also helped to overwhelm indigenous Asian creative effort. Understandably, Asian nationalist leaders were anxious to insure that their people were enabled to achieve expression for the best of their traditional culture. The international recognition now being accorded to Asian dance and drama is a tribute to the quality of these traditions and to the artistic talents that have been devoted to their recreation and support in the manner they merit.

Language offers the principal example of the difficulties that arise when cultural nationalism is uncritically applied. In the Philippines this dilemma became apparent earlier than elsewhere. Among the thirty million Filipinos living throughout the seventy-one hundred Islands some seventy native languages and dialects are in use, eight of which are employed by most of the inhabitants. The introduction of Spanish in the sixteenth and seventeenth centuries provided the first common tongue for communication among the elite and also their first access to a substantial body of written literature. With the arrival of American administration at the beginning of this century and the establishment of a public school system throughout the Archipelago, English became the language of government, education, and commerce. It also opened wide the doors for Filipinos to the accumulated scientific, legal, and cultural learning of the West. The extraordinary progress that Filipinos have made during the past six decades in building a democratic way of life was substantially facilitated by the use of English as a common language among the educated within the Islands and the consequent facility with which they could welcome and digest ideas from abroad.

Filipino writers seeking to portray the intimate insights of family and home, however, found that English was not very effective; for such purposes the vernaculars continued to be preferred. Likewise, the rising generation of political leaders who sought the votes of the educated and uneducated alike were frustrated by the problems of communicating in the numerous dialects in use throughout the Archipelago. In the late 1930s, soon after establishment of the Commonwealth, such considerations plus the desire to have something uniquely their own led to agitation for a national language. A Commission was established to explore the alternatives. Primarily due to the influence of Commonwealth President Manuel Quezon, Tagalog—the language of his youth and of most Filipinos living in the environs of Manila—was selected as the basis for the national language to be known as Pilipino. Tagalog then was the native tongue only of some 19 per cent of the population, as contrasted with Cebuano, which is spoken at home by one out of every four Filipinos.

From the outset this attempt to create and propagate the use of Pilipino has encountered difficulties. Other ethnic groups in the Islands have frequently resented the dominant role of Tagalogs in governmental affairs and some saw this linguistic extension as yet another effort to subordinate them to the influence of Manila. In deference to this feeling, and also in order to make Pilipino more adequate as a means for modern communication, the Commission created words for a modern lexicography. But these new terms remained primarily in the textbooks, even though the study of Pilipino was made mandatory in the schools. The language gaining in use is "movie Tagalog," which differs substantially from the stilted phrases of Pilipino.

But the creation of a national language has not solved the problem of bringing useful literacy to children in the rural *barrios*. Instead, the Bureau of Public Schools, after expert and exhaustive experiments, determined that the only practical course of action was to employ the local vernacular for instruction during the first two years of primary education. This measure proved the most effective to insure that farm children, who receive an average of only four years of education, would be able to read and write about those affairs that mattered to them. English continues to offer the only practical avenue to acquiring professional, technical and scientific skills. The quality of the English employed for instruction in the schools has deteriorated during the past two decades, however, because of wartime interruption of teacher training, the destruction of schools, loss of textbooks, and "language confusion." But competence and confidence in the use of English continues to be the first requisite for excellence in all advanced fields of study. Recognizing this requirement, Filipino parents aspire to a mastery of English by their children as a prized measure of accomplishment and the promise of future success.

Although their individual needs and opportunities differ, each of the new countries of Southeast Asia is wrestling with its version of the language problem. Burma's experience also exemplifies some of the costs of linguistic nationalism. Although 80 per cent of the population in the Union speaks Burmese, the language of the royal court and the more learned officialdom before the establishment of British administration was Persian. With the incorporation of Burma into the British Empire during the nineteenth century, English became the language of administration, and of commerce and education. At the elementary level most schooling was in the vernacular. But all higher education was in English, except for Buddhist religious studies, where Pali was the honored language of the texts. The generation of men and women who manage modern Burma, provide its technical and professional skills, and interpret its laws have employed English for all the formal learning available to them. Yet, the pressure continues for making Burmese the exclusive language of education and government.

The generality of this to the language problem is well exemplified by the 1955 Afro-Asian Conference at Bandung where the leaders of anti-colonialist nationalism found English the most practical linguistic vehicle. With the increasing international integration of knowledge, a new nation that isolates itself linguistically can have scant hope for a substantial role in this enterprise.

From Xenophobia to National Community and Regional Cooperation: The Unfinished Task

The prospects for national survival of many among the new countries of Southeast Asia are dimmed by the present interpretation often given to nationalism. The racial emphasis of many new nationalisms inhibits rational and necessary national action. It also creates friction between the dominant ethnic groups in some of these countries and the minorities that may practice a different religion and speak another tongue and be determined to retain both. Petty jealousies concerning their borders are also vitiating the attention and energies of several new Southeast Asian states, much as they once did in Europe. Nor is the anti-Western bias evident in the pronouncements of some nationalist leaders likely to provide a viable base for building enduring indigenous institutions; it serves chiefly to alienate these societies from the more developed countries whose assistance they can use best. These intellectual perversions of the role of the nation, added to the self-seeking of the manipulators of the symbols of the nation, threaten to destroy the possibility of forming the larger social identifications required for full, self-sustaining development.

The usually unspoken but deeply felt desire of many an ordinary citizen in the Philippines and elsewhere in Southeast Asia is for a larger sense of community. He finds the world an uneasy place, and is fearful concerning what it holds in store for his children. Many of the present proponents of nationalism are highly vocal and quite skilled at capturing the "universe of discourse" and at the same time are most anti-intellectual. But they are rarely countered by men and women who voice the yearning of ordinary folk for a bit more freedom and security in their lives. With the achievement of independence by these new countries, representative forms of government were grafted onto their often feudal social traditions. The frequent failure to achieve effective legal parliamentary or presidential government is a symptom of the unfinished task that confronts those Asians who do care about fostering free institutions in a developing society for their people. While a number of them recognize that the form of ideological nationalism they have known is not historically adequate, they also see the enormity of the responsibility if they are to create such habits of liberal thought and attitude as are essential for development and for democracy. Some among them are puzzled that the Western world, after its own painful experience with certain aspects of nationalism, is not more concerned with fostering those ideas of enlightenment that have molded some nations to the greater service of their people and of man.

{ PART }
III

Culture
and Ideology

"The universe is change;
Our life is what our thoughts make it."
MARCUS AURELIUS
Meditations, IV

Chapter

6

Language, Culture, and Ideology:

The Arab World

CHARLES F. GALLAGHER

Any discussion of Arab nationalism might usefully begin with definitions of the words "nationalism" and "Arab." In the introductory chapter to this book the editor has undertaken the first task. As for specifically "Arab" nationalism, however, one succinct definition is that given by an Arab scholar and government official who writes, "Nationalism is the principal movement through which the Arab peoples are seeking to reconstruct the foundations of their life after centuries of suspended animation."[1]

Two points stand out in the foregoing definition. One is that

[1]Hazem Zaki Nuseibeh, *The Ideas of Arab Nationalism*, Ithaca: 1956, p. 207.

nationalism is not viewed as being confined to any specific
phenomena or limited to particular goals; it deals with life,
unfettered by any qualifying adjective. Most definitions in the
literature of Arab nationalism agree in their refusal to restrict
or circumscribe the nature of nationalism or the field in which
it is to operate. This emphasis on the universality of nationalism
is one striking characteristic of Arab nationalist thought and
there are sound reasons for its existence. The other is the Arab
preoccupation with the past—mention is made of "reconstruction" and of centuries of immobility. This attitude, found so
often in Arab political and cultural thought, confers upon nationalism as a movement a specific historical relativity which
puts it in a category somewhat apart from most other non-
European nationalisms. The Arabs look back longingly to a
golden past while projecting an equally lustrous future so often
described in terms of a revival (*ihya'*) or a renaissance
(*nahdah*), a second coming of righteousness that will restore
the power and the glory and the justice which in their eyes have
been denied them during the centuries of silence and impotence.
With this yearning is interwoven the strong Messianic quality
of contemporary Arab nationalism and its tendency to transfer
to this world values originally reserved for another. The universality of nationalism is the counterpart of the all-encompass-
ing cloak of Islam, and the rebirth on earth is a material
equivalent of the Resurrection (*qiyamah*).

The task of defining "Arab," however, remains. An exact
delineation of that term, which has varied greatly in its content
both in time and space, is more elusive. Up to the time of
Muhammad it was used principally to designate the desert
Bedouins as opposed to the city dwellers of Arabia. But after
the Islamic conquests of the seventh century which created a
state organized and directed by the outflowing peoples of Arabia,
the denomination came to be applied to those who spoke Arabic,
were members of a recognized Arabic tribal lineage, and had
originated genealogically in Arabia. It thus marked off an elite
from the masses of converts throughout the Near East in Syria,
Egypt, and Persia who had become Muslim and had in many
cases adopted Arabic as a working language, but had not become Arabs. Later we find the word generalized to describe,

almost with modern overtones, the culture of the far-flung Islamic empire which grew out of the Arab-founded caliphate at Damascus, and to denote the people who participated in it. Finally, in the later Middle Ages the meaning returned to its original sense, that of the wandering nomad, and it is in this somewhat pejorative context that it was used by speakers of the different vernaculars until very recently. Thus the word has had primarily a social and cultural connotation, and only at times has a secondary political coloring adhered to it.

But the advent of the West in the Arab world at the end of the eighteenth century brought new ideas of nationality and *patria* associated with the concept of a common language and shared cultural patterns. The people in the Near East who first came into contact with Europe, and who had been accustomed to thinking of themselves simply as citizens of Damascus, or members of the Shammar tribe, or Copts, or Druzes, now heard themselves described as Arabs. And a small number of educated Arabs began, from the early nineteenth century, to speculate on their identity in this new "national" framework and to consider exactly what it meant to be an Arab.

This speculation, continuing unabated for the past century, forms the core of Arab nationalist literature. It is perhaps not too much to say that the discovery of "Arabness," in the sense of a postulation and definition of the qualities of Arab civilization and the elements unique to Arab culture, has become the principal objective of most writers on the subject, sometimes to the point of obsession. Later we shall see how the controversial problems of language, race, religion, and historical traditions, among others, have been treated in the development of nationalist thought during the past decades. But these points of often acute conflict tend to be glossed over when the final definition is presented. Thus, at an Arab congress in Paris in 1913, an Arab was defined as "whoever lives in our country, speaks our language, is brought up in our culture and takes pride in our glory. . . ."[2]

Gibb says, "All those are Arabs for whom the central fact of history is the mission of Muhammad and the memory of the

[2] "Kullu Man Kanu 'Araban Fi Lughatihim Wa Thaqafatihim Wa Wala' ihim, Fahum Al 'Arab."

Arab Empire and who in addition cherish the Arabic tongue
and its cultural heritage as their common possession."[3] But the
most inclusive definition of an Arab is that of Yusuf Haikal in
Toward Arab Unity (*Nahwa al-Wahdah al-'Arabiyyah*), where
he says that it is "anyone whose national language is Arabic
and who thinks and expresses his thoughts through its media,
regardless of the racial origins of his parents."[4]

It will be noted that Gibb's definition is the most restricted
of those cited since it qualifies by language, religion, and cultural tradition, whereas the Arabs themselves seem more liberal
in their conditions. The Arab Congress, like Haikal, was willing
to admit almost anyone who wanted to belong; under both their
definitions, for example, those children of the large Greek
minority in Egypt who now attend Egyptian government
schools where instruction is given in Arabic could qualify as
Arabs. Most Western observers would probably agree that
Gibb's description is the closest to the real situation but it is
significant that the Arabs want to express a more far-reaching
ideal, emphasizing the non-isolating, open nature of Arab
society—something which often passes unnoticed. In many
ways, like American citizenship, Arab society resembles a club
in which membership may be obtained by cooperating in certain
good works, in this case by actively sharing in common linguistic, cultural, and emotional attributes. Throughout their
history Arabs on the whole have formed a flexible community,
stretching out to receive and assimilate, in part under the inclusive mantle of Islam. Even today this passive proselytization
and assimilation continue, standing out in sharp contrast to the
exclusiveness of the nationalisms of Europe, Japan, India, *et al*.
This non-exclusiveness goes even a bit further. Arab society,
again like its American counterpart, tends to impress a general
conformity on its organized constituent parts while respecting
individualism and minority patterns on a less general level.
The functioning mechanisms are atomistic and the enveloping
cloak is totalitarian, which may help to explain why the individual Arab tends to be a proud, argumentative, inner-directed
being who often fuses into a passive, unresisting mass conscious

[3] Cited in Bernard Lewis, *The Arabs in History*, London: 1950, p. 9.
[4] Yusuf Haikal, *Nahwa al-Wahdah al-'Arabiyyah*, Cairo: 1943, Ch. 1,
as cited in Nuseibeh, *op. cit.*, p. 89.

of and obedient to the signals given it from above or outside, but a mass which in its ultimate behavior re-creates many of the attitudes of the individual.

In sum, the universality of definition of the Arab and the vagueness and elasticity of the historical community of Arabs provide a third dimension to the sweeping characteristics of nationalism as defined by the Arabs and to the all-inclusiveness of Islam. One senses that the Arabs, fragmented in so many specifics, have yet preserved a deep yearning for a fundamental unity of their life beyond the political considerations of our times. As Nuseibeh wrote: "The spiritual and the material, the political, the economic and the social are interrelated and inseparable parts of a people's life. Whoever succeeds in rehabilitating this essential unity for the Arab people will be its greatest benefactor."[5]

Culture and the Arab Nationalist Thinker

It is customary to think of Arab nationalism as a historically recent phenomenon dating from the mid-nineteenth century. Although this is true in the strictest sense, the roots of Arab nationalism have been nurtured from other more remote sources. For example, the Wahhabi revivalist movement in Arabia in the eighteenth century preceded the nationalist reawakening in the coastal regions by almost a century; its place in the shaping of an Arab nation has not yet been determined. This movement represented the continuance of an Arab-Muslim tradition which had flourished and expanded throughout the Middle Ages, when Islam is usually considered to have been dormant. Modern nationalism goes far back to derive much of its inspiration, as has been said, from the universal state of the caliphate established upon the death of Muhammad in 632 which functioned, first in Damascus and then in Baghdad, with increasing disabilities for six centuries. Part of modern nationalist thought leans heavily upon the "Arab caliphate" established by the Umayyads in Damascus while other elements are more intimately related to the less Arab and more Muslim Abbasid state that followed it.

Above all one must turn back to Muhammad for the principal

[5] Nuseibeh, *op. cit.*, p. 206.

key. Islam is the "central fact" in the history of the Arabs and
Arab civilization has grown, prospered, and waned in its confines. The debt is reciprocal in that to imagine the Arabs without
Islam is as impossible as it is to conceive of the development
of Islam without its Arab carriers. The duality of Muhammad's
role as founder-revealer of Islam and unifier of the Arabs continues to the present day to present the Arabs with a dilemma
not yet resolved. And it is necessary, finally, to consider the
earliest cultural properties of the pre-Islamic Arabs and their
homeland, which in turn shaped the first Arab empire and its
philosophy. The virtues of honor, manliness, and hospitality
prized by the early poets are still important components of Arab
life and help shape to an uncommon degree the ideal of modern
Arab behavior throughout the community which Arab nationalists are intent on building.

The connecting strand on which these items of Arab national
history are hung and exposed to view is the Arabic language.
As can be seen in the definitions of an Arab given above, the
importance of language is paramount in Arab minds, now as
always. In all aspects of Arab culture the immediacy and vivacity
of the verbalization of phenomena is striking. In the beginning
in Arabia there was, literally, the word. The language of Adam
in Eden before the fall was Arabic; only afterwards did this
tongue change and give birth to Aramaic. Ishmael, the son of
Abraham, revived the pure, original language which survived
among the Arabs of the Hejaz. In pre-Islamic Arabia the poetic
koine of the wandering tribal troubadors was shaped into a
common literary tongue which in turn gave rise to classical
Arabic, the language of the divinely revealed Quran. If Islam
is the foundation stone of Arab life, the sacred language in
which it was given to men is equally central. The importance
of Arabic to the Arabs, far out of proportion to what is felt by
most other peoples for their native tongue, however much they
may honor it, derives from this connection. To Arabs it is no
accident that God made his ultimate revelation in Arabic; it
was part of the divine plan which centered upon the Arabs as
the chosen messengers of the truth and upon Arabic as the chosen
language.

Thus the sacred language of classical Arabic, unchanging

and unyielding, became the voice of the Kingdom of God on earth, the caliphate. Islam, both a religion and a state, reinforced the position of Arabic which completed the circle by expounding and illuminating the true and the good for the benefit of men living in the *Dar al Islam*, the House of God. The survival of classical Arabic today as the literary language used in all writing and official speaking depends on this interrelation, and continues to profit by the tradition that no other tongue is fit for the affairs of an Islamic state.

But the relationship of language to the state has in fact changed now that the state is no longer divinely sanctioned. When the Divine Law (*Shari'ah*) was the foundation of government, it was altogether natural that its precepts be expressed in the holy language. Now that the basis of jurisprudence in most Arab countries is an adapted amalgam of European codes, it is not only unnecessary but perhaps also unfitting. The transition from a political doctrine based on revelation valid for all time to one dependent on evaluation through analysis and reason has posed great problems for modern Arabs in many fields, not the least of which is language. The subtleties and intricacies of a subjective Arabic well-equipped to undertake the task of revealing God to man have had to be remolded to express the vagaries of human political behavior and the precisions of science.[6] So far this change has been accomplished with only moderate success. Modern Arab political nationalism has not yet completely found a tongue, although its efforts to develop one are a vital part of its struggle to grow.

To say that the language problem has been in the forefront of Arabic thought ever since the renewal of contact with the West after the Napoleonic invasion of Egypt in 1798 is an understatement. Given the importance of classical Arabic as a vehicle for conveying the truth it is not surprising that the first concern of those affected by the wind of change early in the nineteenth century was not only what to believe and say but

---

[6] Where the church is imperfectly separated from the state, political content resembles religious content. The *za'im* essentially preaches a *khutbah* just as the *khatib* in the mosque in troubled times makes a speech indistinguishable from that of a political leader.

how to express it, and for this reason the Arab awakening was marked from its beginning with a distinctly literary character.

The issue was a dual one, concerning both the relationship of a new world to the traditional means of expression and the fact that this means had in practice decayed considerably. In addition, the first architects of change were Christian Arabs, some of whom, perhaps unconsciously, wanted to use the language after its reformation and purification as a means of modernizing their society and liberating themselves from the often oppressive weight of a dominant Islam. For others a return to the past was to make the language of God a key to unlocking the secrets of a profane present. As Antonius says of one of the first great intellectual figures of the renaissance, Nasif Yaziji (1800-1871), ". . . the problem of how to revive the past became his dominant interest. . . . He became the apostle of its resurrection."[7] If Yaziji tended to lean too much toward purism and the pedantry of the past, another outstanding figure of the times in Syria more nearly balanced revival with innovation. He was Butrus Bustani (1819-1883), like Yaziji a Christian of Lebanon, whose career amply illustrates the new forces then at work in the Arab world. Bustani benefited from the first wave of education then sweeping through Lebanon and attended the Maronite college at Ain Waraqa before going on to study in Rome. His literary accomplishments were remarkable; he compiled a two-volume dictionary of Arabic and an abridgement of it, together with six volumes of an encyclopedia left unfinished at his death but continued by his family. His political activity paralleled his scholarly research, for he founded the pioneer political journal in the region, *Nafir Suriya* (*The Clarion of Syria*) in 1860, and ten years later a review of literature and politics titled *al Jenan* (*The Gardens*). This interrelationship of learning and politics was further exemplified when the Society of Arts and Sciences was founded in Beirut in 1847 by a group including American and English educators as well as Yaziji and Bustani, and again in 1857 with the constitution of the Syrian Scientific Society. In the latter group were to be found for the first time Muslim and Druze associates, among them, significantly, one of Bustani's

[7] George Antonius, *The Arab Awakening*, Philadelphia: 1939, p. 46.

sons, and the Arslan family (one of whose members, Chekib Arslan, became one of the leading pan-Arab nationalists of the early twentieth century). When the Syrian Scientific Society later opened a branch in Cairo, it diffused for the first time its message of common ideals and a common national consciousness to a wider circle and a new region.

A steady drift of the movement from the literary to the political, from general aims to specific grievances, can be followed in succeeding decades. By 1875 a secret society had been formed at the Syrian Protestant College (later the American University of Beirut) and five years later, in 1880, revolutionary placards were posted by society members calling for independence, the recognition of Arabic instead of Turkish as the official language, freedom of expression, and the diffusion of knowledge.[8] The idea of territorial and linguistic consciousness had taken shape, the protest against foreign tyranny had become explicit, and the first vague concept of abstract liberty had made an appearance. All occurred still within the lifetime of Bustani and much stemmed directly from his literary pioneering. A better case for pure research would be difficult to make out.

At the same time as these Lebanese, other discoverers were at work in Egypt. They took a more practical approach than the linguists of the Levant, but their interests remained in keeping with the Arab tradition of letters. Shortly after the French occupation of Egypt had exposed the material backwardness and weakness of the country, Muhammad 'Ali undertook a program of education and Westernization. He established technical schools at home to teach the techniques of Europe brought back by his envoys, and he sent educational missions abroad to ferret out the secrets of Western power. The purpose of both was to produce an intellectual elite, particularly of doctors, administrators, and technicians. In practice the experiment of the government was largely a failure, but it did have

---

[8] In the same year Husain al-Marsafi, a sheikh at Al Azhar, published his famous "Eight Words" (*Al Kalim ath-Thaman*):

Ummah (Nation)	*Watan* (Homeland)
Hukumah (Government)	*'adl* (Justice)
Zulm (Injustice)	*Siyasah* (Politics)
Hurriyyah (Liberty)	*Tarbiyyah* (Education)

See Vincent Monteil, *L'Arabe moderne*, Paris: 1960, p. 36.

secondary side effects of lasting value. The Translation School headed by Rif 'ah Bey at-Tahtawi translated two thousand-odd works from Western languages into Arabic and Turkish. Tahtawi himself was one of the first Arabic thinkers to make a comparison of Western and Arab political institutions and ideas in a remarkable work. He and those who worked around him were important in bridging the gap between mere translation and projection. He explained the West simply but as best he could and without the apologias which were to become a feature of later Arab critiques. The foundation work done in Syria and Egypt during the first half of the nineteenth century made a platform by about 1860 for a cultural take-off which has permanently shaped the modern history of the Near East.

More direct political thinkers soon followed. Jamal ad-din al-Afghani (1838-1897) was probably the most important both in his capacity as promulgator of a reaction to the West with his pan-Islamic revivalism, and in his influence upon almost all the important thinkers of his time and immediately after. Afghani believed in the "regeneration" and strengthening of one of the Islamic states in order to "restore Islam to its past glory." The power of his appeal was and still is considerable, and although his rejection of pan-Arabism eventually placed him outside the main current of Arab nationalist development, the descent of his ideas can be traced through Muhammad Rashid Rida (1865-1935), who compromised to the extent of claiming the caliphate for an Arab member of the Quraish family of Mecca. Rida's notion of an oligarchic republicanism headed by a religious elite but diffused within an area of popular sovereignty and consultative government has been taken up in large measure by the Muslim Brotherhood today. On the positive side Afghani's advocacy of tyrannicide and his championing of liberty struck a responsive chord in the younger generation then suffering from the excesses of Hamidian despotism, just as his endorsement of a strong executive and his doubts about the workability of parliamentary institutions in Islam cast long shadows into the future.

Afghani's influence was transmitted in several important ways. The first was through 'Abderrahman Kawakibi (1849-1903), who took up the theme of liberty, then becoming a subject of importance to the Arab movement, in his work *Taba'i' al Istibdad* (*Attributes of Tyranny*). Kawakibi, representative of one of the best Arab types in his frugality and charity, opposed tyranny with learning and advocated complete freedom of speech and writing as the firmest guarantee against oppressive government. Kawakibi's importance lies in two areas of modern Arab political life: he represented that core of Arab individualism and egalitarianism which is so often found in his native Syria and which made him a hero for those young Syrians who, by quoting him, voiced dissatisfaction with United Arab Republic control over Syria; and he refined the pan-Islamic thought he had inherited from Afghani into a proposal for an Islamic movement headed by the Arabs, whose special position within Islam he underscored. The effects of his work have been enormous, for while Kawakibi prepared the way for a transference of the Arab revival from the predominantly Christian hands in which it had hitherto rested, he also sharpened an area of conflict and uncertainty within Arab nationalism as to how much of it was religiously Muslim, how much culturally Islamic, and how much secularly nationalist—questions which have not yet been fully resolved.

Afghani's most fertile heir was certainly Muhammad 'Abduh (1848-1905). His place in the development of Muslim reformist thought is central and his role in invigorating Egyptian life by combining Islamic tradition with Western progress becomes more important each year. His success at Al Azhar was limited during his lifetime but his influence on modern Egyptians has not ceased to grow, and he has come to represent to many the sage distillation of a Muslim rationalism which can be followed in moderation.

As we have seen, these intellectuals of the late nineteenth century have not been without influence on Arab political thought today. Their effect upon political action may have been even greater, for much of the pragmatic content of Abdel Nasser's philosophy can be found in Afghani's doctrine that direct action to overthrow tyranny is necessary and that the end justifies the means. To the constant concern with freedom expressed by Afghani, 'Ishaq Shumayyil, and their contemporaries was added the glimmering of social concern in the writing of Mustafa

Kamal, who considered the people the only real force, and who founded in 1906 the *Hizb al Watani* (National Party), the first political party in modern Egypt. Kamal's legacy extends throughout Egypt and the Arab world. From him such diverse movements as the social humanitarianism of Khalid Muhammad Khalid and the Socialist Renaissance (Ba'th) Party drew inspiration, while the present military reformist government of the U.A.R., whose debt to Afghani has already been mentioned, also owes much to Kamal.

By 1914 an important transition point had been reached in the development of the nationalist movement. The date is convenient, of course, in that the outbreak of war cut off certain avenues of activity and brought into being a new situation; but in the years immediately preceding it new trends and new approaches began taking shape. The Young Turk revolution of 1908, after causing a surge of hope throughout the Arab part of the Ottoman Empire, retreated into a narrow pan-Turkism whose strong racist bias resulted in an alienation of the Arab nationalists who, until then, had been willing to limit their grievances largely to problems of equal rights for Arabs within the heterogeneous Empire. The Ottoman-Arab Fraternity Society (*Al Ikha' al 'arabi al 'uthmani*), founded in the first flush of enthusiasm after the revolution, existed only a few months before it was banned; it was succeeded by a series of Arab-organized literary or social clubs and institutions which gradually turned, under suspicion and persecution, into political societies whose programs moved irresistibly toward activist philosophies. The earliest ones, such as *Al Qahtaniyyah*, still favored a compromise with the Turks within the Empire, in this case on the basis of a dual monarchy, but soon *Al Fatat*, later to be one of the most influential of all, was preaching the complete independence of the Arabs. Others, like the Ottoman Decentralization Society founded in Cairo, called for home rule, as did the manifesto of the Committee of Reform published in Beirut at the beginning of 1913. The first Arab congress held in Paris that year made the same demand, and it was significant that when the Committee of Reform was dissolved by government order in April 1913, there was a general shutting down of business in Beirut and manifestations of solidarity occurred throughout the Fertile Crescent.

The base of the nationalist movement had by then considerably widened, involving a larger number of persons and embracing several classes. The cultural revival of the preceding two generations had begun to bear fruit. By reactivating the best and soundest parts of Arab culture it had provided a basis for the functioning of several specific fields, of which political activity was a principal one. A line of descent had been established, beginning with the first isolated, enlightened individuals, themselves stimulated by the earliest external military and educational contacts. It continued on to their pupils, in some cases their own offspring, and the next generation of local scholars interacted with the foreign elements in the Middle East. Toward the end of the century these students were becoming leaders of local society, primarily as lawyers and army officers, and in this capacity as a new elite they formed a majority of the membership in the patriotic societies, agencies which in turn transmitted desires for identity, self-respect, and liberty down to the stratum just below.

Geographically, too, and this was a factor of some moment in the Arab world, the field of action had expanded. The nationalist elite on the eve of the war existed not only in Damascus and Beirut, but also in Aleppo, Baghdad, Basra, Nablus, and Jerusalem. And to escape the growing intolerance of the Turkish regime, Cairo, hitherto the stronghold of a separate, parochial Egyptian nationalism concerned primarily with its struggle against the British occupiers, became a rallying point in exile for Arab nationalists of the Levant. So, too, did Paris, whose atmosphere gave a liberal and cosmopolitan touch to the movement which it was to lose later when the West became the oppressor, rather than the supporter, of Arab freedom. By 1914, then, a majority of urban Arabs in the Fertile Crescent was aware of the region's identity and its condition of subservience within the Ottoman Empire, and was beginning to feel a stirring of desire to do something about changing that subservience.

World War I provided the necessary stimulus. In effect, the war shaped the struggle for independence both by tugging generally at the roots of society everywhere, and in particular by forcing the Ottoman Empire into untenable political and military positions marked by a constant hardening of relations.

At the end of 1914 the Turks were still attempting to secure Arab cooperation on the basis of a *Jihad*, or Holy War, and support from Arab religious leaders was desperately courted. But by 1915 the executions of Arab nationalists had begun— the death toll in some of the patriotic societies was extremely high—and *Al Fatat* was already in league with the Sherif of Mecca. By 1916 the revolt in the desert was under way, adding a new dimension to the movement; Arab contingents in the Ottoman army were unsure; popular resentment was general. When the Amir Faisal arrived at Damascus on horseback at the head of the Arab armies in October 1918 and entered the former capital of the Arab empire of the Umayyads, he was greeted by an outburst of emotion and delirium that would have been unthinkable four years before. The uprising in the peninsula and the executions in Syria had done more to popularize the national struggle than any amount of pamphlets and societies, resolutions or congresses. They had given the Arabs martyrs and heroes, two essential ingredients of a successful national myth, the vital emotional decoration for the theoretical sub-structure built up in the pre-war period.

The increasingly harsh Turkish policies of the last years before the war and the conflict itself shifted the focus of nationalist activity from the intellectual to the practical, and at the end of the struggle the dream had apparently become, for a moment, reality: the Arab empire existed once again. But the vision proved to be a mirage when the Western powers proceeded to divide the spoils among themselves. Not only were great expectations betrayed, but the splitting up of the Fertile Crescent into separate and artificial mandated areas so scarred the Arab map and personality that it still determines the wants of today. Zionist infiltration into Palestine, increasing through the period between the wars, did the same thing in another way and continues to do so. The Arabs were gravely wounded psychologically by being told in effect that after they had been encouraged to fight for their freedom they were not fit to govern themselves, and by learning that outsiders were to be allowed to enter their homeland and begin a process of dispossession. They were equally stricken by being told that they must unlearn their self-discovery as Arabs and consider themselves Iraqis, Transjordanians, Palestinians, and Syrians, not to speak of Latakiotes, Druzes, or Lebanese. But to reteach history on whim is not easy, and once a sense of national consciousness is arrived at it is not readily forgotten. The principal result, and the most unfortunate, was that the direction of Arab preoccupations— which had been rightly and healthfully concerned at first with a revival of the best elements in their past heritage, a new finding of self-esteem, and a discovery of the abstract values of freedom and political, if not yet social or economic, justice—now of necessity became neurotically turned against an alien rule which implicitly made a mockery of those earlier strivings. The new rulers had come so recently and in so flagrantly unjust and underhanded a way that their evil was plainly there to be seen and understood by all Arabs. Worse even than the Ottomans, they were bound to the Arabs by no tie of language, culture, sympathy or, for the overwhelming majority, religion. And unlike the Turks, who had at least let well enough alone, they were out to impose their foreign spirit and technique in a way designed to cause a profound inner humiliation of a people which had believed itself on the threshold of a new life. At this juncture the West stood for the negation of all hope for the Arabs; it had brought only death and despair to the Arab soul.

It was natural then that as the interwar period went on, new attitudes were struck and new methods designed to combat these new tyrannies. In these developments there was a certain symmetry of contrast with what had emerged before. The intellectuals and writers of the first wave of the *nahdah* had been in the main progressive pioneers who looked forward to a gradual betterment of Arab society no matter how divided they were in their programs directed to this end. At their best they produced outstanding and important works which are surviving a century-long test of time; they bred a generation of followers who did them honor, including the first heroes of Arab nationalism, the Husains and Faisals who came out better than most of their European political antagonists of the time. Even the more modest efforts of others, judged by the standard of the times, are deserving of at least passing consideration.

But the combined efforts of all these actors had ended in

failure. Although for a while Faisal, and somewhat later Ibn Saud, were popular idols to them, the postwar generation of young Arab nationalists hardened their outlook as their feelings of impotence and insufficiency grew. Their frustration became the keynote of the second wave of Arab reaction to the modern West and has dominated it to the present day—or at least until the mid 1950s, if one may venture from this relatively recent vantage point the idea that sometime around the Suez Canal affair another possibly decisive turning point in Arab national growth appeared.

The thinkers of the generation that grew up after the "year of disaster," as 1920 was labeled, were formed in this new despondent atmosphere of which the harsh rancor of their pens is an expression. Throughout the writing of the thirties, fairly scant in itself, and the greater production of the forties runs a bitter, self-pitying tone. These works are aptly termed apologetics, the defense of a position held against real or imagined attack from outside as opposed to the upholding of ideas in and for themselves. The attempts of writers like Sati' al Husri to prove the existence of an Arab community (*qawmiyyah 'arabiyyah*) implied that there had been a denial of its existence. In truth this was so, for the West had ridden rough-shod over the idea for three decades and an attitude of petulant justification dominated the intellectual climate of Arab national-ism from the Treaty of Versailles onward.

Nationalist literature in the recent past also continued to be derivative of European thought in one of the mainstreams of its inspiration. But whereas the optimistic liberalism of the nineteenth century in Europe had stirred a certain nobility in the Arab mind when wedded with a sound remolding of Islamic tradition, the darker philosophies and the political actuality of the 1930s provided a matrix for the development of local speculations reflecting the character of the times. Husri's requirements that the individual merge himself in the state can be equally desirable for the solidarity of the Islamic com-munity or the all-powerful European nation-state of the twentieth century. The growth of the *qawmiyyah* (com-munity) nationalist tendency and the pallid existence of the *wataniyyah* (local) nationalist concept certainly reflect the strong Arab sense of the solidarity of peoples rather than the ties of territory, but also mirror the increasing importance of blood-folk bonds to European nationalisms between 1918 and 1939. Similarly the search for a national ideology in Zurayq (1938), *Al Wayi al Qawmi* (*National Consciousness*) and Alayili (1941), *Dustur al 'Arab al Qawmi* (*A National Constitution for Arabs*) partakes of the intense preoccupation with this problem in Europe between the wars. Thus a good part of Arab nationalist thought, while itself negating the West, continued to be influenced toward a nihilistic reversal by some of the most negative aspects of the contemporary Occident.

Finally, there is a quality in the post-1920 literature which might best be termed descriptive instead of inspirational. It is possible to read Afghani, 'Abduh, Kawakibi and the best of their contemporaries with a sense of discovery and understanding which accompanies all profound revelation, but it is hard to find much written in later years—dismissing the polemical tracts designed only to convince the previously convinced and enrage the already enraged—that is more than a catalogue of complaints or a listing of projects and proposals for action. And despite a considerable increase in literacy, recent writings have not had the following that one might expect; one finds more students familiar with 'Abduh than with anyone who has been writing during the past twenty years, Gamal Abdel Nasser perhaps excepted. A wide gap has developed between the earlier more purely intellectual approach to pan-Arabism and modern popular feelings about it. While this result is related to the widened base of nationalism, one suspects that it is also in some measure an effect of the failure of recent writers to communicate, as did their predecessors, their concern with the basic questions of reform and social justice which have become for most Arabs the cornerstone of their nationalist aspirations.

Most recently there have been signs of a marked change of direction. Although it is still early to judge, the works of Khalid Muhammad Khalid (*Min huna nabda'* [1950] and *Muwatinun la ra' aya* [1951]) may mark a turning point. In these writings a sheikh of Al Azhar propounds a reformist Islam separated from a secular socialist state, surely a remarkably heterodox position for a theologian from a most conservative

institution. Sheikh Khalid goes beyond the opinions propounded
by Sayyid Qutb in his *Social Justice in Islam* (*Al 'Adalah al
Ijtimaiyyah fi'l islam*), but both agree on the necessity of attending to material wants on a plane of equality with spiritual
needs. And when one considers that not only prominent *'ulama*
of Khalid's stripe and members of the Muslim Brotherhood, but
also the military rulers of the United Arab Republic since 1952
and the leaders of the Ba'th—in short the most powerful formative elements in the most important Arab countries—have all
been injecting a heavy practical dose of social and economic
theory into their political programs, it is apparent how far representative nationalist thought has moved in the past fifteen
years. The parallel of this theoretical change lies in political
action, and there it can be noted how different are the revolutions
in Egypt in 1952 and in Iraq in 1958 from the succession of
barracks revolts which shook the Arab world for almost two
decades after 1936. The apprentice dictators of Iraq and Syria
in those days shared in the mediocrity of the age. If a second
stage of the rebirth of the modern Muslim-Arab world is indeed
now being generated around the social orientation of the community, it is to be hoped that, as happened before, the political
climate will mature in response to the new intellectual flower-
ings that are sprouting up.[9]

Unity and Division

Before the impact of Western ideas touched it, Arab society,
like all traditional societies, had its hierarchy of loyalties.
Depending on local circumstances, these moved upward and
outward from the family and the kin group to the village, clan,
or tribal level, or on another plane to the city. Apart from this
schema, but integrated in counterbalance, was the local linguistic or religious minority loyalty group.

But unlike many other traditional societies, the Arabs had

---

[9] Cf. Jacques Berque, "L'univers politique des Arabes," in the *Encyclo-
pédie Française*, XI, Ch. V, p. 34-11: "The *ummah*, a community dedicated to God, stands in antithesis to the *sha'b*, the profane collectivity.
Just as at the exterior of its limits the blessed 'gathering,' the *jama'ah*,
itself the possessor of particular virtues, is antithesis of the *qawm*, a pure
and simple 'assembling.' "

a communal bond beyond these fixed confines of fidelity. This cohesiveness, waxing and waning through the centuries, has never completely ceased to exist, just as it has never successfully overcome certain fundamental obstacles and flourished to their exclusion. As the historical memory of the Arab Empire and the Golden Age survived to provide vertical continuity with the past, the vague but pervasive sense of identity with all Arabs, and particularly with all Muslim Arabs, has formed a horizontal network stretching out in geography. This awareness provided a consciousness of something beyond the nation-state of the Western world, so that the imported phenomenon of nationalism on entering modern Arab political thought has not only had to struggle against the lesser elements of division but has itself become a dividing force obstructing the completion of unity. The problem of creating what Westerners would call national loyalties thus has been particularly difficult in the Arab world, as the record shows.

The Arab nation (*ummah*) of the past stemmed from the Islamic concept of a brotherhood in common religion. Yet the idea of the nation did exist in political reality, as the accounts of travelers and pilgrims reveal, as late as the fourteenth century. The ease with which Arabs adorn their modern imperialist fancies by claims to areas which have little or nothing to do with the geographical logic of the modern state emphasizes the historical aspect of the brotherhood, just as the truly warm welcome given to ordinary visiting Arabs by their brethren in other Arab countries—something far surpassing that tendered among Europeans or fellow Christians—underscores the living, human fraternity of which they feel themselves a part. In fact, to observers who live among them, the desiccated arguments of scholars about linguistic and racial unity pale beside this impressive phenomenon. The Arab insistence on thinking of themselves as a distinct familial entity cannot be ignored.

As might be expected, the verbal concept of the nation and nationalism has been a central problem for the Arabs. Whether or not the *ummah*, the word for people and community, is derived from the root *'mm* or comes from another source, its overt relationship to the word meaning "mother" established the *ummah al-islamiyah* as something akin to the "children of

Islam," just as one popular name for the Arabs is *banu al-arab*,
"sons of the Arabs." *Ummah* was used in the nineteenth century
and even later to translate the Western word "nation" (*patrie*),
but a part of it retains overtones of a nonsecular nature. The
watan, dwelling place or homeland (from *watana*, "to live in a
place," originally a name for a Bedouin encampment) comes
closer to the sense of *pays*; and Muhammad 'Abduh, among
others, defines it as a physical abode, a focus of rights and duties,
and a center for the exercise of spiritual activities—none of which
conflicts with Western definitions of the homeland. From this
root came *wataniyyah*, patriotism or nationalism, a word seemingly inadequate to the Arab need to describe an emotion encompassing the whole Arab nation, and which has progressively
taken on a coloration of local nationalism with, in the eyes of
many Arabs, a pejorative touch. The word in vogue now is
qawmiyyah (from *qawm*, the *Volk*), implying not so much a
blood unity as one of hearts, and quite opposed to the territorial
idea dominant in *wataniyyah*.[10] Significantly the dominant relationship in this case, as almost always with the Arabs, is a human
one. To people who have on the whole little valued the concept
of land, rootlessness is compensated for by affinities of the
person: the *qawmiyyah al-'arabiyyah* is not defined by lines on a
map but as the "community where Arabs live," and Arabs are,
we may remember, essentially those who behave and express
themselves in a way self-identifiable to Arabs. Thus the elasticity
and the fluidity of *qawmiyyah* nationalism is at once its
strength and its weakness.

What we may then call, for the sake of convenience,
qawmiyyah-nationalism is extremely powerful in the Arab world
today, but it is not by any means supreme. It has to do constant battle with local *wataniyyah*-nationalisms which vary in
content and intensity from place to place. Those areas which
historically had little sense of local or national cohesion, like
Syria, have been the foremost shapers of the *qawmiyyah* and have
constantly pushed the nation of Arabism to the detriment of
Syrianism. At the opposite pole Egypt, with its acute sense

[10] Jacques Berque, *Les Arabes d'hier à demain*, Paris: 1960, p. 46, defines
the *qawmiyyah* as "the effort of the Arabs to adjust to others while
remaining true to themselves."

of solid, uninterrupted existence, was for long and in effect until the Second World War an exponent of Egyptian *wataniyyah*-nationalism; only with hesitancy did it undertake the spiritual leadership of the eastern Arabs and immerse itself in the concept of the *qawmiyyah*. A feeling of historical and geographical apartness respectively tends to keep Morocco and Iraq closer to the particularist nationalists—although, since the revolution in the latter country in 1958, it has been a deeply dividing issue. The importance of religion and minorities shows up notably in Lebanon, where the Christian half of the country, and to some extent the Druze and Shi'a minorities, have a much greater local patriotic (*watani*) spirit than the Sunnis, who feel themselves tied in large measure to their co-religionists outside the country. But in Tunisia, where an exclusive *wataniyyah*-nationalism has at least for the present gained the day, none of these factors seems to have been decisive. Here it would appear that a combination of internal homogeneity, reinforced by an intellectual and social advance over its immediate neighbors, has shaped the country into a singular mold almost approaching at times that of a "splendid isolation."[11]

Social Structure

The class system of the nineteenth-century Arab world has been shaken in the past hundred years in the same fashion as family, village, and tribal loyalty groups. The two-class division, into peasants and landlords in the countryside, and governing and governed in the cities, has for some time been in the process of breaking up into a more complex and diversified society. Bit by bit have been created the new groups of intellectuals, the entrepreneurs, merchants, career military officers, modern students of Western sciences (as opposed to the theological students of the traditional society), and, finally, the new urban proletariat. All of these new groups merit some attention as conductors of nationalist thought.

[11] The events at Bizerte in the summer of 1961 brought about closer relationships between Tunisia and, among other Arab states, the United Arab Republic. It is too early to say whether this signaled a profound change in Tunisian attitudes about the *qawmiyyah* or was merely a transitory response to a political crisis.

The notion of an intellectual bloc requires some definition. It has been properly said that an intellectual is one who uses his mind to observe the metaphysical world, and it has further been claimed in the face of some argument that such intellectuals do indeed exist in modern Arab-Muslim society after having passed through a period of relative eclipse in the centuries preceding the *nahdah*.[12] Agreement may be expressed with both these statements, yet the definition itself is not necessarily germane to all aspects of an investigation of contemporary nationalist activity; the intellectual class in the modern Arab world now largely defines itself in terms far exceeding the strict limits imposed above. It is probable that in many Arab countries at present anyone having a *baccalauréat* or its equivalent would tend to think of himself as an intellectual; certainly anyone with a *licence* or its equal would. Furthermore, a large number of urban middle-class writers, reporters, clerks, functionaries and such who fall far outside the normal definition of an intellectual in the Western world are included both by themselves and by common consent of their fellows. But even though this self-described intellectual group is large and diversified, it maintains an elite character because of the drive to enter it from below. Unlike his Western counterpart, the Arab intellectual can count on honor, prestige, and respect, and he functions usefully if not always altogether wisely or freely in his society. It was very much an intellectual spark that led to the awakening of the last century, and it was scholars who transmitted and transmuted Western ideas into Arab society, trying to alchemize them into more harmonious local resonances. It was the intellectuals who reacted in the period 1918-1939 with bitterness and frustration and introduced the apologetics which have marked so much of recent thought. It is the young intellectuals today in Cairo, Beirut, Tunis, and Baghdad who consider it their task to accept or reject ideas, to discuss and criticize new philosophies; and it is they who are a critical factor in the dissemination of attitudes—despite government pressure in the more authoritarian states—gleaned in their cafes, their clubs,

[12] Cf. W. C. Smith, "The Intellectuals in the Modern Development of the Islamic World," in S. N. Fisher, ed., *Social Forces in the Middle East*, Ithaca: 1955, pp. 190-204.

and from their listening to the radio and reading of periodicals.

One recent and striking characteristic of this group is its passionate involvement in affairs external to the Arab world proper. The young men of Cairo today are probably concerned with the Congo, Cuba, the integration problem of the United States, and Formosa to a much greater degree than the reverse is true of intellectuals in any of the foreign lands mentioned. This statement does not imply that a genuine concern for their own welfare is absent, but recently there has grown a heightened awareness of the similarity between the problems of others and those of the Arab world. One is tempted to hope that a step has been taken to a higher level of empathy which will erase some of the maudlin self-pity with which this class was infected— with, it might be added, some excuse—a decade ago. One other point to be made is the paradoxically greater need for intellectuals and fuller freedom for them because of the absence of a formalized clergy in Islam. Where church and state overlap, the sheikhs of religious institutions may issue a *fatwa* recommending certain acts or declaring licit or illicit this or that kind of behavior in civil situations, but in countervalence is the ability of the pious layman to exercise an individual *ijtihad* (interpretation), or at least to play his part in forming that *ijma'* (consensus) of the community which determines what is proper and improper. It is because of this dualism that the role of an intellectual elite in the Arab-Muslim world is vital in establishing a critique of reason. All kinds of perilous roads leading to isolated *tour de force* solutions can be anticipated, but what is most needed is an effort to integrate a rational modernism into the sound heart of Islamic tradition, a task as important to the future of Arab civilization as any current economic development plan or any project for political federation.

Another crucial group whose recent creation and growth has remolded the society is the entrepreneur class. Arab-Muslim civilization in its halcyon days was strongly commercially oriented, but by the eighteenth century its mercantile *élan* was shattered and its functioning had been reduced to almost ritual operations. European traders residing in the commercial towns of Aleppo and Cairo then became responsible for the fairly simple exchange of cotton, silk, and coffee for Western manufactured goods. In the nineteenth century their role was gradually taken over, first by Jewish merchants in Syria and then by Arab Christians. Thus the Levant (Lebanon and Syria) provided the first example of the growth of a native merchant class, although initially among the religious minorities. At the same time, the outflow of emigrants from the overpopulated Lebanese mountains began to pay a return in the form of capital returning home, and by the first decades of this century domestic money began to go into local small-scale industry. Later, in Syria, the Muslims who at first had remained aloof overtook the Christians in a movement parallel to their later entry into the intellectual sphere, and became entrepreneurs themselves. Issawi's family history as described by him[13] is an instructive example of how successive generations of a Christian family of Damascus moved from ownership of a textile workshop to commercial operations with Egypt in the mid-nineteenth century, and then into the civil service and the liberal professions. In Syria economic development shows another parallel to intellectual growth in the reliance upon local financing; just as Damascus has been for so long the "beating heart" of Arabism and *qawmiyyah*-nationalism and the center of purely Arab as opposed to strictly Muslim thought, so it was also the focus of the first wholly Arab effort in modern enterprise.

In Egypt the impetus was different; here was a case of stimulation by foreign investment which is now replaced by the nationalist state. The process follows Berque's theory that statism is a form of nationalism in which the threatened society defends itself collectively, after individual entrepreneurs have shown themselves unable to take up the challenge, by erecting a state-capitalist organization as first a rival to and then a liquidator of foreign capitalism.[14] The development of nationalist economics in Egypt has followed a course different from that of private mercantilism in the Levant, in part because of the dissimilar background. From the beginning the Egyptian national struggle had economic overtones centered around its attempt to gain equal economic privileges. The pioneer call of Talat

[13] Charles Issawi, "The Entrepreneurial Class," in S. N. Fisher, ed., *op. cit.*, p. 121.
[14] Jacques Berque, *Les Arabes d'hier à demain*, pp. 105 ff.

Harb for a national bank to finance industrial development in 1916 (established finally as the *Banque Misr* in 1920) and his opposition to the renewal of the Suez Canal Contract as early as 1910 presaged much of what has happened in nationalization and Egyptianization since 1957. Egyptian ownership of local enterprises, less than 10 per cent a generation back and only 40 per cent a decade ago, was almost total by 1962.

An entrepreneur class hardly exists in other Arab countries, but in the two regions mentioned above it has served an important innovating function which, in the Egyptian case, needed to be taken over and completed by the state. The net effect of the new industrialists has been to increase autarchy by demands for tariff protection and, notably in Egypt, to widen the degree of popular participation in the national industrial life by bringing in investors and giving them a stake in the country's growth. There the still limited professional classes became shareholders and directors as early as the 1920s and in certain cases, having prospered, they founded their own enterprises. The desire to replace foreign capital and technicians stimulated an at times xenophobic patriotism in Egypt, but also accelerated the establishment of a purely Egyptian business system conducted entirely in Arabic. In an indirect tie-up with the intellectual stimulus and later with that of the all-controlling state, this desire also gave a push to clerical secondary education.

The officer class deserves to be mentioned briefly as another group which has had a well-known influence on the course of political events, if not on the development of theory.[15] The warrior has always been honored in Arab history, and under the Ottomans the sons of notable Arab families held a goodly percentage of the Turkish army's commissions. Their role in winning independence in the secret societies and in the rebellion has been touched on. But as native armed forces began to be built in the pseudo-independent states under mandate between the wars, the aristocratic atmosphere gave way to a more bourgeois and national one. The officers made their way up from more varied social origins than before, representing not any particular class but gradually becoming identified with the nation

---

[15] See the recent study by P. J. Vatikiotis, *The Egyptian Army in Politics* (Bloomington, 1961).

as a whole, perhaps before any other single group. Their broadened view is understandable in the light of their normal reactions to such primary symbols of the nation as the flag, the uniform, and the national anthem, and their being stationed throughout the national territory. In their nationalist fervor these officers, whether followers of the Ikhwan or adepts of the Ba'th party, have often been tinged with a puritanical streak. (This prudish austerity is typical of and explains much about both Nasser and Iraq's late Kassem, as different as they were in other facets of their characters. The role of such men in disciplining corrupt, disorganized societies has been, in the Arab world as elsewhere, noteworthy and valuable.) As soon as their national consciousness became developed and they were in a position to take action, the officers tended to do so, and with violence.

The result was the generation of "coupism" from which the Middle East suffered beginning in Iraq (seven uprisings from 1936 to 1941, in addition to those of 1952, 1958, and 1962-63), taken up in Syria (five between 1949 and 1954), and culminating in Egypt in 1952. While the situation, especially in Iraq, is not yet stable, the last upheavals in the two political centers of the Arab world—Cairo and Baghdad—have been of a nature different from what was seen before, perhaps an indication that the area is beginning to move out of a military adventurist period into something new.

Proletarianization

One might wish to correlate the increased emphasis on social justice in the literature of the past years with the reformist nature of the regimes in Egypt and Iraq and wonder whether the patterns of power are not becoming steadily more popularized, with the deciding voice the wishes and desires of the proletariat, no matter how little the mechanisms of democracy in the Western sense may exist.

The role of the proletariat as a primary instigator and carrier of nationalism comes out most forcefully in the North African version of Arabism, a movement sufficiently separate from the mainstream of Arab nationalist development that it has not been mentioned up to now.

The Arab Maghrib (Morocco, Algeria, and Tunisia) has always been somewhat set apart from the eastern heartland of the Arab world by several important particularisms. If we accept the cultural-linguistic definition of Arabism we cannot discuss racial separateness as an element, but even without that characteristic, both history and geography have given a distinctive cachet to Maghribi national growth within the total Arab framework. In contrast to the Middle East, two fundamentals come to mind at once about North Africa. It has never been a fertile, idea-producing area at any period in its history, whether Punic, Berber, Roman, Byzantine, or Arab, and with rare exceptions it did not develop a traditional urban civilization of the same quality, influence, and transmitting power as those of Cairo, Aleppo, Damascus, and Baghdad.

Whether North Africa's paucity of intellectuals is cause or effect is a pointless argument. In any event those few of whom the area boasts, like Ibn Khaldun and Ibn Battuta, usually came from outside or made their name under external stimulus by traveling and living abroad. A distinguished bourgeois culture existed in Fez, Tetuán, and Salé in Morocco, for a time in Tlemcen and Constantine in Algeria, and more durably in Tunis and the coastal Sahel of eastern Tunisia. It had, however, to be constantly supplied from afar by transfusions of blood, thought, or techniques—whether from Muslim Spain through the caliphate of Cordova and its heirs, or later by the Moriscos expelled from Andalusia, or from the East by the Idrisites, the later Sharifian dynasties, and the recurrent ideas of religious rectification brought back by pilgrims from the Orient. This urban Arab culture of the Maghrib lived an uneasy life, rubbing against but not off on the recalcitrant Berber countryside that hemmed it in and kept it from becoming thoroughly diffused.

Later the colonial history of North Africa further distinguished it from the Arab East, and was crucial in disturbing the timing of the Maghribi nationalist awakening. The small and parochial intellectual class had already been isolated for some time from its Middle Eastern brethren as the Maghrib slumbered on through the eighteenth and early nineteenth centuries in isolated inertia. But it was completely cut off even from the possibility of further ties by the French occupation of Algeria, beginning in 1830, and of Tunisia in 1881. In consequence there was no real Maghribi participation in the Levantine and Egyptian revival of the nineteenth century and, save for an abortive home-made Tunisian stirring around mid-century which came to naught when the French arrived, no equivalent to the Eastern intellectual dawn. It might be added that colonialism should not perhaps be saddled with all the guilt, for there are grounds for suspecting that even without its pall, the dynamism of the East would not have existed. The culture carriers in North Africa, being once removed from the main line, were not sufficiently familiar with their own heritage; and, something always significant in Arabism where language is not simply a phenomenon of culture but a vehicle without which culture cannot move, neither were the intellectuals sufficiently at home in what was theoretically their mother tongue, but was in reality far removed from the decadent *patois* in use.

The settler colonization imposed in North Africa applied another important brake by blocking any movement into the middle class and inhibiting the development of the minuscule bourgeoisie. Apart from a serious splitting of the Maghribi personality through a forced "gallicization," the only mobility encouraged by the French occupation was the creation of a large urban proletariat, aptly described as city nomads, which sprang up in response to the impact of a commercial and industrial exploitation more pronounced in North Africa than in the Middle East.

By about the time of World War II, this swelling force had become a major factor in the area and was ready to be enlisted by whatever leaders it could find. Aspirant leadership groups varied depending on local conditions. In Tunisia after a passing attempt by the upper bourgeoisie to adopt a nationalist posture just after World War I (the old Destour Party), Habib Bourguiba formed the Neo-Destour in 1934 and seized leadership for the *arriviste* merchants of the Sahel and the lower-middle class politicians who saw the advantage of opposing a "popular" party to the ill-organized defenders of the Beylical regime.

In Morocco, where nationalist development was more retarded, the bourgeoisie and some conservative religious figures of Fez played an important part in the first efforts to formulate a nationalist position, beginning in the mid-1930s and coming to a head with the manifesto of 1944. But by the end of that decade the Istiqlal was already attempting to become a mass party, and the resistance movement of 1953-1956 completed the popular coloration of Moroccan nationalism as unknown, underground groups emanated from the silent masses and by violent, direct action inflicted a major change of direction on Moroccan politics. This populism has been disguised to some extent since the return of the king to the throne and the proclamation of independence (1956) because of a continuing confusion in the orthodox religious Moroccan mind between the spiritual and the temporal. But the "popular monarchy," the constant need to adjust policy in answer to internal pressure from the left, the increasingly "self-made" label on the lapels of rising politicians, the strength of the labor movement, in short everything about Moroccan political life today points up the degree of the "proletarianization" of power now prevalent.

The extreme example, however, is Algeria, where the national consciousness, slight to begin with, was trampled out in more than a century of European domination and immigration. The Europeans, who by 1920 formed one-sixth of the population and were a large majority in all urban areas, solidly entrenched themselves as the functioning middle-class element and formed as well a local landed aristocracy. At the same time French intellectual attraction formed, or deformed, most young Algerian thinkers and inevitably ground down the last few traditional avenues of thought that resisted. But as seeming evidence of the fact that nationalist energy, like a psychosomatic illness, will if frustrated in one place erupt somewhere else, the leaders of the revolution and the shapers of the new Algeria have been found and taken from the obscure "classless" sources. Ferhat Abbas, a pharmacist's son, is almost devoid of any Arabic culture; Belkacem Krim, a self-taught former enlisted man in the French army, rose to be foreign minister of the provisional government; others among the revolutionaries were postal clerks, mechanics, farmers, or quite simply without profession. Partly because of this eclecticism in the rise of leaders, and partly because Algeria *in extremis* may have required a kind of positive nihilism, the Algerian motivation today is proudly anti-traditional, anti-intellectual, and anti-bourgeois.

The mythology of all the North African revolutionary movements bears out this general tendency, for nowhere does political man reveal himself more than in his choice of heroes. If a Bourguiba who progressively moves closer to the masses prevails in Tunisia today while the once honored nationalist Moncef Bey is forgotten, the martyrs of the resistance in Morocco begin to take precedence over Muhammad V in many eyes, and the semi-clandestine Muhammad Basri emerges from anonymity to suit the national mood. Similarly in Algeria it is the anonymous grenade thrower, the unknown *fellagha*, and the organizer of the Casbah demonstrations who seize the imagination of a nationalist mass craving identification and self-glorification. It is striking how far we have come from the hero-amir Faisal riding out of the medieval desert, or the hero-officer Nasser overthrowing the corrupt pashas and the idle rich of Cairo. The royal savior and the dashing military figure are not in the dreams of the North African proletariat, which has in this respect leapfrogged a position still widely held in the Arab Middle East.[16]

There is perhaps a relationship to be studied between the "proletarianization" of leadership and the degree of violence practiced by a nationalism inspired from below in a seemingly spontaneous way, rather than as the result of a hierarchically ordered evolution. But what is clear is that "proletarianization" offers greater possibilities for future mobility in political action and in breaking with tradition than is found in more stratified nationalist hierarchies. Taking into account the limitation imposed by the quality of its human capital, Algeria gives every indication of becoming the most experimental, radical and open-ended Arab sub-society in existence.

The Special Nature of Arab Nationalism

It may be a drawback for a writer to see his subject matter in a prototypical or perhaps even unique light, but a summing up

---

[16] Although it is too early to assay it from a historical point of view, the long-term pervasive and direct influence of the European labor movement, as represented in North Africa by the CGT, SFIO, *et al.*, may have been decisive in orienting the Maghribi urban proletariat.

of the emergence of modern Arab nationalism must include several elements which have imparted to it a distinctive flavor. One that stands out immediately is the long gestation period and the slow changeover from thought to action; Arab nationalism grew up in an age when time was not so telescoped as today. Another point is the degree to which nationalism was a part of and dependent on a general cultural revival. Perhaps the Arab world in this century is in the first pages of a renaissance that may ultimately be comparable to the changes that took place in Western society in the fifteenth century. If this is so its roots, still insufficiently studied, may prove to go back deeply into those immediately preceding centuries usually held to be infertile. It is, of course, useless speculation to conjecture that the modern revival could have come about without the catalyst of the West; in fact the awakening was shaped by multiple causes of which the West was an important one, but only one.

In discussing the Arab world, however, an important point should be kept in mind: the continuing sense of historical rivalry with the West, the bipolar attraction and repugnance, and the tension between unity and separateness in the Mediterranean *oikoumene*. The Arabs of the early caliphate took to secular Hellenism but bent it to their image just as Islam claimed to rectify Roman-Byzantine Christianity and return monotheistic truth to a more Semitic mold. There is reason to suspect that the same thing may be happening in our time. Western scientific and political thought are being absorbed while Islam starts to cast about in search of an adjustment to the world order of today. Finally, throughout this whole cloth runs the recurring thread of re-establishment and reconstitution. Nationalism is not only a means of creating a strong new world but a way of bringing about the worldly equivalent of the eternal happiness of paradise. From nationalism's almost indivisible association with the religious tradition comes its need to shake itself free and stand alone. Whether it can do so remains to be seen.

In addition to its peculiarities of development, Arab nationalism confronts special problems today. The insufficiency of the national concept exposes it to attack on grounds of supra-nationalism as well as of localism. Still many Arabs would claim that the nation is simply battling against regionalism and factionalism in this struggle. But sooner or later a decision must be made about primary loyalties and the question solved as to whether the individual Arab state in the future can continue to grow and live organically and command the respect and the allegiance of its citizens. For this reason the United Arab Republic, the first and only living workshop of *qawmiyyah* principles, is important. Upon its course much in the next decade will depend. As with the Holy Roman Empire, it might be considered in all seriousness just how united (complete union, federation, confederation, or alliance), how Arab (rather than Muslim-Arab), and how republican (in actuality and not on paper) a future, unitary Arab state can or should be. For the moment strong centrifugal forces are at work: geographic particularities, established institutions, the imprint of the various colonizing powers, the special economic interests, and the increasingly diversified life habits in each country. But there are also powerful centripetal forces: the unification of the language under the influence of modern terminology aided by the communications media; similar radio, films, and publications; the increasing human contacts with loan teachers, exchange students, pilgrims, and tourists; a heightened awareness of a common historical and cultural fund; and, for the majority, a drawing together in religion.

The degree and nature of the Islamic content of Arab nationalism remains the final overwhelming problem. Westerners may tend to view the separation of church and state in the light of their own experience. But the problem is there for Muslim-Arabs despite the efforts of many to ignore it. The cries for an Algerian Algeria, raised in the city of Algiers in December 1960, at once changed to calls for a Muslim Algeria, but most *qawmiyyah-*nationalist papers in Beirut were embarrassed enough to change the dispatches to read "Arab Algeria," and a spokesman for the Algerian National Liberation Front deplored the incident. It is difficult to find a clearer example of deep popular feelings of self-identification and the trouble these sentiments cause dilettante theorists.

Two signposts might be watched in the coming years to see the kind of relationship nationalism develops with Islam. The first is the case of Tunisia, currently leading the way in separating as much as possible the material and the spiritual, to see if a small, homogeneous Muslim state can become a body in which the highest emphasis is successfully put on the Tunisian-ness of the citizen instead of his Muslim-ness. The second is Lebanon, a fragmented and heterogeneous collection of religious minorities, to see if Muslims and non-Muslims, all of whom claim to be nationalists of one or another kind, can subordinate religious differences to the idea of creating a state which will be a living force and not merely an arbiter between mutually exclusive groups.

If it is true that nationalism is an indivisible by-product of the Arab renaissance, nationalism is also helping to spark a reformation and a reassessment of the role of religion in modern Arab life in its deepest sense. This trend gives it a certain title of nobility. If we reflect, too, that in addition to passing through these two life-crises simultaneously the Arab world also is undergoing an industrial revolution of the nineteenth century Western type, embellished with the social upheavals of the present day, and is being pulled relentlessly into the technological uncertainties of tomorrow, there is reason to attempt a dispassionate yet sympathetic understanding of its difficulties.

Chapter

7

□□□□□□□□□□□

A National Ideology for Development:

Brazil

FRANK BONILLA

Brazil is a nation of pragmatists. Unembarrassed by rigid commitment to ideas or principles, the Brazilian is a skillful temporizer—tractable where others are unyielding, attentive to practical consequences rather than to the dictates of theory. These, at any rate, are traits Brazilians analyzing themselves often point to as central and distinctive elements of the Brazilian personality. Gilberto Freyre, probably the best known student of Brazilian culture, considers the national genius for compromise the key to Brazil's success in Europeanizing the tropics.[1] Other analysts similarly explain Brazil's generally peaceful evolution, in contrast to the more turbulent histories of neighboring republics, in terms of the talent for conciliation and accommoda-

[1] Gilberto Freyre, *New World in the Tropics*, New York: 1959.

tion that Brazilians allegedly inherit from the Portuguese.[2] In contemporary Brazil a quality that is highly prized and widely recognized as extremely Brazilian is *jeito*, which is essentially ingenuity in bending law, regulation, or principle to the moment's need.[3]

Whether or not one chooses to go along with such broadly drawn images of the Brazilian character, major social and political transitions in Brazil have in fact been achieved without the support of formalized political programs or bodies of doctrine and without the mobilization of mass opinion. The major turning points of Brazilian history—the establishment of an independent monarchy in 1822, the shift to a republican form of government in 1889, and the Vargas revolution of 1930—were all ideologically unguided accommodations to underlying economic and social changes. These events were accompanied by substantial realignments of power, albeit within a framework that remained in important ways undisturbed, for the chief contenders were not importantly divided by competing visions of a new society. The absence of widespread violence in these moments of crisis has been celebrated, perhaps justifiably, as a victory of the Brazilian's innate moderation and good sense. But the relative smoothness of these transitions also has been seen as a symptom of the small role played by ideas in the life of a nation given to drift and improvisation.[4]

This unpropitious background sharpens the surprise of finding in Brazil today a well-elaborated nationalist ideology that is more than a makeshift of the moment, that seriously seeks to create for itself a viable intellectual footing. Modern Brazilian nationalists, of course, have plausible theories about why nationalistic thought could flower only at this particular moment

[2] This theme is extensively explored by João Cruz Costa, *Contribuição à História das Idéias no Brasil*, Rio de Janeiro: 1956. See especially pp. 341 ff. and 436 ff.
[3] Roberto de Oliveira Campos, "A Sociologia do Jeito," *Senhor*, July 1960.
[4] "Our greatest successes always smack of empiricism and improvisation imposed by chance circumstance." José Maria Bello, *História da República*, Rio de Janeiro: 1940, as quoted in João Cruz Costa, *op. cit.*, p. 342. Florestan Fernandes remarks, "Our principal political writers have amply demonstrated that the great movements in the political life of the nation were carried out without the support of public opinion and without profound and lasting popular aspirations." *Mudanças Sociais no Brasil*, São Paulo: 1960, p. 89.

in the history of Brazil.[5] But still it is of singular interest that for once theory should seem to run so far ahead of events in Brazil, for nationalism is not a powerful, organized movement in the country. While each of the major political parties claims to be the best defender of the national interest, none is firmly committed to a coherent program that can be called "nationalist." Although politicians in and out of government evidently operate on the belief that the mass of Brazilians is generally responsive to nationalistic appeals, the parties that relied most heavily on those appeals were decisively defeated in the last presidential elections. In the opinion of major Brazilian nationalist thinkers consulted by the writer, the men and the political formulas capable of mobilizing and setting in motion a broad-based nationalistic movement in Brazil have yet to appear. Still, the importance of the ideological groundwork that has been laid, the potential vitality of the nationalist message in a country that is in a process of dramatic growth and consolidation, and the influence wielded by importantly placed nationalists must not be underestimated.

National Unity and Cleavage of Interests

The voices being raised in the name of nationalism in Brazil are many and varied. Pronouncements on the theme come from every side—from politicians, educators, churchmen, social scientists, soldiers. Thus in examining the substantial output of Brazilian nationalist writing, the reader can miss the underlying unity of ideas by focusing on the surface fragmentation of opinion regarding immediate policies or by overattention to the variety of political and personal motives that inspire individual nationalist ideologists. There is a fair degree of consensus about what is intolerable in the present situation and also about what is desired for the nation.

The things nationalist-minded Brazilians want for their country make a familiar list. They want planned action toward a highly productive economy of self-sustained growth controlled

[5] Nelson Werneck Sodré, *Raizes Históricas do Nacionalismo Brasileiro*, Rio de Janeiro: 1960. See also Álvaro Vieira Pinto, *Ideologia e Desenvolvimento Nacional*, Rio de Janeiro: 1960.

by Brazilians, higher standards of living for all, an independent foreign policy, and an end to the alienation and discontent born of prolonged inferior status. Many justifiably see their country as potentially equipped for major hemispheric and world leadership. Because this surface unity of ideas and goals exists and because the current communist tactic is to underplay divisive issues, a casual inspection of nationalist writing in Brazil could also easily fail to spot the bedrock point of discord among Brazilian nationalists—whether the "developed" economy of the future is ultimately to be socialist, capitalist, or some intermediate form of statism.

The intellectual fountainheads of contemporary nationalism in Brazil are the *Instituto Superior de Estudos Brasileiros* (ISEB) and the *Revista Brasiliense*. The *Editora Fulgor*, a São Paulo publishing house, and *O Semanário*, a Rio weekly, have also provided a stream of nationalist writing. The latter two sources are more stridently polemical; since they lack the scholarly pretensions of ISEB and the *Revista Brasiliense*, they are more topical, more aggressive, and more casual in the use of data. As recognized leftist "organs of struggle" (*orgãos de luta*) their function has been one of combat, exhortation, and tireless reaffirmation rather than ideological theorizing.

ISEB and the *Revista Brasiliense* are more ambitious intellectual enterprises. ISEB formally came into existence in the middle of 1955, though the group that gave the new institute its initial impulse had published some significant work as early as 1953.[6] Set up within the Ministry of Education as an independent unit for study and research at the graduate level, ISEB was invested with "full administrative autonomy and full liberty of research, opinion, and teaching." Its objectives were "the study, teaching, and dissemination of the social sciences, especially sociology, history, economics, and political science, with the special objective of applying the categories and data of these sciences to the analysis and critical understanding of Brazilian reality with a view to the elaboration of theoretical instruments

---

[6] *Cadernos de Nosso Tempo* published five numbers beginning in October-December 1953. The founders of ISEB were then still part of an unofficial group called the *Instituto Brasileiro de Economia, Sociologia, e Política*.

that will permit the stimulation and promotion of national development."[7] Just two months later, in September 1955, the *Revista Brasiliense* appeared in São Paulo, professing similar aims but without the official sponsorship or the organizational resources of ISEB. Like ISEB, the *Revista* sponsors affirmed that the guidelines for a truly national program and ideology of development could flow only from the study in depth of Brazil's economic, social, and political problems.[8]

Although the *Revista Brasiliense* and ISEB went into action almost simultaneously and their ideological lines over the subsequent years have been the same in almost every particular, there was absolutely no overlap between the organizers of the *Revista* and the ISEB group. The ideological gulf between the "left" nationalists of the *Revista Brasiliense* and the "right" nationalists among those who had created ISEB came momentarily into the open in 1958. This clash between the *Revista* and ISEB occurred over an ISEB publication that irritated leftist nationalists on two principal points—first by arguing that the Brazilian bourgeoisie can still take the leadership in the process of national development, thus averting a more violent and costly socialist revolution; and second by taking a conciliatory attitude with respect to foreign participation in the exploitation of Brazil's oil resources.[9]

ISEB was reputedly "fascist" in its beginnings as it is now reputedly "communist." But the fact is that from the start various

[7] *Decreto* 37608, July 14, 1955, published in the *Diário Oficial* for July 15, 1955. The idea of creating ISEB originated among a group of young but strategically placed advisers to the government during the last months of the Vargas regime. The group came to be known as "*O Grupo Itatiaia*" after a national park where they met for weekends of study and discussion.

[8] See *Revista Brasiliense*, No. 31, September-October 1960, pp. 1-3.

[9] The book in question was Hélio Jaguaribe's *O Nacionalismo na Atualidade Brasileira*, Rio de Janeiro: 1958. No issue before or since has so clearly polarized nationalist feeling in Brazil as did the fight to establish *Petroleo Brasileiro, S.A.* (Petrobras), the state oil company. Since October 1953 Petrobras has had a monopoly on the exploration, extraction, and refining of Brazilian oil, though a small number of private Brazilian refineries have been allowed to continue operation. Foreign companies participate only in the marketing phase, chiefly of imported oil products required to make up the difference between Petrobras production and national needs. The story of Petrobras is of undeniable importance in the development of Brazilian nationalism but is not essential to the exposition of nationalist ideas as such.

points of view have been represented in the group. The book that provoked the attack from the *Revista Brasiliense* also split ISEB, leading eventually to the withdrawal from the *Instituto* of the author and some of his colleagues. ISEB's work has not been distinguished for its doctrinal purity. The irreconcilable division of minds that produced the open rift in 1958 was already foreshadowed in the introduction to the first major publication of the founding group, *A Crise Brasileira (Cadernos de Nosso Tempo*, October-December 1953), a comprehensive analysis of Brazil's situation that also outlined a policy of national development. In his prefatory remarks, the writer who was acting as reporter for the group stated:

> The author himself shares certain reservations that arose in the course of the discussions. These recognize especially that the socialization of the means of production, recommended in the report, cannot be carried out without taking into account the objective conditions of maturity that the economic structure and the various sectors of production in the nation may show. That reservation does not appear in the text, but it should be emphasized that it is made purely from an economic-sociological point of view and constitutes in no way a tactical concession to those interested in the private ownership of the means of production.

ISEB thus began activities with a heterodox group that gave promise of providing a setting in which genuine debate and scholarly work might be possible. Clashes of personality, factional disputes, and doctrinal squabbles have marred and discredited the *Instituto*'s work. Yet ISEB is important and perhaps unique in being an officially sponsored institution for research and study that set out deliberately to formulate a national ideology of development. The fate of ISEB might have been quite different under a regime like that of Getúlio Vargas, which it was designed to serve. The *Instituto* is remarkable in having managed to survive and operate despite indifferent support from the government, great internal problems, and powerful enemies.[10]

[10] A special supplement of a Rio daily, *O Globo*, on March 25, 1960, was entirely given over to an attack on ISEB by a group called "The National Committee for the Defense of Democracy." On November 11, 1960, the

At this writing the future of ISEB is in doubt. But whatever its fate, ISEB has in the last six years unquestionably shaped the thinking of a substantial number of importantly placed Brazilians through its extensive publications, courses, and public lectures. By the end of 1960 ISEB had a large array of original and translated works in print and in preparation.[11] Thirty-eight students successfully completed the year-long graduate-level course that ISEB offered for the fifth time in 1960. That course normally requires full-time attendance and is primarily open to middle-level government functionaries and military officers. The course covers five major fields: economics, sociology, political science, history, and philosophy.[12] In addition to the regular course, special seminars, conferences, and short courses were presented during the year in Rio and in other major cities. In the academic vacation period during January and February of 1961, one hundred or so students gathered on twenty-five evenings for a compressed version of the full ISEB course. They heard lectures nightly on such themes as "The Worldwide Anti-Colonial Movement," "Relations of Power and Economic Development," "Philosophy as a Metropolitan Conception of the World," "The Philosophy of the Process of Development: Theory and Contradictions," and "Sociological Aspects of Imperialism."

ISEB lectures could hardly be expected consistently to provide solid substance of a scholarly quality on all of these themes. If a propagandistic note creeps in or on occasion dominates a presentation, that should also occasion no surprise. Of first importance is the fact that so many of the titles do point to key problems and place them within the context of a specific discipline. The desire to bring the knowledge of social science systematically to bear on the analysis of Brazil's present situation

Corrêio da Manhã announced that the election of Janio Quadros meant the sure death of ISEB and printed an advance epitaph on its editorial page.
[11] Unfortunately no one of the works originally in Portugese is available in English translation.
[12] The alumni association of ISEB graduates began publishing a column in O Semanário, the nationalist weekly, in April 1961, with the avowed mission of carrying on the job of disseminating the ISEB ideology of Brazilian development. Until it stopped appearing in mid-1961, O Semanário claimed a circulation of about 59,000. O Semanário, No. 756, April 19-26, 1961.

and prospects for growth is perhaps ISEB's most notable contribution and reflects strongly the imaginative and serious effort of the founding Itatiaia group. In this effort the Brazilians were innovating in an area where more advanced countries continue to lag. The early work by the originators of ISEB set an intellectual standard for nationalist theorizing that has strongly influenced both in content and style nationalist writing of whatever political inspiration in Brazil. The group moreover succeeded from the beginning in identifying Brazilian problems at a level of analysis and abstraction that anticipates and illuminates problems in quite different national contexts. Thus, unexpectedly and in demonstration of the breadth of Brazilian thinking, this survey of current nationalist thought in Brazil can begin with a comparison between the first major pronouncement on national problems and policy of the ISEB founders and a recent publication of the Center for the Study of Democratic Institutions in the United States.

Economic Development, Planning, and the New Rationalism

Most of the comparisons that follow are between two documents published seven years apart: *A Crise Brasileira* appeared in 1953, *The Economy Under Law* in 1960.[13] The first was, as has been noted, a joint pronouncement of the *Instituto Brasileiro de Economia, Sociologia, e Política*, the forerunner of ISEB. Many of the ideas put forward in it have been echoed repeatedly in later nationalist writings. *The Economy Under Law*, published by the Center for the Study of Democratic Institutions, is accompanied by an extensive discussion among consultants of that organization.[14]

---

[13] Hélio Jaguaribe, "A Crise Brasileira," *Cadernos de Nosso Tempo*, October-December 1953, No. 1; W. H. Ferry, *The Economy Under Law*, Santa Barbara: 1960.
[14] The Center for the Study of Democratic Institutions is an offshoot of the Ford Foundation's Fund for the Republic. According to its masthead, "The work of the Center is directed at clarifying basic questions of freedom and justice, especially those constitutional questions raised by the emergence of twentieth century institutions. Among the areas being studied are the economic order, the political process, law, communications, war as an institution, the American character." The Itatiaia

The striking convergences of thought in the two documents are not catalogued here as evidence of the generality and hence "correctness" of the views stated. Even less are the comparisons intended as an affirmation of the basic harmony of interests of advanced and underdeveloped nations. But this exercise can, at the same time that it reveals central aspects of nationalist thinking in Brazil, also caution development-minded nationalists who often speak as though development will provide a perfect resolution to present difficulties. As the lines to follow clearly show, the advanced nations have not by-passed or resolved all the important problems that are now in the forefront of attention in "immature" countries. Finally, the ideas outlined here underscore a genuine common problem and possibly a present danger for all nations—that is, the question of the functions and mechanisms of planning in a democracy and the increasing acceptance among social scientists, especially non-economists, of planning functions at the national and international level.

For the moment, in Brazil, the core objective of nationalism is economic development. However broadly or with whatever varying emphases the "developed society" may be defined, at the heart of the vision is a smooth-running, highly productive, industrial apparatus whose control lies within the nation and whose product is primarily divided according to some equitable arrangement among Brazilians themselves. If Brazil were a truly underdeveloped nation, or perhaps somewhat more developed than at present, Brazilian nationalism might have a more revolutionary cast. As it is, no nationalist group has come forth for a maximum mobilization of national resources behind a drive for development, including the regimentation of consumption and production that such an effort would require. Increased direction and central planning of development by the state are generally accepted keystones of nationalist doctrine, but the actual legal and administrative framework within which such state activity would function is seldom spelled out.

---

group among whom the idea of ISEB was then germinating similarly set out with "a program of work consisting of the clarification of problems related to the economic, sociological, political, and cultural interpretation of our time, with particular emphasis on the analysis of contemporary political ideas and phenomena and the systematic and historical study of Brazil simultaneously from the economic, sociological, political, and cultural point of view."

This search for a viable middle road between capitalism and socialism is a basic link between much of the nationalist writing in Brazil and the questions currently being raised by some thoughtful Americans.[15] Both points of view begin with the conviction that the present moment is critical, that the existing economic system is inefficient and is failing to realize the full social potential of present technology, and that the state must reclaim the political functions that have been gradually allowed to slip into the hands of powerful private corporations. Brazilians, who are most absorbed by problems of growth, do not discount the fact that some "spontaneous" growth has already occurred, but say that private enterprise, and especially *foreign* private enterprise, cannot be expected to formulate and even less to finance a well-coordinated plan for development.[16] The United States's problems are of a similar order; they are basically connected with establishing norms for growth and distribution of income. Says Ferry, the author of the basic paper in *The Economy Under Law*:

> It is no longer a private affair that the steel industry has been producing at less than a 55 per cent rate, nor that the petroleum industry has no idea what to do about excess capacity, nor that the auto builders and others are laying off employees (or not hiring) because of automation and foreign competition. The rationalizing and equilibrating mechanisms which are supposed to correct such situations simply do not function and the nation suffers.[17]

Political and legal direction of the economy is an imperative not only to prevent internal dislocations but to make possible

[15] The views quoted here from *The Economy Under Law* are chiefly those of the author of the basic paper, W. H. Ferry, and those of A. A. Berle, who supported Mr. Ferry's position in the discussion that followed. Mr. Berle, a former ambassador to Brazil, reputedly met with an unexpected rebuff from former Brazilian President Quadros on a special mission to Brazil in 1961. Though there were official denials at the time of any clash between the two men, and some of the local press chided President Quadros for his alleged rudeness to Mr. Berle, the incident was a source of satisfaction to many Brazilians, including many who would indignantly disavow the label of "nationalist."
[16] Ignácio Rangel, *Recursos Ociosos na Economia Nacional*, Rio de Janeiro: 1960.
[17] W. H. Ferry, *op. cit.*, p. 28.

a firm and coherent foreign policy. The need for political control
of the economy is justified on approximately the same grounds
by Mr. Ferry speaking about the United States in 1960, as it
was for Brazil by the ISEB founding group in 1953. The Ferry
statement runs as follows:

> No one has claimed that an "unintervened" market
> would result in a rate of national growth commensurate
> with obligations to our own citizens and to those abroad
> whose situation is both desperate and of selfish importance
> to us. Such basic economic decisions will have to be brought
> into the realm of public responsibility. . . . Otherwise our
> future will continue to be determined by economic choices
> made privately, choices having to do with domestic matters
> such as the rate of growth and type of capital investment
> and internationally with the amount of foreign investment
> and the type of regime with which business is to be done.[18]

Once the economy has become "deprivatized," the early *ISEBistas*
tell us, foreign policy ". . . ceases being merely tutelary of
private interests that adjust one another to become a system
of concrete interests at the service of internal necessities."[19]
Both of the documents explicitly confront the basic dilemma of
forging a path between capitalism and socialism. Ferry calls
for creativity and imagination in legislation and for the invention
of new forms of organization; the Brazilians coin the phrase *a
desprivatização da economia* to describe the gradual politicizing
of the economy that they propose. Both documents recognize and
lament the fact that the process is one of drift rather than
directed movement toward the planned society. Hard pressed by
his fellow consultants to distinguish his point of view from
socialism, Ferry replied: "I think there is something brand new
emerging here as well as in Europe which is certainly not capitalism. If you wish, you can call it socialism. Several of my less
friendly critics suggested that the new fascism was being proposed here. Naturally, I don't agree to that statement."[20] *A Crise
Brasileira*, seven years before, had made the same point.

[18] *Ibid.*, p. 22.
[19] *Cadernos de Nosso Tempo*, October-December 1953, p. 160.
[20] W. H. Ferry, *op. cit.*, p. 31.

Pure capitalism does not exist in any contemporary nation. And in all countries there is a growing tendency to transfer the control of production from private to public initiative, even though past experience with nationalization has dissipated a certain hopefulness about the excellence of such a transformation.[21]

Thus the extension of political controls over the economy is favored chiefly as a means of rationalizing and accelerating economic growth, and secondly as a means of bringing areas where collective interests are at stake back into the framework of responsible governmental action. The politicians do not have to prove that they are better managers than the corporate executives; the affirmation is simply that matters of collective interest must be handled through public institutions.[22]

The crisis of our times, say these men, is not only institutional but moral as well. The general condition in Brazil and the United States, as they paint it, is one of profound alienation; the individual lacks any vision of a collective or private design that can invest his life with meaning. The institutional machinery is inert because it lacks direction and is therefore incapable of motivating and sustaining action. There is an absence of what ISEB thinkers call "a project" and what A.A. Berle refers to as "the transcendental margin." As Ferry states:

Most men, however successful, are not satisfied with their lives. An epidemic of alienation spreads as people feel their own destinies slipping out of their control. The sense of unease is pervasive, because there seem to be only trifling choices to be made about central issues. Our well-being in a world of want makes us feel guilty, but not guilty enough to make a profound political issue out of it. We ignore poverty and hardship and inequality in our own midst.[23]

The nationalist diagnosis of the Brazilian state of mind parallels Mr. Ferry's.

[21] *Cadernos de Nosso Tempo*, October-December 1953, p. 146.
[22] W. H. Ferry, *op. cit.*, p. 35.
[23] *Ibid.*, pp. 8 and 9.

In the Brazilian case it is the very generalized absence of a collective project—the lack of will in the collectivity, the state of waking sleep-walking—that gives to the nation the aspect of a geographical place, a *topos* where things happen, where rather than being made, history, in its most commonplace facets—in government, administration, in personal relations—merely occurs.[24]

The *ISEBistas* have a ready formula to fill this lack; what is required is a national ideology of development. The "project" that can galvanize the disoriented, alienated masses is to build the economic power and consolidate the political sovereignty of the nation.

To an important extent the new social power of the state and nation flowing from new forms of loyalty and participation is seen by *ISEBistas* as springing naturally and inevitably from ongoing economic changes. The ideologist's job is to give intellectual substance, coherence, and direction to the social processes in motion. Nationalism is at once a way of expressing fundamental changes occurring in Brazilian society, and of anticipating and orienting further change. As the central value of economic development, say *ISEBistas*, nationalism is not only appropriately but inevitably the key to mobilizing human resources for the task of development.

The Americans, more squeamish about open talk of power and already disillusioned with productivity goals, seem to flounder at this point. The following exchange between A.A. Berle and Scott Buchanan, former Dean of St. Johns College, shows the Americans fumbling toward the idea of a secular religion equivalent to that which *ISEBistas* find ready at hand in nationalism.

Berle: There will always be dreams of some kind, and in any group of dreams in a country as large as this there will be a central core which is more or less common to society. Each individual will go beyond that in various ways. The central core represents the hopes and

[24] Oscar Lorenzo Fernandez, "Análise Existencial da Realidade Brasileira," *Cadernos de Nosso Tempo*, No. 4, April-August 1955, p. 161.

dreams and future pictures that a society or a considerable part of a society has chosen as the hoped for goal.

Buchanan: You certainly don't mean as a sort of energy to run your economic system with.

Berle: I mean exactly that. I mean the central core is the source of the additional margin or energy over and above sheer human survival that is required in a highly organized society.

Buchanan: Whose values? Is this hitching up God to drag the economic machine?

Berle: You are adding a few additional ideas.[25]

There is a touch of irony in the fact that as the Brazilian ISEB seemed about to expire, Berle and Ferry were calling for the creation of a parallel institution in the United States. They proposed as a first step in national planning, "the creation of a forum wherein planners can get together and understand one another and coordinate what they are doing." Commented Berle: "What you might like to have would be a group of men in the University who were rather systematically and intentionally trying to do the job that, say, St. Augustine did in his day and a lot of other men of advanced values have done since."[26]

Economic Nationalism and the "Peripheral" Economy

Nationalist theorizing in Brazil is thus committed to and draws its chief strength from the idea of achieving rapid economic development within a framework that would place effective control over the nation's wealth and productive apparatus in the hands of Brazilians. Since there is general agreement that the task of first priority is a determined build-up of the economy, as far as possible from within, nationalists of all political inclinations are for the moment fairly uncritical defenders of national business groups. The right of national entrepreneurs to lead in the process of industrial development is affirmed even though, when pressed, nationalists of the left and of the right readily confess that they have no illusions about the motives or inten-

[25] W. H. Ferry, *op. cit.*, pp. 66 and 67.
[26] *Ibid.*, p. 57.

tions of the industrial and commercial groups. National business leadership is not widely credited with having either the vision or the disposition to serve or defend national interests, except in so far as these interests coincide with the profitable conduct of business.

A fundamental issue dividing economists and laymen in Brazil is, then, whether the nation is capable of continued growth at an acceptable rate on the basis of its own resources, and under what conditions foreign investment will advance rather than hinder the achievement of an autonomous developed economy. One would think that a reasonably objective answer to this question could be readily produced, but no such reply has been forthcoming. All treatments of the problem, however scholarly they may pretend to be, candidly or implicitly begin with assumptions that make the results at best inconclusive. Information about many key factors is simply not available. In any case, the important thing is to see beyond both the anti-United States "hate" literature and the reassurances of friendly "free enterprisers" with respect to this point.

Nationalists prefer to speak of the Brazilian economy as "peripheral" (*periférica*) rather than underdeveloped. The uneven development from region to region and among sectors of the economy has meant that in certain areas Brazil has advanced well into a phase of sustained growth at high levels of productivity and technology while in others it continues in a primitive state. The outstanding fact about Brazil is not "underdevelopment," it is asserted, but rather the multifaceted dependence on the major industrial powers (notably the United States) that Brazil shares with other "peripheral" nations.[27] The nature and degree of that dependence and how it may be broken are major preoccupations among nationalists.

Brazil is clearly far from being in a situation that is in any realistic sense close to that of a newly emancipated colonial nation. Brazil has not had the kind of crippling experience of colonialism that many such nations have suffered; it very amply meets all the conventional criteria of political scientists for sovereign nationhood. To speak of a "rupture in the comple-

[27] Ivan Pedro de Martins, *Introdução a Economia Brasileira*, Rio de Janeiro: 1961, p. 167.

mentarity" of the Brazilian economy and the systems of the major industrial powers with which the country now trades, as some nationalists do, may be premature.[28] Yet the country has advanced sufficiently to think realistically of itself as a reasonably autonomous unit and even to consider seriously competing for foreign industrial markets in the near future. The country is not quite ready to stand alone, but for a variety of reasons—economic, political, and psychological—Brazilians have begun to feel that they have a true option to exercise with respect to choice of creditors and the conditions under which foreign investment will be accepted.

Accumulating evidence of the rapacity, ruthlessness, and indifference to the national interest of foreign operators is no more difficult in Brazil than in any other country where important resources have been developed by private foreign investors. Leftists and others have not neglected this kind of pamphleteering, but there has also been an effort to make a case against private foreign investment that rests on more than an indictment of particular corporations or individuals.[29]

One line of argument has been that withdrawals in profit remittances and other forms quickly leave a negative balance for the country in private capital invested. That is to say, it takes a very short time for a foreign investor to withdraw the equivalent of his initial investment in profits and to become a drain on national capital rather than a contributor. This seems to have been in fact the case in Brazil and elsewhere in Latin America between 1938 and 1955, the period that has been studied most carefully.[30] Under strong encouragement during the administration of President Kubitschek, the net flow in Brazil has been generally positive since 1955, but many nationalists argue that the shift is temporary and that the new investments were won only at the cost of unreasonable concessions to foreign investors.

[28] Cándido Mendes de Almeida, *Perspectiva Atual da América Latina*, Rio de Janeiro: 1960.
[29] The variety of approaches can be seen, for example, in Caio Prado Junior, *História Econômica do Brasil*, 5th ed., São Paulo: 1959; Aristóteles Moura, *Capitais Estrangeiros no Brasil*, São Paulo: 1960; Osny Duarte Pereira, *Estudos Nacionalistas*, São Paulo: 1960, Vols. I and II.
[30] Aristóteles Moura, *op. cit.*, see also United Nations, *Foreign Capital in Latin America*, New York: 1955.

Some nationalist-minded economists also feel that reinvested profits earned in Brazil should not be considered a contribution of new "foreign investment," since such profits represent capital accumulated internally. There are at this writing no limitations on foreign remittances in Brazil, so that nothing impedes a firm from going through the motions of exporting and bringing such funds back in as new investment. That part of the argument is therefore somewhat academic for the moment. Interestingly enough, the practice of financing expansion and new development out of earnings, which has been challenged in the United States as an illegal form of public taxation by corporations,[31] has not drawn much attention in Brazil.

Another practice protested by nationalists is that of allowing foreign companies to raise capital through local bank credits on the basis of patents, equipment, or other guaranty. The fact that foreign banks and investment companies are allowed to accept deposits in Brazil and lend these funds to foreign companies is a further irritant to nationalists, who see both mechanisms as ways in which locally generated capital is often deflected from truly productive investment.[32]

What constitutes a reasonable profit rate and how such rates may be calculated is another focus of argument. The leftist nationalist weekly, *O Semanário*, early in 1961 listed some forty companies, most of them foreign, with profits ranging from 30 to 500 per cent per year. The conservative *Conjuntura Econômica* has reported an average annual profit rate of 23.6 per cent of "nominal" capital (declared capital investment) for 7,104 corporations in 1959. These rates were calculated on the basis of financial statements appearing in the *Diário Oficial*. Steel industry profit rates were 37.1 per cent, rubber 46.7 per cent, mining 49.8 per cent. *Conjuntura Econômica* does not show foreign and national company profit rates separately.[33]

---

[31] "Expansion and new development are being more and more financed out of earnings, and there is less recourse to the stock market and other sources of capital by the large firms. Thus present customers are buying new plant and equipment for Corporation A without receiving anything in return. . . ." W. H. Ferry, *op. cit.*, p. 20.

[32] Sergio de Magalhães, "Investimentos Estrangeiros," *Revista Brasiliense*, No. 23, May-June 1959.

[33] *Conjuntura Econômica*, Vol. XV, No. 2, February 1961, p. 136.

Though such charges can seldom be fully documented, even these high profit rates are widely suspected of being understated through various bookkeeping and other devices. The hidden movement of funds and goods through over- and under-billing is notorious, especially with respect to coffee.[34] Moreover, the revelations of large-scale business fraud and tax evasions are sufficiently frequent to make such charges credible. At any rate current regulations are so permissive and so ineffectually applied that it is impossible to arrive at any clear picture of the full import of the financial transactions of business firms, especially the non-corporate enterprises.

The alternatives that have been suggested include the importation of foreign technology without foreign capital (i.e., the hiring of technicians), importing capital without private companies (through intergovernmental and international agency loans), and a concentration on the mobilization of idle resources through a build-up of internal and external markets permitting full use of the nation's productive potential. Experiments are being made with other forms of financing that seek a combination allowing a maximum use of private foreign capital while keeping financial and managerial control in Brazilian hands. Certainly less capital would be required for future growth if the country were prepared to accept some regimentation, but no group has presented the alternative in quite that way. The austerity program initiated in early 1961 was designed to save free enterprise, though it may paradoxically bring the first legislation in support of the constitutional provisions against abuses of economic power as well as closer regulation of the financial operations of foreign companies.

The urgent dilemmas of the moment, however, are how to curb inflation and how to deal with the nation's crushing indebtedness. It is to meet these pressing obligations that Brazil needs foreign help desperately. On these problems, unfortunately, nationalism as a point of view provides no special clairvoyance. When one descends to the level of weighing the day-to-day policies of the government, nationalists are to be found on every side of the issues. There is little likelihood that private foreign investment will be shut out from Brazil in the

[34] Ivan Pedro de Martins, *op. cit.*, pp. 234 *et seq.*

near future; but the pressures on foreign enterprise to demonstrate a capacity and willingness to integrate effectively with
the national economy will continue to mount.

The New Political Independence

Despite the abundant signs that a fundamental reappraisal
of national capabilities was in progress, the strongly independent
line in foreign policy initiated by the Quadros government excited considerable surprise, apprehension, and perplexity. Two
months after Quadros took office in January 1961, a Rio edi-
torialist quipped that the new President was playing the part
of a Frondizi of Argentina for three days of the week, of a
Fidel Castro for another three days of the week, and that of
Nehru on Sundays. By an adroit combination of conservative
economic reforms and an independent foreign policy, the President, it was generally believed, had been seeking to neutralize
opposition during the rough period of adjustment to basic exchange reforms imposed soon after his inauguration. Quadros'
refusal to speak against the Cuban revolution despite United
States pressures, his readiness to explore the advantages of
diplomatic and commercial relations with socialist countries, as
well as his friendly overtures to neutralist leaders were all
presumably concessions to nationalist sentiment at home that
were expected to make the new austerity more palatable. In
the months that followed, Quadros' innovations in policy
emerged as part of a coherent and carefully thought out effort
to construct a determinedly independent Brazilian policy aimed
at wresting the greatest political and economic advantage possible for Brazil from the existing crisis in international relations
within the hemisphere and in the world at large.

Although these measures did not in fact mollify the more
intransigent nationalists, they were a triumph for nationalist
ideas. The departures in policy won wide acceptance almost at
once, confirming the broad appeal in Brazil of a line strongly
affirmative of national sovereignty. These moves met with general approval even before it became clear that they would not
jeopardize the country's chances for much needed help from

abroad.[35] Apparently, as nationalist thinkers had been saying all along, the firmer and more independent Brazil's position on international issues, the greater the disposition of creditor nations to accommodate new demands.

Many assumed that the Quadros government would be forced to compromise that independent line in some respect in exchange for the economic concessions granted in the United States and elsewhere. The repeated statements of confidence in Quadros by President Kennedy and other United States spokesmen were as often taken as indications of some tacit diplomatic understanding as of a new and genuine respect for Brazilian independence on the part of the United States. The delicacy of the situation was reflected in the lengths to which the government went to avoid the appearance of having been influenced in its economic policies by external demands. The quick and public approval of Brazil's exchange reforms by the International Monetary Fund proved enough of an embarrassment that it was felt necessary for the Minister of Finance to deny explicitly that there had been any capitulation to the Fund in the planning of those reforms. The IMF, affirmed the Minister, had been informed concerning Brazilian plans only as an interested agency.[36] Whatever the facts of the matter, these efforts reflected both the government's calculation of the public mood and its desire to project a new and self-assertive image.

[35] A survey of opinion among legislators and the broad public in Brazil carried out in late 1960 and early 1961 showed widespread support among all political sectors, including the traditionally conservative upper class elements, for a foreign policy expressive of Brazilian independence along the lines undertaken by the Quadros government and carried forward by the Goulart regime that followed. See Lloyd A. Free, *Some Implications of the Political Psychology of Brazilians*, Institute for International Social Research, Princeton: 1961.

[36] An official release appearing in *International Financial News Survey*, March 17, 1961, publication of the International Monetary Fund, gave a rather different impression. It stated: "The Government of Brazil has consulted the International Monetary Fund with regard to changes in its foreign exchange system which become effective on March 14, and which are designed to simplify the system and to introduce more realistic rates of exchange. The Government has notified the Fund that it intends to proceed to simplify the system further. *The Fund has agreed to these changes on the understanding that the new system is to be a temporary one and that it represents a step toward further simplification of the country's exchange system.*" [Italics added.]

The international reactions to this new note in Brazilian foreign policy and the meaning of the internal support this policy apparently enjoys cannot be appraised without considering that for many months there was more talk than action demonstrating a determined independence. Even this talk was accompanied by repeated affirmations of the government's commitment to free, private enterprise, of faithfulness to Western ideals, and of respect for established international obligations. Such restraint and tactfulness coincides with the ISEB thesis that it is the practice of neutralism and not its display that must be systematic.

A newspaper analysis of the concepts of neutralism and neutrality by a key adviser to both the Quadros and the succeeding Goulart governments further illustrates the pragmatic cast that marks Brazilian thinking on this theme. The writer carefully distinguishes between neutrality (a simple refusal to take sides) and neutralism (a genuine move toward an independent position). Neutralism, he notes, may be both tactical and ideological and may or may not include an effort to create a third power bloc. After weighing carefully the pros and cons ("maximizing the advantages and minimizing the disadvantages"), he concludes that the present world situation "justifies neutralist experiments of a tactical type. Delicate as is all navigation on uncharted seas . . ."[37] The present urgency of the need for new markets and the need for greater leverage in the "capacity to extract economic concessions" are clearly posed as the moving considerations for the tactical experiments to come. With reason thus wed to prejudice, a fairly solid closing of the ranks on this issue is possible.

The new independence is thus anchored in practical aims. Brazilian leaders can proceed with caution and restraint because they pursue fairly concrete objectives and are only secondarily concerned with the sheer emotional satisfactions of shaking off real or apparent subservience to United States foreign policy aims. Because the new policy is fundamentally also a drive for

[37] Roberto de Oliveira Campos, "Sôbre o Conceito de Neutralismo," *Corrêio da Manhã*, March 12, 1961. As an "orthodox" economist and a persuasive defender of free enterprise and foreign participation in developing the Brazilian economy, Mr. Campos is not popular among nationalists of the extreme left. He was formerly associated with the *Instituto Superior de Estudos Brasileiros*.

new power, it goes beyond being a simple expedient to deal with the present economic crisis. Involved as well are the consolidation of Brazilian leadership in the hemisphere, prospective markets for Brazil's expanding industrial production, and the enhancement of Brazil's position as a world power through participation in the development of newly freed African nations.[38]

In the rather blood-chilling exercise in *Realpolitik* which closes *O Nacionalismo na Atualidade Brasileira*, the author outlines a policy in which, by judiciously playing all the actual or potential major power blocs off against each other, Brazil will eventually emerge as a major power in itself, completely equipped with a store of advanced ballistic missiles and atomic weapons.[39] There is no reason to doubt that this kind of hard-headed analysis of future possibilities is going on wherever such decisions are being made in Brazil. The new outlook has recently been quite succinctly stated by a former Minister of Finance in a newspaper defense of his dealings with the International Monetary Fund: "Let us not create anew in Brazil the impression that to deal with the Monetary Fund and other credit agencies of friendly countries is an act of submission or *entreguismo. We are already too big and too powerful to feel shy about contending with other nations.*"[40] [Italics added.]

Revitalizing the State

The resolution of tensions stemming from internal political problems does not promise to be as readily achieved as the apparent consensus on a firmer line in international policy.

---

[38] President Quadros in April 1961 created a Brazilian Institute of Afro-Asian Studies. Among its objectives is "to promote the comparative study of development in Brazil and African and Asian countries with a view to a mutually beneficial exchange of experiences, techniques, or solutions." The Institute celebrated its first major conference in April 1962. The new interest in Africa also promises to open Brazil's formerly racially exclusive foreign service to a small number of distinguished Brazilian Negroes.

[39] Hélio Jaguaribe, *op. cit.*

[40] Lucas Lopes, in *Corrêio da Manhã*, March 2, 1961. *Entreguismo* is the nationalist epithet for the act of opening Brazil to foreign penetration or control. Ignácio Rangel, an economist with the National Economic Development Bank writing in Rio's *Última Hora*, April 17, 1961, says: ". . . if imperialism is unable to impose its will on tiny Laos, why should it be able to make us bend our knee."

Nationalists have in fact tended to skirt these issues just as they have shied away from a close examination of the operations of national business groups, except for those most directly linked to foreign investors. Yet this area is one in which the country shows significant lags that seriously inhibit the achievement of the political integration that must accompany desired economic growth and independence. As often happens, an account of these omissions is almost as important to an understanding of nationalist thinking as is the examination of its major themes.

Few political events present such formidable resistance to logical analysis as does a presidential election in Brazil, a fact no less true when the choice of the electorate is as forthright and decided as it was in the presidential contest of October 1960. President Janio Quadros' clean sweep of the national vote in that year was widely celebrated as symbolic of Brazilian progress along the road to effective democracy. The election was noteworthy in several respects. The campaign and the election itself were unmarred by any important incidence of fraud or violence. A candidate in opposition to the government in power campaigned with full freedom, won easily, and was duly installed in office with the blessings of the outgoing chief executive. Yet Quadros' election and brief tenure of office served to throw into glaring focus many of the frailties of Brazilian political institutions.[41]

The choice of candidates and the lineup of forces for the presidential race in themselves pointed to the absence of logically articulated or more than momentarily crystallized connections among parties, personalities, and political principles. But the weakness, confusion, and lack of organic links with defined sectors of the electorate evident in the parties during the campaign was as nothing compared with the general paralysis that followed once the dimensions of Quadros' personal victory were established. *For several months no one knew or would publicly venture a firm prediction about any important policy decision or appointment that the new President would make.* The suspense was genuine—the parties, the press, and the private citizen

---

[41] Frank Bonilla, *Janio Vem Ai; Brazil Elects a President*, American Universities Field Staff Reports Service, Vol. VII, No. 2, East Coast South America Series, October 1960.

gave themselves entirely to what was openly acknowledged to be a guessing game. The *União Democrática Nacional*, the party that had made Quadros its candidate, was as much perplexed in victory about its future role as were its rivals in defeat.

The presence in Alvorada Palace of a powerful personality such as Quadros highlighted not only the persisting weaknesses of Brazilian party structure but also the debilities of the chief institution in which party power theoretically should have its arena of action, the legislature. A distinguished jurist, who has written extensively on nationalist themes, remarked in an interview with the writer:

> My greatest fear for the future has to do with underlying institutional problems, primarily the lack of discipline of our legislators. Our senators and deputies are each a Sputnik in his own individual orbit; neither parties nor voters can control them. The executive has to court each man individually to get a majority together. Our whole system of representation must be overhauled or we may face serious trouble.

A well-known nationalist columnist and state legislator painted for the author much the same picture of how the legislature operates.

> The Congress is powerful but vulnerable to pressures from organized interests—probably not too many are bought outright but their links with specific interests are so notorious that congressmen have lost prestige. Janio's investigations are not just aimed at cleaning up the government but are his way of getting something on as many congressmen as possible so that he can make them do his will.[42]

With the transfer of the national capital to Brasilia, 600 miles inland atop the isolated central *planalto*, these problems of control and organization within the legislature were magni-

---

[42] These remarks should not be taken as indicative of any concerted anti-parliamentary campaign among Brazilian nationalists. In fact, relatively little attention has been given to such concrete problems of political organization.

fied. But over and above the uncertainties and inconveniences of operation in the new capital, the most striking and persistent note in the months after the election was the indecision of the parties with respect to relationships with the Executive and with respect to any policy the new President might conceivably embrace. Dissident factions seeking to revitalize and give some distinctive meaning to party platforms appeared in every major party—"the compacts" of the *Partido Trabalhista Brasileiro*, the "new wave" of the *União Democrática Nacional*, and the "young wing" of the *Partido Social Democrático*. None of these reformist groups succeeded in seriously challenging the control of the entrenched old-line politicians. To compound the fragmentation and confusion among the standing parties, there were also loose coalitions among *deputados* across party lines. The older of these blocs was the Nationalist Parliamentary Front (*Frente Parlamentar Nacionalista*), and the newest, the *Ação Democrática*, which proposed to counter the influence of Communists within the Nationalist Front.[43]

Quadros' style of government also served to accentuate the great discretionary powers that a Brazilian president commanded. During his time in office there was a massive daily flow of decrees and memoranda from Alvorada Palace. In the first few weeks of his government he dismissed all civil service appointees engaged after September 1960, suspended all government hiring for one year, established an eight-hour day in two four-hour shifts for civil employees, ordered budgets in all ministries to be pared by 30 per cent, and established military men as direct presidential representatives to municipal and state governments. The last of these measures further undercut the power of legislators and the political parties. All these moves were capped by the now famous SUMOC (Superintendency of Money and Credit) Instruction 204, a first step in eliminating existing preferential exchange rates for certain kinds of transactions.

The publication of Quadros' memoranda (*bilhetinhos*) to cabinet ministers and other high officials often before the men

---

[43] A 1960 listing (Osny Duarte Pereira, *op. cit.*, Vol. I, p. 5) named 67 of the 326 members of the Chamber of Deputies as Front members. The *Frente* included a sprinkling from all the major parties, but 23 of the 67 men listed were members of the *Partido Trabalhista Brasileiro* (PTB). The PTB had 66 deputies in the Chamber.

concerned had had a chance to see them soon began to draw criticism as unnecessary high-handedness and a flaunting of power. The *bilhetinhos* ranged over matters large and small. On a not untypical day Quadros instructed the Minister of Public Works to organize a work group to elaborate a master plan for the nation's telephonic communications, requested the Minister of Foreign Affairs to withdraw from the Senate the nominations for ambassadorships to Prague and Praetoria, and ordered the mayor of Brasilia to collect and sell all the old paper from government offices and to use the proceeds for welfare activities.[44]

This kind of personal attention to detail, the long hours of work the President put in daily, and his informality of dress and indifference to protocol served to certify Quadros' promise to give the nation a clean, efficient, shirt-sleeve government with plenty of hard work and no special privileges for anyone. Quadros' winning margin of a million votes is widely attributed to the success of this moralistic appeal among middle-class voters who felt themselves victimized by the uncontrolled spending, wastefulness, and misuse of public funds that had characterized past governments. The problem is, of course, a more or less permanent feature of government everywhere, but there is no question that it has reached alarming proportions in Brazil. The danger lies in that moral reform begins to take the place of politics, obscuring the considerations that should be guiding political choices. Thus the SUMOC Instruction 204, mentioned above, was presented to the public chiefly as "an end to self-deception and a confrontation of economic truth," when in fact it had far-reaching implications that have nothing to do with truth or falsehood.

Another more elusive political problem that Quadros' career serves to highlight is the silent veto power that the armed forces apparently continue to exercise. Quadros' candidacy was often described as imperiled by his lack of military "coverage" (*cobertura*); the campaign was punctuated by rumors that Quadros would be barred from taking office by a military coup. This threat was believed dissipated by the overwhelming victory of the new President at the polls, but occasional rumblings continued to be heard right up to the time of his unexpected resig-

[44] *Corrêio da Manhã*, March 1, 1961.

nation. The subsequent crisis threw into the open the frankly interventionist spirit that prevails in certain sectors of the armed forces. But unless unmasked by dramatic events such as those attending the Goulart succession in 1961, reporting on politics within the armed services is shrouded in a uniquely circumspect rhetoric. The vague and allusive terms of news stories touching on the political activities of military men make it almost impossible to conjure up any realistic image of the concrete actions or relationships that lie behind the events such reports purport to describe. A lead article in a 1961 number of the magazine *Visão* covering the career of Minister of War Marshal Odylio Denys, who served under both Juscelino Kubitschek and Janio Quadros, abounds in this kind of verbal mystification. Of Minister Denys, the article reports:

> After the events of November 11 he became so indispensable to the maintenance of the democratic regime in the nation that the government and the Congress found it indispensable to keep him on active duty. . . .
>
> Months before the elections [Quadros' in 1960] it was known that no matter who the victor was, he would continue as Minister of War. The reins of the army were firmly in his hands. It would be difficult to unite them in other more able, more respected hands. . . .
>
> Many observers imagine that Denys does not view well the changes of command carried out to consolidate the position of the new government. They are deceived; these changes are carried out by Denys himself. . . .
>
> At another period the departure of General Osvino from command of the III Army provoked political restlessness. This, however, died at birth, thanks to the prestige of the Minister of War. . . .
>
> The moderating power exercised by the democratic army headed by Denys will without doubt still be called upon to intervene many times and in many domains.[45]

[45] *Visão*, March 31, 1961, pp. 20-23. The November 11 date in the first quote refers to the military movement that permitted Juscelino Kubitschek to take office after his election in October, 1955. A nationalist point of view of those events is given in Plínio de Abreu Ramos, *Brasil, 11 de Novembro*, São Paulo: 1960. This book was originally a thesis for the 1959 course of the *Instituto Superior de Estudos Brasileiros*.

This kind of reporting makes it impossible to tell just how Marshal Denys "became indispensable to democracy," or what special abilities he has that "put the reins of the army firmly in his hands" while other distinguished officers of equivalent rank stand by in presumed impotence. How did "the political restiveness" that was stifled at birth by the marshal's "prestige" manifest itself? What is the nature of the numerous future interventions that were predicted other than those that were carried out in the public view in ensuing months?

Highly placed and otherwise well-informed and outspoken Brazilians tend to give reticent and evasive answers to such questions. The same circumlocution common in press accounts crops up in conversation. The army is defended on all sides, and surprisingly with special vigor by leftists, as an essentially democratic institution, well leavened by middle-class elements, with a high degree of national responsibility and a sympathetic understanding of the needs and aspirations of popular groups. The army, we are told, "is not available for *golpes* [coups] but does live intensely the political problems of the nation." Other clues suggest that the contribution of leftists to the maintenance of this happy myth may be little more than a form of whistling in the dark intended to forestall opposition or win favor. The armed forces have arbitrated every major political shift since the advent of the Republic in 1889. The changes have been almost entirely bloodless and all have represented some modest gains for democracy. Still, it is common knowledge that a man's military career is not helped by his being outspokenly leftist, and there are few signs that the conservative top military command is disposed to relinquish its discreet tutelage over the nation's affairs.

A few of the nationalist theoreticians face up to these varied problems of internal political structure. They tend to discount the importance of the fragments of nationalistic organization that exist within the major parties and the congress, or that are periodically mobilized for electoral ends. The crisis as they conceive it is one of leadership—of the emergence of a "dynamic sector" for the task of national development. That dynamic sector, as noted earlier, is conceived as destined to come from appropriately politicized and self-aware national entrepreneurs, the technical and managerial sectors of government and business (the "non-parasitic" elements of the middle class), and some intellectuals, gradually incorporating mass support. The question of whether a specific nationalist political organization is required for the task remains open. Thus the fortification and regeneration of the state rather than the immediate organization of new political parties or the revitalizing of old ones is the chief concern of these thinkers.[46] The people, they feel, must be brought to defend and have growing confidence in public power despite the many deficiencies of political institutions. Quadros' efforts to bring efficiency and honesty to the national bureaucracy were in line with the belief of former ISEB ideologists, now among his advisers, that the mass mobilization of political loyalties in support of national economic objectives can only build upon a new kind of confidence in the State and the government.

A Tomada de Consciência

The cerebral, analytical, and instrumental approach to problems of ideology that gives a distinctive mark to Brazilian nationalism may be no more than a reflection of real gains in the scientific understanding of the place of ideas in society. This practical stance may even be just another manifestation of the ingrained pragmatism that, as has been noted, is often attributed to Brazilians. But one should not lose sight of the fact that though nationalism may of its nature be an ideology for young nations, in Brazil the elaborators of nationalist ideology are men heavily scarred by the ideological wars of the last three decades. While such men decry the exhaustion and impotence of old ideologies and the absence of new visions that can give a moral and emotional charge to contemporary life, they give little evidence of being themselves gripped by powerful feeling or commitment. As an ideology formulated in part by and, to an important degree, in behalf of the nation's social technicians and economic programmers, the new nationalism has been weighed more with an eye to its usefulness than for its mere capacity to

---

[46] "Para una Política Nacional de Desenvolvimento," *Cadernos de Nosso Tempo*, January-March 1956, p. 47. These ideas were also expressed to the writer in numerous personal interviews with nationalist spokesmen.

charm. The new nationalism is a credo for men of power with a job to do rather than for zealots out to refashion the world.

There is unquestionably a strong current of anti-United States feeling both open and latent in nationalist thinking, and manifestations of this hostility tend to dominate the impressions United States observers form concerning nationalist views. Still, nationalist writers in Brazil with almost religious regularity disclaim that hatred of the United States or any other country is an important element in contemporary nationalism. Occasionally these disclaimers seem only to be a ritual preamble to vicious attacks. Nevertheless the irrational fanaticism directed toward outsiders and the ingenuous tendency to self-glorification common to nationalism in many other countries are at the moment without doubt secondary features of Brazilian nationalism. Not hate but moderation and reasonableness bordering on the coldly cynical give a unique stamp to the new nationalism. The key recurrent phrase in the utilitarian rhetoric of the programmers of the development ideology is *tirar o melhor partido*, that is, to maximize gains. *Nationalism is the ideology of the moment for these men because it is "possible" and because it satisfies present needs.*

The present need is, of course, for a guiding set of principles and objectives for the task of national development. The present possibility rests on a particular appraisal of the nation's situation in which a counterpoint between two concepts—*alienação* and the *tomada de consciência*—has a central part.

The state of *alienação*, the incapacity until recent times of Brazilians to think or act for themselves, is directly linked in this analysis to the dependent state of the Brazilian economy. The condition of *alienação* is the mark of the colonial mentality in which man and nation are mere objects rather than active agents of history.[47] Though it springs from a particular set of economic relationships, *alienação* is not Marx's "estrangement"

[47] Álvaro Vieira Pinto, *op. cit.* See also Cándido Mendes de Almeida, *op. cit.*, and Michel Debrun, *Ideologia e Realidade*, Rio de Janeiro: 1960. The barrenness and superficiality of political thought in Brazil up to the present time is thus seen as flowing from historical conditions. "From none of the efforts at political theorizing registered in Brazil up to the present has there flowed the formulation of an ideology organically linked to Brazilian reality and capable of supporting political action with a truly national meaning." Guerreiro Ramos, *Introdução Crítica à Sociologia Brasileira*, Rio de Janeiro: 1957.

nor the Freudian "discontent" with civilization or work.[48] It is specific to the fact of colonial dependency and the domination within the country of an elite that is outwardly oriented and lacks organic links with the mass of the population.

The polar state, the *tomada de consciência*, or the achievement of national self-awareness, becomes possible when the bonds of dependency are broken, when the country passes from a simply reflective economy to one attuned to a development with a rhythm and direction rooted within the nation itself. A qualitative change in the self-awareness and vitality of the nation takes place as greater numbers are incorporated into the economic and cultural mainstream of national life. The man in the street not only acquires the idea of the nation and the possibilities of economic development, he is himself possessed by those ideas.[49]

One can challenge details of this thesis. The patent difference in the actual experience of colonialism and consequently its psychological effects on Brazilians as contrasted with, for instance, Congolese, hardly justify applying the same terms to these phenomena. Were the effects of United States cultural penetration as devastating and definitive as they are occasionally depicted in these analyses, the United States would not be confronting the profound crisis in its relations with Latin American nations that it does today. There is some argument as well about just when the beginnings of nationhood in the sense outlined above date from in Brazil; few nationalists would take the process beyond the rise to power of Getúlio Vargas in 1930. How far the *tomada de consciência* can be said to have advanced in the interim also depends on what aspects of Brazilian life one chooses to emphasize; estimates vary sometimes with the mood of the same writer. The national illiteracy rate is still above 50 per cent and reaches nearly 80 per cent in some states. In rural areas hundreds of thousands still live on the edge of starvation, there are staggering imbalances in regional per capita incomes, and the illiterate masses of the rural

---

[48] Karl Marx and Friedrich Engels, *The German Ideology*, New York: 1947. Herbert Marcuse, *Eros and Civilization*, New York: 1955; Daniel Bell, *Work and Its Discontents*, Glencoe: 1958.
[49] Álvaro Vieira Pinto, *op. cit.*, p. 18.

and urban slums remain without franchise or other effective political voice.[50] Balancing this forbidding panorama are the dramatic gains in industrialization, the expansion of an internal market for national manufactures, proven capacity to produce and adapt new technology, a growing internal capital market, and, perhaps most important of all, the beginnings of economic planning within a framework that is attentive to regional as well as national needs.

One part of the quarrel is thus about the facts of Brazilian reality at this moment; it rages on because so little is known about many crucial aspects of that reality. What is important is that Brazilian nationalists have correctly perceived the unplanned, nonvoluntaristic elements in the process of becoming a nation. Their complaint that sociologists in Brazil and elsewhere have failed to gauge the importance of the growth process in nations and its links to problems of economic and social development is amply justified.

There are doctrinal squabbles as well about details of theory and tactics. If ideology flows from and is made possible by particular combinations of historically determined factors, how active a role is the ideologist to play? Does nationalism theoretically or strategically mean that the class struggle is superseded or is to be carried on only within circumscribed limits? What is the place of education in the process of national development?[51]

There is little to be gained by detailing here the full byplay of theory and polemics on such issues. The main elements have already been traced in this account. National integration as a social process in Brazil has made substantial advances in the last three decades. There remain profound internal tensions rooted in persisting class and regional inequalities. No one can give a sure reply as to whether the country will be able to consolidate its process of economic development and social integration without some violent internal clashes. Everything that

---

[50] Miguel Osório de Almeida, "E Morrem Mesmo: O Subdesenvolvimento Brasileiro," *Senhor*, February 1961.

[51] See Roque Spencer Maciel de Barros, *Diretrizes e Bases da Educação*, São Paulo: 1960. This book provides a chronology of a long-standing and at times bitter controversy over proposed legislative reforms in Brazil's problem-riddled educational system.

serves to awaken Brazilians to national needs and objectives also serves to crystallize class interests. The fragments of nationalist organization that exist are torn between the impulse to promote unity for the task of economic and political development and the temptation to exploit emerging class consciousness among the groups to which they look for mass support (farm tenants and workers, urban workers, lower middle class). Politicians in and out of government will continue to seek to exploit patriotic and nationalist sentiment electorally and as a support for policy. Power seems likely to remain in the hands of the ruling elite, which is increasingly open to a rising group of nationalist-minded technicians and planners. The action of these men promises to be no more radical in social policy than it has to be for them to remain in power and to move judiciously toward the national goals that have been outlined.

By focusing attention on the *external* barriers to national self-realization, nationalists of the right and left are in effect buying time for established power groups within Brazil. The current insistence on basic social reform in United States policy in Latin America seeks in part to shift the political pressures flowing from deeply rooted inequalities back on the internal groups resisting real changes. The new American policy, if applied with courage and energy, may eventually conquer the skepticism and disbelief of many who passionately want a redistribution of power, wealth, and privilege in Brazil and elsewhere in Latin America. Those now in privileged positions are less likely to accept a genuine social revolution, even one financed for them by the United States. The theorists of nationalism in Brazil have yet to face squarely the magnitude, and the potential for conflict, of the internal task of national integration that lies ahead.

{ PART } IV

Caste, Race, and Nation

"*A branch cut off from the adjacent branch must of necessity be cut off from the whole tree also. So too a man when he is separated from another man has fallen off from the whole social community. Now as to a branch, another cuts it off, but a man by his own act separates himself from his neighbour when he hates him and turns away from him, and he does not know that he has at the same time cut himself off from the whole social system. Yet he has this privilege certainly from Zeus who framed society, for it is in our power to grow again to that which is near to us, and again to become a part which helps to make up the whole. However, if it often happens, this kind of separation, it makes it difficult for that which detaches itself to be brought to unity and to be restored to its former condition. Finally, the branch, which from the first grew together with the tree, and has continued to have one life with it, is not like that which after being cut off is then ingrafted, for this is something like what the gardeners mean when they say that it grows with the rest of the tree, but that it has not the same mind with it.*"

MARCUS AURELIUS
Meditations, XI

Chapter

8

□□□□□□□□□□□

Hindu Society and the State:
The Indian Union

SELIG S. HARRISON

The contrast between a more or less continuous Chinese imperial establishment and the utter discontinuity endemic to the Hindu political experience engages the scholar and confounds the Indian nationalist. In defense of his commitment, the nationalist disputes the historical evidence while denying that the hoary past can, in any case, have much to do with the capacity of India today to sustain a unified modern state. Beyond this he reminds us that the British Raj coincided with the Industrial Revolution, which is to say that India, left on her own, might have found in the prospect of subcontinental transportation and communication the invitation to unity that had always been missing. But to concede what might have been is not to erase the long view of what did in fact happen in India. The study of Indian nationalism has as its natural point of departure the all too evident indisposition of the architects of Hindu social and religious institutions to erect a superstructure of pan-Indian political unity.

Some interpretations of Indian history juxtapose Chinese "this-worldliness" with Hindu "other-worldliness" and let it go at that. The explanation for the Hindu political default lies, it is said, in a preoccupation with the eternal cycle of rebirth which was logically accompanied by a certain inattention to the chronology or ultimate purpose of earthly affairs. What is an eternity? In Hindu imagery the answer is explicit. According to the *Brahmavaivarta Purana*, a standard mythological "day" in the infinite life of Brahma the Creator lasts 4.32 billion years.[1] The twentieth century falls in the fifty-first year of the present Brahma life span, and when this runs its course amid a universal dissolution at the end of a Brahma century, the timeless sequence resumes all over again in a new cycle of 311.04 billion years. There is no one Creation or Doomsday. There is really no essential difference between yesterday and tomorrow. Both are denoted by a single Sanskrit word (*kal*) which is used interchangeably and takes on meaning only in relation to the tense of its companion verb.

Hindu notions of space and time and of all terrestrial life as something of an illusion do indeed seem to mock the issue of political power and how it is to be organized. But the Hindu tradition nevertheless embodies in the *Arthashastra* one of the most rigorously precise codifications of the political art to arise out of human experience; and the *Dharma* or social law to which all Hindus answer lays down stern ethical guidelines for secular statecraft. It is not as if the king were exempt from the concern of the Hindu lawmaker. He is subject to his own particular *Rajadharma* with its injunctions against the excesses of tyranny as well as of personal immoral indulgence. From the outset the Hindu tradition had a strong "this-worldly" streak. It accorded a definite place to statecraft in the general social scheme of things. What it failed to do was to define in unambiguous terms the basis of the legitimacy of the state, or indeed to concern itself at all with the question of how many state structures there should properly be within the Indian universe.

[1] Heinrich Zimmer, *Myths and Symbols in Indian Art and Civilization*, The Bollingen Series VI, New York: 1946, pp. 3-19.

This absence of any pan-Indian political conception comparable to the comprehensive "Middle Kingdom" of the Chinese is not fully conceded by some Indian and foreign scholars who point to the *ekchatratipatyam* (literally, "one umbrella") ideal of the Hindu ruler, even in ancient times, to bring all of the Indian subcontinent under a single hegemony. Though the ideal was real enough, the critical fact nevertheless appears to be that it was not joined up with a doctrine of legitimacy. The pattern of Chinese civilization was set in the period of the Warring States when the emperor came to be accepted as combining in his person the authority not only of the dominant secular ruler but also of the high priest who alone was qualified to transmit the sacred tradition on earth. In the India of the pre-Christian era, however, the power of the prince and of the Brahman evolved in tandem from earliest times. Max Weber has made a persuasive case in assigning the highest importance to "this different configuration of political and theocratic power . . . independent priests standing beside a strictly secular prince."[2] The prince needed the Brahman at his side to confirm his obeisance to the Dharma in the eyes of the populace. At the same time the actual claim of the prince to his power was derived less from ethical right than from his personal leadership qualities and the competence of the Brahman in his role as magician and sorcerer intervening with the gods. Moreover, and here was the central point of difference, while the Chinese literati of the day were gathering around a single imperial pontifex, the Brahmans "in this epoch of innumerable splinter states . . . faced a plurality of petty princes without a legitimate lord paramount from whom to derive their power. The concept of legitimacy was rather simply that the single prince was ritualistically correct when and to the extent to which his behavior, especially toward the Brahmans, conformed with the holy tradition."[3]

An accident of history at its inception, the duality of political and priestly prerogatives was to harden into a permanent feature of the Hindu order. Because the Brahmans established no church machinery by which to contend for temporal power, as

[2] Max Weber, *The Religion of India*, Glencoe: 1958, p. 141.
[3] *Ibid.*, p. 141. See also Amaury de Riencourt, *The Soul of India*, New York: 1960, for suggestive comparison of the Indian and Chinese cases.

Mackenzie Brown observes, "they were dependent upon the king for earthly support,"[4] and one king was as worthy of their attentions as another. No Hindu ruler was specially situated to claim a unique pontifical authority. The evolving doctrine of *karma* implied a seemingly limitless series of autonomous and often contradictory ethical codes for each of the disparate social groups being accommodated in the expansive new Hindu system. In this atmosphere devoid of a universally applicable social ethic, there was no impulse to search for such a political ethic and there was, on the contrary, nothing to stop the progressive degeneration of Indian political life. While the Legalists in China had to operate in the shadow of the legitimate "Son of Heaven," the Indian forerunners of Machiavelli whose means of pursuing power for its own sake were spelled out with unabashed detail in the *Arthashastra* had a field of wide open opportunity.

Broadly sketched, the historical backdrop against which the scenario of the modern Indian nationalist effort has been and continues to be enacted is a splotchy tableau of sudden imperial brilliance followed invariably by the dim obscurities of collapse and disintegration. When a dynasty did manage to unite considerable territory under its banner, this was most often a unity confined within one of the ten major linguistic regions which were taking form along the lines of natural geographic divisions —Assam (Assamese), Andhra (Telugu), Bengal (Bengali), Gujarat (Gujarati), the north-central Gangetic plain (Hindi), Karnataka (Kannada), Kerala (Malayalam), Maharashtra (Marathi), Orissa (Oriya), and Tamilnad (Tamil). Multiregional empires spanning all of north or central or south India were the exception rather than the rule, and only the most exceptional of the empire-builders went on to carve a still larger subcontinental imperium out of the jungle disorder of Indian political rivalries. The Maurya and Gupta dynasties head-

---

[4] D. Mackenzie Brown, *The White Umbrella: Political Thought from Manu to Gandhi*, Los Angeles: 1958, p. 18. See also Daniel H. H. Ingalls, "The Brahman Tradition," in Milton Singer, ed., *Traditional India: Structure and Change*, The American Folklore Society, Philadelphia: 1959, p. 7. Professor Ingalls outlines the distinction between what was a numerical minority of Brahmans in the ambit of royal power and the larger number of ascetics and "stay-at-home traditionalists."

quartered in the Gangetic heartland; the Chalukyas and Rash-
trakutas of the midlands and the Cholas of the Tamil country
were able to reach out unimpeded from their local bases of
power only until they encountered the outer limits of another
imperial domain. A common social order was spreading to the
four corners of the geographically self-contained Indian subcontinent without respect to political boundaries. But in the
absence of a common political conception to go with it, the
Hindu order was unable to make a concerted stand on its home
ground against the united onslaught of the Moguls and then
the British.

The Hindu Past

To the intellectual leaders of the Indian renaissance at the
turn of the century, the fact that Hinduism had survived the
vicissitudes of nearly four thousand years while a procession
of other civilizations had come and gone seemed in itself an
answer to those who made much of the record of political disunity. The creation of an enduring social order out of the
influx of diverse tribal and racial groups which it had been
India's fate to experience was compensation enough for the
omission of a lasting political order. Rabindranath Tagore in
particular said pointedly that if the Hindus had not achieved a
Universal Empire it was because they were more concerned to
establish a Universal Society pervaded by universally acknowledged religious values. "The vital strength in different civilizations is variously embodied," wrote Tagore in 1904. "The heart
of a country lies wherever the peoples' welfare is centered. In
England the overthrow of the state might mean peril for the
nation—that is why politics there is such a serious affair. In
our country there would be danger only when the social body,
samaj, became crippled."[5] India's "true and deathless strength"
lay in her "genius for unification. Her problem was the problem
of the world in miniature. . . . India tolerated differences of race
from the first and . . . her caste system is the outcome of this
spirit of toleration. For India has all along tried experiments

[5] Rabindranath Tagore, "Society and State," in *Towards Universal Man*,
New York: 1961, p. 51.

in evolving a social unity within which all the different peoples
could be held together. . . . This has produced something like a
United States of a social federation whose common name is
Hinduism."[6] Although caste had become grossly distorted and
it would be impossible in modern times "to build a political
miracle of freedom upon the quicksand of social slavery,"[7] the
institution itself had a core of timeless validity and the rehabili-
tation of Hindu society on the bedrock of its ancient ideal of
the harmonious and closely-knit village community was not
only possible but offered, in Tagore's view, the only salvation
for India. The last thing for what he called the Country of the
No-Nation to do was to imitate the model of Western
nationalism.

"If we cherish the desire of paying our all for buying a
political nationality," argued Tagore, "it will be as absurd as
if Switzerland had staked her existence in her ambition to build
up a Navy powerful enough to compete with that of England."
Pondering where the "organized selfishness" of nationalism
would lead the world, he asked what place there could be in a
world of fiercely contending nationalisms for "those who have
lived and suffered, have loved and worshipped, have thought
deeply and worked with meekness, but whose only crime has
been that they have not organized. . . . I know what your advice will be. You will say, form yourselves into a nation and
resist this encroachment of the Nation. But is this the true
advice? that of a man to a man?"[8]

But Tagore's case rested on the assumption that an India
held together in a necessarily tenuous social network could not,
even if she tried, compete on the terms of the new homogeneous
nationalist states, and this was intolerable self-disparagement to
his contemporaries of the renaissance period. It was something
else again to emphasize as Swami Vivekananda did that India
need not make the effort to compete politically because hers
was a more important mission of spiritual leadership for which
she alone had the special qualifications. The message of Vivekananda and those who later carried on his crusade for a Hindu
revival carefully refrained from suggesting, however, that

[6] Rabindranath Tagore, *Nationalism*, New York: 1917, pp. 135-136.
[7] *Ibid.*, p. 144.
[8] *Ibid.*, pp. 43-44.

Hindu society could not hold its own in the developing nationalist rivalries. Their clear implication was that a revitalized Hindu community, sure of itself and able to draw on rediscovered spiritual resources, could make whatever adaptations might be necessary to consolidate the requisite state power for a competitive role in the modern world. "Strength, strength is what the Upanishads speak to me from every page," exclaimed Vivekananda. "What we need is strength."[9] The past was not a specter to them because they looked to it for mystic inspiration rather than political instruction. Tagore's warnings did no more to forestall the imitation of Western nationalism than Gandhi's subsequent emphasis on the *Sarvodaya* economics of village self-sufficiency or the present-day dissent registered by Jaya Prakash Narayan and Vinoba Bhave. In the face of the state-power chorus of so many politically aware Indians, Narayan sounds a lonely and faintly tragic note when—in the Tagore tradition— he exalts the *Gramraj* ideal of a decentralized society of small units "which promotes direct human relations. In the modern city even neighbors are strangers. There is hardly any intercourse or contact between them and this strengthens impersonal foci of power. Society becomes something like a machine."[10]

Post-independence India has acted on the unmistakable assumption that an industrially undeveloped country must indeed imitate the model of the integrated nation-state if it is to get a fair share of the worldwide technological advance and if it is not to fall easy prey to others who might outdo it in exploiting the new technology. Tagore may have been right, it is reasoned in effect, but even if this were so his course would be too risky today. However, the substantial consensus now existing on the adoption of the value of nationalism has been achieved without resolving, at the same time, the very considerable lingering ambivalence on the issue within Indian society in general and even among some of those elements most urgently committed to nationalist aspirations.

For the nationalist also behaves as a member of caste and

9 Swami Vivekananda, *Complete Works*, Almora, Advaita Ashram: 1948, III, pp. 237-242, cited in Chattar Singh Samra, "Subhas Chandra Bose: An Indian National Hero," in *Leadership and Political Institutions in India*, Princeton: 1959, p. 69.
10 Jaya Prakash Narayan, "The Concept of Gramraj," *Bhoodan*, May 29, 1957, p. 1.

regional units which often call for a loyalty directly contradictory to the claims of the national loyalty. Although a comparable ambivalence is no doubt found in certain elite groups in most of the undeveloped countries now experiencing social change, the Indian case appears to be an extreme one both because of the scope of diversity in the Indian subcontinent and because the Indian federal system gives unusually well-defined political recognition to this diversity. All of the fourteen states of the Indian Union are more or less linguistically homogeneous units conforming in most cases to the boundaries of India's ancient linguistic territories; and though there are some exceptions, the limits of the more significant politically operative caste units tend to be congruent with linguistic alignments. The drafters of the Constitution of January 26, 1950, deliberately incorporated the millennial divisions of Hindu society into the very structure of the Union in the express belief that the problem of unity in the Indian subcontinent was a special one calling for a unique balance between national and regional claims.

Cutting across and overlapping the linguistic-caste map are still more fundamental groupings setting off the Muslim (9.92 per cent of the population) and Sikh (1.74 per cent) minorities from the Hindu majority. The Hindu-Muslim and Hindu-Sikh problems would have posed profound dilemmas in and of themselves even if Hindu society had itself gotten off to a politically unified start four thousand years ago. But the apparent political incapacity of Hindu society has left a legacy of self-doubt which serves to exacerbate inter-communal adjustments today. Unsure of its own strength and cohesion, the Hindu majority magnifies the threat presented by non-Hindu minorities which remain, for their part, on guard against an outburst of pent-up Hindu militance. Still, this is not to say that the Hindu majority has yet been able to find in confronting the minorities the unifying sense of identity that it has not found in its confrontation with a whole world of non-Hindus. The caste and regional groupings which delimit the political consciousness of most individual Hindus have the status of autonomous sovereignties, as it were, attached only in the most precarious manner to the loose subcontinental framework that is Hindu society. Their claims are made on the individual in his capacity as a Hindu quite as pointedly as a pan-Indian Hindu appeal which has virtually no authentic historical points of reference. In terms of their history, as we have seen, most Hindus would be hard put to find much sense of identity with a trumped-up ideal of Hindu nationalism; and yet they are also unable to gratify their emotional hunger for a modern political identity through the narrow outlets of caste and regional allegiance. It is consequently a persistent central question in Indian politics whether the effort to evoke a pan-Indian Hindu consciousness can be given some new psychological fillip it has never had before, and if so, how a militant Hindu nationalism would relate itself to the presence of forty-three million Muslims and eight million Sikhs.

Hindu tradition acquires its potentially enormous unifying strength from the pan-Indian character of its principal symbolism. The *Vedas* projected the unity of the motherland on a subcontinental scale and the pilgrim centers beckoning the orthodox in all parts of India are situated, as if by a clear design, in the four corners of the subcontinent. The *Ramayana* and the *Mahabharata* provide a common fund of tradition for Hindus throughout the country. Nevertheless, this overarching unity of the Hindu tradition has yet to prove itself powerful enough, politically speaking, to cancel out the pervasive effect of the centrifugal forces built into Hindu social institutions. The present analysis will accordingly consider the stresses within Hindu society before assessing the possible relevance of the Hindu tradition and its symbolism in the development of Indian nationalism.

Caste in Transition

The caste order with its division into four *varnas* (Brahman, Kshatriya, Vaisya, Sudra) common to all parts of India has the appearance of a pan-Indian caste structure in which all Hindus enjoy a close social relationship to one another. In actuality the fact that the linguistic boundary is also in most cases the caste boundary alters the image to suggest a radically different picture of self-contained regional caste structures. Caste ties limit inter-dining and inter-marriage to an endogamous unit (*jati*) which may be native to one or two villages or may embrace an entire linguistic region, but which rarely crosses linguistic frontiers. In the traditional idealized Hindu society the caste network served to give a social discipline to functionally integrated villages which had little relationship even to the neighboring villages and none at all with the social systems of villages hundreds of miles away. Then the change from a closed to an open society in the eighteenth and nineteenth centuries enabled castes for the first time to establish internal solidarity over relatively far-flung areas. The old spirit of live-and-let-live which was central to caste changed almost imperceptibly into a new competitive urge as regional alliances of kindred local caste units took form and caste became a vehicle of modern economic and political competition. Instead of acting as a solvent of caste, economic and political change in an egalitarian dispensation has prompted each caste to seek assurance that it is more equal than the rest and, in the case of low-caste Hindus, to fasten onto caste identity with a special tenacity as the most probable guarantee of self-protection against the entrenched higher castes. The constitutional provisions for certain minimum levels of civil service posts, legislative seats, and school admissions to specified out-caste and low-caste groups have turned out to be the instruments of a constantly sharpening caste consciousness. The Backward Classes Commission appointed to safeguard the interests of the lower castes has enumerated as eligible for protection under these guarantees a total of 2,399 "backward" communities, excluding untouchables, 913 of the major ones numbering in themselves some 116,000,000 people.

It may well be of considerable significance that the newly-rich individual in Hindu society does not normally shed his caste identity for a new and higher economic class standing. He is not only caught in the tight web of a caste circle which is formed around religious sanctions but faces, in addition, the unified refusal of higher castes to his social ascent. Both the rich pacesetters and the poor stragglers in a caste find it equally necessary to make their way together up the ladder of social mobility. The emblem of their success in claiming a higher status is the emulation of previously forbidden high-caste Sanskritic ritual, which accounts for the invention of the term

"Sanskritization" by some scholars[11] to characterize what is happening, or seems to be happening, in Hindu society under the stress of economic change.

What is actually taking place beneath the surface of a complex social landscape cannot, by its nature, be easily perceived or comprehended, and the political implications of the changing role of caste are, as a consequence, anyone's educated guess. It can be argued, for example, that the containment of the process of social change within the existing caste hierarchy implicit in the concept of "Sanskritization" would suggest a great degree of stability in Hindu society. As Lloyd and Susanne Rudolph see it, the coalescence of politically assertive caste lobbies makes possible a process of democratic interplay and accommodation among groups which would not otherwise occur among individuals who are not yet politically mature or even, to any great extent, politically activated. "Caste," they argue, is in a sense "anti-caste."[12] The political clash of caste interests is viewed as a healthy feature of a transitional period destined to end in greater social justice and thus eventually greater individualism. Others have argued that the pursuit of equality on the part of subordinated social groups can provide precisely the dynamism required for economic growth in the less-developed countries.[13] No doubt sooner or later the emergence of new economic lobbies and the competition among a growing number of ambitious individual operators will tend to complicate and disrupt a contest between rigidly demarcated social groups. But the process of disruption may take what is, in terms of the evolving Indian political drama, a dangerously long time.

The comparative studies of Marion J. Levy are highly suggestive in considering the political implications of caste in India.

[11] See especially M. N. Srinivas, "A Note on Sanskritization and Westernization," *Far Eastern Quarterly*, Vol. XV, No. 4 (August 1956), pp. 490, 493.
[12] Lloyd I. and Susanne Hoeber Rudolph, "The Political Role of India's Caste Associations," *Pacific Affairs*, Vol. XXXIII, No. 1, March 1960. For an extended presentation of the present author's views on the changing role of caste, see "The New Caste Lobbies," in *India: The Most Dangerous Decades*, Princeton: 1960, pp. 96-136.
[13] Everett J. Hagen, *An Analytical Model of the Transition to Economic Growth*, Center for International Studies, Massachusetts Institute of Technology, Cambridge: 1957, esp. pp. 60, 65, 87-88.

The common overriding loyalty to a national feudal hierarchy
and an emperor—and hence to a national state—which gave
Japan the social control for its modernization stands in remarkable contrast not only, as Levy has argued, to what has already
occurred in China, but also to what may well be taking place
in India. The "conscious social engineers" of the early Tokugawa
period required each feudal lord or *daimyo* to spend a part of
every year at the Shogun's court or to leave his family in his
stead. "The only solidarity in Japanese social structure that
offered any threat to the primacy of the obligation to one's over-
lord was the family bond," writes Levy, "and by this hostage
system the Tokugawa tied them together as far as the *daimyo*
were concerned."[14] Loyalty to a hierarchy of overlords which
became increasingly rigid "took clear precedence over loyalty to
one's family. . . . Even if an individual were to lose or be
separated from his family, he could not lose or be separated
from the entire hierarchy of persons in positions of power over
him."[15] Administrative posts came to be hereditarily determined
through "a sort of civil service by adoption" in which the *daimyo*
might go outside his own family or even across class lines into
the ranks of the *samurai*. The conflict between the aggrandizement of one's family and the proper performance of office so
typical of China was not in nearly the same measure a difficulty
in Japan "because one's family and one's office were combined."[16]
In China the orientation of the family head "was not first, last
and always to someone over him in the general social hierarchy
of power and responsibility" but rather to the family itself; and
if he should be able to enhance the interests of the family at the
common expense, the responsibility was not his but that of the
sovereign. Still, in practice, it was most often to the family interest to remain within the bounds of the established order and it
was in the personal interest of the ambitious individual, in turn,
to trade on his family identity for his own advancement. The

[14] Marion J. Levy, "Contrasting Factors in the Modernization of China
and Japan" in Simon Kuznets, W. E. Moore, and J. J. Spengler, eds.,
Economic Growth: Brazil, India, Japan, Durham: 1955, p. 528.
[15] *Ibid.*, p. 532.
[16] Marion J. Levy, "Some Aspects of 'Individualism' and the Problem of
Modernization in China and Japan," Center for International Studies,
Princeton: 1957, mimeo., p. 41.

system exercised considerable social discipline on its members until industrialization offered job opportunities outside the traditional spheres which did not depend so heavily on family antecedence.

By contrast with both the Japanese and Chinese cases, the discipline of Hindu society has never extended for long above the level of local caste units, and the social control that did exist in a particular local area rested on low-caste acquiescence in a Brahman supremacy which is now being challenged in nearly all parts of India. Moreover, the distinguishing feature of Hindu society, one should bear in mind, was the geographic diffusion of caste in separate local hierarchies. When Rabindranath Tagore visited Japan he was struck by this "civilization of human relationship. Your duty toward your state has naturally assumed the character of filial duty, your nation becoming one family with your emperor as its head. Your national unity has not been evolved from the comradeship of arms for defensive and offensive purposes . . . but it is an extension of the family and of the obligations of the heart in a wide field of space and time."[17] In India, on the other hand, "there is no common birthright. And when we talk of Western nationality we forget that the nations there do not have that physical repulsion, one for the other, that we have between different castes. Have we an instance in the whole world where a people who are not allowed to mingle their blood shed their blood for one another except by coercion or for mercenary purposes? And can we ever hope that these moral barriers against our race amalgamation will not stand in the way of our political unity?"[18]

The protestations of contempt for caste widely expressed among Indian intellectuals are in a sense expressions of the discomfited realization on the part of each individual intellectual that he is to some extent the prisoner of his own caste identity. For all of his cosmopolitan exposure, the most Westernized Indian with the most clearly articulated intellectual commitment to nationalism cannot lightly shrug off this identity. The bearers of the nationalist ideal are caught in the pull and counterpull of ambivalent loyalties as much as, or more than, the unlettered

[17] Rabindranath Tagore, *Nationalism, op. cit.*, pp. 90-92.
[18] *Ibid.*, pp. 146-147.

multitude. The view that they are, if anything, more unhinged
emotionally by this ambivalence has been presented with insight
by Edward Shils in his pioneering study of the Indian intellectuals. Caste not only asks of the Indian intellectual a positive
loyalty incompatible with his nationalist loyalty; as Shils observes, it also negates the sense of identity between the nationalist intellectual and all those beyond the pale of his limited caste
circle. The "troubled sensitivity" discernible in many Indian
intellectuals is a sensitivity to "the discrepancy between pride
in one's nation and attachment to its symbols on the one hand,
and the absence of any sentiment of affinity with one's fellow
nationals on the other."[19] If the Indian intellectuals are, as so
many of them are wont to complain, "cut off from the people"
more than the intellectuals of most countries, "the caste system
must take some of the blame. . . . It is the caste system perhaps
even more than the crushing ubiquity of other human beings
which makes the upper-caste Hindus, from whose circles most
Indian intellectuals are recruited, fundamentally and humanly
insensate to the mass of the population who belong to the lower
castes. Indian intellectuals . . . cannot enter the minds of their
fellow-countrymen."[20]

Regional Languages and Hindu Identity

The intensity of the desire to bridge the emotional gap separating them from the mass of their fellows suffices, in Shils'
analysis, as an explanation for movements led by intellectuals
favoring the indigenous regional languages as against English,
exalting the glories of the regional past, and pressing the claims
of one region as against another in national politics. But when
he derogates the regional movements as inspired by "a few
back-country types, a few zealots and traditionalists,"[21] he is,
in effect, simply glossing over much of the strongest stuff of
Indian history. For the regional languages are, like his caste, a

[19] Edward Shils, *The Intellectual Between Tradition and Modernity:
The Indian Situation*, The Hague: 1961, p. 70.
[20] *Ibid.*, p. 71.
[21] *Ibid.*, pp. 72 ff. See the present author's discussion of language policy
problems in India in "The New Regional Elites," pp. 55-95, in *India:
The Most Dangerous Decades, op. cit.*

badge of the intellectual's heritage as a Hindu. This is indeed the case with all Hindus, those who are not intellectuals as well. Although the common fund of Hindu cultural lore found its first expression in Sanskrit, it was through the secondary transmission and amplification of this cultural legacy in the regional languages that the substance of the Hindu tradition was carried to most Hindus. Folklore is often only a variation of themes from the *Ramayana* and the *Mahabharata,* and commentaries or translations based on the story of Rama are to be found in all of the regional languages; but even more important is the fact that the *bhakti* movement which popularized Hinduism and made it intelligible to a mass public was a movement conducted in the language of each region. In place of metaphysics and high philosophical flights the pioneers of the new movement a millennium ago preached an emotional Hinduism offering salvation through *bhakti* or uncomplicated devotion to God. The case of the Tamil hymns of the Nayanars and the Alwars embodied in the Saivite *Tirumurai* and the Vaishnavite *Nalavira Prabhandam* was only the first of a long historical sequence in which the regional language became the medium of a sacred liturgy central to the regional practice of Hinduism. Like Buddhist and Jain reformism the *bhakti* movement emphasized the use of the regional languages as a means of reaching the lower castes, and thus had an important part in the actual shaping and evolution of these languages. The traditional Sanskrit meter could have been transposed to the still not fully formed regional media, but instead the *bhakti* poets went out of their way to adhere to the native or *desi* meters characteristic of each language as it was spoken, and thereby to capture its flavor and make more effective emotional contact with would-be devotees. The special significance of *bhakti* in this sense lies in the coincidental fact that it came at a time when the regional languages had already acquired a tentative shape and were peculiarly ready to respond to external stimuli. The stamp of the *bhakti* movement can be found today in the most treasured sacred literature of nearly every linguistic region. The regional languages developed as the literary vehicles of a popular religious revival extending over centuries, and thus acquired a linguistic legitimacy denied to a mere *patois* or folk language. Recorded expressions of the *bhakti* spirit during the centuries of Islamic assaults on Hinduism became a strong link for each region with its past. It was for this reason that the regional languages provided the obvious outlet for the burst of new cultural creativity which followed the nineteenth century influx of Western social and political thought.

While the high station given to English as the passkey to intellectual and administrative employment under the Raj made it the principal "prestige" language of the educated, the period of British rule also witnessed a literary renaissance in the regional languages behind the façade of the Western-oriented elite culture. To some extent the early products and even many of the contemporary manifestations of this renaissance must be classed as second-rate imitations of English models—the work of "back-country types" who were not up to the intellectual standard of the more accomplished English-speaking leadership of the day. But there were quite different examples—Bankim Chandra Chatterjee with his Bengali historical novels, or Guruzada Apparao in Telugu or Subramaniam Bharati in Tamil—who render any generalization inadequate. As the languages of common speech the regional languages were, in any case, the inevitable media for the mobilization of a mass independence movement. Bal Gangadhar Tilak with his weekly *Kesari* (*Lion*) had started to preach his political message at the turn of the century in a simplified popular Marathi, and Gandhi as the rising star of an invigorated Congress movement was quick to perceive that grass-roots pamphleteering would necessarily have to be conducted in the regional languages.

Gandhi himself was most at home writing in his own Gujarati; and it was a central article of the Gandhian faith that after Independence English should be supplanted by the regional languages in education and administration. Nationalism in the Gandhian conception could not be nationalism if it did not mean the coming of age of the indigenous Indian languages. Meaningful education and cultural creativity would always be the exception rather than the rule so long as a foreign language dominated Indian intellectual life; a linguistically alienated leadership could not be expected, in his view, to lead an authentic national regeneration. The shift to the mother tongue first began to take place in pre-Independence years in the secondary schools, where textbooks were readily available in the regional languages and where the professional pedagogical consensus was clearly on the side of the use of the mother tongue. But it had been the use of English as the medium of instruction which had given Indian students their relative facility in English and had made it possible for them to grasp university lectures conducted in a foreign language. Once the shift was made in the secondary schools and English became simply one of a number of courses of study—comparable, let us say, to French or Spanish in an American high school—the new college entrants began to arrive increasingly ill-prepared for meaningful study through the medium of English.

By the time Independence came, the advocates of the mother tongue were pressing for a complete changeover to the regional languages as the media of higher education. At the same time proponents of Hindi as the Union language were insisting on its introduction as the nationwide medium of instruction. In the resulting impasse the non-Hindi regions have tended to stand by the retention of English as the surest means of forestalling the imposition of Hindi. Yet the pressures building up from the bottom clearly threaten to displace English as the medium of instruction in most non-scientific university classes by the use of the regional language or at least, for the transition period when teachers are learning to shift linguistic gears, of a bilingual jargon mixing English with the regional language. No enforcement sanctions, constitutional or otherwise, are available to the central government should it wish to prevent universities from converting to the regional language; and though the present English-educated professorial generation has slowed down the transition, in time, possibly at the end of a decade, the regional languages will be in general use as the media of university education.

Here it should be explained, before proceeding further, why the prospects for the spread of Hindi as anything more than a second or third language in the non-Hindi regions can be so blithely discounted. The primary factor is the resistance to Hindi on the part of votaries of other languages, notably Tamil, Bengali, and Marathi, which have a far more impressive and far more ancient literary heritage. In contrast to most regions of

India, where there was a single dominant linguistic tradition, the sprawling, culturally disparate Gangetic plain was the locale of a multiplicity of competing traditions with its powerful dialect variations of Braj Bhasha in the so-called western Hindi belt and Avadhi in eastern Hindi territory, and in the added complication of the later Urdu heritage of the Muslim elite. Thus, unlike the educated elite of Bengal, which can claim as much familiarity with Tagore as with English-language literature, the literati of the Hindi region do not share a common literary tradition. The would-be developers of a standardized Hindi complicate what would in any case be the difficult task of choosing between words drawn from the different dialects by insisting, with purist zeal, on virtually complete Sanskritization. This means expunging from the Hindustani which is spoken in most towns of the Ganges plain all traces of the Urdu and Persian words left over from centuries of Hindu-Muslim interpenetration, and the introduction in their place of new expressions, adapted from Sanskrit words, which are literally unintelligible to most people in the Hindi region. There is considerable question, in short, what Hindi one is talking about in referring to "Hindi" as the national language. And so long as the very character of the language remains indeterminate on its own native terrain, it is unlikely to radiate outward into the non-Hindi regions, nor can it be expected to acquire standing as the general medium of university education beyond the limits of Hindi territory.

Region or Nation?

When the changeover to the regional languages does occur in the universities, and it seems only a matter of time, the political impact on the course of Indian nationalist development may well prove critical. The most concrete immediate consequence may well be in a change in the rules governing national civil service examinations to permit the optional use of the regional languages as the medium—a development of critical importance in a society in which government employment enjoys such high esteem and in which educated unemployment is so often the unemployment of frustrated aspirants to the national bureaucracy. The attractive power of government employment can be expected to give decisive prestige to any language permitted as the medium of the civil service examination. Nominally, the Home Ministry has been committed since 1955 to acting on the injunction of the Congress Party high command that both Hindi and the regional languages should be given status as optional media for the examinations. But action has been delayed because of an anxious recognition that this would be a kind of Rubicon for Indian nationalism, a premature step across the narrow divide separating an India led by a cosmopolitan national elite educated in one common unifying language from another emergent India whose rising political and administrative leaders tend to read, think, and write most comfortably in their own regional languages.

The source of this anxiety lies in the probability that narrow intellectual horizons will become narrow political horizons, and in the fear, most particularly, that a new generation of civil servants increasingly exposed to parochial political appeals may prove less dependable as a "steel frame" in moments of surcharged political conflict. To inhale the political atmosphere in the towns and small cities which are the foci of political life in each linguistic component of the Union is to detect the scent of bubbling new movements voicing an assortment of regional grievances in frank antagonism to the national leadership in New Delhi. It is not too much to say that the vitality of Indian political life is now at its peak not in New Delhi at all, but rather in ten separate regional arenas. Intellectual activity in all regions of India is to a considerable extent the pulp culture of popular writers who address themselves to the growing numbers of new literates in the regional languages, and this is a pulp culture which, if the record to date is any guide, seems destined to be parochial in its horizons. The growth of this pulp culture reflects the scope of partial literacy accompanying the expansion of education on a colossal scale. In rural India most children who go to school at all leave before reaching the fifth grade; less than one child in five, and in many rural areas not more than one in ten, are receiving full elementary education, according to recent surveys. The growth of a vast audience of partial literates at a time of general decline of educational standards, aggravated by a transition from English to the regional languages, has to some extent choked off cosmopolitan impulses in the journalism and literature of the hinterlands; and this process of intellectual compartmentalization has contributed, inevitably, to a political compartmentalization as well. Harking back to the real or imagined glories of the regional past, the political manipulator has a free field. He need not compete with a nationalistic appeal to a shared pan-Indian political past, for there is no single past on which all Indians can look back with equal pride. He can make of the fratricides of the past a summons to new vengeance—or for the victor, new aggrandizement.

The development of Indian political life since Independence has witnessed the steady growth of regionally based forces and the corresponding erosion of the system of national party competition which was implicitly envisaged by the drafters of the Indian Constitution. Even in the relatively stable political climate of the 1957 elections, regional forces won more seats in the state assemblies and the lower house of the central parliament than any national party in opposition to the Congress Party. The free-wheeling candidate running as an independent on strictly local issues and ready to bargain with the highest bidder among the national parties has become a ubiquitous Indian political type. At the same time the regionalization of Indian politics has carried with it an additional, potentially ominous, development in the mushrooming rise of militant parochial parties which are in no mood for bargaining and which have as their *raison d'être*, in fact, the elimination of the national party presence in their territory. In only one case, that of the so-called Dravidian movement in the Tamil region, does a powerful movement with strong mass appeal raise the demand for outright secession of a region of India from the Union. This is merely the most extreme manifestation, however, of a disaffection felt in varying degrees of intensity in other regions, and given significant if less strident expression in well organized political movements.

Precisely because it is an extreme case, the Dravidian movement in the Tamil region provides an interesting case study against which to measure other regional movements in India. Launched in 1945 as the *Dravida Kazagham*, or Dravidian Federation, by leaders associated with the non-Brahman Justice Party, the "Blackshirts" abandoned the polite parliamentary efforts to win representation for lower castes in government and schools which had been characteristic of the Justice Party, and defiantly proclaimed the non-Brahman majority (97 per cent) of Tamilnad as a separate national group entitled to sovereign independence from the rest of India. Members were enjoined to sign a pledge to support separation, and adopted the black shirt as a symbol of the alleged north Indian Aryan exploitation of the once-glorious Dravidian South with its more or less self-contained political and culture history extending over nearly 3,000 years. The movement split in 1949 when some of its younger militants formed the *Dravida Munnetra Kazagham* or Dravidian Progressive Federation; and though this splintering as well as subsequent factionalism within the new D.M.K. has somewhat vitiated their potential, the two leading Dravidian groups, together with several smaller offshoots, exercise what is nonetheless a potent destructive force at the expense of the dominant Tamil Congress Party. The growing strength of the Dravidian movement has been apparent in the fact that the city government of Madras has been under D.M.K. control for protracted intermittent periods, and apparent, also, in D.M.K. gains in the 1962 elections to the Madras legislature.

The fact that the Dravidian movement is essentially a social protest of the Tamil lower-castes against Brahmans and even elite non-Brahmans at the pinnacle of the regional social structure makes it no less serviceable as a vehicle for the protest of the region as a whole against alleged north Indian racial and economic oppression. Indeed, as an alliance of aggrieved Tamil castes—among others, the Nadars, the Maravars, and the Adi-Dravida untouchables—the "Blackshirts" typify the political potential of regional caste groups united behind a catch-all slogan against a "foreign" scapegoat. In the case of the Tamil non-Brahmans, the interlopers blamed for most of the region's troubles are the Brahman—depicted as a north Indian Aryan fifth columnist—and the northern Gujarati or Marwari traders. Both epitomize the cosmopolitan elements of a Hindu social order in which regional caste groups hold a strong sense of their local interests and identity. The Brahman is also a symbol of a Hindu hierarchy of color awareness in which the Tamil non-Brahman sees himself placed at the very bottom. The very word in Sanskrit (*varna*) for the four basic caste divisions of Brahman, Kshatriya, Vaisya, and Sudra literally means color. There are in India's ethnic kaleidoscope Brahmans who are darker than non-Brahmans, but the caste hierarchy descends in a general sense from a fair Brahman downward, and the Tamil non-Brahman is often the darkest of the dark in the subcontinent.

The relevance of the Tamil case as part of a general examination of regional political movements in India is enhanced by the effect such a strong non-Communist expression of regional chauvinism has had on the growth of Communist power in the area. For in general the pattern of Communist strength in India has corresponded to the pattern of Communist identification with regional forces. Andhra and Kerala are the two regions in which the strongest Communist organizations have developed and in which the most powerful Communist vote-getting power has been demonstrated. They are also the regions in which the Communists have been able to appropriate regional patriotism for their own political advantage. The contrast presented by Tamilnad is striking, for here the Dravidian movement cornered the market on regional protest and Communist footholds have been restricted, in the main, to constituencies in which the Dravidian movement has been willing to strike an occasional electoral bargain.

The Tamil Communists have been handicapped in their effort to win regional influence by the national Communist line on Indian unity which has been in effect since 1953. After a long separatist phase in which the Indian Communists maintained that India was not a single national entity but consisted, in actuality, of separate regional sovereignties, each possessing the inherent right to secede from any larger body politic, the Party reversed itself in late 1953 in a flip-flop coinciding with the post-Stalin Soviet decision to accept the Indian Union under Nehru as an established fact. Though the right of each "national" unit within the Union to secede could not be denied by a party faithful to the Leninist scriptures, the critical pronouncement signifying the change of the line held that "the right of secession should not be confused with the *expediency* of the formation of separate states" —which remained in each instance for "the working class" (i.e., the Communist Party) and its allies within each national group to decide. It had accordingly become "inexpedient" under existing circumstances for Indian nationalities to exercise their separatist rights.[22] This meant, in the Tamil case, that the separatist demand was to become the political property of the Dravidian movement for the greater part of a decade in which Tamil Communist strength would remain at a standstill. But the Communist line on nationality is an open-ended one, subject to change without notice whenever it is judged "expedient" to change it in the "national" interest. The determinant of the line in the years ahead is likely to be the vulnerability of pan-Indian political institutions to capture by the Party and its allies—which is to say that if power in New Delhi should, in fact, come to appear unattainable, the accent on national solidarity exemplified in the 1962 Party election platform could be softened in a flash to justify joining ranks with non-Communist divisive forces.

The Relevance of Hinduism

It is because the centrifugal stresses built into the Indian Union are subject to persistent exploitation, and because he himself feels the disquieting tug of parochial loyalties, that the nationalist who is a Hindu experiences a pervasive frustration leading him to seek out some undiscovered new political identity. His caste and regional loyalties are in a deeply significant sense related to his identity as a Hindu, as this analysis has suggested, but they cannot encompass it in its totality and they lack, by their nature, the grand sweep of a loyalty addressed to pan-Indian Hindu symbolism. There is nevertheless a relatively uncomplicated clarity and coherence in the commitment of loyalty to Maharashtra or Bengal or Tamilnad which has yet to be imparted to an allegiance asked in the name of all of India in its confrontation with the exterior non-Hindu world.

An attempt to give the issue of Hindu political consciousness its due place and importance in a discussion of Indian nationalism is to some extent hampered by the inconclusive character of the efforts which have been made during the period of Nehru's secular leadership to mobilize anti-government political action

[22] "Questions and Answers—Nationalities and the Right of Secession," *Crossroads*, September 6, 1953, p. 10.

around a frankly communal Hindu banner. The so-called Hindu Right—the *Jan Sangh* party as the most significant example— has gained in vote appeal, but only within the five-state northern belt extending from the Punjab on the west to Bengal on the east; it is in these states that, together with the Hindu *Mahasabha*, the *Jan Sangh* vote for candidates for the lower house of Parliament increased from 8.5 per cent in 1952 to 15 per cent in 1957, and that the *Jan Sangh* increased its strength in legislative assembly seats from 46 to 115 in the 1962 elections. The image presented by the *Jan Sangh* next to a Congress Party with Nehru as its leader is a pale one, so that it has been easy to conclude that the Hindu communal appeal has been rejected by the electorate. Furthermore, because of the strong components of obscurantism, revivalism, and economic conservatism in the Hindu Right program, it is commonly assumed that a natural contradiction exists between a modernist appeal and a "Hindu" appeal, and that the latter must inevitably lose out in the twentieth century to some form of socialist party running on a bread-and-butter platform. The study of Indian politics has given relatively little attention to the possibility that a nationalist political movement offering a modernist economic and social program will itself manipulate Hindu symbolism to evoke a sense of pan-Indian solidarity.

Following the lead of Prime Minister Nehru, the Indian leadership has so far scrupulously avoided the use of Hindu symbolism. The case for nationalism in the first decade of Independence was reduced to the austere rationality of the proposition that unity offers the only route to modernity. At the same time the efforts of Nehru and some of his close intellectual followers to articulate a positive conception of Indian nationalism as a synthesis of Hindu and Moslem cultural influences have implied a recognition that the appeal of modernity may need the extra accent of a more specifically Indian theme. Modernism in the Western image, argues the Indian Muslim educator S. Abid Husain in one of the more notable of these efforts, leads to a common but not a national culture.[23] And it is a national culture that India must have for its survival. The basis for this common culture is

[23] S. Abid Husain, *The National Culture of India*, Bombay: 1956, p. 112. Nehru's own articulation is typified in *Discovery of India*, New York: 1946, esp. p. 241.

said to be found not only in the fusion of Hindu and Muslim influences in a new "Hindustani culture"[24] which had already taken place during the Mogul centuries, but in a special mental atmosphere[25] arising out of climatic and geographic factors peculiar to India, in a common national temper and mind.[26] To another prominent Indian Muslim, Minister of Education Humayun Kabir, this characteristically Indian temperament is expressed in a certain "philosophical outlook which has determined Indian culture in all of its various manifestations . . . a spirit of toleration."[27] The retired Indian diplomat K. M. Panikkar, a Hindu, speaks similarly of "the differentiating mark of Indian culture, a respect for the faiths and beliefs of others."[28]

But what happens when people do not behave in a spirit of toleration and mutual respect? The Nehru-style articulation of a liberal Indian nationalism has nothing in reserve to deal with the irrationality of particularist appeals, no larger symbolism of its own to bring forth in competition with the parochial symbolism of its opponents. All that Nehru can do when something goes awry with his nationalist ideal, as in the 1960 Assam riots when some 50 persons were killed and nearly 50,000 Bengalis fled their homes, or in the Hindu-Muslim clashes at Jubbulpore and Aligarh in 1961, is to deplore and exhort and utter what comes close to the language of despair. His response to the Assam debacle was an outcry that India had become for him "a haunted place . . . with all kinds of ghosts and spectres pursuing us—ghosts of the past, of our feelings, our conflicts." It was an ashamed confession that "our superficial covering of what you like to call 'nationalism' bursts open at the slightest irritation. The language question for them had become a symbol of their individuality, of their existence as Assamese, of their future. And when a thing becomes a symbol like that, rightly or wrongly, it becomes difficult to deal with. It becomes above reason."[29]

Disarmed and increasingly at bay, the older generation of leaders committed to a liberal nationalism seems somewhat inept

[24] Husain, *op. cit.*, pp. 13, 60, 80-83.
[25] *Ibid.*, p. 2.
[26] *Ibid.*, p. 6.
[27] *The Basis of Indian Culture*, Information Service of India, 1955, p. 14.
[28] *Ibid.*, p. 2.
[29] *Parliamentary Proceedings*, September 3, 1960, Cols. 6714, 6717, 6723.

and out of date in the eyes of a new generation impatient to come abreast of multiplying economic and political problems. It is the unashamed conviction even today of quite a few strategically placed Indians that an alternative must be discovered; and that it will have to be found, if not, as some say, in an Indian form of the Communist new religion, then in an equally "contemporary" political appeal which taps the deep emotional reserves of a time-honored Hindu faith.

Hinduism, we are told, has become irrelevant in the face of the scientific spirit;[30] but it all depends upon what one has in mind. If by Hinduism one means to denote the mythology and superstition that pass for religiosity at the village level, that is one thing, and here it can be agreed that popular Hinduism as now practiced is patently incompatible with the assumptions of modernism. In time, popular Hinduism is likely to be transformed, if not altogether undermined. But this is far from saying that Hinduism, broadly speaking, will lose its hold, for the heart of Hinduism is not necessarily to be found in its popular embodiments. When Radhakrishnan contrasted "the bewildering polytheism of the masses and the uncompromising monotheism of the classes,"[31] his purpose was to suggest that the true guardians of the faith were to be found among the classes. The Westernized Hindu who does not kneel down before the gods and who has intellectually rejected the philosophy and theology of Hinduism may not be emotionally disengaged; he may still continue to think of himself as a Hindu and to take this identity most seriously. Edward Shils in his study of the Indian intellectuals found "a quite elaborate religious consciousness, ranging from the performance of religious exercises early each morning, the daily reading of a sacred text, and the temptation to 'go into the forest' to an ineffable sense of the working of a trans-individual power or a belief that there is a ruling spirit in the universe." Even those "without very intense religious sensibility speak in religious metaphors. The Hindu pantheon permeates their imagery."[32] The question of a Hindu political identity appears

[30] For example, see Barbara Ward, *The Interplay of East and West*, New York: 1957, pp. 138-139.
[31] S. Radhakrishnan, *The Hindu View of Life*, London: 1927, p. 32.
[32] Edward Shils, *op. cit.*, p. 64.

to be separate and distinct from that of the disintegration of traditional religious forms under the impact of materialist thought. And this is a question that cries for attention in the light of the past half century of Indian political evolution.

It is not germane here whether, assessing the sequence of events leading up to Partition, one points the finger of guilt at the Hindus or the Muslims or the British or possibly all concerned. It should be enough to remind ourselves that the political consciousness of modern India has been to a very great extent a Hindu political consciousness. "The will of India at first to be a self-governing dominion within the Empire and later to be an independent nation," writes W. Norman Brown, "was the will of Hindu India . . . the stubborn fact remained that nationalism was a phenomenon of the Hindu community, and this community provided the strength and direction of the Congress."[33]

Faced with what was in some measure a cultural and even religious as well as a political onslaught, Hindus and Muslims alike reacted to British rule in a series of revivalist movements glorifying their own cultural achievements. In the case of Hindu India the initial response led by Ram Mohun Roy was a plea for a return to the original principles of Vedantism and for a regeneration of Hindu life through the incorporation of what was best in the influx of Western culture. The Brahmo Samaj sought to go even further in adapting the new spirit of reform to the Hindu revival, and this led, in turn, to the counterreaction of the ultra-orthodox pandits, of the zealots of the Arya Samaj and in time of Ramakrishna and Vivekananda. As against the Brahmo Samaj, Ramakrishna pleaded the virtues of the traditional Hindu ascetic ideal and defended the symbolism in Hindu worship which was under attack by the ultra-modernist Samaj. Subsequently, Vivekananda as his disciple stepped into the political arena with his inspirational message; and as Nehru has written, though his "gospel of nationalism was not in any way anti-Muslim or anti-anyone else, nor was it the somewhat narrow nationalism of the Arya Samaj, nonetheless Vivekananda's

[33] Cited by Stanley Maron, "The Pakistan Movement as a Cultural Crisis," a paper read at the Ninth Annual Meeting of the Association for Asian Studies, Boston, April 4, 1957, p. 7.

nationalism was a Hindu nationalism, and it had its roots in Hindu religion and culture."[34]

There was a strong chosen-people note in Vivekananda's assertion that the Hindu "has been the blessed child of God always," that "ours is the only true religion," and that "if there is any land on earth that can lay claim to be . . . the land where every soul wending its way Godward must come to attain its last home . . . it is India."[35] "India's gift to the world is the light spiritual,"[36] he declared, and it is in her spiritual mission that India may look for the secret of her own national consolidation. For in India "religious life forms the centre, the keynote of the whole music of national life." The one common ground for India with its great diversity "is our sacred traditions, our religion, and upon that we shall have to build."[37] As a consequence, he went on to say, "unity in religion is absolutely necessary as the first condition of the future of India." This did not mean raising the sword against Muslims, but it did mean their gradual peaceable absorption into a Hinduism irradiant with the lost spiritual power of its pristine days. He looked to a future twenty-five years hence in which "the whole Indian world would be once more Aryan" and in which every man of letters would be a Sanskrit scholar.[38]

What Vivekananda said was to be of peculiar importance, because while he spoke in the nominal language of religion, his listeners heard the message of a new political nationalism. Echoes of the evangelistic summons preached by Vivekananda all over India on his triumphant return from the World Parliament of Religions in 1897 carried over into the more strident credo of Aurobindo Ghose, with his declaration that "nationalism is a religion that has come from God," and his announcement that "when it is said that India shall be great, it is the Sanatan Dharma, the eternal religion, that shall expand and extend itself over the world. . . . The Sanatan Dharma, that is nationalism."[39] And a decade later in Maharashtra, the militant Hindu nation-

---

[34] *Glimpses of World History*, London: 1934, p. 437.
[35] Swami Vivekananda, *From Colombo to Almora*, Madras: 1897, p. 5.
[36] *Ibid.*, p. 10.
[37] *Ibid.*, p. 38.
[38] *Ibid.*, p. 62.
[39] W. T. Bary, *et al.*, *Sources of the Indian Tradition*, New York: 1958, pp. 730-731.

alist Bal Gangadhar Tilak paralleled Vivekananda with his insistence (in *Gita Rahasya*) that the *Bhagavad Gita* teaches the importance of action as well as contemplation, and that violence in a righteous cause is thus morally justifiable. The Hinduism of the *Gita*, wrote Tilak, "preaches that the whole of one's life should be turned into a sacrifice (*yajna*)," and this is indeed "the essence of the entire Vedic religion."[40]

Although one could quote at length from the scripture of extremist Hindu movements and their flamboyant leaders—Veer Savarkar of the *Mahasabha*, or M. S. Golwalkar of the *Rashtriya Swayamsevak Sangh*, or R.S.S., the militant (and quasimilitary) elite corps of the Hindu Right forces—this would in the present context amount to a most extraneous and misleading exercise. For the Hindu extremists were a marginal force throughout the period of the freedom movement and were no more able to challenge Gandhi in pre-Independence years than they have been able since 1947 to compete with Nehru. Their appeal has lacked the radical commitment on economic matters and the generally pervasive modernism of the one twentieth century Indian political figure who did offer a serious challenge to the Gandhi-Nehru leadership, and whose popular appeal rested in considerable measure on his identification with the Vivekananda-Tilak tradition.

The story of Subhas Chandra Bose can be told as nothing more than the exotic political adventure story of the Führer-like figure who organized the wartime Indian National Army and aligned it with the Axis in the cause of Indian Freedom. But the intensity of the devotion to the image of Netaji (Leader) on the part of a wide spectrum of Indians is a phenomenon demanding more searching investigation. Many an Indian who does not share with the close political partisans of Bose a disbelief in the finality of his death in a 1945 plane crash nonetheless cherishes the same intense wish that Bose "or someone like him" could somehow turn up one day on the figurative white charger. The tintype of Bose is given equal honor alongside that of Gandhi and Nehru in many Indian homes because Indian nationalism draws on a curiously ambivalent tradition. Gandhi struck a deep current when he spoke in the time-honored lan-

[40] *Ibid.*, p. 724.

guage of *Ahimsa* (non-violence). But it was no less the real thing
in Indian nationalism for Bose to invoke the tradition of the
Kshatriya and the Shakta,[41] and to insist, as Arjuna did in the
Gita, on the righteousness of violence in a righteous cause. In renunciation and the immolation of self in the chosen mission, said
Bose, one can find realization.[42] Embracing Vivekananda as "the
spiritual father of the Indian nationalist movement," he organized a student group at Calcutta University whose declared object was "to bring about a synthesis between religion and nationalism, not merely in the theoretical sphere but in practical
life as well."[43] For a time he thought of a life of renunciation in
the role of a *sadhu*, and looked to a retreat in the Himalayas as
his eventual goal. He made a well-publicized decision to stay a
celibate which also contributed to the Bose legend, though in the
wartime years which were to be his last he did marry in Berlin.

The popular image of Bose which took form during his prewar career as a declared rival of Gandhi and Nehru in Congress
Party councils was an image streaked unmistakably with the
colors of a fervent Hindu commitment. The mystic quality so
characteristic of Bose was most striking in autobiographical
speculations on the nature of reality which blended a certain
sneaking acceptance of marginal features of Shankara's doctrine
of Maya with Vivekananda's activist ideas, Aurobindo's asceti-
cism, and Hegelian notions of synthesis. Though reality cannot
be dismissed as illusory, it is "relative and not absolute. . . . This
reality is not static but dynamic [and] ever-changing."[44] It
would be difficult to imagine Nehru perceiving "the terrible
beauty of the smile of Kali in flashes of lightning,"[45] or solemnly
affirming a faith that "reality is Spirit working with a conscious
purpose through time and space," that "the world is a manifestation of Spirit," and that "just as Spirit is eternal, so also is the

[41] Chattar Singh Samra, "Subhas Chandra Bose: An Indian National
Hero," *op. cit.*, p. 77. Mr. Samra is preparing a book-length extension
of this study. The author is indebted to him for assistance in research
on Bose.
[42] Subhas Chandra Bose, *An Indian Pilgrim: The Autobiography of
Subhas Chandra Bose, 1897-1920*, Calcutta: 1948.
[43] *Ibid.*, pp. 67-75.
[44] *Ibid.*, pp. 139-140.
[45] Kali Charan Ghosh, "A Saint Turns Patriot," in S. R. Sharma, ed.,
Netaji, Agra: 1948, pp. 60-61.

world of Creation." Creation, Bose argued, does not and cannot end at any point in time, likening his religious thought in this respect to the Vaishnavite conception of the Eternal Play (*Nitya Leela*) of conflicting forces.[46]

The attachment of Bose to his Hindu heritage did not mean that he was in any sense a conservative, a traditionalist or a revivalist. On the contrary, the most revealing implications of the Bose record are suggested by the totality and urgency of his commitment to modernization and Westernization. He frankly contended that India "must have a political system—a State— of an authoritarian character,"[47] "a dictatorial government by a strong party bound together by military discipline . . . as the only means of holding India together."[48] The next phase in world history, Bose predicted, would produce "a synthesis between Communism and Fascism, and will it be a surprise if that synthesis is produced in India?"[49] He took a radical line on economic matters, looking to a "left-wing revolt" which would benefit "the masses . . . of the peasants and workers, and not . . . the vested interests, that is, the landlords, capitalists and money-lending classes," attacking Gandhi's economic views as capable of "unreserved acceptance by any Indian industrial magnate," and anticipating a wholly new monetary and credit system for the country. He cited the Ataturk example in advocating the Roman script[50] to bridge linguistic differences. At the same time, he sharply distinguished what he was advocating from the communist pattern, stressing that "Communism today has no sympathy with nationalism in any form," and contrasting the place of religion in traditional Indian and Russian society. "Owing to the close association between the Church and the State in Russian history and to the existence of an organized Church," declared Bose, "Communism in Russia has grown to be anti-religious and atheistic. In India, on the contrary, there being no organized Church and there being no association between the

---

[46] Subhas Chandra Bose, *An Indian Pilgrim*, *op. cit.*, p. 141.
[47] Subhas Chandra Bose, *The Indian Struggle*, London: 1935, p. 344.
[48] *Ibid.*, p. 346.
[49] Jagat S. Bright, ed., *Important Speeches and Writings of Subhas Chandra Bose*, Lahore: 1946, p. 371.
[50] *Famous Speeches and Letters of Subhas Chandra Bose*, Lahore: 1946, p. 27.

Church and the State, there is no feeling against religion as such."[51]

In post-Independence India the dominance of Nehru has given a secular cast to the political landscape which might not last long should bedrock forces come to the surface in future upheavals and realignments. Significantly, the secular nationalist Asoka Mehta, chairman of the Praja Socialist Party, has stressed that socialist ideology "will have to become increasingly nationalism-conscious and integrate within itself vital elements of our culture. Social awareness and national consciousness will together discover a new political fecundity." In particular he has suggested that politically conscious youth attracted to the Hindu extremist R.S.S. will in many cases grow dissatisfied with "the pot-bellied elements" of the movement and will then be responsive to other political invitations. Their training and respect for discipline "and the contempt for concepts of democracy and individual freedom instilled by the R.S.S. would attract them to the Communists, but their nationalism and idealism would be alienated; and though a section will undoubtedly go over to the Communists, a very much larger section will find understanding and hope in the Socialist Party."[52] For their part, the existing Hindu Right parties hope for accretions to their own ranks and appear to be making a few faint efforts to cash in on populist and pro-planning slogans on economic matters. The 1962 election platform of the *Jan Sangh*, for example, though retaining a bias against the public sector of economic development, talked of a minimum monthly wage of 125 rupees ($24) and pledged that if put in power the party would see that prices, wages, interest rates and profits would be "correlated . . . so that all sections of society become co-sharers in the increase in the national income."[53]

The critical question with respect to the future of Indian nationalism may well be whether social awareness and national consciousness can, in fact, discover together a "new political fecundity," and in this revivified union gain the strength to overpower the centrifugal forces threatening the Indian Union.

[51] Subhas Chandra Bose, *The Indian Struggle, op. cit.*, p. 348.
[52] Asoka Mehta, *The Political Mind of India*, Bombay: 1952, p. 31.
[53] Bharatiya Jan Sangh, *Election Manifesto*, Delhi: 1962, pp. 15, 3-4.

Indian nationalism will not be secure, however, if the effort to consummate such a union is left to the messianic xenophobe who equates Hindu glory with Muslim humiliation. In the last analysis the question becomes whether the vital elements of Hindu culture can be integrated into Indian nationalism within the larger framework of an over-all South Asian accommodation guaranteeing the security of the 45,000,000 Indian Muslims and of the predominantly Muslim state of Pakistan. An examination of nationalism in Pakistan would underscore problems of national consolidation comparable in scope and character to those in India, and would bring us back in full circle to the process of interaction governing political development in the two new states. Each in fearing for its own national integrity suspects that the adversary would not hesitate to strike in a moment of weakness or disarray. The progressive debilitation of political life on both sides of the border is likely to be arrested only if a confident and large-hearted nationalism can find sustenance within one or the other body politic.

It was the late national patriarch, Acharya Narendra Dev, who stated the challenge to the political imagination of the Indian leadership in its boldest terms. "So long as we do not feel secure in the integrity of our national self," he said, "we cannot take big decisions and risks and meet the challenge of our times."[54]

[54] *The Pioneer*, Lücknow: October 3, 1951, p. 1.

Chapter

9

Race and National
Identification:

The Republic of South Africa

EDWIN S. MUNGER

Nationalism there undoubtedly is in South Africa, but what do we mean when we talk of a South African nation? The original inhabitants—Strandlopers, Hottentots, Bushmen—have died out or are approaching extinction. South Africa for all practical purposes is peopled by comparatively recently adopted children. The first relatively modern invaders were Bantu-speaking Africans who occupied more than one-half of the country by the middle of the seventeenth century. The progenitors of the Afrikaners came next, taking the western Cape and later joining the British to halt the advancing Africans and still later to subjugate most of them. The first British contingents arrived in the first half of the nineteenth century and the Indians in the second half. The Coloured (mixed) community is in a measure representative of the indigenous groups and is alone in showing signs of a national rather than a sectionally chauvinistic attitude.

But if South Africa is not a nation, it does contain two powerful and competing nationalisms—African (10,000,000 persons) and Afrikaner (2,000,000)—revolving around each other like a binary star and far outshining the weak light of a nebulous South African nationalism. Thus not South African but Afrikaner and African nationalisms overshadow the country. Significantly, the man in the street—black, brown, or white—is familiar with the term "nation," although not as it is used in this book. The Afrikaner habit of speaking of *ons nasie* (our nation) to mean Afrikanerdom is recognized by other groups. Likewise, the concept of a Zulu "nation" is widely accepted. But the English word "nation" can never be a direct translation from the Zulu *Umhlobo*, which refers to "type" or "kind" and has a sociological rather than a political connotation. These two strong nationalisms inside the same borders show remarkable parallels in their form and provide a unique opportunity to test the theories suggested in the introduction to this volume.

The first stirrings of African nationalism followed the emergence of Afrikaner nationalism by about a century. Although African nationalism is barely at the beginning of its intermediate, developmental phase, its time lag behind Afrikaner nationalism has now shortened to about thirty years. After 1910, Afrikaners were allowed a peaceful if difficult path and came to political power at the close of their intermediate phase. Afrikaner nationalism is today in its final phase, although the process of full maturation has been warped by the threat of destruction. Africans, on the other hand, will probably not be allowed pacific procedures. Their ascendancy will come nearer the middle of the intermediate phase. If external forces did not appear to dominate South Africa's future, one might venture to predict that an African break-through would require at least a decade of active participation in what is now the exclusively "white" sphere; as it is, African political participation has begun in one form in the limited powers of the Transkei "parliament."

The Two Nationalisms: A Historical Sketch

Africa is the last of the great continents to make either a peaceful or a revolutionary transition from colonialism to nationalism. Prime Minister Harold Macmillan, in his famous "Winds of Change" speech delivered in Cape Town in 1960, told the Afrikaner M.P.'s that "in the history of our times yours will be recorded as the first of the African nationalisms."

Anti-colonialism, the seed of Afrikaner nationalism, has a long history in South Africa. The early Boers ("Boer" is the Dutch word for farmer) who rebelled against the tyrannical rule of the Dutch East India Company's governor in the eighteenth century were the first anti-colonialists south of the Sahara. Although Ethiopia has been autonomous for centuries and Liberia was founded as an independent state in 1847, the first African country actually to free itself of colonial rule was South Africa.

In 1836 the Afrikaners trekked to the interior away from British rule, and only seventeen years later, in 1853, the Transvaal Volksraad declared itself independent of the "civil or Church laws of the Cape Colony," and was recognized as such by the British Government. The first Transvaal war was fought after the British forcibly occupied the country in 1877 and ended with Transvaal independence in 1881. In sympathy with the cultural and political autonomy gained to the north, various *taal* or Afrikaans-language movements sprang up during the late nineteenth century in the intellectually more advanced British Cape Colony. The defeat of the Boer Commandos between 1899 and 1902 led to the constitution of South Africa in 1910. Afrikaner nationalism became full-blown in the new Union when the political nationalism of the north was extended to the south and wedded to the cultural nationalism flourishing there. Thus *Die Burger* was founded in Cape Town as the first Afrikaans daily in 1915, and appropriately had as its first editor a former Dutch Reformed Minister, the Reverend D. F. Malan, who later became with equal appropriateness the symbol of unity in the reconstituted National Party and the first prime minister of the Union in 1948. The powder horn, a symbol dating back to the early nineteenth century Voortrekkers and their many fights with African tribes, is retained today as the emblem of the National Party.

Afrikaner nationalists, like others in this century, soon realized that political independence does not satisfy nationalist aspirations if the symbols of the state are alien and economic control remains in foreign hands. Thus there was a bitter and successful struggle for Afrikaans language rights from 1905 until 1925; the fight for a co-equal South African flag was won in 1934, leading to the eventual disappearance of the Union Jack in 1958; and the battle for republican status ended in Afrikaner victory on May 31, 1961. The fight goes on for Afrikaner "equality" under the present massive South African English and foreign control of the country's industry and foreign trade. There are separate Afrikaans banks, insurance companies, savings societies, and cooperatives, just as on the cultural side there are Afrikaans universities and Afrikaans versions of the Red Cross (*Noodhulpliga*) and Boy Scouts (Voortrekkers). In the communications field the battle of nationalism is carried into the linguistically segregated newspapers, magazines, and radio.

The right of self-determination in South Africa has had a consistent appeal. The Boers and the latter-day Afrikaners—now a majority of the white population—had enjoyed the spiritual support of most of the world in the struggle against British colonialism. Subscription lists were filled in Boston and Baltimore for the Boers, and Boer sympathies divided the British people. But half a century later it is the African people of the Union who have the spiritual support of Americans and most United Kingdom citizens. Afrikaners who once profited from foreign sympathy are assailed on the same principles as they, in their turn, have become a colonial power inside South Africa.

Before Afrikaners gained even their first goal of language rights, the African National Congress had been formed in 1912 to begin its still uncompleted struggle for the same equal treatment by Afrikaners that the Afrikaners had wrung from the British and their descendants within South Africa. Bantu tribes had engaged in many wars, some successful, in protest against the gradual subjugation of the country east and north of the Kei River. There had been cross-tribal arrangements but none taking in Africans throughout the Union. Gradually the Bantu drifted to towns looking for work—usually the poorest paid and most unattractive jobs. Significantly, one of the first real labor strikes stemmed from the urbanization of Africans of various tribes on the Witwatersrand and the menial work assigned to them. In 1918 most of Johannesburg lacked a water-borne sewage system. African sanitary workers "downed buckets" and demanded sixpence a day more. The strike was linked to the demands of the new African National Congress for political change, loosely described as socialism, and was broken by imprisoning the leaders and using African police as scabs. In the 1920s Clements Kadalie, a remarkable Nyasaland African, organized African workers on a large scale in the Industrial and Commercial Workers Union and pressed for higher wages. The African National Congress led innumerable protests and continued preeminent in African politics until it began sharing leadership in 1960 with the Pan Africanist Congress, organized in 1958 principally by defecting A.N.C. members. Both these branches of the African nationalist movement, with the overwhelming mass of Africans behind them and with overseas support, continue to push for elementary human rights.

Both Afrikaner and African nationalism have grown out of a deep sense of pride, both were spurred on by deep humiliation, and both found sympathy from the outside world in their initial stages of development. South Africa therefore differs markedly from most European and Afro-Asian countries in a weakness rooted in its lack of a single unifying nationalism. Emergent African nationalism is akin to nationalism in underdeveloped parts of the world, while Afrikaner nationalism has had more in common with nationalism in Europe. But both are similar in that the political aspects of nationalism preceded separate linguistic developments. Afrikaans resembles Norwegian in that it was promoted as distinct from the prevailing languages (Dutch and English on the one hand and Danish on the other) as an expression of political nationalism. African nationalism in the Union stands above different linguistic groups for which a common language (such as Hindi in India) has not evolved. The language of African nationalism in South Africa is at present English, just as the languages of nationalism through most of the sub-Sahara are English and French.

The Non-Nationalists

If we look for the moment beyond Afrikaners and Africans, we find three important sub-groups in the Union below the threshold of nationalism: the 1,300,000 English-speaking white people; the Afrikaans-speaking Coloured community of 1,500,-000; and the 480,000 in the "Indian" group.

There is no convenient way to describe the English group, an indication of their strong sense of being South African rather than members of a discrete sub-group. This lack may also be taken rightly as a symbol of the bridge between Britain and English-speaking South Africans. The Union Castle Steamship line is a little like a ferryboat across the Irish Sea. "English" nationalism in South Africa is not clearly differentiated from nationalism in Great Britain. The only noteworthy English-speaking association on narrow political lines is UNESSA (United English-Speaking South Africans), a feeble organization led by an Irishman and linked to a half-baked revolutionary group. Its principal function is to issue, on behalf of the English section, strong statements which are usually highly unrepresentative and serve to infuriate the Afrikaners.

The tie with Britain has become weak, however, and there is no longer wide support for a Dominion Party. The Sons of England, a patriotic organization, is viewed as anachronistic by many local English. If English nationalism is subconsciously diffused by a form of dual loyalty, it is also unheard in the strident noise of the market place where most English energies are spent. With the principal exception of the eastern Cape and the plantations of Natal, the English farming community has disappeared or blended into the countryside. The English in business are concentrated at the seaports of Cape Town, Port Elizabeth and Durban, or in Johannesburg, the terminus of flights from Europe. For all of them ties with Great Britain are a matter of everyday practical importance, despite the loss of Commonwealth status in 1961.

The attitude of British-descended whites toward nationalism in general has gone through three phases. In the 1920s South Africa reflected some of the British anti-nationalism and antipatriotism that was summed up in the famous Oxford debate refusal to fight for king and country. This attitude was transmitted through South African newspaper editors, nearly all of whom were born in Great Britain, and through the English-medium universities whose faculties were likewise drawn from "home." But still a sense of imperial mission remained stronger on the outposts of empire than in Britain itself.

In the 1930s the militant nationalism of Hitler and Mussolini repelled the South African British and caused them to draw closer to the United Kingdom. There was criticism of Afrikaner Nationalism, but Dr. Malan's tiny group was then ineffective and the main proponent of Afrikaner Nationalism, General Hertzog, had made his peace, in a sense, with General Smuts (for the English) by joining the South African Party. This "smelting" occurred in the crucible of the Great Depression.

The breakup of this alliance in September 1939 unleashed the present Afrikaner Nationalism, which in turn created a spirit of greater anti-Afrikaner Nationalism among the British-descended South Africans in the 1940s and 1950s. Thus a dislike of nationalism in general spiralled into a specific dislike of Afrikaner Nationalism.

This feeling in turn explains why the "English" in South Africa consider UNESSA and its "nationalistic" statements as "cranky." The spirit of the "English" South Africans is not grouped around a central core of nationalism, but is identified with rather wide and elastic bonds. The resilience of these ties is proved by the remarkable cohesiveness of the English-speaking section through thirteen years of Afrikaner Nationalism. Despite incessant propaganda, the National Party has gained only a tiny minority of "English" votes and has depended upon the greater growth of the Afrikaner population and upon recapturing Afrikaner *Sappe* (voters for Smuts' South African Party) to swell its political strength. Although "English" support for the National Party did well up in 1962, this was due to external and internal threats more than to Dr. Verwoerd's gesture of including for the first time two English-speaking ministers in his cabinet.

The respective sizes of the white voting groups have long threatened obliteration of an "English" nationalism. To have solidified formally would have been to lose. Thus the "English" have been tactical voters and without exception have sacrificed the leadership of "their party" to Afrikaners. They have compromised on one issue after another in seeking to split Afrikaner Nationalism—successfully in the 1930s and so far unsuccessfully in the 1950s and 1960s.

A natural result of the "English" voters' everlasting readiness for tactical compromise was a repudiation of the United Party by a significant minority and the formation of a more liberal Progressive Party under an Afrikaner leader but with largely English-speaking support, including many South Africans of Jewish belief. Its adherents, especially in Natal, are both less anti-Afrikaans in a cultural sense and more pro-African than the bulk of United Party supporters. While the party captured a dozen sitting M.P.'s from the United Party, all but one were wiped out in the 1961 election. Still, a rich white suburb of Johannesburg elected its M.P. on a platform of merit and not color as the desired basis of the franchise, the first success of its kind in South African history. Further to the left, such "English" as Alan Paton and Patrick Duncan created a Liberal Party from all groups—a few Afrikaners but mostly "English" and Africans.

An English group-sense is also weakened by the feelings of the 103,000 members of the "English group" who are of Jewish descent. Under the pressure of anti-Semitism from both Afrikaner and English (although by 1962 this pressure was not nearly as strong as it is in the United States), and fearing African rule, South African Zionism is probably the strongest Zionism in the world. South African Jews have sent more money per capita to Israel than any Jewish group in the world—far exceeding the American—and a higher percentage of settlers has gone to Israel from South Africa than from the United States or any other country where Jews are relatively prosperous. In the days after South Africa withdrew from the Commonwealth, South African Jews not infrequently expressed the thought that they might have to go to Israel.

To the Jews must be added another white group which, although of Afrikaans descent, is socially, economically, and politically divorced from Afrikaner Nationalism as the Nationalists define it, and whose members are sometimes referred to as "anglicized Afrikaners." Although they speak English at home, this term is often resented. They claim to be South African and not Afrikaner or English, but as a group they have little cohesiveness. Some of them sing *Die Stem* as their national anthem, and others abhor it. They are South African for want of being anything else, but their position tends to be amorphous.

Within the so-called "Indian" community exists an understandable ambivalence. Since the days when a young lawyer named Mohandas Gandhi was arousing his people in Durban, the emotional tie with India has been kept firm by discrimination against Indians in South Africa. But divisions of loyalties between the land of their birth and the sub-continent of their origin have been fomented by the Hindu-Muslim split and by political differences between the South African Indian Congress and the Indian parent organization. Indian leaders meanwhile have sought to forge close bonds with African nationalists, but the Indian masses, many in daily competition with Zulus, have fearful memories of the worst rioting in the history of the country in 1949, when Zulus murdered and raped them and pillaged the Indian areas of Durban. Thus to seek the protection of Afrikaner policemen heightens the ambivalence. Only in the last few years has Afrikaner Nationalism conceded that the Indian community has a permanent future in South Africa.

The 1,500,000 members of the Coloured community, descended from Hottentots, Bushmen, Europeans, and "Malay" slaves from Java, with more recent additions of newer European and Bantu "genes," are a distinct and relatively stable community. They speak European languages (more Afrikaans than English), follow formal religions (more Christian than Muslim), and in the urban areas have achieved a middle-class personality. They fight against a particularistic national-group feeling because it runs contrary to their integration into the white community, and have fewer urges towards separate nationhood than any other major group. They tend to say, "We belong to South Africa," as opposed to the more common cry, "South Africa belongs to us." At the same time they find it relatively easy to accept the broader symbols of a South African nationalism; *God Save the Queen* and *Die Stem* are both sung on occasion, for example, and neither rankles the masses. Coloureds willingly served South Africa in two world wars and their veterans are

proud of it. A few individual friendships in South Africa bridge
the color chasm, but perhaps the only group affection is between
Cape Afrikaners and Cape Coloureds, who share a common
history, and, for many, a common ancestry. The middle-class
function in creating nationalism is demonstrated by the fact that
the Coloured community has proportionately the strongest middle class and the greatest intensity of class feeling as well as the
strongest sense of South African nationalism.

In summary, we can assess South African nationalism by
quoting Lincoln's admonition in his first inaugural address:
"Though passion may have strained, it must not break the bonds
of affection." This kind of humanism has little meaning for all
people in South Africa, because there is little affection for all
people. As the title of G. H. Calpin's book shouted, "There are
no South Africans." Even the English, Afrikaners, and Coloured
people who draw together against the *swart gevaar* (black
danger) do so out of fear, not in mutual affection.

The Search for Cohesion: Imitation

The two powerful nationalisms in South Africa have both been
deeply affected by that historical period during which, in a
common but distinct process of moving toward nationalism, they
entered a mimetic stage. Most Afrikaners first looked abroad
for a model in the 1930s, just as most Africans are taking their
first real look abroad today. Afrikaner nationalism just before
its final rise to power in 1948 was affected by the nationalistic
ideologies of pre-World War II Europe. Whatever was anti-
British looked attractive to Afrikaners; to many, Hitler and
National Socialism were preferable to Chamberlain and democracy. According to a court decision on a libel action, Dr.
Verwoerd, then editor of the party newspaper in the north,
Die Transvaler, supported Nazi Germany.[1] Various Nazi imitations sprang into existence, such as Oswald Pirow's New Order
and the anti-Semitic "Grey Shirts." The *Ossewa Brandwag*
(Ox-wagon watch) was more indigenously Afrikaans and gained

---

[1] But it must also be said that Verwoerd opposed the *Ossewa Brandwag*
so strenuously that a group of angry O.B.'s surprised him in his drive-
way one night and threatened to kill him.

significant strength throughout South Africa. In time it challenged the *Nasionale Party* as the torch bearer of Afrikaner
Nationalism.

All these movements had a superficial quality, their vitality
vitiated by distance from the European source and traditional
antipathy to Britain. The *Nasionale Party* led by Dr. D. F. Malan
clashed with the O.B. (as the *Ossewa Brandwag* was known)
during World War II. Afrikaner Nationalists attacked the O.B.
for Nazi associations and a bitter struggle ensued until the O.B.
was smashed in 1944. British propaganda against Germans in
World War I, later exposed as false, contributed to the
Afrikaners' very slow realization, during World War II, of the
mass murders of Jews. As the facts became evident and the
issues clarified, most Afrikaners saw World War II in a different
light and their contribution to the war against the German Reich
was strengthened.

A few individuals who privately believed in National Socialism
are still active as members of the *Nasionale Party*, but they are
far outnumbered by those who see it as conflicting with traditional Afrikaner values and who accordingly oppose it. Newspaper editorials in the "English" press of South Africa and in
Britain in the 1940s anticipated a full-fledged Nazi government
in South Africa by 1960. Professor Keppel-Jones, formerly of
Natal University and now of Queens in Canada, is one of many
who continued to apply the Nazi "image" after it had ceased to
be the model; he predicted in his history of the future, *When
Smuts Goes* (1948), that the great pogrom would take place in
1956. In fact, however, that was the year a Jewish group
presented Dr. Malan with a silver plate as the "Moses of the
Afrikaner people." Subsequently nationalist politicians inaugurated a number of synagogues, including the Great
Synagogue in Johannesburg, opened by Finance Minister Eben
Dönges, one of those associated with anti-Semitism in the 1930s.
The Afrikaner government has given extraordinary aid to Israel
in critical times, and Dr. Malan was the first head of state to
visit the new Israel. Today English clubs have more anti-
Semitic barriers than Afrikaans clubs.

In extremis, Afrikaner Nationalism may yet imitate the fascist
dictatorships of Europe, but for at least fifteen years these models

have been thoroughly discredited by the majority of Afrikaner leaders. Despite prevailing world judgment at the time, both Malan and Strijdom, although staunch segregationists, were anti-Nazi in belief; details of Malan's successful undercover fight against Nazism inside Afrikaner Nationalism have recently come to light. Nevertheless the influence of former Nazi supporters in the Nationalist caucus grew in 1961-1962, and led to strenuous attacks by the white opposition. However, the end of the mimetic stage of Afrikaner Nationalism was pointed up in 1962 when opponents of the so-called "anti-sabotage" law compared it to laws in Ghana, Hitler Germany, Spain, the Soviet Union, and Portugal. Certainly, the oversimplified "Nazi" label often attached to the Nationalist Party is an anachronistic epithet. The law—wise and necessary or vicious and oppressive—is not borrowed from abroad but is South African.

African nationalism, on the other hand, is only now at the mimetic stage. Despite greater education, higher incomes, more urbanization and deeper grievances, African nationalists in the Union have lagged politically behind their contemporaries elsewhere on the continent. One reason is not far to seek: stringent laws backed by a powerful police force and army. One must also include, seemingly paradoxically, the higher material standard of living achieved by successive African generations in the Union. When the famous American Negro actor Canada Lee visited various African political leaders in 1949 during the filming of "Cry, the Beloved Country," his comment to the writer was, "They never had it so good and they are afraid to die." In a sense, the material advances of Africans in the Union make revolutionary changes inevitable—and postpone them.

As models for African nationalism, three possibilities suggest themselves: democracy, communism, and neutralism. The last is an African- and Asian-created stance which may or may not be adopted *after* a nationalistic movement has succeeded, and as such has limited interest for Africans in the Republic at this stage. The preferred choice is very clearly Western democracy. In this choice Africans are deeply influenced by the Western milieu within which nearly all their leaders have been forged. For decades they have overheard the Afrikaner cries for political rights and for fair treatment in the market place by the English-speaking whites. On every hand Western democracy is extolled as the ideal, and in nearly every English-language newspaper Africans are told that Afrikaners do not practice it, and that if they did Africans would reach some of their cherished goals.

But such Western democratic techniques for gaining power as political parties, electoral campaigns, and ultimately the ballot box have never been freely offered to Africans in South Africa and are almost non-existent for them today. In the compromise of Union, the British government agreed to the exclusion of African voters from the common voters' roll outside the Cape Province. The British had hoped that the example of the Cape would extend to the other three provinces. Instead even these civil rights, which had been practiced only in the Cape Province, were withdrawn in 1936, and in 1959 even the representation of 9,000,000 Africans by three white M.P.'s was ended. The trade unions as a vehicle for political pressure are also effectively closed to Africans by discriminatory legislation. It is clear that any normal avenue of peaceful political expression common to the democracies of Western Europe would be summarily closed to Africans by legislation and machine guns.

The reaction has been a trend toward communist leadership of African nationalism. Thus the general strike of May 31, 1961, was led by three militant Marxists and former (if not present) adherents of the Communist Party of South Africa. Although this general strike failed, and the overall African leadership is by no means communist, the trend is in that direction. The practice of Prime Minister Verwoerd's government of labeling almost all African nationalism "communist" goes a long way toward building up an image of "communism" as a desirable ally in the minds of Africans, although the purpose of such tactics is to influence the leaders of the West to give the government their political and military support. The writer encountered an amusing twist in Windhoek, Southwest Africa, from African laborers who had gone to Walvis Bay to see the Soviet fishing fleet calling there. They returned surprised that the people the South African government was so against and afraid of were not "black" but "white."

Communism would seem, on the face of it, to have a great potential appeal to the ill-informed African mass. The reported economic achievements of some communist countries can be held up as inspirational models for African nationalists. But whatever the potential appeal communism has had, realization has never been approached. The Communist Party has had pitifully few successes since 1922, when Afrikaner miners went to the scaffold singing "The Red Flag," most ironically the song of an anti-black communism, for the party's greatest appeal in South Africa has always been to white citizens. Today it is to the anti-racist section of whites and, since 1950, to a group of Indian intellectuals.

The Communist Party never had more than 1,500 members while it was legal, and of this number fewer than a quarter were Africans. Although the Stalinist purge of the white Communist leadership in the 1920s represented an attempt to shift South African leadership from white to black hands, it was premature and wrecked the party organization; communism might otherwise have gained ground in the Great Depression, and really made strides when Soviet military efforts in World War II were earning the plaudits of the South African press.

For a generation most African nationalist leaders have fought against communist infiltration. In considering communism as a possible model, Africans in the Republic have so concentrated on their antipathy for local white Communists and their efforts at infiltrating African nationalism with the aid of African allies that the African nationalist leadership has never been able to raise its eyes to the world level to judge—for good or ill—the possibility of communism as a model.

Until recently, all potential communist-model nationalisms were white and European, a severe handicap in an atmosphere of white vs. black. Racially mixed parties at the Soviet Legation during World War II did erase certain doubts, but since the expulsion of the Soviet representatives from South Africa in 1956 the image of communism as "white" has grown.

Whereas the old Communist Party was inter-racial, the successor "Congress" movement is racially segregated, a series of "congresses" organized roughly according to race. The white members of the old Communist Party belong to and dominate the Congress of Democrats, a lily-white organization, and the principal one of the Congresses.[2] The subordinate organizations

[2] The racially integrated Liberal Party of South Africa says it is anti-fascist, anti-communist, and anti-apartheid.

include a weak Coloured Congress (with a white president), the strong Indian Congress, a weak trade union Congress (SACTU), and the African National Congress. The A.N.C. is by far the largest Congress unit and has the only relatively independent personality. The C.O.D. has from time to time manipulated the upper echelons of the A.N.C., sometimes by the simple means of giving a hungry man a job at fifty dollars a month. But it has failed in its efforts to extend to the grass roots, white or black.

Nevertheless, in a curious reaction against what some Africans, and especially the youth section of the A.N.C., felt was communist influence in the A.N.C., the Pan Africanist Congress was formed in 1958. It made rapid headway and was overtaking the A.N.C. in influence when its anti-pass campaign against the requirement that Africans carry internal passports came to a bloody end in the March 1960 Sharpeville massacre. Is the Pan-Africanist reaction more anti-white or anti-communist? It is difficult to judge. The dominant sentiment varies from one P.A.C. member to another. Because the "outsiders" allegedly manipulating the A.N.C. were both white and communist the question is not fully answerable.

The foregoing outline explains in part the focus of attention within African nationalism upon communism inside South Africa, and why communism outside is scarcely considered as a matrix on which to pattern African nationalism. African nationalism in the Republic thus lacks a strong theoretical model, for even though Marxism has little attraction, liberalism too will be ineffective so long as the ends of Western democracy remain divorced from the means of reaching them. In general, the A.N.C. wants full rights for all South African citizens, and the P.A.C. wants "Africa for the Africans" without specifying whether this slogan means expulsion of or cooperation with Europeans, Indians, and Coloured. In any case, the P.A.C. wants Western democracy for Africans, even though under prevailing conditions communist techniques have sometimes been adopted as a means of reaching Western democratic goals. Inconsistencies must clearly arise to make this curious marriage unstable, and the possibility that communist means will lead to communist ends is obvious.

Class and Nationalism

Within the two nationalisms there is no serious challenge to the consensus that class and other sectarian loyalties must be submitted to the national need. Afrikaner dogma thunders from a thousand platforms in behalf of what former Prime Minister Strijdom called "white Christian civilization"—as though civilization could only be white and Christian. This cry in turn is matched, as an overriding consideration for African nationalism, by a hatred of the very concept of color as a determinant of civilization, and a resolve to grind it into the red dust of Africa. It is perhaps remarkable, and a tribute to a small handful of whites with different ideas from those of the Strijdoms, that relatively unsophisticated Africans make a distinction between their opposition to the laws of some whites and "anti-whitism" in general. The year 1961, however, marked the rapid growth of African hatred for those people called in Xhosa the *Amaburu*, or Afrikaners.

The skewing of classes so that Afrikaners lack a normal size lower class and Africans a normal size upper and middle class means that the role of the upper class in importing foreign ideas (fascism, democracy, or communism, for example) is of less importance within Afrikaner nationalism than in other countries. But the existence of two juxtaposed nationalisms means that the upper class of South Africa as a whole—the whites—does act unwittingly as the importer of ideas for consumption by the lower class as a whole—the Africans. Whereas, ironically, Afrikaners once leaped to import nationalistic ideas in their struggle against the foreign and local "English," they now feel compelled to draw a curtain against such ideas and influence.

Class structure is of more marked significance to Afrikaner than to African nationalism. But divisive forces in both nationalisms rising out of the clash of interests are always relatively weak in the face of the powerful cohesive identification flowing from the clash of the two opposing nationalisms.

The transition of Afrikaners from an essentially rural people with their political strength embedded in *platteland* (prairie or rural) seats to their present position after the trek to the cities, the loss of some "tribal" mores, and equal dependence upon rural and urban worker constituencies has not produced a visible conflict of interest within the ethnic group. Taxes are still arranged for the benefit of the farmer and, with the rapid rise in the value of old farms, special care has been taken to help farmers avoid heavy death duties. Petitions at National Party Congresses may raise protests from the Nationalist consumer, but they can never be very loud without attracting criticism for dividing the *volk*.

Classlessness in Afrikaner society is reflected in almost every family's possessing the ultimate symbol of upper-class status: a servant. Income and number of servants can be directly correlated among the Afrikaners, with one important exception: at the lowest end of the Afrikaner income scale, such as among the railroad workers, there is a rise in the number of servants per family because having a servant becomes an absolute status necessity. To "live like a Kaffir" is the ultimate in degradation. Throughout the poorer "white" rural areas (where the population is still predominantly African or Coloured) there is a strong undertone of resentment against the National Party among its supporters for spending "too much money" on African schooling and hospitals. Opposition United Party speakers—away from their relatively liberal colleagues in the cities—gain a local popularity by attacking the government for "doing too much for the Kaffirs."

Another indication of "classlessness" among Afrikaners is the relatively small number of Afrikaner surnames. There is scarcely an Afrikaans surname with strong upper-class connotations. Afrikaners are also prone to extended family relationships, with a multiplicity of cousin ties; thus most Afrikaners recognize relatives throughout every walk of Afrikaner life.

In the early phase of nationalism, nearly all Afrikaners were in one class—uneducated if sober and industrious farmers, plus a sprinkling of educated *predikante* or ministers. This homogeneity was not peculiar to Afrikanerdom, but was indicative of the general poverty of all South Africa until the discovery of gold and diamonds. In the intermediate phase, wide class differences arose as some of the Afrikaners went into a new world. The gap between the educated and prosperous, on one hand, and the semi-educated and poor, such as the *bywoners* or landless farmers, on the other hand, reached its height in the 1930s. Afrikaner nationalism received an impetus from organized efforts to "rescue" the "poor white" Afrikaners, as described in the next section.

By 1961 middle and lower-class Afrikaner groups were able to gratify their wishes for higher levels of consumption. Egalitarianism marks Afrikanerdom once more, and the wide gap between the *arm blanke* (poor whites) and the cultivated Afrikaner has been greatly lessened. Maturation of Afrikaner society has led to a further marked blurring of social boundaries as all classes have become consumers at a fairly high level. Although social mobility is high, the paths from the bottom of Afrikaner society to the top have become routinized and there are few shortcuts. It is no longer a unique distinction to be an Afrikaner pharmacist, admiral, bank president, or diplomat. The greater complexity of society and increased international interdependence, especially in the business realm, have led to changing loyalties. An Afrikaner firm is at the apex of cigarette selling in the world, with notable successes in Great Britain, Europe, Canada, and Australia. The Afrikaner managerial team recognizes that its own loyalties have broadened and that it now looks back upon South Africa as a whole rather than upon Afrikanerdom alone.

The hypothesis that replacement of a bi-class by a tri-class social system precipitates crises in leadership does not apply with full force to Afrikaner or African nationalisms because of their unique interrelationship. Although Afrikaner nationalism has matured, it has never faced greater outside threats than it does today, threats that produce a concomitant call for unity. Nevertheless, minor crises of leadership are developing in the once politically homogeneous Afrikaner *volk*. The first time a National Party caucus vote for a new prime minister failed of unanimity was in the 1958 choice of Dr. Hendrik Verwoerd. By 1962, however, Verwoerd dominated his party by the force of ideas to a greater extent than his predecessors.

In viewing the Afrikaner and African middle classes, one is struck by the lack of a middle-ground meeting place for the creation of a South African nationalism. Today a truly unified middle class for the whole country would be composed of lower-class Afrikaner workers and upper-class Africans with unusual skills or in business. Instead of providing the basis for the construction of a single national society, however, such groups are the very point of the most explosive contact.

Beneath the monolithic exterior of African society are greater tribal than class differences. The extended family system and the fact that nearly every African family has members or relatives in both the city and the tribal reserves also militate against the emergence of a true class system. In this kind of social structure the detribalized African workers constitute a modern "tribe." Even in the cities, however, most minor altercations and practically all the more significant mob fighting by Africans are still on a tribal basis. Yet it is only in the city that African nationalism finds a unity across tribal lines in its struggle. And the heat of this lengthy struggle (the African National Congress itself, as we have seen, dates from 1912) tends to melt new and tenuous class divisions.

Financially Africans are only beginning to gain significance. The traditional head (or hut) tax on all Africans has given way to a graduated income tax. It is unlikely that a majority of Africans subject to this new tax actually pay it, but the figures are still revealing. In 1958 there were 1,025,749 income tax payers, of whom 920,743 were white. Among the 2,448 Africans, only three reported incomes of over $22,000. Once Africans reach the level of paying income tax, however, the distribution of taxpayers by categories of income is similar to that of the whites.

Under General Smuts' administration Africans of the upper stratum, as defined largely by education and income, were exempted from various segregation laws, such as that requiring the carrying of passes. Whether or not this tolerance would in time have produced an upper class of Africans "loyal" to the whites is dubious. Some Afrikaners were themselves "anglicized" by being drawn up into the "English" upper class, but this move eventually intensified Afrikaner nationalism. Today discrimination against Africans, from the college graduate in his business suit to the rural laborer in his blanket, is a strong force in overriding class consciousness among them. In African society the change from a bi-class to a tri-class system involves the replacement of traditional authorities by detribalized African leaders. Because the latter are unusually able and the former often inept, the old gives way to the new with fewer crises than might be expected. As with the Afrikaners, the need for unity and for the strongest leadership in the face of the ever present "enemy" makes the man who divides an unpopular one.

Although Africans in the Republic are quantitatively the most technologically advanced African group on the continent, occupational specialization is largely confined to the upper classes and has restricted the growth of nationalism in the lower classes. Thus the Africans of the rural areas, with their traditional tribal agriculture, are relatively quiescent, as are the gold mine laborers. Although some of the latter are specialized, they are kept from contact with nationalizing influences by the residential compound system. Nationalism's penetration of the lower classes is increased by their degree of urbanization and cultural Westernization, coupled with the high visibility quotient every African carries with him—a circumstance that also forces the upper and middle classes into an identification with the lower class and thus broadens the social base of nationalism. The staying power of tribal authority—even after two hundred years of contact with Western culture—was striking until it was weakened in recent years by government control and manipulation of the chiefs and traditional authorities. African nationalism has moved into the vacuum. The chief in the shadow of government power rarely emerges as an alternative pole of loyalty to the urban African politician. The situation is the opposite of that in the enclave of Basutoland and in Swaziland, which adjoins South Africa, where British toleration and encouragement of traditional authority have allowed it to become a conservative force resisting the growth of nationalism. Swazi and Basuto loyalties have as yet to be transferred from the Swazi and Basuto peoples to the territories named after them.

The nearly total exclusion of Africans from the Western political system and the workings of the "pass laws" might drive Africans back to their traditional tribal political systems in the Republic were it not that the "hated" government is attempting to encourage just such a development. The result is an extension of nationalism into the lower class to a greater extent than would otherwise occur. A wobbly government syllogism runs as follows: urban areas with African "agitators" are politically disturbed; rural areas without "agitators" are quiet; therefore, send the "agitators" to the rural areas. This final step was extensively carried out in the year following the Sharpeville massacre of March 1960. The result, however, was not the anticipated tranquillity in the countryside, but rather an extension of unrest and disorder to many rural areas. History may record that the base of African nationalism was broadened at a critical time with the assistance of Afrikaner nationalism.

In surveying the entire development of Afrikaner and African nationalism, we see clearly that class has been subordinated to a kind of group interest by almost all sections at almost all times. Now, as in the last century, being white counts for more than being skilled or rich. The labor movement from 1900 to 1930 was predominantly English (including Cornish) and Welsh. The idea of the unity of the working class—white, black, brown —thus lost out first among the British workers. When the Afrikaners trekked to the cities during the depression and grew in numbers until they formed the bulk of white workers, they merely extended the racial practices already being followed. Old-time white labor leaders had hoped that the creation of an Afrikaans proletariat would lead to a Labor Government, but the call of Afrikaner nationalism combined with his racial fears made the non-communist Afrikaner worker the close ally of the Afrikaner farmer and the new Afrikaner industrialist.

The wobbly Communist line in South Africa has already been mentioned. Starting off with an appeal to all "working men," it was twisted during the Stalinist purges of the 1930s toward the attainment of a "Native Republic," and a potentially flourishing organization was destroyed because of Moscow's insistence that Afrikaner and English working men be told to fight for an African republic in which they would have a minor position because of their race. This line was reversed less than a decade later, but by then many of the ablest comrades had been expelled and the sympathy of most white unions permanently alienated. What has survived is the policy of the 1930s that the party must be kept small and that African nationalism must be encouraged through African organizations. There is thus a high degree of theoretical knowledge, discipline, and flexibility within a small party. But still the party places its greatest emphasis on nationalism and not on class; consequently all Africans, no matter how bourgeois, are considered in a common stream along with all whites who support the African cause.

Nor has there been much reason to consider class on the noncommunist African side in the political struggle. Clements Kadalie's Industrial and Commercial Workers Union of Africa, formed in 1919, has been the most successful African union in South Africa. It set a pattern of fighting for African rights, both economic and political, without reference to a class pattern involving whites, and it resisted attempts by white Communists to control it at a time when this policy was the party line. Subsequent African organizations have been formed on a racial basis (although not always with racist platforms) addressing their appeal to Africans of all classes. Almost all have continued to resist being turned to communist ends by Communists of whatever race, some, such as the African National Congress, with mixed success, others staying well clear of communist manipulation. Where the goal is the overthrow of the government, which the Communists want, or even sweeping reforms such as some African organizations seek, there will always, however, be a measure of cooperation in a common cause between the Communists and African organizations.

Until the recent change in the character of the multi-racial Liberal Party from a parliamentary party to one of all-out identification with democracy for all and hence with the African cause, the Communists had no competition in the "freedom struggle" from any organized democratic parties. The Liberal Party was born economically capitalist and staunchly opposed to totalitarianism of right and left. Although some elements in it moved toward underground tactical popular front alliances with Communists in 1962, the Liberal Party has not sought to introduce class issues as a means of either dividing or uniting the population. Its relative weakness both within the white electorate and among the African mass is itself indicative of how Afrikaner and African nationalism have polarized political forces. In an alternate sense, however, they have also prolonged class concepts, and may be viewed as two huge feudal classes divided by color. South African society thus lacks a true middle class and its integrating value of a *South African* nationalism. Class in its fullest sense has become synonymous with color.

Massification

The possibility of including all social classes within one nation through massification derived from a high level of technology is characteristic of the Afrikaner case. Afrikaners have a national concern for the *armblanke* (poor whites). The intermediate phase of Afrikaner nationalism was given a strong impetus by the centenary celebration of the Great Trek of 1834-1838. The enthusiasm then engendered was channeled in 1939 into the *Reddingsdaadbond* (relief action society) to uplift the poor whites (mostly Afrikaners, then 45 per cent of the total Afrikaner population) and to make them strong components of the Afrikaner nation. Similar manifestations involved even far-flung offshoots of Afrikanerdom in Kenya, Argentina, and Angola. The *trek boers* of Angola were "rescued" and rehabilitated with a sense of devotion. The so-called "civilized labour policy" on the government railroads during the depression of the 1930s had replaced African pick and shovel workers with Afrikaner laborers at higher wages. Prime Minister Hertzog, backed by General Smuts, saw his first responsibility as prime minister not to all the people of South Africa but to his own people, the Afrikaners. The cry that "our government" must help "our people first" is still heard whenever a particularly costly Coloured school or African hospital is built. The wife of a minister in the Verwoerd cabinet explained to the writer her opposition to the present expansion of Coloured education because "our people need help first"!

A massification of African society deriving from a high order of specialization has yet to occur. An obvious contributing factor is education. In 1960, of the 10,000,000 Africans, only 250,000 had passed primary school, 70,000 had passed junior high school, 15,000 had passed high school, and but 2,000 had been graduated from a university. Although South Africa has outstripped other African countries in producing African university graduates locally, the Republic has fallen far behind in the numbers of

Africans receiving degrees abroad and in the rate of producing graduates at home. The demand for secondary school education by Africans has been so tremendous as to force a dangerous expansion in relation to the number of trained teachers available. From 1949 to 1960, the number of secondary schools rose from 94 to 288. School matriculation passes, roughly equivalent to high school diplomas, dropped from 47 per cent of the candidates in 1953 to only 17 per cent in 1960, although the absolute number of successful candidates increased.

That nationalist symbols and ideologies may be transmitted by a cosmopolitan group before social, political, and economic structures are articulated to the point of immediate function is clearly revealed by the particular South African circumstances. Day by day, Africans can examine in minute detail the paraphernalia of nationalism laid out at full length by Afrikaners in public actions and in their press. It is simplicity itself to take a *stryddag* (struggle day—a party meeting) speech of the most emotional content and to substitute "African" for "Afrikaner." Almost every charge the Afrikaners lay against the "English"— one-time political control, domination of finance and commerce, exclusive private schools—can be trebled when Africans want to accuse Afrikaners. There are more than enough heroes to fill both pantheons. But whereas African society in the Republic has enough immediately available talent to give meaning to the less complicated political and economic structures of, say, Uganda or even the Congo, such structures in South Africa are in many ways more complicated than those of Western Europe. Unlike Ghana with its cocoa monoculture and its gold and diamond mines, South Africa has a diversified fruit and grain export trade and giant steel mills; it produces a fifth of its gasoline from coal, and manufactures such complicated machinery as the gold mining equipment sold to Ghana.

Most whites in South Africa believe, correctly, that there are not enough educated and skilled Africans to take over all the administrative and technical posts in such a complex society at present levels of efficiency. Most whites miss the point that the development of Bantu leadership in Africa has not meant that every non-African was immediately displaced, and that, furthermore, no country (including the United States and the Soviet

Union) develops at a comparable stage without employing technicians from outside the national group. Current derogatory comments on African technical and administrative abilities are but new words to an old tune. In South Africa in 1910, when trucks were supplanting horse-drawn wagons, it was commonly asserted by whites that "the native will never be able to drive mechanical vehicles." By contrast, senior government civil servants in 1962 excuse various signs of inefficiency by pointing out that three million whites (in practice largely restricted to Afrikaners) "must" furnish the administrative talent for a country of fifteen million. There is a significant number of civil service posts where "non-whites," limited though they are in training opportunities, would immediately improve the caliber of performance. The Cape Town City Council has had notable success with Coloured traffic policemen, but the government has prohibited the hiring of more of them and legally barred the employment of "non-white" parking meter inspectors!

The only efforts to give Africans necessary training are made with an eye to the growth of the "self-governing Bantustans" (the Government prefers the expression, "Bantu Homelands") in which such trained people may apply their talents over a wider area. The skills possessed in African society thus are often gained despite, as well as in some measure because of, the presence of a cosmopolitan group which is ambivalent, to say the least, about passing on a wide range of skills or giving opportunities for their employment. Nonetheless Africans who show skills are given jobs in which they can use them, and may reach labor supervisory but not managerial levels in "white" firms.

It is a common sight among the soaring skyscrapers and honking traffic of Johannesburg to see a crowd of Africans wearing their tribal blankets en route to their first mine employment. Many who wait confused by a traffic light are from outside the Republic and have never driven in a motor car. The contrast with a succession of poised urban Africans wearing smart single-breasted suits and carrying briefcases is a measure of the distance spanned in a few years. The interaction between Afrikaner and African and the daily cultural contact despite *apartheid* laws, especially in urban areas, enormously accelerate the rate of change among the undeveloped African group in the Republic.

The transition from a rural, almost subsistence economy to a highly intricate money economy is one the Afrikaner has but recently completed. The Africans are as yet only in midstream. Many deep South African problems are obscured by the still deeper racial issue. They include the Afrikaner's transformation within a generation from a general farmer—often a poor and even landless one—to a prosperous exporting farmer or factory foreman or bank manager. A hundred years of industrial revolution in Europe are being compressed into twenty years in South Africa. It is surprising that more non-racial disorders and dislocations have not taken place, and that South Africa is among the nations of the world with the fewest strikes and industrial disturbances. While absence of strife in this area can have one explanation for African workers, it is also true of white workers and was so for twenty-five years before the present Afrikaner Nationalist government came into power.

The inherent complexity of new economic techniques and the nature of modern ideologies has led to the necessity of mass recruitment into the new social, political, and occupational groups. For Afrikaners, the path has been a straightforward one as they have moved from being a pastoral people with few occupations to a half-urban people in a complex economy with great occupational diversity. For Africans, the first factor is the movement from a simple rural society to a complex urban society; second comes the movement from African society (really societies) to Western society; and third, the operation of the color bar at almost all levels of society.

The Afrikaner, of course, has been faced with only the first factor. He has his church and other institutions to follow him to the city, and also his political power and racial advantage in seeking work. Nevertheless Afrikaners have had an extremely difficult time in making this one transition. Great tears in the traditional fabric of Afrikaner mores are evident in the frequency of juvenile delinquency, prostitution, and loss of religious belief among those Afrikaners who change under the city's impact. In the lower class this disorganization shows in their "sexsational" reading matter. Upper-class Afrikaner reactions are conveyed by numerous Afrikaans poems contrasting pure rural life with evil city life.

Africans face all these problems several times over. Many studies, such as Laura Longmore's *The Dispossessed*, a study of the sex life of African women in Johannesburg, reveal the disintegration of African mores under pressure. But before these society-destroying influences have run their course, Africans are confronted with forces emanating not only from the Industrial Revolution, as outlined above, but also from the political forces of the French, American, and Russian Revolutions.

The African professional classes have been the most successful in breaking barriers into urban occupations; racial barriers are higher in commerce and industry. One result is a form of labor bootlegging. An African may be employed as a laborer or semi-skilled worker in a small shop, and actually perform skilled tasks for which he can usually demand under-the-table bonuses. In large factories jobs are declassified from skilled to semi-skilled to allow the use of African workers. Afrikaners have shown no greater reluctance than other employers to use such tactics; in fact, they have taken the lead in shifting clothing factories to the borders of the African reserves where the ceiling on employment of skilled Africans does not apply.

That new industrial techniques lead to the necessity of mass recruitment into new occupations is as true for Africans in the Republic as it has been everywhere else. It means that thirteen years of Afrikaner Nationalism, with essentially conservative and traditional economic policies, have seen the continued movement of Africans into urban and so-called European areas, and greater economic interdependence than ever before in South African history. If this mobility is possibly not as great as the movement of Africans to the cities from 1940-1947 under a war-time industrial boom, the stream was certainly not reversed as the Nationalists promised. Extraordinarily strict measures in 1960-1962 kept down and slightly reduced the African population in Cape Town, after a rapid burgeoning from 1948-1960. In 1959 Dr. Verwoerd said that the final reversal of the African movement to the "European areas" would not come until 1970. While this estimate is more realistic sociologically than the naive predictions of the Nationalists in 1948, it may be even more naive politically in the face of internal and external pressures on *apartheid*. This shattering of the original economic theories and timetable of *apartheid*, backed by a host of laws and political exhortations, has come from the apparently inexorable pressure for mass recruitment. Most of the social and political grievances of Africans are intensified when occupational recruitment is not accompanied by recruitment into new social and political groups. Nationalist practice has accelerated the eventual breakdown of segregation by allowing more economic integration while assuming that only a man's hands may be recruited, omitting the rest of his person. It was not until 1959—eleven years after *apartheid* started in earnest—that this fallacy was recognized and the Bantustan theory was seriously advanced in an effort to meet the problem.

Communications

Mass communications have of course accelerated the recruitment of both Africans and Afrikaners to the cities and to their respective nationalisms. The accompanying "revolution of consumer expectations" is largely completed among Afrikaners, while most African appetites are still merely being whetted.

Long before living standards started to rise, the first cultural movement among Afrikaners was built around the *Afrikaanse Patriot*, published near Cape Town in 1876. Afrikaner nationalism also received a massive organizing boost with the establishment in Cape Town in 1915 of the first modern Afrikaans paper, *Die Burger*, under the editorship of Dr. D. F. Malan, later prime minister.

Although there have been African-owned newspapers, it is striking that the African press today is European-controlled, even though African-edited. Ragged papers are started throughout Africa by Africans, but Republic Africans who have, on the whole, greater capital and more journalistic experience to start papers do not do so on their own. The reason lies partly in the competition of the so-called "English" newspapers, read by large numbers of urban Africans. In fact, Republic Africans lead the sub-Sahara in literary and newspaper readership. One out of every four readers of some "European" dailies are Africans, and this "newspaper integration" is so potent for Africans who read English that it smothers efforts to establish a daily

African press. Educated Coloured people also regularly read publications aimed at Afrikaners.

Despite the lack of African daily papers, it cannot be said that any one newspaper in the whole country has a significant influence on all groups, although the often sensational *Sunday Times* of Johannesburg is widely read by English, Afrikaners, and Africans throughout the Transvaal. Less than 10 per cent of the English read Afrikaans papers and less than 35 per cent of the Afrikaners read *die Engelse pers*. Perhaps 95 per cent of the upper classes of all groups and races read the English press as a first, second, or third paper.

Magazines mark another distinction between the previously rural Afrikaners and the Africans, as evidenced by the low cultural and moral tone of many best-selling Afrikaans magazines. In the last decade a better quality became apparent in *Die Huisgenoot* (a magazine like *The Saturday Evening Post*) and in *Sjarme (Charm)*.[3] All African magazines are still tailored for detribalized Africans and are also cheaper than their potential competitors aimed at English readers. Picture magazines such as *Drum, Zonk,* and *Bona,* which are similar to *Ebony* and *Life,* have national circulations. The first two are sold throughout English-speaking Africa, while *Bona* has various vernacular editions. Sex, violence, African politics, and African achievements are the main fare.

State-controlled Radio South Africa provides four programs —English, Afrikaans, a commercial channel in both these languages, and a Bantu program. The Bantu service, the largest of all, is backed by a large and well trained African technical and editorial staff. "European" radio programs are, however, commonly heard by Africans. A proposed shift from AM to FM is calculated to control reception of foreign broadcasts at some future date, but at present the thousands of Africans who own radios capable of short wave reception are free to listen as they please to London, Peking, Moscow, etc.

The absence of television stems partly from a drive to shield Africans, but more importantly from the presence of the old

[3] Much earlier *Die Huisgenoot* had been a publication of literary merit, so much so that Mrs. Verwoerd wrote her M.A. thesis on its cultural influence.

Afrikaans-English split. It would be inordinately expensive to produce Afrikaans programs of the same quality as English programs, which could be purchased abroad; hence the struggle over European languages, and not finances, keeps South Africa behind such poorer African countries as Southern Rhodesia, Nigeria, and Egypt in the use of television.

Motion pictures and the theater are ideally adapted to the aims of Afrikaner nationalism because audiences can be restricted and the "black" man kept from looking over the "white" man's shoulder. Films for Africans are censored differently from those for whites, but there is virtually no restriction on plays. Imported books are occasionally banned; more often, however, the expensive hard-cover edition is allowed in, while the cheaper paperback with a sensational cover, the one more likely to be purchased by Africans, is kept out.

But despite restrictions of race, the African population of the Republic receives in ample measure the force of Western culture. Political ideas from abroad are not really blocked, because of the wide circulation of the English language press. Paradoxically, there is no country in Africa where more forceful personal attacks can be made on government officials without reprisals than South Africa. Although the English press does screen out some economic news favorable to communist countries, the communist-edited newspaper with the greatest circulation in Africa was published in the Republic until 1962. And in addition to what they learn from the usual media, nowhere in the world can a higher percentage of "underdeveloped people" see so easily, many of them every day of their lives, the benefits available to more fortunate men. Furthermore, because some cream spills over to the poor relation, there is a distinct taste for a better material life. Africans in South Africa have four times as many automobiles (100,000) per capita as do the citizens of the Soviet Union (575,000). In some smart downtown Johannesburg clothing stores, one-half of the higher priced men's suits are sold to Africans. In the tribal reserves, where there are fewer European "models" to advertise what a high standard of living can mean, local-boys-made-good return from the city as walking advertisements. Expectations of economic advance are high throughout both urban and rural African society.

In spite of the open nature of the communications media and the daily interrelation of white and African society in the streets and in offices, however, the door is virtually closed to cultural and political contact of one group with another across color lines. The three white representatives of the Africans who sat in Parliament until they were removed in 1959 were not important for their tiny voting strength, but as voices of some African opinion. Their replacement by tribal political structures has not been accepted by the majority of Africans, and the clumsy arrangements for chiefs to have "ambassadors" in urban areas provide a hopelessly inadequate outlet for politically conscious city Africans.

The Absence of Universal Symbols of Nationalism

Traditional symbols of nationalism scarcely apply for all of South Africa. Even before the Crown disappeared with the advent of the republic, it had carried little weight with Afrikaners. They demonstrated their wartime dislike of Britain by refusing to stand in theaters for *God Save the King;* on many occasions their rude rush for the exits provoked a free-for-all fight with those who regarded it as a sacred hymn. Today the anthem is *Die Stem* ("The Call")—one of the best written and most moving of national anthems—but its historical allusions to the creak of the trekker ox-wagons have deep meaning only for the Afrikaner. When Afrikaners sing *ons sal offer wat jy vra* ("give what you ask") and "live and die for South Africa," the meaning applies only to the Afrikaner nation. One has only to hear the anthem sung by Afrikaners in Afrikaans and then on a very rare occasion by the "English" in English to know the tremendous emotional difference. There is now, however, a growing number of "English" who do sing it in Afrikaans with a sentiment approaching that of the Afrikaner. But neither the old nor the new anthem has emotional significance for the African population. All the African sub-groups recognize *Nkosi Sikileli 'Afrika* ("God Bless Africa")—not *South* Africa—as their anthem even when it is sung in different tribal languages.

Another indication of the lack of an all-embracing South African nationalism is the fact that, despite the great fortunes made in the country, there are almost no great philanthropists. Universities, art galleries, libraries, and research of all kinds cry out for assistance, but few significant bequests have been made. Cecil John Rhodes was pre-Union English and scarcely counts. The wealthiest South African magnate, Sir Ernest Oppenheimer, died without leaving a substantial charitable bequest, although his wise son made large gifts in his father's name. The sons and grandsons of such earlier mining magnates as Abe Bailey and J. B. Robinson also show a deep concern for South Africa. But on the whole Afrikaners have become rich too recently, perhaps, and Africans not at all, to encourage the expectation of giving on a truly national scale.[4] Even though there is some giving by individuals on a country-wide basis, the narrower appeal of the group to which the donor belongs far outruns any sense of general South Africanism.

Military policy, too, responds to ethnic particularism. Official defense policy now has shifted to concentration upon internal rather than external dangers. The government explicitly recognized the lack of South African nationalism in 1960 when it pushed the organization of voluntary Commandos (a Boer War term) among the Afrikaans-speaking whites alone. New Centurion tanks were sold to Switzerland while armored cars were bought from Britain and sub-machine guns from Belgium. These measures marked a change in the answer to the question whether the country's citizens would defend it in time of war. In World War I thousands of Africans performed manual labor in France as members of the "Native Corps," and the Cape Coloured Corps did transport work. In World War II the Cape Corps continued and, in practice, its soldiers in North Africa were armed, although no Africans were armed to oppose Hitlerian racialism. General Smuts had 25,000 Zulus trained to fight an invasion, but they were never used. Today the defense forces, even though they have expanded rapidly from 1960 through 1962, include only whites. The successive narrowing of the categories of dependable soldiers has a striking counterpart in the attitude toward disloyalty.

---

[4] Substantial numbers of Afrikaners are worth half a million dollars, but their wealth is tied up in land and has not been easily divisible without handicapping the new generation.

The loose fabric of South African nationalism is evident in the handling of treason charges. In law treason is a crime punishable by death; in practice it draws a lesser punishment than rape. When *English-speaking whites* failed to shoot their way into Johannesburg on the Jameson Raid of 1895, old Paul Kruger said the prisoners taken in the ill-fated adventure would be shot, but they were nearly all out of jail in a few months. When *Afrikaners* took up arms against the state in the 1914 Rebellion and killed government soldiers, most of them were free within a few weeks. When *Africans* were on trial for treason in Pretoria during the period 1956 to 1961, it was clear that even if they were not acquitted, their sentence would have been a few years in jail, not hanging. These lenient penalties for treason suggest that men do not feel the same loyalty toward South Africa that characterizes nationalism elsewhere.

Nationality as a symbolic concept tends to be identified only with love of one's immediate physical surroundings. Thus the Cape Afrikaner, English, and Coloured people abroad may share a nostalgia for the western Cape, and have been known to abandon successful careers to return to its extraordinary beauty and salubrious climate. Elsewhere in Africa, the longing for "their" country by South African Africans often puzzles other Africans, who fail to see a compatibility between antagonism toward the laws of the country and love of, say, the cattle and hills of Zululand.

And indeed South African nationalism finds its greatest expression outside the country. Thus to hear "Natalians" (whites from the most "English" province) speaking wretched Afrikaans in a London tube is to listen to a pathetic search for a national symbol as they strain to set themselves apart from the English people around them. A Zulu or Afrikaans folk song or a "Malay" dish sometimes provides a link among English, African, Coloured, and Afrikaner South Africans in a foreign land and a sense of comradeship virtually impossible to duplicate within the borders of the country. When the Springboks (the most prestigious of South African white sporting teams) play abroad, there is fairly wide national support from all sports fans. But when the Springboks have played Britain or New Zealand in South Africa, the African and Coloured fans have rooted wildly for the visitors and are now barred from Bloemfontein stadium on that account. Conversely, white citizens take a sporting pride in the accomplishments of African (South African) boxers in overseas rings, but not when they are matched with a white boxer in an adjacent country.

The blooming of South African nationalism abroad while it wilted at home was most marked during World War II. Gangs of Afrikaners assaulted individual soldiers in uniform on the streets of Johannesburg. When a group of soldiers retaliated, a pitched battle with rocks as ammunition was quelled only by the use of tanks. Yet in North Africa, where 50 per cent of the South Africans were Afrikaners, a real comradeship was forged in the face of Rommel's legions.[5] The leadership of professional Afrikaner generals such as Dan Pienaar was outstanding. Thousands of English and Afrikaners returned home after VE-Day determined to keep their battle-born unity and to tackle their country's looming racial problem.

This new spirit faltered when the home front passed insensitively over the valor of the all-volunteer troops and turned to renewed peacetime commerce. The disgruntled soldiers may even have provided the narrow margin of victory for Dr. Malan's National Party, just five scant years after it had been crushed on an end-the-Hitler-war platform in 1943. The wartime spirit of cooperation did give birth to the Torch Commando, led by "Sailor" Malan, an R.A.F. Fighter Ace. But the Commando ran into differences over the role of Coloured ex-servicemen, whose exclusion diluted the moral basis of the movement, leaving it an auxiliary of the predominantly "English" United Party. The leader of the United Party, Prime Minister Jan Christian Smuts, allowed party hacks to block the entry of the ablest ex-servicemen into politics and thus added to his reputation of surrounding himself with weak "yes men."[6] Finally, the English and Afrikaans war comrades found themselves enmeshed in the long-established division of their respective language groups, a split accentuated by bitter divisions at home during the war.

---

[5] The figure is generally given as 60 per cent Afrikaners, but this was a wartime propaganda gimmick to secure Afrikaner support. Toward the end of the war a number of "poor white" Afrikaners enlisted to serve on the home front for financial reasons.

[6] A decade later, in 1958, the United Party did try unsuccessfully to enlist the support of the "veteran group," whose businesses and families were by then in the mid-stream of life.

Many men of both groups have described to the writer how they drifted away from a common loyalty as they re-absorbed the attitudes of their own section.

South African nationalism is thus limited for the most part to the formal concepts of citizenship. All citizens carry the same passport and are subject to laws passed by the same parliament even though such legislation may not apply equally to all citizens. Although there is a cultural similarity in the dress and many of the food habits of the middle-class Africans, Afrikaners, and English, they themselves do not recognize it nor appreciate it when it is pointed out.

There was, however, an unprecedented degree of national feeling inside South Africa when Prime Minister Hendrik Verwoerd went to London in March 1961 for the Commonwealth Conference. A thin pro-Commonwealth unity bound the two white groups, as well as a majority of the Coloured and Asians and a minority of the Africans, although the unity of the last three groups was based upon a feeling that apartheid was best attacked inside rather than outside the Commonwealth. It is striking that more persons in South Africa—in terms of numbers of individuals—can be united in opposition to the government than in any other single cause.

The great unifying agency of war against an outside danger has never come to forge a common South African loyalty. The two world wars did not constitute an immediate danger and were primarily fought by the white groups. In contrast, the sower of disunity—civil war—plagued white-black relations for a long century, only to be succeeded by a white-white war whose seeds of hatred still bear unusually bitter fruit. But the generation of Afrikaners who remember the Boer War has had much of its hurt assuaged, while a sense of grievance has been deliberately encouraged in succeeding generations as a device to foster Afrikaans unity.

The Two Nationalisms Today

African nationalism can be considered to be in an intermediate stage in some respects, but in others it is only beginning. Nationalistic values have not shifted downwards, but are still held most intensely by the better educated and more prosperous

African upper-middle and upper classes. This continued restriction of attitude accounts in part for the relative lack of violence. While it may be said that Africans as a whole have little to lose and much to gain from violent revolution, it is also true that African *leadership* has a great deal to lose. Succeeding generations of upper-middle class Africans have built a material stake in their community that they risk with reluctance. A driving devil-may-care sense of dedication is more evident in the youth, and accounts for the greater militancy in 1960 of the Pan Africanist Congress. Nationalist slogans and symbols are spread through the African schools and in various communications media. After the Sharpeville massacre in 1960, Bantu announcers on the government-controlled radio network played patriotic African songs with revolutionary words in the vernaculars until, much later, they were discovered and fired.

African trade union activities have been gaining ground, although technically they are illegal. European employers have pressed for legalization of African unions to allow at least a hypothetically non-political outlet for workers' grievances.

Despite the low economic position of Africans, the patterns of their economic power have become quite complex. When an African gasoline station owner can show a yearly profit of over $60,000 and a number of Africans own a string of businesses or several farms, economic complexities have developed. But African rural advance has been retarded because of the general practice of communal ownership of land in the tribal reserves.

The sense of dedication of many persons in politics tends to lack continuity and is related to the effect of charisma. While there is a decline in the "messiah" concept among Africans, continual harassing by the police and restrictive legislation make the building of a solid organization difficult. An individual who can gather a number of supporters rapidly will soon leap into prominence. But there is no single leader or group of leaders with whom interested outsiders, including the South African government, could deal directly. Left alone, it is likely that African nationalism in the Republic would soon develop its own distinctive pattern and lose its dependence upon foreign example, but given conditions inside the country, there remains a dependence on foreign ideas, as indeed on foreign capital. Nevertheless, it can be said that African nationalists in the Republic are not waiting for foreign allies to do all the work for them. Those who contact other African nationalists outside South Africa usually return home with renewed faith in the quality of their own leadership. It is but another aspect of the growing anomaly that in all of sub-Saharan Africa, the greatest depth of African leadership is in South Africa.

The intermediate stage of Afrikaner nationalism is virtually completed in all its aspects. Loyalty values have shifted to the middle and lower groups (though one must bear in mind the truncated nature of the Afrikaner lower class). Nationalistic slogans were widespread in the schools by 1950. Compulsory legislation required all Afrikaans-speaking children to attend schools taught in that language, and the curriculum in most parts of the country is adapted to "Christian National Education," as opposed to British liberal education. In 1961, the Administrator (Governor) of the Transvaal called upon all white schools to inculcate the importance of defending white, Christian education.

Because of the danger to Afrikanerdom of allowing divergent parties, the one dominant National Party remains, but it covers broad differences of opinion. From 1957 to 1961 there was a sharper separation of the party into left and right wings; a regional split of opinion between the Cape and the Transvaal also developed. Throughout the country many ministers, professors, businessmen, and newspaper editors formed an intellectual minority favoring some liberalization of racial policies, but they were opposed by the vast majority of Afrikaners. By 1962, liberal ideas inside Afrikaner nationalism were less well focused, although they were being diffused to more people than ever. The government's capture in 1961 of the Afrikaner race relations university group known as SABRA and the withdrawal of the Afrikaans churches from the World Council of Churches are but two indications of a wider organizational change in an attempt to hold the race line. But at the same time non-racial ideas gained wider currency than ever among middle-class and upper-class Afrikaners. Anomalously, a number of Afrikaner intellectuals have moved well to the left of even the opposition United Party, which is repugnant to many of them because of its alleged British "jingoism."

The National Party continues to flaunt its racist theories before the world, but in practice narrow financial self-interest has often carried more weight. Thus ideological pronouncements that Africans must be removed from certain parts of the western Cape have been countermanded because of pressure from Afrikaner farmers; the removal of certain white traders from African reserves has likewise created a wave of white protest and the withdrawal of some demands. Middle-class and lower-class Afrikaner groups have at last been able to gratify their wishes for higher levels of consumption. Afrikaner trade unions with Nationalist goals took over from the relatively liberal British-oriented unions by 1955, and the contemporary issue has become social protection, not expansion. Despite substantial Afrikaner opposition inside the party and vociferous protests by workers of all races outside the National Party, a law to reserve (i.e., protect) jobs for members of a particular race (usually white) in such industries as the manufacture of clothing was passed and gingerly applied. This concern reflects the marked egalitarianism within Afrikanerdom noted in our discussion of class.

Rivalry among Afrikaner institutions is shown most clearly in the church-state split. Party pressure forced several churches out of the World Council of Churches and threatened outspoken theological professors with dismissal. But relatively liberal Afrikaner *dominees* (ministers) have continued fighting with some success, and those holding positions in various synods were re-elected in the Cape and Transvaal during 1961.

Afrikaner nationalism has not only passed through the middle and late stages of transition to full nationalism, but under the peculiar conditions of South Africa it is about to be submerged in a "white nation." Because "English" whites and many Coloured people feel compelled to seek shelter under the Afrikaner tent—even while some despise and bicker with their fellow occupants—this white-white-Coloured integration in the face of African nationalism foreshadows the end of exclusively Afrikaner nationalism. At the same time it does not create a total South African nationalism, but further hardens the white/black division.

A major step in the process for many Afrikaners was the establishment of the long-sought republic on May 31, 1961, following the referendum of the white population. The release from a narrow Afrikaner loyalty is evident in this private comment of a senior government official: "Just as the Voortrekkers gave way to the Boers (a broader group), and the Boers gave way to the Afrikaners (a still broader group), so now people like myself who think of ourselves as Afrikaners must lose our exclusiveness in a broader citizenship. I wrote my old father, who was born in the Orange Free State Republic and helped defend it in the Boer War, that an old book is closed and a new one opened. On polling day, I voted for the republic and for the dissolution of the National Party as we have known it."

South Africa as Nation

Despite its divergent nationalisms, South Africa is one of the most cohesive and economically integrated countries in sub-Saharan Africa. It has the most complex economy with the largest and most diversified exports, the best transportation network, the highest literacy rate, the strongest army, and the highest material living standard for both the total population and the African majority in all of Africa. Blessed by generous natural resources, including the world's largest gold production, South Africa could look forward to tremendous expansion and a rapid rise in living standards if a political specter did not dominate the scene. The thesis of these pages is that it is the failure to move toward unified nationhood which has plagued continued South African progress. There is in the country little willingness for all to function within a South African loyalty. The lack of consent and consensus means that the governed do not have a capacity to set outside limits to government action. Obedience is built upon fear and compulsion, rather than given voluntarily in a truly national society.

The reason is clear if we realize how fully the government meets Afrikaner desires and how little it meets African desires in regard to participation in policy making, taxation and military service, equal application of the law,[7] and access to political

[7] There is a much greater element of justice and independence in South African courts than is generally recognized outside the country. It was

communication. The lack of African participation at these levels is a measure of the untapped potentiality of the African people in South Africa to consent and contribute to a broad nationalism. It thus follows that the lack of African acceptance prevents attainment of the stage of mature nationalism which permits the use of a lower order of overt force. The growing strength of the police and army to meet internal African attacks is a marked characteristic of South Africa today, just as the absence of a need for force within Afrikanerdom points to a maturation of their ethnic nationalism.

The incomplete national integration of South Africa is a prime example of how an unfinished transition serves irrationality and may be more painful than no integration at all. South Africa's political uniqueness—with European-type nationalism on one hand and Afro-Asian-type nascent tribalism and nationalism on the other—is strikingly important in the economic field. South Africa had had a booming development for seventy-five years and its current growth rate is a consistent 4 per cent. From the start of this boom through World War II, there was no doubt that there was sufficient loyalty for South Africa among those engaged in finance and business (whites) to create the confidence necessary to an articulated economy. That confidence still holds for Afrikaner nationalism today, or, in the field of economics, for a broader white "nationalism." And until recent years the loyalty of the African section of the population, only gradually moving into a money exchange economy, was not required. But it has become a factor just at the point where, according to a number of reputable economists, South Africa has reached an economically self-sustaining "take-off" point. The very idea of doing without investments from abroad was not even considered before World War II.

The unusually high returns on industrial equities, at times over 12 per cent for "blue chips," are not due to the under-

widely and wildly charged that the defendants in the drawn-out "Treason Trial" would be "railroaded" in a "police state." In fact, one of the judges accused of being a government "stooge" was sharply critical of the public prosecutor before the defendants were all freed. But racial inequities often occur. A number of European men have been freed in "immorality" cases in which the African women charged with cohabiting with them were convicted in a separate trial. An improvement on the American South is that racially mixed cases cannot be tried by a white jury but must go to a judge and assessors.

developed nature of the country and consequent economic risks, but rather to the political fears of local and foreign investors. Ownership of equities and property exists among a wide range of whites—those people whose loyalty was previously the key to confidence—but there is virtually no ownership among the African mass.

How dominated South Africa is by Afrikaner and African nationalisms may be shown by asking some questions fundamental to the consideration of nationalism in any country.

1. How is the concept of treason handled?

   Afrikaners: Treason to the goals of Afrikanerdom is equated with treason to the state. Thus one of the single most effective opponents of communism in southern Africa, was "banned" under the "Suppression of Communism Act" because of his denunciations of communism are interspersed with denunciations of the tenets of Afrikaner nationalism, although he sympathized with its battle against British imperialism.

   Africans: Conversely, cooperation with the government is treason to African nationalists. When nine policemen were torn to pieces in a 1960 riot in Durban, the fact that four had black skins appeared to make no difference to the African assailants.

2. What is the status of Church-State relations?

   Afrikaners: Despite a valiant and continuing struggle in some quarters, the white Dutch Reformed churches have aligned themselves with the government and those who disagree are exiled as heretics. Few concur in the statement of the leader of all the Reformed churches, Dr. A. J. van der Merwe, when he said in 1961 that the preservation of Afrikanerdom is not the role of the Church.

   Africans: The breakaway of many Christian groups from European-oriented churches has given rise to over 2,000 African-oriented churches. Their identification is with African nationalism.

3. How do family loyalties conflict, if at all, with political sanctions?

   Afrikaners: The call of nationalism is greater than the call of the family, because nationalism is extolled as the real defense of the family.

Africans: The spirit of African protest in a sense makes all Africans members of one family. Thus family, clan, and tribal loyalties are merged in one obsession: a redress of grievances.

4. How does the economic structure aid or retard the expression of nationalistic loyalty?

Afrikaners: Their economic well-being and high standard of living are supposedly protected and are to be saved through their nationalism.

Africans: Their standard of living, low compared with that of the Afrikaners—but not compared with that of Africans elsewhere or with that of many Asians—is to be tremendously improved by the success of their nationalism.

5. How is the military recruited, from which groups, and with what reigning ideologies?

Afrikaners: The military is recruited almost entirely from the white group, and largely from among Afrikaners. Afrikaner nationalists are in almost all key positions of authority. The police and the army, along with the volunteer *skiet-commandos*, are the military extension of Afrikaner nationalism.

Africans: They have no real military force. None is legally armed.

The division, then, is almost complete. Afrikaner and African nationalist have almost nothing in common for which they would die together for South Africa. The question in the reader's mind may well be whether there are any Afrikaner nationalists at all who see the great chasm and the immediate prospects of falling into it. The answer is "yes." At the very top, strangely enough, Prime Minister Verwoerd is aware of many of the conflicting nationalistic forces we have discussed. Unlike his unimaginative and unintellectual predecessor, J. G. Strijdom, Prime Minister Verwoerd says that he knows that *baasskap*, or permanent domination of white over black, will not work. The significance of the dramatic parliamentary announcement in early 1962 that the Transkei Bantustan is to be "independent" is not that actual authority will be exercised by incumbent Chief Kaiser Mantanzima or his successors. The South African government will be extremely reluctant to give up control of

key ministries such as defense and foreign affairs, however
rapidly the new Transkei government eliminates local segregation. The announcement is significant, rather, in that it marks
the acceptance by influential Afrikaners of the concept of African nationalism and the giving of at least lip service to African
independence. Recognizing the co-existence of African nationalism along with Afrikaner nationalism is a deep psychological
shift on their part.

However firmly the Africans embrace their new "states," and
a poll by a staunchly liberal organization shows wide acceptance
by Transkei Africans, the Bantustans do not grapple directly
with the problem posed by the denial of elementary political
and social rights to Africans in so-called "white South Africa"
in which they, the Africans, constitute a majority of the population. Dr. Verwoerd tries to solve the problem by providing
for urban Africans to vote in Bantustan elections, as Italian
workers in Germany vote in Italian elections, but the issues
which concern the urban African are not those of the Transkei
or Zululand. His concerns lie within his present community,
where he and his father and in some cases his grandfather have
worked and lived. Thus an accommodation of races remains to
be worked out in "white South Africa" even if and when the
Bantustans begin to function.

While it is possible that the two powerful nationalisms might,
with bloodshed and chaos, be merged into a single South African
nationalism, this solution is not likely in any near future. Neither
Afrikaner nor African nationalism will submit to the other.
And yet few foreign observers fully assess the centuries of
intimate interaction and association of Afrikaner and African
in South Africa. There is a bond that will persist even under
radically changed social mores and political patterns. The
mimetic period for Afrikaners is over, and for Africans it has
never fully materialized. The nationalisms emerging from the
southern tip of Africa will be the product of the *vleis*, *vlaktes*
and *kwiinduli nemilambo*,[8] dear to the people of South Africa.
Stirrings of a new accommodation are evident in the increase
in multi-racial gatherings in urban areas and could be seen

---

[8] Like the nationalisms, a precise translation is not possible; approximately "marshes," "plains" (in Afrikaans), "hills and rivers" (in Xhosa).

during a visit to the Transkei in 1962, where individual Afrikaner nationalists were finding and will find a *modus vivendi*
within an African power structure.

If one insists on a projection of how the two nationalisms will
interact in the 1960s and 1970s—and the South Africa problem
seems peculiarly to call for attempts at resolution—one may
anticipate a southern Africa with an economic common market
and a variety of political units. There will not be white states
and black states marked by rigid racial segregation. But one
does foresee, for example, the white *cum* Coloured population
exercising effective political control in the western Cape. In
some of the overwhelmingly African societies important economic and social roles will be played by whites, including substantial numbers of Afrikaners. The Coloured people do occupy
a unique and pro-South Africa position. The Indian community,
with support from Asia, could be a stabilizing influence. Finally,
the economic leadership of the English-speaking whites and
their democratic heritage must weigh in the scale. Today, white
and brown minorities are ground between two powerful stones,
but they could become first a buffer and later the cement of a
new brand of nationalism in southern Africa. And one stresses
"southern" Africa because Basutoland, for example, will not
agree to rule by Afrikaner nationalism but it must be an integral
part of the southern African economy.

Although neither would at this time proclaim this new pluralistic political pattern, such an evolution (which might not lack
revolutionary periods) would accomplish many of the goals of
Afrikaner and African nationalisms. Afrikaners are less interested in dominating Africans than in not being dominated themselves. Conversely, Africans on the whole do not aim at what
some would feel is just retribution, but rather at control of their
own destinies.

These concluding comments do not fit the "volcano" thesis
for the resolution of divergent nationalistic aims. But experience
with volcanoes shows that they are often puny when they do
erupt. One cannot see eruptions in South Africa which really
solve the problem of the interrelationships of 15,000,000 people.
Only revolution involving intervention by a major foreign power
is likely to be more than a revolutionary phase in a basically

evolutionary situation. This view is not now acceptable to Afrikaner or African nationalists. But neither was there initial
acceptance of the present equilibrium in India and Pakistan,
Israel and the Arab states, or Eire and Ulster, when conflicting
nationalisms had, and may still have, tragically bloody moments
in longer periods of coexistence. As one who witnessed the
savagery of the Belgian ejection from the Congo and the subsequent ebbing back of that element which had fled in understandable panic, the author doubts the *Götterdämmerung* view
often held abroad about South Africa.

The parallel evolution of Afrikaner and African nationalisms
in South Africa, even when it points to African nationalism
struggling with its forerunner, provides generically common
experience in a predominantly Western and Christian society.
Indeed, African nationalism in South Africa is more "Western"
in its organization and form, although not necessarily always
in its political orientation, than African nationalisms elsewhere
on the continent. The binary nature of nationalism in South
Africa will persist even as it evolves into something new and
South African.

{ PART } V

Class, Values, and Nation

"*Intemperate optimists talk as though you could get something for nothing; or at worst, as though the only payments owing on account of human progress were payments in advance. But the truth is, that Destiny always charges twice for the benefits it sells us—once before the goods are delivered, and again, when the preliminary efforts have been crowned with success, in an indefinite series of deferred payments, afterwards. In other words, men have to work for every mental or material advance they make and, when they have made it, can enjoy the fruits of their labours, only on condition that they give up the privileges which were theirs before the advance was made.*

"*. . . The advance from primitivism to civilization, from mere blood to mind and spirit, is a progress whose price is fixed; there are no discounts even for the most highly talented purchasers . . . . When man became an intellectual and spiritual being, he paid for his new privileges with a treasure of intuitions, of emotional spontaneity, of sensuality still innocent of all self-consciousness . . . .*

"*Human Bondage, in the words of Spinoza, is the price of Human Freedom. The advantages of the first state (and Human Bondage has many and substantial advantages) are incompatible with those of the second. We must be content to pay, and indefinitely to go on paying, the irreducible price of the goods we have chosen.*"

ALDOUS HUXLEY
Beyond the Mexique Bay

Chapter
10

□□□□□□□□□□□

The Costs of
Anti-Nationalism:
Argentina

K. H. SILVERT

The oft-quoted testamentary remarks of Bolívar, his final despair, remain an excellent benchmark for a sentimental appreciation of modern Argentina. "There is no good faith in America," said Bolívar, "either among men or among nations. Treaties are paper, constitutions books, elections battles, liberty anarchy, and life a torment." Bolívar went on to advise that, "The only thing one can do in America is emigrate." These sentiments, and especially the sour admonition to move away, are entirely conventional in today's Argentina, a land caught up in three decades of regression and dissolution. The intellectual reflection of this counsel of despair is found in a preoccupation with explaining why a country of such material promise, human richness, urban exaggeration, and past progress should now find itself stagnant, a prey to "tropical" politics in the upper reaches of society and to apathy and irresponsibility below.

To explain the Argentine experience demands a theory of failure, a search for what prevented an initially amazing growth from becoming self-sustaining. Although Argentine economic statistics are highly dubious, certainly that country was one of the world's richest in the first quarter of this century.

From 1860 to 1930 the Argentine Republic experienced one of the most spectacular developmental processes in world history. . . .

During this period of progress, the economic and monetary institutions kept up with [social] needs. Without any guide other than that of not slowing down the natural movement of the country and of private initiative, the governors supplied the few laws and decrees necessary to guarantee and promote individual and collective progress in a climate of liberty and justice.

All economic indices of that period also indicate the prodigious growth . . . as much in what are called "basic" or "social" investments (level of public literacy and of cultural and technical progress, public health, communications and transportation systems, organization of the public administration, public services and the police power of the state) as in the realm of private economic activity (foreign and domestic commerce; agricultural, industrial, mineral, and fisheries production; systems of commercialization and credit institutions, etc.). And to this generalized progress there contributed in obvious fashion the extraordinary stream to the country of foreign investments, which climbed to around four billion dollars in 1930. . . .[1]

All the standard ingredients for self-sustaining, self-generating growth seem to be present—both rational ones (capital, trained population, urbanization, and so on), and mystical and irrational ones (climate, "race," and the like). And yet, for three decades the country has staggered from revolution to dictator-

[1] Walter Beveraggi Allende, "Economía y finanzas," *Argentina 1930-1960*, Buenos Aires: 1961, pp. 243-244.

ship to depression and into the hopelessness of today's military rule.

The widely shared taxi-driver explanation is a condemnation of corrupt governments and more often than not a slurring of one or another of Argentina's numerous immigrant groups—Italians or Spanish Galicians or Jews or what-not. Economists lament the fiscal illiteracy of the Perón regime and the unwillingness of Argentines to take their orthodox austerity medicine like men, or at least like gentlemen. Historians like to start with the 1930 intervention of the military in political affairs, and then grimly trace the juggernaut through intervening Conservative oligarchies, military dictatorships, the Perón adventure, the Liberating Revolution of 1955 to 1958, the civilian governmental period of Frondizi from 1958 to 1962, and then the present thinly disguised military reappearance. Recently interpretations less concerned with symptomatology have begun to be heard, attempting to relate social disorganization to the more profound facts of national character, values, and social structure. The following quotation is typical of this new search:

> Argentina today can be described as an economic enigma —a basically resourceful country that has undergone a period of economic stagnation during a decade of almost unprecedented economic expansion throughout most of the world, a country making a serious but largely unsuccessful attempt to take the road of steady economic growth. . . . Of course, economic factors play an important role in determining whether or not economic development occurs. . . . But Argentina's experience between 1945 and 1955 and its failure to recover . . . suggest that something of more vital importance lies behind the troubles besetting the nation's economy. . . .
>
> An analysis of the Argentine "national character" . . . will demonstrate that some cultural traits of the bulk of the population are inimical to the emergence of social relationships which would enable individuals to act concertedly in the pursuit of common goals and interests. This feature, i.e., the fact that Argentines are a "conglomeration" of people rather than an organic "commun-

ity," together with the fact that those same cultural traits
also constitute a powerful barrier to the appearance of
"Western-capitalistic-like" economic initiative in the bulk
of the society's members, is and has been in the past a
fundamental impediment retarding the nation's economic
growth . . . the basically passive, apathetic value-orientation
profile of the Argentine society must be regarded as the
critical factor limiting the possibilities of steady, long-run
economic development.[2]

Questions of values and ideologies underlie all social happenings, of course. But this analysis will not rest content with
palpating the value system, for consistent with the theoretical
introduction, our interest focuses on the relationship among
values, social structure, and social institutions, with particular
reference to the nation. Certain assumptions concerning the
value structure will have to be made, despite the absence of
corroborative studies, in order to help in the definition of the
limits of probable and possible institutional change. These assumptions can be put in terms of those dilemmas, paradoxes,
or contradictions with which so much of the recent literature on
Argentina has been concerned.

1. A contradiction affecting the entire society is the clash
between the leveling effects of mass communications and a very
high degree of urbanization on the one hand, and on the other
the failure of the political mechanism to escape the corset of an
extraordinarily narrow definition of interest. Argentina's class-
bound politics assume that no public measure can be good for
almost everybody, that the benefit of one group is the automatic
loss of all others. Life is an inelastic pie, and a bigger piece
for *fulano* necessarily means a smaller piece for *sutano*. The
Perón period offers a notorious example of this sub-national
thinking. Argentines take it as axiomatic that increased freedom of action for lower groups between 1945 and 1955 implied

---

[2] Tomás Roberto Fillol, *Social Factors in Economic Development: The
Argentine Case*, Cambridge: 1961, pp. 1-3, *passim*. For another recent
publication underscoring the concept of "dilemma," see also Arthur P.
Whitaker, "The Argentine Paradox," *The Annals of the American
Academy of Political and Social Science*, Vol. 334, March 1961, pp.
103-112.

a necessarily restricted freedom for others, and that with the fall of Perón nothing could have been more natural than a return to restriction of freedom for those below and a regrowth of freedom for those above.

Economic statistics bear out the practice of these narrow views. Between 1945 and 1951, wages rose by about 35 per cent in real terms, and then leveled off. But, after the fall of Perón, the reaction set in; real wages dipped suddenly and in 1958 reached the level of 1945 once again. After a short pause in this process, the new economic policies of "orthodoxy" established in late 1958 continued the politics of greed with the following effect:

> According to the statistics issued by the Central Bank, in 1958 the participation of the labor sector in the distribution of the national income was 53.3%, compared to the 46.7% which represented the share of proprietors, professionals and *rentiers*. These figures changed strikingly in 1959, when the former shrank to 45.8% and the latter rose to 54.2%, meanwhile there having been produced a global drop in gross national income of 4.8% and in consequence a drop of 6.6% in the income per capita, if the rate of increase of the population is taken into account.[3]

When labor had some power, "economic sanity" dictated a redistribution in its direction; when middle and upper groups regained power, "economic sanity" implied a redistribution back to them. Whether either policy in truth served the end of general development is a matter never realistically discussed by the opposing groups.

2. Another inconsistency, very closely related to the first, is the failure to adjust a fairly advanced degree of industrialization to responsible entrepreneurial attitudes and to an appreciation of the possibilities inherent in mass consumption. The impediment is once again the inability to see the society as in some respects total and interdependent. The power of industrialization, then, is employed to maintain a degree of social inequality preventing the growth of healthy markets and thus inhibiting

[3] Leopold Portnoy, *La realidad Argentina en el siglo XX: Análisis crítico de la economía*, Mexico: 1961, p. 10.

the further economic expansion of the country. But this power is used also to create a brave new world of material expectations the denial of which prompts a loss in morale and a further disturbance to the economic machine.[4] The intensity of the industrial stimulus to general change should not be underestimated.

In spite of the depression [of 1929], a new industry was developing itself. The quantity of workers doubled between 1935 and 1941, and by the end of the war industry represented a higher percentage of the gross national product than farming and cattle raising together. The process of industrialization and of massive urbanization initiated then took on a dizzy speed in the following decade. In the four-year period of 1943 to 1947, about a million persons moved to urban areas—that is, about 20% of the rural population of 1943.[5]

3. The politics of oligarchy in a mass society and the economics of privilege in an industrial society are paradoxes met by a third in the individual himself. The high degree of specialization demanded of the individual in Argentina, especially in the cities, coexists with the widespread holding of traditional values which do not permit the citizen to guide himself by a set of impersonal loyalties toward all the others operating within the system of mutual dependency. The narrowness of the loyalty horizons and the failure to accept the state as the ultimate arbiter of secular dispute weaken social institutions and invite autocratic personalism, whether directed toward change or the mere continuance of the *status quo*. The complicated and long-range predictions required for the maintenance of such a complex economy and polity as that of Argentina cannot be made. Not only is it impossible to know whether any particular president will finish his term, but, even in a metropolis of six and a half million inhabitants, there is no certainty that the electricity will

---

[4] Easily available sources for a study of the Argentine economy are United Nations Economic Commission for Latin America, *El desarrollo económico de la Argentina*, 1957; the periodical statistical bulletins of the Argentine Central Bank; Ricardo M. Ortiz, *Historia económica de la Argentina*, Buenos Aires: 1955; and Leopoldo Portnoy, *op. cit.*
[5] Roberto Cortés Conde, "Partidos políticos," in *Argentina 1930-1960*, *op. cit.*, p. 139.

remain on either through dinner or through an operation in the children's hospital.

The common element of these three paradoxes, clearly, is that economic development and occupational mobilization have taken place in a context of insufficient acceptance of the values of the nation-state. The survival of localistic, sub-national views and loyalties archetypical of the traditional society affords a first explanation of the malfunction of social institutions, as measured by the criteria of the developed world. But because a working adjustment does exist, the Argentine situation does not fit neatly into the categories of social order as they have been derived from the major currents of European experience. The "paradoxes" of which we have been speaking are paradoxical only in terms of the elements necessary to continued development; they are not paradoxical in the sense that they are incoherent, not understandable, or mutually incompatible in terms of the experiences of a static daily life. That the results are policy confusion, an ultimate halt to economic growth, and the politics of force is, of course, exactly fitting to the situation.

To demonstrate the thesis that Argentina remains in a pre-national condition, we must look at the organization of government and the relationship between leaders and followers. A close examination of the Perón administration is also required, for if it is true that Argentina supported a fascist state, then this argument concerning the non-national character of the government must fail, for fascism is essentially a national and thus "modern" form of organization.

The Articulation of the Political Mechanism

Simplicity is the most striking characteristic of Argentine politics. The lack of complication and the failure to achieve a high degree of articulation of the nation's power groupings are also in consonance with the set of traditional values still widely held. While the *structure* of the economic institution has managed a fairly high degree of modernization despite the continued rooting of certain *functions* in an older order, the political institution has remained much more intimately related to prenational structures as well as functions. Charisma, the charm factor of

personalism, remains vital to the mobilization of widespread
public support, and the essential fragility of the entire mechanism is demonstrated by the ease with which the military have
been manipulating the state. Their freedom of action is not so
much a demonstration of military might as it is of civilian
weakness. Personalism and naked force have been the two essential ingredients of the mobilization of political power in the
last three decades; the so-called "popular will," although often
invoked and even occasionally called upon to act, has in truth
been but the creation of the manipulations of essentially anti-
democratic demagogues. Recent history unequivocally supports
these statements concerning the essentially superficial nature of
allegedly "national" Argentine politics.

Argentina's last truly free election of a civilian president occurred in 1927. This mandate, extended to Hipólito Yrigoyen,
was revoked by the military in 1930; although the coup was
based on a fair degree of popular support to begin with, the
dictatorship of José E. Uriburu ended in 1931 as a mere military adventure with overtones of Italian corporativism. Succeeding Conservative governments depended on simple electoral
fraud to give their governance a semblance of democratic legitimacy, but their authority rested directly on a combination of
oligarchical economic and military power.[6] The baldness of the
hypocrisy is revealed in the name commonly given to this epoch
—the "Period of the Patriotic Fraud." The reason is that the
Conservatives argued that they were forced, as a matter of
patriotism, to falsify the vote, for otherwise the ignorant populace would vote against its true interests, knowledge of which
was a merit only of the Conservatives. By the middle of World
War II, the Conservative governments had entirely lost their
ability to confront the changing local and national scenes. The
military returned themselves to direct authority in 1943, a move
made possible, and to military eyes "necessary," by the utter

[6] It is not necessary to list the standard works on recent Argentine political developments. Specialists already know them, and any non-specialist
can find them easily enough. I might mention only a fairly recent work
of merit, Alfredo Galletti, *La realidad argentina en el siglo XX: La politica y partidos*, Mexico: 1961. Otherwise, see Fillol, *op. cit.*, and the appropriate works of A. P. Whitaker, G. I. Blanksten, J. J. Johnson, J. J.
Kennedy, R. Alexander, *et al.*

simplicity of the patterns of power distribution and the shrunken universe of political discourse recognized as pertinent. The emergence of Perón in 1944 and 1945 and his attractiveness to certain parts of the public—a political magnetism not seen in the country since the early days of Radical Yrigoyen during World War I—added other dimensions of power. Still, the fall of Peronism was essentially a response to changes in the views of certain leaders and not to the complex, sweeping movements which one attributes to truly national and popular politics. The succeeding provisional government of President Aramburu (1955 to 1958) made no pretense of being other than a military interregnum, even though it earned widespread praise and support among middle and upper-class groups. The election of the civilian Arturo Frondizi in 1958, a polling which did not permit the candidacy of avowed Peronists, appeared at first to offer some promise of the complicating mechanisms of true party politics. But that administration chose not to attempt to develop and then rely upon the mechanics of a pluralistic society, but instead played about among the all too evident power centers to maintain a most precarious existence until its fall in early 1962. A highly confused and divided military leadership has once again arrogated to itself the responsibility for "maintaining the constitution" in the face of almost absolute public helplessness. The hard surface of military rule or the mottled aspect of Machiavellian balancing and intriguing have been the two masks of Argentine politics since 1930. The masks, most unhappily, do not disguise reality—they *are* the reality of Argentina's situation of weak government.

The political absoluteness which is a natural corollary of political simplicity is nowhere made so evident as in the manner in which political parties define their own functions. Instead of viewing themselves as the guardians of a part of the truth and as holding only a limited responsibility for the nation's destinies, party leaders see themselves as the vessels of universal truth and their parties as simple mechanisms with which to gain power. Even the quasi-official historian of the Radical Party, the most professional of all Argentine parties, permits himself these words:

356 : *Class, Values, and Nation*

> We are not just a political party . . . we are a force of
> national and continental history which consists in impart-
> ing constitutionality to Independence . . . in giving to the
> Nation through its people firm bases for its authentic de-
> velopment, which conceives of the Republic as a moral
> idea. . . .[7]

This Messianic view of politics leaves no room for a legitimate opposition; the erection of an ideological structure on moral
grounds held to be universal condemns dissenting voices not
as mere human error but as heresy. The dismaying inclusiveness
of this view of Radicalism is really no less than the bald statement made by General Rawson the day after he led the military
back to overt power in 1943: "Now there are no political parties,
but only Argentines." In his turn Perón employed his newly
erected party structure as a direct arm of government, as in
totalitarianisms. Although the succeeding military government
actually encouraged a limited play of party politics except for
Peronists, official proclamations deplored such activities, clearly
implying a belief in the innately evil nature of parties.

> And finally, we appeal to all the inhabitants of the Re-
> public to postpone all tendentious and partisan interest to
> the higher interests of the collectivity. Let republican
> austerity be the guide of our conduct and let solidarity in
> the common effort permit the prompt gaining of those ends
> for which our people long.[8]

Even the professional politician Arturo Frondizi, when his
turn came, demonstrated the same implied disdain for party
politics by his constantly reiterated statement that he was the
"president of twenty million Argentines," and not the exponent
of a self-consistent and necessarily only partially valid set of
views supported by a continuing, responsible, and extended
party organization. President Frondizi demonstrated in much
more basic manner the inefficacy of his country's political struc-

[7] Gabriel del Mazo, *El radicalismo: Ensayo sobre su historia y doctrina*,
2nd ed., Buenos Aires: 1951, as quoted in Galletti, *op. cit.*, p. 40.
[8] Message prepared by General Pedro Eugenio Aramburu on assuming
the provisional presidency of the nation after the deposition of General
Eduardo Lonardi in 1955, as quoted in Galletti, *op. cit.*, p. 209.

ture by the profound about-face he made after assuming office. During his campaign he projected the image of the classical Latin American left-leaning intellectual—anti-clerical, anti-imperialist generally, anti-American specifically, economically autarchical, in favor of industrialization, opposed to foreign business, and so forth. After election, he allied himself openly with the Church, took Argentina into a close alliance with the United States, welcomed foreign investments, and turned his back on nationalistic recipes for economic development to embrace an austerity program, monetary stability, and other measures normally deemed sound in the United States and Western Europe, but viewed as anathema by Latin American proponents of economic nationalism. These new policies could be adopted only because his followers, though they were deeply opposed to them, were powerless to stop the executive. In turn, the taking of this line was a measure not of Frondizi's strength, but of his weakness. If the Radical Intransigent Party had not the power to prevent the change, then it follows that it did not have the strength to support its own president and that Frondizi had little national bargaining power with which to confront his ideological opponents—a fact borne out by the ease of his deposition, accomplished without a break in the normal rhythm of Argentine life.

Clear consistency also was shown by the successor government to the Frondizi administration, one of the earliest acts of which was to disband all political parties.

Evident within the structure of the government itself are the lack of pluralism and the directness of the manner in which public power is applied. The strong executive pattern is a constant; the judiciary is weak and without prestige; and the legislature has never at any time been able to exercise the deciding voice in the setting of public policy. Indeed, one of the earliest acts of the Frondizi administration was the destruction of the integrity of the Supreme Court and the criminal courts of the Federal District, and one of the first acts of the government which followed was to disband Congress. The expression of fundamental decisions comes from within the executive establishment itself, even though those decisions may have been made elsewhere. Although there are rudimentary interest groups established outside the formal organization of government, the institutionalized power centers extend their heads directly into the executive. The country's basic decisions are made *in camera*, the result of deliberation among the heads of the organized power groups. The armed forces, the single most obvious source and avenue of extra-state pressure, of course represent other groups and ideologies as well as their own professional interests. As a consequence, all aspiring interests attempt to exercise influence over the military establishment; even far leftists sometimes speak wistfully of the possibility of talking some disgruntled level of the army over to their point of view. The Church, agrarian interests, industrial groups, and the labor unions all bring their plaints and their points of view to bear directly on the executive and often upon the leaders of the other power establishments, at best using the legislature as a sounding board and the courts, when possible, as some kind of interim source of juridical legitimacy.

The workings of the mechanism are transparent, the channels of access clear, and the results apparent to all through the media of mass communications and the pronouncements of the interested parties themselves. Executive decisions, however they may have been reached and with what concessions and through what bargaining, may be in themselves the decisive political acts of the state, but they are limited in their scope and effectiveness by the very simplicity of the structure. In short, the Argentine government is intrinsically weak, a debility stemming from several fundamental causes:

First, the simplicity of the political institution of which we have been speaking not only makes for decisions which are a response to the crudest of pressures, but also inhibits the subtlety and refinement of measures which, by promoting general development, might work to strengthen government itself.

Second, the state is not firmly established as the ultimate secular arbiter of Argentine public life. The other institutions competing for men's loyalties permit a high degree of protection from the dictates of the state. Although the Church immediately springs to mind, the matter is much more complicated. A failure to recognize the supremacy of the state in the arbitration of secular dispute leaves many areas of life, such as the family, outside the reach of governmental determination. Class status also plays a fundamental part in the unequal and uneven application of the law, as does simple economic position. The impunity enjoyed by the far right scions of upper class families over the last twenty-five years for their racist demonstrations, shootings, bombings, and burnings are undeniable evidence of the truth of this statement.

And third, the combination of a simplified structure and a lack of acceptance of a broad social area as legitimate to political action reduces the amount of obedience or attachment to the rule of law which any Argentine government can expect, thus increasing the need for direct police and military enforcement of the law, or else permitting a wide latitude in such daily events of life as parking a car or painting political slogans on walls. This executive dependency on the police and the weakness of the legislature were well illustrated in mid-1961 when members of the national gendarmerie peppered the Congress building with small-arms fire in a protest concerning equipment and pay, incidentally at the time Congress was considering charges of police torture. Their punishment was a salary increase.

Simplicity, party weakness, the immediacy of action of pressure groups, and an exaggerated dependence on direct sanction within a severely limited sphere all describe not only Argentine politics, but also generic Mediterranean political thought and practice. An innate distrust of the state coupled with the direct representation of economic and occupational interest in the government are destructive of party strength, erode pluralism, and deny the sweeping grandeur possible to enlightened political action in its broadest senses. Such results stem directly from the conscious desire of leadership groups and the value structures of the societies involved—they are the politics of anti-nationalism indigenous to Spain and Portugal, but also clearly visible in Argentina and such other Latin American countries as Colombia. Syndicalism and falangism are two of the ideologies evolved in the Mediterranean world in the attempt to permit some economic development without the usual cost in terms of class structure and national organization.

The theory of Mediterranean syndicalism is essentially a complication of the idea of hierarchical order of medieval society. The Doctrine of the Two Swords is amended to become the Doctrine of the Six or Seven or Eight Swords, depending upon the number of institutional pillars created to become the fasces, so to speak, of quasi-modern traditionalism. The purpose of this institutional ordering is to subsume class to hierarchy, preserving a kind of Latin *Führerprinzip* and leaving inviolate the privileges and powers of the traditional, thus escaping the effects of "massification." While Marx was writing his attacks upon the evils of industrialism from the vantage point of the northern European, southern Europeans too began to attempt to protect themselves against the fully revolutionary implications of the changes of the last century. Mosca, Croce, and others were the intellectual scions of the period, reflected in Hispanic America by the work of Ortega y Gasset, whose *Revolt of the Masses* was not a kind of early *The Lonely Crowd* in Spanish, but rather an appeal against mass man from the stance of the traditional universalist whose humanism stems from a medieval base.

The good society pictured by the syndicalist would have the individual firmly rooted in his institutional place. His representation in government would not be a result of his individuality or of his mere citizenship, but rather a function of his place in the institutional order of events. Public decisions would then result from the interplay of the institutional oligarchs, and not from the deliberations of groups and men elected at large from a citizenry escaping its occupational bonds in an act of political selection and decision formally and somewhat substantially indicative of equality. The secular state could not become supreme in its area; mass man would be tamed by being herded into institutional kennels, safely under the tutelage of the leader.

Although it does not exemplify a pure form of falangist or syndicalist practice, the recent Argentine experience does exemplify it in modified form. The weakness of the state, the strength of competing institutions, and the accent upon class-bound politics wedded to hierarchy and obedience within the occupational function all define Argentine practice; and all are incompatible with the fluidity and self-adjustment required for the voluntaristic human mobilization of democratic development. Because the modern nation-state carves out an area of secular and impersonal politics, the traditional man with his notions of religious order, ecumenical and thus exclusivist and anti-democratic politics, and occupational hierarchy must dedicate himself to anti-national endeavors. The failure of Argentina to emerge into a relatively stable existence despite its high level of economic development can certainly be attributed in major part to the unwillingness or inability of decisive power groups to accept the necessary impersonal secularism of the modern, interdependent society.

It should be remembered that falangism and syndicalism are not fascism. The essential difference is that the fascist government does indeed attempt to establish the supremacy of the state, while the syndicalist subscribes to an extended oligarchical form legitimated by religious sanction. The Perón period in Argentina well exemplifies this difference, despite the many times that regime has been carelessly labeled as "fascist" in other countries. The following discussion of Peronism also illustrates the limitations of the leader-follower relationship of which we have been speaking, as well as the prenational politics of Argentina even in the throes of a harsher than usual dictatorship.

Peronism and Leadership

The Argentine leader cannot create a modern set of national values by signing a decree or speaking from a balcony. He can extend the effectiveness of his government by chipping at the power of rival institutions only through the exercise of great skill and effort. Unless he whips together a mass movement striving for frank and complete revolutionary change, the leader is restricted to the employment of two types of authority: he can be content with the immediately available power derived from the existing play of intra- and inter-institutional forces, or he can attempt to modify this situation by gaining a measure of external power through the mobilization of new domestic groups or the enlistment of foreign support. In matters of program, as distinct from the question of the composition of his sources of power, he is restricted either to the path of administering the tides of the *status quo* or to a mild reformism. In explaining his actions to himself and others, however, he can indulge in the strongest ideological statements from center-left to right in tone, or else be a simple eclectic. But no matter what the basis of his power, the profundity or superficiality of his program, or the style of his explanations, the non-revolutionary leader cannot escape the limitations inherent in the prenational orientation of the elite, nor the confining contradiction of leading a people of traditional values who are flexing the muscles of a substantially developed economy.[9]

These limitations apply to Perón as well as to his successors. The matter of categorization here becomes crucial to further analysis, for if the foregoing synthesis is correct, then the Peronist government was not effectively totalitarian, whatever other unhappy things it may have been. A totalitarian state employs the political institution to work its will directly upon the citizen without the interference of intervening buffer institutions or the restraints of a rule of law or a less than universal ideological justification. These conditions simply did not prevail in a total pattern in Argentina between 1946 and 1955, although the lack of juridical and ideological constraint did and still does exist.

If we use secondary criteria of totalitarianism derived specifically from the European fascist examples as our baseline, the Argentine experience diverges in significant points:

[9] Little attention is given in this statement to the political left. The reasons are that we are not considering the possibility of social revolution and that, of course, all Argentine governments since 1930 have leaned more or less sharply to the right. The Argentine left has had scant chance to mount fullblown revolution in the last two generations, although the present chaotic situation and the availability of certain fringe Peronist groups are changing this perspective. But it should be remembered that leftist leaders are no less the captives of their culture than their political opponents. They have delivered themselves up to endless bickering, conspiratorial practices, unreal policies, and short-lived coalitions entered upon through wishful thinking more than a real concord of belief and interest. *Fidelismo* has also served to accentuate romantic dreams and to underscore the extranational nature of at least part of the left in a country crying for a healthful national integration. The fraying away of the left Socialists and Radicals, Communists, Trotskyists, and other left fringe groups was also hastened by the actions of ex-President Frondizi, who persuaded many of them during his campaign that he would be a left-leaning president, only to present them after his election with a conservative caricature of their own economic determinism, as mentioned earlier in the text.

The middle-class base for German and Italian fascism must be contrasted in Argentina with the mass lower-class backing for Peronism. In Argentina, it is true that important middle-class groups were also involved, and even a significant number of persons of upper-class extraction made themselves available for leadership positions. The participation of the traditional rural elite was especially important in the culturally more colonialist provinces such as San Juan and Tucumán. In no class sense was Peronism revolutionary; the movement squeezed classes together, especially by raising the lowers, but did not change class order or strive for a substantial loss of class status among any groups.

The relatively high degree of technology necessary for police state control, eminently true of Nazi Germany, could not be said to describe Argentina. Even Italian fascism lost some of its effectiveness through an institutional "leakiness" caused by technological deficiencies.

Charisma was of great importance in the three systems, but in Argentina the full measure of organizational consequences did not flow from the personalism of Juan and Eva Perón, especially in the internal administrative operation of the government. Most of the persons holding important leadership positions of a formal nature in the Peronist hierarchy followed career paths normal both to the pre- and post-Perón epochs. Max Weber's definition of the charismatic corporate group does not describe the Perón administration:

> The corporate group which is subject to charismatic authority is based on an emotional form of communal relationship. The administrative staff of a charismatic leader does not consist of "officials"; at least its members are not technically trained. It is not chosen on the basis of social privilege nor from the point of view of domestic or personal dependency. It is rather chosen in terms of the charismatic qualities of its members. The prophet has his disciples. . . . There is no such thing as "appointment" or "dismissal," no career, no promotion. There is only a "call" at the instance of the leader. . . . There is no hierarchy. . . . There is no such thing as a definite sphere of authority and of

competence, and no appropriation of official powers on the
basis of social privileges. . . .[10]

A mystical ideology of nationalism was true of the three governments, but Argentine *justicialismo* was almost an after-
thought, an intellectual appendage to justify the "leadership
principle" and dignify the regime. Argentine nationalistic ideology was restricted largely to attacks on foreign countries in
speech and press and to mystical glorification of the nation, but
devoted itself little to the task of assuring the relative position
of the state as the supreme social institution. Only very late
in the Perón administration was ideology designed to begin to
grapple with the country's institutional organization over the
issue of church-state relations. The result was an open break
with the leaders of the Catholic Church, the burning of Church
properties, excommunications, and the passing of a divorce law
and other punitive legislation. The process ended with the overthrow of the government, forced back into its accustomed compliance in such matters.

Militarism was an important component of Peronism as of
German and Italian fascism, for Perón assumed power primarily as a consequence of his military position and the previous
actions of the armed forces. But of course both Hitler and Mussolini assumed power in some measure despite the military, and
employed their armed might for war, a purpose alien to the
ideas of Perón, despite brave words about Argentine hegemony
in the southern part of the continent. It would not be unfair to
state that the military functioned in almost directly opposite
manners in the Argentine and European experiences.

A controlled economy—the total identification between economic and political interests and the growing indistinguishability
of controlling personnel that came about in Italy and Germany—
was not matched in Argentina. Despite a degree of governmental
intervention unsurpassed in previous history, the Argentines did
not reach the degree of control exercised in Chile, Mexico, and
Uruguay. Although Peronism did recruit some new million-
aires from among its own ranks, it is difficult to say whether

[10] Max Weber, *The Theory of Social and Economic Organization*, tr. by
A. M. Henderson and Talcott Parsons, Glencoe: 1947, p. 360.

such acts were substantially different from the same kind of political insurance practiced in other Latin American countries. In any event, Peronism contributed to building a new class of industrialists, but stopped far short of dispossessing pre-existing wealthy groups or instituting total mobilization of the economy for national ends. The motivation for the economic measures of Peronism rested in autarchical nationalism, as in the Mexican case, in statism, as throughout Latin America, in anti-capitalism, an almost universal article of faith among both traditional conservatives and leftists in Latin America, and probably only in a very minor degree on any self-conscious ideological principles concerning the role of economics in a fascist society.

Racism was entirely incidental to Peronism, even more marginal than it was to Italian fascism. Indeed, the Perón administration defended certain ethnic minorities against the extreme measures desired by certain parts of the urban upper class.

Perón's search for support outside the existing power structure led him to herd the lower-class groups into captive trade unions. This black populism appealed especially to the less skilled workers, such as packinghouse employees, and to new migrants to the city, coming out of the countryside in response to the growing industrialization of the metropolitan centers. Despite the substantive difference between this process and the recruitment of déclassé middle-class persons in Germany, some observers have attempted to save the totalitarian category for the Peronist regime by labeling it as "Fascism of the Left." S.M. Lipset, for example, writes:

> [Another] . . . type of social movement which has often been described as fascist is Peronism. . . . Unlike right-wing antidemocratic tendencies based on the more well-to-do and traditionalist strata and those tendencies I prefer to call "true" fascism—centrist authoritarianism, based on the liberal middle classes, primarily the self-employed—Peronism, much like Marxist parties, has been oriented toward the poorer classes, primarily urban workers but also the more impoverished rural population. . . .
>
> The phenomenon known as Peronism—anticapitalist populist nationalism which appeals to the lower strata in

alignment with the army—is, of course, not unique to the
Argentine. In Brazil, Getulio Vargas developed the same
theme a decade earlier, was also identified with fascism,
and continued to retain the support of the workers after he
left power. . . . If Peronism is considered a variant of
fascism, then it is a fascism of the left because it is based
on the social strata who would otherwise turn to socialism
or Communism as an outlet for their frustrations.[11]

Several very serious quarrels can be picked with this statement, the most important being the loose and interchangeable
use of "fascist," "authoritarian," and "totalitarian." All fascism
and totalitarianism is of course authoritarian, but not all authoritarianism is totalitarian and fascist. Peronism employed the
ideology and public style of fascism, but performed no revolutionary functions in a class or structural sense, governed internally by juggling already existing power centers in a fashion
typical of states in immediately prenational situations, and above
all was unable to establish the unquestioned supremacy of the
state. The regime even toppled in traditional semi-developed
Latin American style, victim of a *coup d'état* led by a military
vanguard and supported by an important and significant body of
public sentiment.

Much doubt also can be cast on the seemingly logical view that
the persons who became Peronists would otherwise have become
socialists or communists. Certainly Peronists have not flocked to
the Marxist banners upon the collapse of their own movement.
What is most probable is that, at least in any short or intermediate run, persons susceptible to following the traditionalist politics of syndicalism are not apt recruits to the essentially developmental and nationalist appeals of any of the modernizing camps,
whether Marxist left or Liberal moderate. The intellectual atmosphere on this point might well be cleared by understanding
that in Italy Mussolini presided over a mixed regime—part
Mediterranean traditional syndicalism, part modern totalitarianism. The rather purer forms of the one are found in Portugal,
and of the other in Nazi Germany. Both Mussolini and Perón,
after all, were leading Latin peoples with Latin cultures.

[11] *Political Man: The Social Bases of Politics*, New York: 1960, pp. 170-
173, *passim*.

But Peronism did succeed in setting class against class more sharply than in any other period of Argentine history. The movement clearly and self-consciously counterposed liberty and authority and opted for the latter; in more hidden fashion it also opposed honesty to dishonesty, and also chose the latter in all senses. Reason, too, was made to cede to demagoguery. If Peronism did not change the relative position of Argentina's social classes, only pressing them together in their economic aspects, it did temporarily reduce social distance in a psychological as well as economic sense. There is no contradiction in the fact that the more equitable income distribution and greater feeling of participation on the part of lower elements was accomplished in part through the fomenting of overt class antagonisms.

The regime, nevertheless, did not change the land tenure system or the prevailing patterns of distribution of great wealth. Although the style and ideology of leadership were novel, the recruitment patterns changed only slightly, and the sources of succeeding opposition leaders were unaffected after all was said and done. Not even the pre-Perón distribution of opposition parties was effectively destroyed, for they all returned to their usual sickly bloom within a year after the fall of the dictator. These "accomplishments" of Peronism simply do not describe the workings of a totalitarian fascism.

Peronism responded to many basic needs in Argentine political life, and succeeded eventually in betraying all of them. Any reasonably modern society must somehow recognize and make provision for the desire of large groups of citizens to participate in the civic experience; Argentina also needs some kind of national, integrated identity, and a means for the routine settlement of secular dispute. Perón gained outside support by promising to meet these needs and by devising a poor man's neo-fascist ideology to explain his actions. But he employed worker support only to construct a General Confederation of Labor as an added institutional pillar in the emergent syndicalist structure, not as a free labor movement. He did not change the institutional order; he only amended it by extending its already existing configuration. Through corruption and inefficacy, a failure to understand why he really had gained mass support, and his ultimate commitment to traditional values and sources of power, Perón perverted what might have been the positive developmental aspects of his policies and left his country with the twisting legacy of a lower class infected with neo-fascist political beliefs and an opposition stained with his own style. And by denying even the traditionally thin Liberalism to which middle and upper groups had become accustomed, his kind of authoritarianism guaranteed the hatred even of wavering Argentine democrats.

The Argentine political tragedy resides in the fact that the political integration of the popular classes was initiated under the sign of a totalitarianism which succeeded in providing, in its fashion, a certain experience of political and social participation in the immediate and personal aspects of the life of the worker, nullifying at the same time the political organization and the basic rights which constitute the irreplaceable pillars of any genuine democracy. The immense task to be carried out consists in gaining this same experience, but relating it in an indissoluble manner to the theory and practice of democracy and freedom.[12]

The importance of Peronism should not be underestimated, however. The effects were profound precisely in those two areas least strongly inhibited by institutionalized power—ideology and style. Unable or unwilling as Perón was to change the basic contradictions in the structure of social values, economic practices, and mass versus traditional politics, his ideological prods and his simulacrum of populism have left the problems inflamed, a continuing source of infection and pain. Not only did the dispossessed became aware of their status and taste some of the fruits of an artificial participation, but now even the integrated middle and upper groups are willing to admit the possible alienation of some of their fellow citizens.

Dismantling the work of the Perón administration in an organizational and immediate policy sense was not an inordinately difficult task, and certainly nothing to compare with what would have been a transition from totalitarianism to limited democracy. Despite the damage he wreaked on the nation's

---

[12] Gino Germani, *Politica e Massa*, Minas Gerais: Estudos Sociais e Politicas da Faculdade de Direito, No. 13, 1960, p. 189.

economy, there is good reason to believe that many of the difficulties would have existed even without the badly directed interventionism of the Perón era. The constitution of 1949 was calmly
repealed, elections organized, and by early 1958 the government was legally re-established in regular constitutional fashion.
Ideological confusion has hindered all politics since the end
of Peronism, but since both policy horizons and public power
remain limited, the play of politics continues to deal with
problems superficially and merely manipulatively. Peronism was
not born in social revolution, nor was it immolated in it. And the
politics of post-Perón Argentina remain traditional prenational
and essentially syndicalist in nature.

The Heritage of Anti-Nationalism

The military government of 1955-1958, presided over by an
unstable group of predominantly Liberal army officers, attempted
to restore the politics of formal democracy based on a coalition
of upper and middle groups. The armed governors, somewhat
abashed at their role, sought to establish a kind of democratic
market place without the Peronists, but otherwise characterized
by a large measure of civil liberties. They succeeded in this end
well enough to supervise substantively good and honest national
elections for all groups except Peronists. Otherwise few decisive public acts were taken, the government assuming that its
basic function was to provide a healing cushion of time between
the fall of Perón and a constitutional civilian successor regime.

In early 1958 Arturo Frondizi, the candidate of the center-left
Radical Intransigent Party and supported by the Church, the
Peronists, and the Communists, was elected president. The military divided on the advisability of permitting the new government to assume office, but finally moderate counsels won the day
with the understanding that Frondizi would be inhibited by the
military from following policies of either an allegedly Marxist
or allegedly Peronist nature. Thus began the uneasy three
years, marked by three dozen attempted military *coups* of many
political hues, which finally culminated in the collapse of the
Frondizi administration in early 1962 and the assumption of
power by the extreme interventionists among the military.

Frondizi was seen overseas as a progressive politician who followed free enterprise policies dedicated to a rapid healing of the nation's economic problems antecedent to a political reconstruction. He was considered inside Argentina as an opportunist and a Machiavellian juggler always ready to retreat when necessary to maintain his precarious hold on power. Whatever may have been his motivations and those of his inner group, the Frondizi regime, measured by any yardstick, was a total failure. Frondizi's economic policies did not succeed in raising productivity, distributing income more equitably, or reducing balance-of-payments difficulties, although inflationary pressures were stopped short of becoming run-away. His social policies did not reduce interclass tensions; indeed, the immediate reflection of his economic measures was to intensify such conflict, as was stated in the introduction to this chapter. And his political "integrationist" policy of attempting to woo Peronists into the Radical Intransigent Party failed before the absolute strength of the Perón movement itself and was, of course, the immediate cause of the military strike which removed him from power.

The Frondizi government can be best understood as yet another Argentine attempt at syndicalist organization. The government made no attempt to follow Liberal political policies, but instead fomented the very politics of institutional hierarchy employed so strikingly during the first seven years of the Perón administration. It is clear that Mr. Frondizi presumed that he could gain the support of enough of the organized power groups to be able to contain the military until such time as he could muster sufficient strength to submit them entirely to civilian control. To that end, he wooed the clergy, insisted upon turning the General Confederation of Labor over to Peronist control, and hoped that his economic policies would weld industrial and agrarian groups to his movement. He also sought to go outside the standard fasces to find extra support, much as Perón had done when he established his captive trade union movement in the first instance. The Frondizi government sought the added margin of power in the international sphere, soliciting and receiving strong support from the United States. All this maneuvering was still not enough, for the policies followed remained antithetical to the very economic development for which all the material and ideological sacrifices were being made. Traditional values and organization remained inconsistent with economic development; Argentina was not and is not in a primary economic crisis which can be solved by economic means. It is in a political and social crisis which has affected the formerly healthy economic machine.

The economic policies of Mr. Frondizi and his foreign advisers only exacerbated Argentina's problems, leaving the country much worse off after his truncated rule than before. The political party system is now in shards, democratic procedures are even more discredited, the military have become ever more deeply convinced interventionists, and a national weariness has replaced the enthusiasm of the immediate postwar years. As yet no political solutions are in sight, despite the promised return to a moderate and civilian administration implicit in the elections of July, 1963. The basic sin of the Frondizi government was that it betrayed the democratic process in the ideological conviction that a policy of neo-syndicalist "integrationism" and naked economic determinism was the only viable solution. The self-delusion of the military that they are the ultimate defenders of the constitution against the Peronists and Communists proves itself in the utterly regressive nature of their politics of consolidation by force in the midst of delay, confusion, and vacillation. The failure of Argentina's large middle classes is their continued identification only toward the top instead of toward the total nation. And the insufficiency of major parts of the literate lower group is their yearning for a Peronist politics of romanticism and authoritarian leadership.

As there are Romance languages, so are there Romance politics. For long it has been a common saying that Europe stops at the Pyrenees. The Iberian peninsula and its offshoots, Western though they may all be, are the only part of the European cultural community so consistently lagging in integrating any effective degree of modernism. Underdeveloped, undefined, and understudied, they have gone their way, the subject either of neglect or of a beneficent Pan-Americanism of a rather sticky hands-across-the-border variety. But there can be little doubt that eventually, in the long and dolorous run, the Iberian community will emerge into the modern world. In the meantime,

Argentina will probably continue to serve as one of the more striking cases of resistance in the Romanic world to the value and institutional requirements of development. All Latin America offers case after case of differing accommodations of traditional values to a certain ingestion of the modern, especially in the areas of industrialization and mimetic ideology. But Argentina's experience is still the most notable because of the country's extraordinary degree of urbanization, industrialization, and cultural Europeanization.

There will be no effective solutions in Argentina until that country puts aside its paradoxes, its attempt to have the best of the traditional and the best of the modern. Argentina clearly demonstrates that machines and Europeans and big cities do not guarantee self-sustaining development and stability. Equality before the law, public secularism, and guarantees of participation in the total nation remain ineluctable parts of the total situation that is the modern state.

Chapter

11

▭▭▭▭▭▭▭▭▭▭

Development
and the Cultural
Reinforcement of Class:

Israel

EDWARD A. BAYNE

Unevenly, but inexorably, immigration into the state of Israel continues. By the early summer of 1961, Israel had welcomed its millionth newcomer since the founding of the state, *de jure*, in May of 1948. The continuing flow of Jews from Europe, Africa, and Asia served constantly to emphasize, fifteen years after independence had been recognized by most of the world, that Israel is a modern Jewish phenomenon created by just such immigrants, who have been drawn or driven from more than threescore cultures. These people seek a new freedom for themselves and for the Jewish nation in this still-disputed enclave on the southern shores of the Mediterranean Sea—an arid, unpromising land, but rich in a long history that their ancestors had helped to create, history which much of the world reveres.

The motivating ingredient for this renewed statehood was altogether human, a socio-religious dynamic known as political Zionism, whose most effective prophet was a nineteenth century Viennese journalist named Theodor Herzl. He had seen and felt the separatisms that were to disintegrate the Austro-Hungarian Empire, and had observed in France the anti-Semitism that festered there despite the supposed "Enlightenment" of European civilization. This Jewish nationalist did not live to see an independent Israel (he died in 1904), but he did witness the first steps of modern Jewish settlement in Palestine. Most important, he encouraged the formation of a body of men and women, originating chiefly in the restless Jewish communities of Eastern Europe, who were willing to devote their lives selflessly to the creation of a new Israel. Herzl's legacy thus rested upon two significant elements: the concept of a Jewish state in which the intermittently persecuted Jewish society could be free (as it had not been free since the sack of Jerusalem by Titus in 70 A.D.); and a determined elite who would wage war and diplomacy, would buy and build, conspire and construct to bring the dream into reality. These appear to be two classic components of nationalism, in this case founded upon five millennia of religious unity and a great measure of cultural exclusiveness, and finding in modern Zionism a coloration, at least, of social democratic utopianism.

This modern dress of Zionism—post-Enlightenment, post-Napoleonic—has antecedents in almost every century of Jewish history ranging from the momentary charisma of false messiahs to the constant religio-secular determination to maintain ties with the Mosaic "promised land." As an expression of nationalism, it may thus be characterized as an outgrowth of the fact that Jewish consciousness includes both a religion and a people, a combination that until now, at least, has provided a stalwart historical example of societal durability. The idea of a separate and independent "peoplehood" has never been lost.

Today, the concept has become a living Jewish state. It is not, perhaps, totally fulfilled; it is subject to complicated and continuing bitter Arab resentment and to profound social problems within; but it is an increasingly viable and modern nation-state. The elite, grown older in the sixty-odd years that have momentously passed since the first Zionist Congress in 1897, or partially replaced by a selection of equally fervent second-generation Israelis, constitutes the leadership of the state and the administrators of its spiritual legacies in a remarkable secular achievement. Although it occupies only a short period in Jewish history, the creation of the state of Israel has been a model of dynamic nation-building, beginning with the modest agricultural settlements in then Ottoman-ruled Palestine, going on with the legitimization of the idea of a Jewish home by the British Government during World War I, the epoch of growth during the British mandatory period, the heightened pressure for an independent Israel brought about by the Hitler pogroms against European Jewry, and finally, when the British withdrew in 1948, ending in a war with the resentful Arab states that affirmed independence. The process had its moments of glory, but it has left in the region remainders that continue to smolder, a danger to peace.

Within world Jewry, however, Zionism has never been accepted by all Jews, nor perhaps even by a majority of them. Most, probably, have had a familial sympathy for the Zionist cause, but not to the extent of sharing physically in the struggle it has represented. The dialogue between those who believed that an earthly redemption—liberty—could only be realized by political independence, and the opposed "assimilationists" who have found individual satisfaction and an adequate cultural freedom in certain Western countries (notably in the United States, where there are three times as many Jews as in Israel) continues around the definition of the true Jew. Must he be a Zionist? And must a Zionist be an Israeli?

Opposing this modern Zionist view is a great body of cultural history and the historical fact that long before the Roman Empire Jews had been dispersed more or less happily, if more or less deliberately segregated by social and economic function as well as by the suspicions of the host peoples in the lands in which they found themselves. Contemporary Jewish rationalism which (no less than "Christian" rationalism) separates the religious element from the social—or tribal—character of Judaism, seeks to make a break with Jewish history, dissociating itself from a fundamental ingredient of Jewish nationalism, or any acceptance of the reality of spiritual ties expressed in communal terms. Citizenship, no matter how emotionally phrased, is not the same as nationality.

It is the view of the most prominent Zionist, David Ben-Gurion, Israel's longtime prime minister, that "Israel has been the decisive instrument . . . for enabling Jews in search of freedom to find it." He explains that he has always believed "that the Jewish people needed a country to which Jews in search of freedom could go as of right and where they could, by their own labor, create a society where the Jewish spirit and culture could thrive naturally on their ancestral soil . . . ." But he further has pointed out that "not every Jew has to come to Israel. No Jew has to do anything that he does not want to do. If he is a free man, he does what his conscience dictates and nothing else . . . ."[1]

The assumption of a nationalist orthodoxy that marked nineteenth century Italian, German, and Polish patriotic sentiment, which modern Zionism has intellectually taken for its own in its modern expression, is thus moderated theoretically by a degree of *laissez-faire*, even though a certain evangelism continues. It was as much to warn assimilating Jews of continuing world anti-Semitism as to express nationhood that Israel tried and condemned Adolph Eichmann, the Nazi executive of the Hitlerian "war on the Jewish nation." As the continuing immigration indicates, Israel is a symbolic and real refuge for all Jewry in times of actual or suspected oppression, and in this sense an ultimate national home for all Jews. Perhaps more than could ever be admitted, a majority of world Jewry quietly acknowledges the state's image within their consciousness of Jewishness, an acknowledgement measured in part by the support for the establishment and development of the state that has been forthcoming, and in the real alternative of citizenship in time of stress that it represents.

Political and Cultural Integration

More than a million of Israel's two million Jews were born after 1940, and have known no political reality other than an

[1] In conversation with the author, March 1961.

independent Israel beleaguered by its Arab neighbors. They have been part of a state that has been struggling for a rapid social and economic development supported by large injections of international assistance. For the younger half of the Israeli people, the country is normalizing. Cultural diversities, even skin coloring, that continue to present immediate problems of social integration for their parents appear to fade into relative insignificance in the schools where all learn in the Hebrew language, in the army, or on the soccer fields. For youth, a consciousness of being Israeli has emerged.

The citizen army particularly, where virtually all able-bodied Israelis must serve, acts as a great leveler and melting pot. It is, for one thing, the principal marriage mart, and for another, the agency of Israel most dramatically defending the state. For everyone, it is a somewhat rough but chauvinistic common experience wherein the nation's security is a seriously studied business with few frills or comforts. The national conviction that vengeful Arab neighbors can be held in check only by a readiness for instantaneous and "massive" retaliation adds immeasurably to the intensity of the military experience, led by the small but dedicated and honored permanent officer corps. The "secret weapon" of the Sinai campaign of 1956, when Israel, although logically overextended, managed to sweep the Egyptian forces aside and win the field, has frequently been cited as the product of the easy relationship between officers and men (and women) that places a great reliance upon individual initiative and improvisation in the field. The essential "democracy" of the command line indicated here is perhaps a symbol of the total military experience as a social training for citizenship in the state, but it is an even clearer demonstration of an urgent patriotism, common to all.

Later, as civilians, some Israelis lose part of this idealistic martial egalitarianism. Exclusiveness returns as a result of continuing parental attitudes and standards of living and education, but as in any citizen army the fundamental equality of experience will have left a residue of attitudes toward governmental institutions that reflect a broad fraternal approach. Few Israelis, if any, are fearful of "militarism"; they think of the army as a citizen force devoted to a democratic society, even though other observers are sometimes apprehensive of the Israeli command in the social dynamics of a state where external security necessarily causes a constant tension, and where defense represents as large a proportion of national resources as it must.

The emergent consciousness of an Israeli character is too new, however, to be defined in tangible terms. The young state's arts and literature bear the mark of the developed cultures of Europe from which its intellectual leadership has come and to which it continues to look for aid, approval, and alliance. Broadly, perhaps, Israel has the flavor of an Eastern Europe of several decades ago, with startling admixtures of a brassy "Atlantic" style. Yet the Israeli national personality sacrifices elegance to earnestness of purpose. As the state has become more affluent during its short history, the emphasis of conception has only slowly moderated from strict functionalism to more life-enhancing patterns both in social organization and in material matters. At first, mere shelter at the cost of pleasant architecture was characteristic, for example. The frequently stark but functional collective agricultural settlement, the *kibbutz*, which served during the pioneering years as a concentrated labor device, a stockade in a hostile area, and a crucible of socialist idealism, has long ceased to grow in Israel as a form of social organization, giving way in agricultural settlement to the more liberal, cooperative but individual family-oriented *moshav*. As the economy has deepened, becoming more industrialized and mechanized, the limited training objectives that were once adequate are now unsatisfactory; higher skills are encouraged and readily absorbed in an economy already within the "take-off" stage.

The early limitation of skills is explainable when the pattern of immigration is noted. Israel first of all needed people as soldiers and workers and deliberately encouraged Jews to come from everywhere. Its pre-independence Jewish population of about 600,000 was sufficient neither to meet the threats from outside nor to develop the country from within. Moreover, the purpose of the state, never to be forgotten, was to provide a home for Jews. More than half of the million who have arrived since independence came from the underdeveloped areas of Asia and Africa, and not all of those who came from Eastern Europe (making up a majority of the remainder) originated in communities of high technology. This immigration pattern continues, and nearly 80 per cent of those who arrived in 1961 came from North Africa. The needs of this mass of underprivileged people for training and education, often in the fundamentals of sanitation and literacy, have been tremendous, and higher levels of education have been necessarily inadequate. Great reliance was placed upon the army as a training and linguistic agency. Ordinary teachers had to be trained as well and schools built, in a program that has resulted in an increase in school population, from 130,000 in 1948 to 600,000 in 1961, with an increase in teachers during the same period from 5,900 to 23,500, chiefly at the elementary levels. The burden of cost had to be shared with students at higher levels, and it still costs as much to attend high school as to attend the university.

Moreover, the immediate need during the early years of the state was for simple skills for the construction of basic housing, the development of land projects with elementary techniques, and the creation of basic services to handle the influx of people. The ease with which employment could be found and the low standard of skill required to perform the great bulk of tasks tended to discourage motivations for education particularly among those who found Israel's standard of living, precarious and austere as it was, far superior to what they had left in primitive countries. The aspirations of many of the immigrants were too quickly satisfied, perhaps as much by the new cultural freedom they sensed as by the generally higher standard of living already

TABLE I

JEWISH IMMIGRATION BY CONTINENT OF BIRTH

	North and South America, Europe and Oceania	Asia and Africa
1919-1948	89.6%	10.4%
1948-1951	50.3	49.7
1952-1954	21.8	78.2
1955-1958	34.4	65.6
1959	67.0	33.0
Cumulative Percentages:	46.0%	54.0%
Numerical Totals:	425,564	500,273

Source: *Statistical Abstract of Israel, 1959-60.* Vol. XI, Tel Aviv: The Government of Israel, 1960.

available. The result has been a continuation of the imbalance of the skilled few and the unskilled mass, one aspect of the principal social problem confronting the state since, striving for unification of its people, it must usher most of them through an acculturation process.

As occasional dramatic results demonstrate today, however, Israel has not neglected the higher training of a selected few. Institutions founded in Palestine during the period between the two world wars, such as Hebrew University and the Technion technical college in Haifa, expanded as rapidly as possible and have begun to produce the technical leaders who are now taking their places in the economy. With the Weizmann Institute, which equals in talent most European centers for basic scientific research, Israel is already making important contributions in basic physics, in water desalinization processes, and in new techniques for increasing productivity in arid agricultural areas. Israel's recent launching of high-altitude solid-fuel rockets, ostensibly for meteorological rather than military research, and the operation of two nuclear reactors for both research and energy purposes are some results of the attention the country has been paying to the development of higher skills. Although in many cases such achievements do not rest completely upon Israeli training, since most of the scientists and engineers involved have drawn at least part of their techniques from foreign institutions, a satisfactory body of skills and experience now exists in the country and should reproduce itself as opportunities and necessity for advanced education develop for a larger number of young Israelis. Whether this intellectual resource will be adequate to maintain the general rate of cultural development depends also upon motivation, a factor that is not always measurable.

The process of general and not only educational growth has taken time, and the perfected government has yet to emerge. In public administration and in industrial entrepreneurship, the builders of Israel have been confronted with as many difficulties as in any other aspect of the society, and—in view of the country's rapid pace of development—more than are met by most developing countries. The problem begins, in Israel's case, with the fact that in a Gentile world, the Jew was rarely welcomed to perform *all* the tasks of government. There were, literally, scores of functions in which the Jew had had no traditional experience, and frequently these were in key aspects of administration. The more successful Jews of the world who had gained experience in modern industrial management were not the Jews who came to Israel in large numbers. Those who came from such developed areas of Europe as Germany, for example, were persecuted refugees without capital and, often, without quick spirit to rebuild.

Israel's conscious decision to include in Zion all Jews of whatever estate, from oriental as well as from Western areas, has turned out to be more costly socially than could have been expected. The oriental sector of the population has had only moderate enthusiasm for modern statehood, although an increasing awareness of the democratic process and of a citizen's voting power can be noted as a result of avid electioneering by the principal political parties, if for no other reason. But the problem reaches more profoundly, and the gap in skills and aspiration that divides oriental from Western Jewry, or to a lesser extent from the native Jewry of the generally immigrant state, is tending to become structural. The leaders of Israel speak ominously of the "Levantine" quality of the nation that will result from the loss of the spirit of *halutziuth*—that dedicated pioneering through the application of science, dynamically uniting intellect and morals in egalitarianism, an ethic which has inspired Israel's elite.

A recent study[2] emphasizes the grave national difficulties of integration which, despite such unifying agencies as the army and the elementary school system, and the efforts to unify oriental and Western Jewry in housing developments and agricultural projects, persist to the point of active demonstrations of protest by the oriental population against the upper class and color prejudice. A survey of Israeli personal incomes revealed that the poorer half of the population received only a quarter of the national income and the upper half received three-quarters. Unhappily, the halves are largely divided into the Eastern and Western elements of the population; in one sample, orientals were shown to earn only 76 per cent of the national average, while Europeans earned 112 per cent.

[2] *Fifth Report, The Falk Project for Economic Research in Israel*, Jerusalem: 1961.

The problem of income differentials is further exacerbated by the fact that Asian-African families of the same income level and composition as European families nevertheless spend significantly less on education—and that this difference even increases with length of residence in the country. Thus there is no "natural" tendency for these differentials to disappear.[3]

The report further points out that the country's per capita "educational capital" has been decreasing, while the tangible capital ratio has been increasing at a rate of 6 to 8 per cent per year during the last decade. The low income level of the oriental group is in part a function of an increase in family size of 60 per cent, a growth which in turn tends to intensify their unfavorable economic situation.

These gaps in skills, education, and earning power (not to mention other indices of difference such as food habits, saving patterns, clothing) are tending to isolate communal groups. It is already common in Israel to regard Moroccan immigrants as a behavior problem, and for political parties to be somewhat ostentatious in promoting a single oriental candidate among a majority of Westerners. As the above cited report mentions, "the connection that is generated between membership in a particular community or duration-of-residence group and low economic status brings about a feeling of discrimination and inferiority, creates social and cultural barriers and tensions, and may cause the isolation of certain groups."[4]

Lacking massive injections of skills and talent, Israel must rely upon the talents built into certain sectors of the economy during the days of the British Mandate. There had been a Jewish Agency, a private and democratic "government" that represented the Jewish minority before the British authorities and the Arab majority in Palestine. The agency became the nucleus of the government of Israel upon which, together with the remnants of the British Mandatory government, the present complex of institutions has been built. Today, in almost all departments, the Israeli Government may be termed a modern responsive instrument for democratic rule, subject to a parlia-

[3] *Ibid.*, p. 20.
[4] *Ibid.*, p. 121.

ment. However, the technical aspects of administration had to be learned in a very short time under the difficult conditions of rapid population expansion, intermittently severe warfare, and pressured economic development.

The fact that Israel continues to operate without a written constitution (although a special body of Basic Laws, passed under particular conditions, is beginning to provide a written constitutional base) has postponed the formulation of a number of important legal definitions of the state's role. The most notable of these must be a statement of the division of authority between church and state. In the years of Dispersion, most Jewish communities relied upon *Torah*, the basic Jewish religious law and revelation as expounded by the community rabbi. Except for the need to abide by the secular laws of the country in which it found itself, the community tended toward theocracy. Indeed, it has been said that at least part of the freedom sought by the early Zionists was freedom from this kind of closed theocratic rule. However, in today's Israel, in the absence of either a constitutional or a public consensual division of authority between church and state, the issue remains vague and subject to political pressures from the more militant religious bodies. The secular leaders of Israel have avoided the creation of a rigid constitution (and probably have lost the psychological opportunity to create one, since the state is more than fifteen years old) on the grounds that until an Israeli national personality emerges, a constitution cannot properly reflect its political values. And in fact, during a period when flexibility has been an essential for the executive to build and protect the state in an atmosphere of high emotional intensity, the absence of a constitution has been of benefit.

The absence of a rigid defense against the encroachments of religious restrictions upon secular liberties (in marriage law, food preparation, and various Sabbath restrictions, for example) has, however, raised the specter of theocracy. The loyalties of the less acculturated elements of the immigrant population, moreover, may be assumed to be as much directed toward religious unity as toward the secular unity of the nation. The state does not attempt to be anti-religious, although it may be assumed that the Establishment is opposed to the restrictions of orthodoxy in the interests of freedom and the furtherance of the enlightened pioneering spirit; on the contrary, the workings of parliamentary government have obliged the granting of concessions to religious forces. Religion, after all, provided the "national" law of Jewry during the centuries of the Dispersion— it is not easily exchanged and some loyalty to it must be assumed to be deeply ingrained in all Jews. For those whose inner convictions have been "liberated" by the Enlightenment, the state is supreme; but for those who have not experienced this rationalism, religion—the law of Moses—claims ultimate loyalty and defines the dimensions of the community.

What results for the less religious Israeli, perhaps, is a *henotheism*, a social faith that makes a finite society the object of loyalty and trust, a feeling which may be intensified by the concept of duty that is Judaism's gift to ethics. For the majority of Israelis, physically circumscribed by the Arab wall and the Mediterranean Sea, orthodoxy or religious rationalism provide the choices within the frame of the present national scene.

Social and Economic Integration

In the industrial economy, as in government, there was also a structure that had grown up before independence. Jewish settlements, most of which had been imbued with the ideology of social democracy, had joined together for common purposes, for health facilities, adult education, marketing, and a miscellany of essential services. Many of these arrangements involved nonagricultural labor. Gradually there evolved an over-all mutual aid organization—Histadrut (the General Confederation of Israeli Labor)—which in the circumstances acted as both labor union and entrepreneur. When independence came in 1948, and the country's urgent requirements for a rapidly expanded industry were immediately apparent, the Histadrut filled an entrepreneurial vacuum. It became a behemoth of Israeli industry, commanding more than 30 per cent of the country's basic enterprises in services as well as manufacturing, and by its size somewhat intimidating both foreign and local businessmen, many of whom logically suspected that it enjoyed unusual governmental favor since it was essential to the state, and also since the main political party of Israel, the Mapai (the Israel Labor Party), was heavily recruited from the Histadrut's ranks. As time has gone on, however, the "labor" aspect of the Histadrut seems to have become less convincing to its rank-and-file membership, and there have been numerous incidents in which workers, who are technically owners of the enterprises, have struck against management for better wages and working conditions. While the government has generally sponsored a policy of a "mixed" economy, and has taken a number of politically important services away from the exclusive control of the Histadrut, the fact that nearly 90 per cent of Israeli industrial workers belong to the agency gives it a strong voice in obtaining general benefits at the expense of the remainder of the economy. The fundamental egalitarianism of the Histadrut and the Mapai party has tended to equate the wages of workers with those of professionals, with the result that Israeli labor has taken a larger share of the economic benefits of the country than its productivity justifies. In 1961, for example, textile production in Israel could be generally reckoned as costing 45 per cent more than in the United States, an unfavorable factor only slightly modified by a recent change in exchange rates.

Gradually, however, the industrial economy has expanded outside of the Histadrut complex. A few foreign investors have entered Israel despite the continuing security problem in the Middle East, and the government itself has undertaken industrial development in cooperation with private capital. Industrial employment expanded from 73,000 workers in 1950 to more than 170,000 in 1959, and the value of industrial output quadrupled.

Industrial progress has been more than matched by the pace of agricultural development, into which a high proportion of investment has been channeled for both security and economic reasons. Since independence there has been an increase of nearly 150 per cent in the amount of land cultivated, and Israel, which once had to import nearly 85 per cent of its foodstuffs, now produces more than 70 per cent of the food consumed by its population, which in the meantime has increased two and one-half times. In cotton, the application of modern agricultural science (and certain price incentives) has given Israel the highest rate of productivity per acre in the world, more than twice the average yield in the United States. In sugar beets and vegetables equally dramatic records have been established, although total production, of course, has been relatively small since Israel is about the size of New Jersey and nearly half of its land is desert. A great hurdle confronting the further expansion of Israeli agriculture, particularly in the production of fats and protein, is the shortage of water. By mid-1964 Israel will have completed the facilities for drawing about 54 per cent of the presently unused waters of the Jordan River valley into its southern Negev wilderness. However, even this supply, usage of which will undoubtedly be contested by the Arab states, will not expand agricultural horizons to autonomy; Israel is likely to remain a net importer of fats and cereals for some time to come, even with a theoretical population limit of four million.[5]

The state's economy has been registering considerable gains each year, and despite one of the largest per capita expenditures in the world for military costs (taking nearly half of the national budget), the gross investment rate has approached 25 per cent of the gross national product. This massive capitalization has occasioned an almost constant inflationary pressure, which has been kept within measurable limits by such involved and frequently unorthodox means as multiple exchange rates and internal subsidies. Nevertheless, each year has been marked by public reactions from various sectors for relief from the rising cost of living, which has been mounting despite the fact that the national product has increased in recent years at a rate of nearly 10 per cent. There is virtually no unemployment, although the lack of skills indicates a certain amount of hidden unemployment. The government's ordinary budget is generally in balance, although the effects of wage increases and rising service costs in general have occasioned a small deficit in recent years. The development budget, which depends almost entirely upon foreign loans and contributions, constitutes the largest single aspect of economic expansion.

[5] The 1961 census reported Israel's population at 2,173,923. The majority of citizens live in the three major urban districts of Haifa, Tel Aviv, and Jerusalem. Increasingly, the country is taking on the image of an industrialized modern city-state.

On foreign account, the economy of Israel shows its weakness as a developing country. The annual trade imbalance exceeded $250 million as of 1961, and has been increasing yearly as the economy has matured. In total balance of payments, however, Israel has actually added modestly to its cash reserves in recent years (its mid-1963 level totaled more than $400 million) as a result of foreign investments, contributions, German reparations, and personal restitution to German Jews (a program that may amount to as much as $2 billion over a decade), and capital loans from such institutions as the International Bank and the Export-Import Bank. Since the beginning of the state, the United States Government has provided more than $750 million in grants for immigrant settlement, food surpluses, economic and technical assistance, and development loans.[6] In all, counting borrowings from all sources and the sale of Israel Government bonds to American Jewry, the influx of capital has been massive, while the debt load has been held to less than $700 million, chiefly in long-term obligations incurred for the development of water resources and industrial expansion. With a per capita annual income of more than $500, a gross national product of more than the equivalent of $15 billion, and a short but effective record of growth, Israel has been accepted by the world's bankers as a good credit risk.

For all of this considerable progress, the task of economic development and social integration is obviously incomplete, and Israel continues to run a considerable risk of structuring its society with sharply defined economic distinctions. Wide gaps in income levels exist, despite a high graduated taxation rate. While it is true that Israel is a democratic state, and that the Jews of the world rarely experienced the feudal pattern of society that left its class mark on Western civilization, a less uneven distribution of wealth would appear to be desirable if the egalitarian dreams of the founders are to be realized. Israel obviously must rely upon its own people if it is ultimately to achieve full economic viability at the high standard of living it has set as its goal. It lives in a hostile environment, confronted with a geography that shows only climatic aridity and virtually

[6] The United States ceased its technical assistance program in Israel in June of 1962, but not, presumably, its capital assistance in various forms.

no natural resources except a little oil and a few minerals, of which the chemicals of the Dead Sea provide the principal source. The country must therefore rely upon a "value-added" economic formula of raw imports re-exported as finished goods.

Suffering the limitations of a small state, Israel will depend more and more upon foreign trade. This eventuality has already been foreseen in some measure; within a few years Israel will have more than a million dead-weight tons of ocean shipping to carry its goods, and its exports have been showing a modest increase and an increasing diversity each year. Efforts to open markets in Africa and Asia have been slowly rewarding, and, as standards of merchandise and sales techniques have improved, markets for its finished goods in the United States and Europe also have expanded. More than half the value of Israeli exports still depend upon two items: the traditional Palestinian citrus fruits and the more lately developed polished diamonds—an example of the value-added formula, since Israel must import the raw stones for processing.

Israel has already recognized that in the long run it must become part of a larger trading area to survive. It is a signatory to GATT (General Agreement on Tariffs and Trade), for instance, and shares in such international institutions as the International Bank and the Monetary Fund. In its early days, many observers assumed that its economic future lay in the Near Eastern states, but as development on both sides of the border has proceeded apace, there seems to be less and less basis for a growing trade. It is thus no accident, aside from Israel's predominant cultural affinities, that it has been seeking membership in the European Common Market, although so far without encouraging results, at least partly because Europe has not yet defined the political dimensions of the future of the economic community itself.

Given a continuation of the needed capital resources and no worsening of either the regional or global security situation, Israel can continue to demonstrate that it has passed the "take-off" stage of development. Its prospects for further growth both externally and internally would seem to lie rather in the political arena, and ultimately to be based upon a resolution of its social problems.

The Politics of Nationhood

Even before the day of independence, when Israel established a parliamentary government, the councils of the Jewish Agency and the World Zionist Congress that had nursed the concept of Israel into being were noisy with political debate. To a large extent the differing ideologies represented were products of the European cultures from which Zion's leaders had come; they were bound together by the common determination to create a Jewish and democratic state. The eastern Europeans, Jews of Russian origin particularly, had grown up in an atmosphere in which the language of political protest was that of the nineteenth-century Social Democrats; they superimposed this view upon the concept of Zionism, which they saw as a dedicated pioneering with a content of scientific humanism. Germans, and other western Europeans, tended to represent a bourgeois liberalism. The orthodox religious contingents saw in Zionism an opportunity to establish a *Torah*-ruled community in the image of Old Testament times. As a senior Zionist in Israel once remarked, "Israelis are born into political parties," each determined to fill the all-embracing dynamic of nationalism with a specific ideology—not always liberal or democratic.

When the state undertook to establish its first legislative body, known as the Knesset, this rainbow of largely European political ideologies colored its membership from the beginning. As the election statistics in Table II demonstrate, there has been a remarkable rigidity in vote distribution, even though Israel has drawn a majority of its citizens from areas where nineteenth-century political ideas had never penetrated, and despite the changes wrought in Jewish life by the rapid development of the state since independence. Only in the decline of minority parties, representing temporarily unintegrated bodies of immigrants, or the Arabs who have remained in Israel and who constitute about 10 per cent of the population, has there been any improvement. In the first election, these minority interests claimed more than 13 per cent of the votes, while in the 1961 polling, less than 6 per cent of those voting found it necessary to express their individuality in this fashion, rejecting integration in one of the larger parties. For the separated and unintegrated Arabs, both Mapai and Mapam, center-left and leftist parties led by Jews, maintain associated Arab parties to counter the Communists, who have traditionally been the protest group for the Arab minority in the country. However, the

TABLE II

KNESSET ELECTION RESULTS

[Seats held by each party]

	1949	1951	1955	1959	1961
Mapai (Labor)	46	45	40	47	42
Herut Movement	14	8	15	17	17
National Religious	16*	10	11	12	12
Mapam (United Workers)	19**	15**	9	9	9
Achdut Ha'avoda (Labor Unity)	**	**	10	7	8
General Zionists	7	20	13	8	17—
Progressives	5	4	5	6	—
Agadut-Poalei Agadut (Religious)	*	5	6	6	6
Communists	4	5	6	3	5
Minority parties	9	8	5	5	4

Source: adapted from *Israel Government Yearbook, 5722 (1961-1962),* Tel Aviv: The Government of Israel, 1962.
* In the first Knesset, the religious groups all voted under a Religious Front.
** In the first and second Knessets, Mapam included voters later forming Achdut Ha'avoda.
— Following the crisis which made the 1961 elections necessary, the General Zionists and Progressives joined to form the Liberal Party.

Herut party of the extreme right and the religious groups have not been regarded as potential sources of alternative government, even though the adherence of many oriental Jews to the Herut has been persistent and gives some prominence to the possibility of its growth as a conservative alternative to Mapai, equally capable of temporary compromise with the religious parties. Secular politics has therefore centered upon a left-right spectrum reaching from the leftist Mapam and *Achdut Ha'avoda* to the General Zionists (now, with the Progressives, known as the Liberals) on the right, a spectrum so fractionated that the Mapai emerges as consistently dominant—a qualified form of "one-party" rule.

The leadership of government from the beginning has thus fallen to the left-of-center Mapai, led by the most prominent Zionist of all, David Ben-Gurion. However, his premiership has necessarily rested upon uncomfortable coalitions, which exclude the Herut but usually have included the religious groups whose interests are more easily accommodated, provided concessions are granted in matters of religious law. Herut's philosophy is expansionist and ultranationalistic, and by the proportional representation system under which Israel votes, it tends to retain its somewhat scattered strength. The problems of coalition rule are many, and Mapai has not been able to achieve a majority in the 120-man Knesset. Although philosophically a labor-oriented group, it has been forced to rule through "national" governments frequently more conservative than it would like, but rule it has.

In reality, while the Knesset is democratically supreme and Israel's court system is totally free and revered for its integrity and general legal purity, the country's executive leadership stems principally from the Mapai party and constitutes an "Establishment" of ardent, earnest Zionists whose devotion to Ben-Gurion tied a divergent group of administrators closely together. The Establishment reaches into all aspects of the government and the professional military, and its existence from the early days of the *Yishuv* (as the pre-independence community of Jews in Palestine was known) made the state possible. The group, of somewhat fluid membership as older Zionists retire or die off, is composed of perhaps 150 persons who maintain an atmosphere of youth and tireless energy. It constitutes an elite, which, although democratically committed, has become habituated to its position of power.

The Israeli experience with the Establishment is worthy of study wherever new governments are coping with the problems of nationhood. The existence of this capable and democratic leadership suggests a workable alternative political formula available to developing countries that all too often flounder into disillusionment under self-government and turn to dictatorship. The Establishment of Israel has never entrammeled the democratic process, but has kept it flexible and somewhat limited in administration, and thus has been able rapidly to accomplish many of Israel's national objectives. The dual problems of maintaining the country's defense in a hostile region and developing an institutional fabric on which the state could grow have been formidable and their solution a major achievement.

As time has gone on, the maturity of Israel has begun to make itself felt in a questioning of the power of the Establishment and a seeking of means to broaden the basis of executive power. To a large extent, the losses suffered by the Mapai party in the 1961 special election (and the reasons that required the holding of this special election) can be attributed to a growing minority dissatisfied with the system. In the long-term view this development can be assumed healthy, and consistent with Jewish democratic history. Elites and nobility have never been a part of Jewish religion or culture, but the country owes much to the devotion of the Establishment in founding the state and bringing it to its present stage.

The Nation and the World

Although neither Israelis nor world Jewry might accept such an observation without argument, it can be said that Israel's primary foreign preoccupation appears to be with the majority of world Jewry living outside Israel, largely in the United States. The result has been a certain duality in the conduct of Israeli foreign policy. There is an international role for Israel as there is for all nations within the family of nations, and there is a role special to a government seeing itself as the self-imposed guardian of the interests of Jews everywhere. For example, although Israel is committed by institutions and predilections to Western values, in its relationship with Soviet Russia a note of neutralism is retained. Russia still contains nearly two million Jews, some of whom might be released to swell the ranks of the Zionist cause. The Jews of the Dispersion have not only been the source of manpower for the new state, but have provided an essential element of support, both moral and financial. In general, while admitting that this support has been helpful and at times critical, the dedicated Zionist has been irritated by the fact that a majority of world Jewry has not chosen to emigrate to Zion.

The search for definitions of the Jewish relationship to Israel is constant and frequently acrimonious, and like all foreign policy is related to a domestic problem. It is the fear of many leaders of Israel that without continuing injections of Jews from the developed countries of the West, the constant influx of largely unskilled and Eastern Jews may modify the material potentialities of the state and lower its standards of achievement.

From the beginning of statehood, Israel's foreign policy has had an urgency about it which, in light of the active resentment of the surrounding Arab states, was not overstatement. Once independence had been achieved survival was essential, and it is more than a routine requirement that puts every able-bodied Israeli from 18 to 45 into the military reserve. While the United Nations and interested great powers of the West, such as Britain, France, and the United States, might seek to maintain the peace in the Near East, Israel has chosen a more realistic defense of its highly vulnerable territory, and on occasion has undertaken punitive campaigns and even a preventive war to impress upon the Arab leadership that its determination to survive is unwavering. In the doing, Israel has not always been tactically righteous, and has frequently been condemned by the world for its aggressive stance. But since Arab leaders do not and politically, perhaps, cannot make peace with Israel in the continuing hostility of the area, now complicated by the entry of Russia into regional affairs, Israel's preoccupation with defense would seem to have been justified.

The regional legacies of Israel's independence remain bitter problems. The continued existence of former Palestinian refugees living in surrounding territories of Jordan and the Egyptian-administered Gaza area along the Mediterranean coast is the most difficult one to solve, since neither Israel nor the Arab states desire to absorb these people. The rivalry in recent years, however, has assumed the aspects of cold war rather than hot. A regrettable arms race of major proportions between the United Arab Republic and Israel nevertheless continues. The result is a continuation of potentially explosive tension.

Israel has on several occasions tried to negotiate with its Arab neighbors, seeking either directly or through the United Nations a means to discuss the outstanding problems of border rectification, Jordan River water rights, the use of the Suez Canal which Egypt continues to block, indemnification of Arab refugee property rights in Israel, and the fundamental issues of peace and disarmament. However, the basis for a substantive interchange is lacking because on the one hand the Arab states do not officially recognize the legal existence of Israel and remain technically at war (although in a state of armistice) with a Zionist band; while on the other hand, the idea of Israel as an exclusively Jewish state has been embedded in Zionist thought from the beginning. The hardening of this concept in Israel has made any re-absorption of the Arab refugees, only some of whom came from the area comprising Israel, virtually impossible.

Israel's foreign policy has been dominated by this situation from the beginning, and it has affected its relations with all countries. Its recent development of friendly contacts with emergent African states and its determined effort to build satisfactory ties with such non-Arab nations in the region as Turkey, Iran, and Cyprus have been given emphasis by the necessity to balance the threat posed by the Arab countries.

A democratic state, Israel has natural ties with the West in the global arena, although even these predilections are modified when Israel's immediate survival is thought to be at stake. Israel has an increasing interest in Europe for both economic and cultural reasons, and perhaps someday will become a significant bridge between Europe and the Orient because its own population and cultural history represent a mixture of East and West. Israel has also sincerely desired to become a part of a regional organization, contributing to the peace and further development of the Near East.

The Strength of Israeli Nationalism

Embedded within the dynamic of nationalism which is modern Zionism and which has created the state of Israel, at least three significant elements can be perceived that are pertinent to a "social acceptance of the state as the impersonal and ultimate arbiter of human affairs." In Israel's case particularly, the historical factor seems unique in its prominence. Few other peoples have exhibited the durability of nationality that, however widely the Jews were scattered, preserved a sense of Jewishness embodying a rigid supernatural loyalty and a tribal exclusiveness. It lasted for millennia substantially unaltered until the effects of the Enlightenment upon European thought introduced an alternative humanistic set of loyalties, now translated into a modern state. The translation, however, has not affected the whole of the world's Jewish population in the same way— or even the majority of them, as we have seen.

Other loyalties, especially to other nation-states, have intervened, resulting in an acceptance of a reasonable cultural freedom and political pluralism in other countries.[7] The phenomenon of Israel, like its foreign policy, has its duality. For the Israeli, the centuries of Jewish history, drawn particularly from the Old Testament as a chronicle of a nation, have given a fundamental legitimacy to the concept of nationhood, while for the "assimilationist" Jews in other societies, the Bible remains the book of early revelation at least to the extent accepted by the non-Jewish world, and specifically by Christendom. As a result, the incompleteness of Israel lies not wholly in the problem of viability of the territory in the Near East, but in the fact that most Jews do not yet have more than a sentimental, familial loyalty to it. The historical factor has therefore aided in enrobing the modern achievement of Zionists for Zionists, but at the same time has illustrated its fundamental shortcomings as a universal appeal if taken by itself.

It is doubtful that in modern times an Israel could have been created if the motivation was only a common religion and millennia of relatively communal living, or the oppression Jewish communities have suffered in Western societies. A spirit of messianism was required—as European nationalism of a century ago had indicated—and this was provided by the ideology of social democracy which the founding leadership inherited and superimposed upon Jewish history and the Jewish ethic. Israel's contemporary leader, Ben-Gurion, who performed the function of a prophet, has phrased it thus:

> All of the fruitful, redemptive, progressive and uplifting values of man are included in the vision of Messianic redemption. These values include action for the conquest of the desert, for the absorption of immigrants, for the security of the state, and also the unflinching effort to

[7] Note here the fact that in the general exodus from Algeria upon independence, the vast majority of Algerian Jews elected to move to France, not to Israel, even though the French Jewish community is largely Western and not oriental as are the Algerian Jews—i.e., Ashkenazi as opposed to Sephardic.

achieve a society built on liberty and peace, equality and justice among the nations. This vision must be the mainspring of the education of the younger generation . . . .[8]

This idealism, sometimes happily described as "scientific humanism," has become a highly modified social democracy in the realities of modern Israel, with its mixture of peoples of differing backgrounds and the exigencies of economic development and administrative management necessarily dependent upon resources and influences from other countries, especially in the early formative years. Nevertheless, the sacrifices of blood and wealth and the inner discipline these required to form the state stemmed from an acceptance of this dream, possessing both negative and positive values.

Even these ingredients would have been insufficient had there not been still a third element to carry out the dynamic of Zionism. More than twelve million Jews of the world, sharing a common experience and religious ethic, if not the same immediate cultural history in the secular sense, could be made aware of this messianism only by an elite, a self-chosen "pioneer" force that by example and exhortation would transform any inherent but awakened sense of being *déclassé* into a positive idealism, of turning aliens in an alien land into determined nationalists and modernizing a historico-religious image into the tangible reality of a commonwealth. The present Establishment of Israel, as we have noted above, is that elite.

While the progress of Israeli statehood from dream to reality has been extremely rapid, largely as a result of the participation of a far higher proportion of educated, modern people than most emergent nations of today enjoy, the ideal has been moderated into a political reality that is more democratic than socialist. It would appear to be a moderation of the rigidities of the vision; but even more, the development of a less doctrinaire approach to Israeli patriotism can be adjudged to be helpful to the growth of liberal democracy within, and to an improvement in the relationship between the Israeli and his fellow Jew of the Diaspora. In a small state, a triumphant

[8] From the *Proceedings of the Jerusalem Ideological Conference, 1957,* Jerusalem: 1958.

socialism imbued with negative elements of Marxian class consciousness might well be a force for separatism, the Jew of the Dispersion being the object of rivalry. Israel would cease then to be a hopeful gesture of Jewish unity, but rather an element of factionalism in the totality of Jewish cultural nationality.

Alternatively, a more open society could become a city-state within a larger culture, brought technically closer in an age of easy communication. Israel then could accept its historical geography and its inherent symbolism with grace in a rationalist era, with no compulsion to evangelize all of Jewry to a narrow messianism. It would become, perhaps as most of the world is becoming, provincial.

In the making of the state, these three ingredients seem almost classically obvious: a sense of historical unity; an ideology containing its own redemptive qualities and promise; and a committed elite led by a generally accepted prophet. The physical consolidation of the state into a relatively viable national unit is a matter of pragmatic organization of men and resources, survival and common sense. For the immigrants, whether from the Western or Eastern worlds, Israel has been a spiritual means of "modernizing"—in cultural freedom and with relative economic liberty—since both streams of immigration may accurately be said to have come from countries and cultures outmoded by other and freer societies, particularly in the West. On this same plane, the Jews of the Dispersion who have either found personal "modernization," or have not yet become awakened to the desirability of development may look with logic upon Israel as a symbol of a religious tribalism and remain physically separate from it so long as their own environment provides an acceptable measure of cultural freedom.

Nevertheless, Israel's own credentials remain formidable. Whether it is a contemporary nationalized form of city-state, replete with its particular internal loyalties and international responsibilities, or part of a larger cultural and political milieu, the Israeli is already a citizen of what he sees as a clearly defined national entity. He seeks to survive and to prosper, and whatever sacrifice is required to achieve survival or success the state can easily mobilize by a wave of the flag in the name of Israeli freedom.

Chapter

12

□□□□□□□□□□

The Elite, Industrialism, and Nationalism:

Japan

LAWRENCE OLSON

Nationalism as a political force uniting the Japanese people in a self-conscious nation-state began with the Meiji Restoration of 1868 and the train of events which followed. Until then the internal organization of the country for many centuries had been feudal. Control over regional principalities was exercised by the military regime of the paramount feudal clan in what is now the city of Tokyo. This regime rested on a usurpation of power in medieval times from the legitimate civil authority headed by the Emperor. Its policies and the goals it promoted were extremely restrictive. It preached loyalty to itself, not to the nation Japan, and fought change with an archaic view of man that confused ethics with economics and urged self-knowledge and self-denial to control pestilences, price fluctuations, and the law of supply and demand. In this premodern Tokugawa dispensation, classes and occupations were rigidly compartmentalized, social and geographical mobility was regulated by a system of sanctions and barriers, and regional authorities were checked by decrees and beset with spies. For nearly three hundred years the country was deliberately sealed off from the world, and although the basis was laid for the popular foreign view of Japan as an exotic civilization, neither internally nor externally was Japan a nation in the modern sense.

However, there were in Japanese society in the middle of the nineteenth century certain marked attributes of nationality that could be used to support the idea of a unified, integrated nation, assets that were waiting to be exploited by leaders with a nationalist mentality. In the first place, there was an old, common language with a large literature. Language and literature, moreover, were exclusive, difficult for the non-Japanese to learn and understand but available for quick and easy communication and for transmittal of the "value" among the people themselves, once literacy was achieved and modern means of communication established. The multiplicity of tongues that has been such a barrier to national unity in many countries was not a problem for Japanese leaders. There was a common race, highly uniform in physical characteristics, unaccustomed to the idea of living with minorities or changing the constitution of the race by absorbing them. Xenophobia was obviously strong. The single native religious cult, Shintō, though devoid of ethical content and inadequate as a carrier of religious sentiment in the Western sense, had never lost its force at the level of primitive, protective folk belief. On the other hand the political power of Buddhism, competitive in medieval times with the secular authorities, had been crushed, so that rather than acting as a barrier to nationalism, religion was subordinate to the state and could be identified with a state cult.

All these attributes of race, language, and religion were made more peculiarly Japanese by the fact that Japan was a small island country, close enough to the mainland of Asia to make contact when it wished, but far enough away, at least in premodern times, to control the inflow of foreign and the outflow of Japanese people, things, and ideas, and to enforce long periods of isolation. The viewpoint of the Japanese islanders in the modern period has reflected this geographical isolation: they have been uncosmopolitan, inclined to extremes of eager imitation or arrogant rejection of the non-Japanese world, and apt to vacillate between feelings of insecurity and complacency toward the narrow but comfortable known island world of Japan.

Beyond such basic counters of national identification as race, religion, and language, certain less easily described attitudes and values were present which could be used by leaders self-consciously building a modern nation-state. It is clear, for example, that traditional Japan was a status-bound society. The individual was submerged in the group and in the performance of obligations toward the group, or toward persons standing for the group, which the prevailing social ethic required. Concepts of majority and minority opinion were alien; in cases of disagreement some sort of adjustment theoretically was required, because the group had substance beyond any or all of its members, and had to be preserved. The origins of this ethic are not the subject of this essay; but the opportunity for free realization of individual human possibilities, which is at the base of the Western view of man, was absent from the Japanese view. Personal development, if possible at all, was regarded as validating and deepening the terms of status. After accepting unequal status as ordained fact and also accepting the status given him, each man had the right as well as the duty to develop himself within his place. In some such terms as these many modern Japanese have sought to reconcile democracy with Confucian benevolent paternalism, and to claim the attributes of an egalitarian philosophy for what was essentially an authoritarian social prescription.

Respect for authority was thus a social habit inculcated in the Japanese by centuries of ethical teaching and minatory regulation. However, the loyalties felt by Japanese individuals were not solely to their family heads. Duty to one's lord might, and often did, conflict with emotional ties with one's family. This conflict was seized upon by writers who saw its dramatic possibilities, but there was no question which should take precedence in a feudal society. The Chinese exalted filial piety above other virtues; the Japanese ideal, on the contrary, was the *samurai* who would sacrifice his family for his lord. A habit of paying fealty beyond the family thus was ingrained long before modern leaders appeared who could focus these loyalties on a new, centralizing object. When it is appreciated that diligent performance of one's obligations was as important as acceptance of one's place, it is not difficult to see how a consensus of belief and behavior could be enforced once it had been reached.

Here, too, the way had been pointed much earlier, as early as the middle of the seventeenth century, when scholars began to write and teach doctrines dangerous to the usurping Tokugawa. The exponents of *kokugaku*, or "study of the country," in reaction against Chinese Confucian influence, went back to the original chronicles of the Japanese race and there rediscovered and re-emphasized the legitimacy of the unbroken Imperial line, eclipsed but not eradicated by generations of feudal rule. An intellectual movement began to recover the Japanese past. At a time when, in the West, William Godwin's *Political Justice* and the militant pamphlets of Thomas Paine were the scriptures of a new faith in rational progress and perfectibility, in Japan half-legendary classics were being reinterpreted and a new orthodoxy based upon primitive creation myths expounded. As the nineteenth century passed, more patriots spoke out for a restoration of the Emperor to real power. Some of them were punished for their pains, but they became martyrs to later patriots. On the ideological level, then, the leaders of the Meiji Restoration had native materials ready at hand for the centralizing, nation-making course upon which they were to embark after 1868. A homogeneous, vigorous people accustomed to hierarchy was at their disposal; and in the Emperor a symbol of unimpeachable legitimacy was available which, if carefully protected and used, could carry the full ideological burden of Japanese nationalism.

What kind of men were to lead in the creation of a new state from these raw materials of nationality, social belief, and ideology? The leaders of the Meiji Restoration are not to be regarded as "new men," protestants inspired by Western revolutionary doctrines to throw off tyranny. Nor did modern Japanese nationalism originate as a movement of the "masses" from below, led to the barricades by middle-class intellectuals with radical ideas. Tokugawa society was full of protest and ripe for reform; but in 1868 most Japanese were illiterate peasants, capable of sporadic revolt against specific abuses but conservative in outlook from time immemorial and in no sense prepared to foment social revolution.

The Meiji Restoration was essentially a *coup* directed by a few leaders against a suffocating feudal rule. The rigid feudal order established by the Tokugawa, to the maintenance of which many generations of ingenuity were devoted, had been breaking up for two hundred years when the Western powers first appeared as a threat in the middle of the nineteenth century. Cities had grown up around the castles of feudal lords, and a richly human, pleasure-loving culture flourished, despite all the grim edicts issuing from Tokyo. From the luxuriance of genres like *kabuki* and color prints can be implied the failure of Confucian classes to stay in place. Merchants, though theoretically at the bottom of the social scale, acquired wealth and married their daughters to *samurai*, military retainers of hereditary rank who had social eminence and administrative responsibility but no money to pay their debts in a long era of enforced peace and idleness. This mixture of an elite, bureaucratic tradition with commercial experience and initiative foreshadowed the emergence of the modern Japanese governing class.

As the Tokugawa grew more bewildered at the complexities of their isolated, hothouse society, *samurai* of a few feudal principalities distant from the center saw the chance for a new order, with more freedom to trade and scope for political action and adventuresomeness. Though they had been cut off from the whole course of the Industrial Revolution, some knowledge of Western medicine, engineering, and military science had filtered into the country. In addition, word had long been coming from abroad of the Western penetration of China. With the appearance of Western ships on the Japanese horizon, the time had come to cast off the restraints of the backward-looking Tokugawa.

Modern Japanese nationalism began with centralization of power imposed for a variety of reasons, selfish and patriotic, economic and political, but always imposed from above. Nationalism's ultimate drift in pre-World War II times was not toward a revolutionary consummation of a people's need for freedom and autonomy, but rather toward a chauvinism, richly got up with myths and creeds, imposed by a secular elite with origins in a restless military bureaucracy and the old Imperial Court and supported by urban commercial interests and rural land-lords. Whereas in many other countries nationalism has been a reaction against colonial rule and a struggle for independence, in Japan the major motive of modern national leaders was de-fense against the West; they sought to forestall colonial domina-tion and, by establishing a new nationalist orthodoxy, to match the strength of the colonial powers in an imperialistic age. Their earliest and most memorable slogan, "A rich country, a strong army," reflects these essentially conservative goals. Moreover, they are remembered as a group rather than as individuals. Though young and possessing an uncanny perceptiveness re-garding what they had to do to make Japan a modern state, they were unmemorable as people, lacking in color and without charisma. Of all the group who led in the first era of reform, only Saigō Takamori stands out as a memorable figure, probably because he was an anachronism in the new age and eventually died revolting against it. Young Japanese are more likely to remember him than the more constructive others, Ōkubo, Itō, Kido, Itagaki, and the rest, members of a collectivity called the "Meiji leaders" who together led modern Japan on the road to world power in the late nineteenth century. Among them were no Mazzinis, Rizals, or Simon Bolívars, nor are there any Nehrus or Nassers among the conservative leaders of Japan today.

This elite displayed a rich talent for group action in the practical sphere, and they attacked their problems with vigor. The governing desire of the leaders was for national power, for themselves, to be sure, but also for Japan in the world. Emerg-ing in an imperialistic era, they knew that a new nationalist ideology would mean little without guns and ships to support it, and factories in which to build them. The alternative to national strength, they believed, was domination by colonial powers, perhaps even colonial status. Distrust of the outside world was mixed in their minds with curiosity about its technological achievements. As they set about the tasks of modernization they were disposed to limit change to the technical sphere and, by fostering traditional attitudes of harmony and consensus, to enfold and neutralize subversive beliefs and ideologies that might come into the country with the new machinery. What they failed to appreciate, ultimately, was that the experience of what was "Japanese" was bound to change as successive occasions of technical innovation and institutional reform introduced new needs in every sphere. Time could not stand still; the history of the last hundred years of Japanese development has been a story of the tension between change and the drag of the past, between a society industrializing, moving into great cities, and becoming ever more complex, with new needs and demands, and a governing group which, though itself changing slowly, still was bent upon expanding national power, if need be at the cost of popular needs. By the 1930s this tension was to issue not in a triumph of modernism but in ultranationalism, war, defeat, and the discrediting of a whole archaic cosmology.

Because they had had some commercial experience and even some local manufacturing experience before the Restoration, the Meiji leaders perceived the key importance of investment incentives and entrepreneurial skill in the industrialization process. Unlike the plantation colonies of Africa and Southeast Asia, Japan was not to remain a country where land was the basic unit of value and risk capital went primarily into gold bangles and real estate. The great merchant-traders of the closed, pre-Restoration era lacked, on the whole, the aggressive spirit of the new age, and few survived to become leaders of Meiji capitalism. However, as a protective framework of credit and finance was built up, new entrepreneurs appeared, some of them ex-*samurai* or former feudal lords who had been pensioned off and who capitalized their pensions to engage in banking and productive enterprise. A capitalist economy was not established overnight; at first the government itself tried to go into business on a socialist scale, but after a few years of trial and error the foundations were laid for the modern Japanese economy.

In this economy the aggregate of alien capital investment was kept small by design, and no foreign minority existed to control retail trade and money-lending. The government maintained direct control of a few strategic industries such as rail transport and munitions, but the rest were turned over to a few Japanese entrepreneurs whose social origins and education were identical with those of the political elite and whose view of what was desirable for society and the "national polity" coincided to a remarkable degree with that of the officials of the government. By bestowing judicious favors and benefits and by a process of intermarriage and social confederation, the government leaders welded themselves to the big business class. From this union arose what has been called "community-centered entrepreneurs,"[1] leaders of a capitalism in which state influence on the economy was pervasive but rather vague and implicit, and where responsibility was diffuse but rested on a high degree of consensus about national goals and a relatively uniform view of society.

The desire of this business-bureaucratic elite to effect technological change without revolutionizing society led to some spectacular achievements and some peculiar distortions. The leaders perceived early that they must educate the peasant labor force in literacy and basic skills for new factory jobs, while at the same time taking advantage of old habits of thrift and frugality to accumulate capital for investment and tax money for immediate overhead costs of the new state. In the early stages of industrialization the labor force was relatively mobile, but from the end of the nineteenth century the new urban factory class was frozen in the service of a few firms which gained control over each major branch of industry. These firms, and especially the greatest ones, the *zaibatsu*, were in a sense new feudal principalities, commanding the total loyalty of their worker-subjects, limited only by their higher loyalty to the Emperor at the top of the whole structure. The shift from farm to factory was made with as little disruption of social attitudes as possible; many factory workers were housed in dormitories, enfolded in a paternalism which saw the job as a social relationship rather than as a cash contract between worker and employer. Since harmony and consensus were the social ideals of the elite, they

---

[1] Gustav Ranis, "The Community-Centered Entrepreneur in Japanese Development," *Explorations in Entrepreneurial History*, Vol. 8, No. 2, Cambridge: Harvard University Research Center in Entrepreneurial History, Dec. 1955.

fell back on these principles in grappling with the labor disturbances that became more and more frequent. "Conciliation societies" urged labor and management to observe the proprieties of decorum and place, but behind these societies ultimately stood the police. Japanese labor has had a bloody history; it has been weakened by the enterprise-centered nature of the industrial labor force and by a heavy tradition of paternalism, and its excesses have often been met by brutal repression.

In the economic sphere, then, the ideal of the prewar Japanese elite was an educated but tractable labor force which could be controlled by appeals to traditional social values and attitudes and which was, or so the leaders supposed, for all intents and purposes inexhaustible. Ideas of individual initiative or industry-wide pride of craft rather than loyalty to the firm as the main motive of worker-productivity were foreign and subversive, and labor unions, which had a brief existence in the 1920s and early 1930s, were systematically repressed.

In politics the prewar record shows a growing awareness that Western-modelled institutions must be allowed to grow, coupled with a reluctance to permit the real participation of the people in power or their sovereignty over the political process. Here the main task of the leaders, as they came to see it, was to erect an ideology that would "handle" imported institutions and neutralize them without destroying the inner meaning of centralized political controls. Their gropings for a method may be studied beginning with the Meiji Constitution of 1889, in which the sovereignty of the Emperor is explicitly stated. The Constitution was the beginning of a half-century of political innovation that was to see the electorate steadily widened and more and more Japanese accustomed to the activities of parliaments and party politics. But these institutions, though modelled on those of the progressive West, lacked their essential inner power, which was instead carefully reserved to extraparliamentary organs not responsible to parliament or people. And even while Constitution and parliament were being granted, the construction of an ideology of ultranationalism was being undertaken which would insure the prerogatives of the bureaucracy.

In Shintō the Japanese elite found native materials for a cult of the Emperor as spiritual and temporal head of a family-state, its folk unique because they were a people descended through the Emperor from unique gods. He was the focus and apex of their loyalties. This myth did not have to be rationally believed; it had merely to be repeated, and for this purpose an "amuletic" vocabulary[2] was devised that came to stress such mystical, unifying concepts as *kokutai* (National Polity), *kōdō* (Imperial Way), *yamato damashii* (Japanese Spirit), and the like. In Confucian ethical teachings the leaders found a code of conduct that fit authoritarian purposes and built it into their new educational system so that, instead of developing personality, Japanese schools produced indoctrinated citizens to fill slots in an over-all national design.

Political parties at first perplexed the governing elite, and the earliest methods for their control were crude—bribery or outright suppression. Before long, however, the government learned how to form its own party and to maintain control in loyal hands. Because authority was imposed from the top, Japanese politics suffered from inordinate factionalism; as in other spheres of life, personalism prevailed over principles and emotions over original thoughts. Political relationships, like economic ones, were given a social nature, but when true deviants appeared, they were recognized as such and systematically suppressed. In view of the personal experience of the Japanese with the "thought police" in the 1930s and 1940s, it is not surprising that many intellectuals have been led to interpret their modern history in Marxist terms, setting up the "feudal absolutism" of the ruling class against the deprived proletariat and regarding rice riots (in 1918) or riots against foreign treaties (in 1960) as harbingers of revolution. In the words of one of these intellectuals, "prewar nationalism in Japan came to be most powerfully embodied in the political oligarchy which had ruled Japan since the Meiji Restoration, [and] nationalism as a movement among the people did not acquire any strong autonomy or independence, and played a role subsidiary to the chief actor in the drama."[3]

The foregoing summary has emphasized the overriding na-

[2] Ivan Morris, *Nationalism and the Right Wing in Japan*, New York: 1960, pp. 427-428.
[3] Masao Maruyama, "Nationalism in Postwar Japan," Japan Institute of Pacific Relations, Tokyo: 1950. A Japanese version of this essay is in Maruyama, *Gendai Seiji no Shisō to Kōdō* (*Thought and Action in Modern Politics*), Vol. 1, Tokyo: 1956, pp. 149-166.

tionalist goals and ideals of the Japanese governing elite and related them to certain beliefs and attitudes already present in the society which could be used to develop a self-conscious political nationalism. Under talented leadership centered in the bureaucracy and big business groups, Japan's modernization was directed along lines believed essential for the creation of the national power to compete with other world powers of the age. The spectacular results of these policies are a matter of history. In rapid succession Japan won two wars, profited greatly from staying out of a third, and by 1920 had come to be regarded as a world power.

At the same time it should not be supposed that the Meiji leaders were able to limit change to the technological sphere, or that, by permitting the establishment of formal political institutions modelled on those of Western countries, they could totally exclude Western ideas. A democratic religion (Christianity), Western literature, a taste for Western arts, and perhaps most significant, experience with new political processes— all these entered and found some lodgments where they appeared likely to take root and persist. Many intellectuals were stirred by Western ideas, including concepts of political liberty, in the early years of the Meiji period; later Marxian thought, with its emphasis on class struggle and revolution, powerfully attracted them after the Russian Revolution and World War I. By the early 1920s the last of the Meiji "oligarchs" had passed from the scene, to be succeeded by a new generation of bureaucrat-politicians. In the decade following 1918 parliamentary government acquired more real influence, following world trends; the electorate steadily widened, and intellectual controversies flourished concerning the proper form of government for Japan and the nation's course in world affairs. During the early days of the League of Nations and the Weimar Republic, "democracy" became a popular word in Japan, and civilian parliamentary regimes were even successful in reducing somewhat the formal influence of the military bureaucracy over the Diet and policies of the cabinet.

As nationalism turned to militarism in the 1930s, the educated classes included many who did not believe the myths of State Shintō. Many loyal Japanese struggled to rationalize the irrationalities of *kokutai* and to reconcile the emotional appeals of such nationalist articles of faith as the Emperor with their perception of parliamentary democracy as the real need of Japan if it were to become a nation of truly "high culture," equal to the West in every way. Doubt was widespread within Japan concerning the wisdom of overseas adventures in Asia, and the drift toward war with the West was not unaccompanied by protest.

Thus it is true that Japanese nationalism has been more than merely an "accented medievalism."[4] As the face of Japan changed during industrialization, social change followed slowly behind. But hierarchy and submission to authority still characterized the social structure, and the social lag was increased by deliberate government policies inculcating self-sacrificial ideals. Overpopulation was deplored in statements addressed to the world and population pressure was used as a justification for aggression, but at home nothing was done to reduce the birth rate. The countryside was regarded as the storehouse of ever greater quantities of food and traditional virtue, and the gulf in living standards between country and city deepened throughout the prewar period. The government continued to regard the myriad small industrial establishments as a sponge to take up surplus population moving from farm to city, and the technological gap between large and small industry was not closed. Urban workers maintained close connections with their origins in the countryside, often, in the case of women, returning there permanently after a few years in the city. Despite growing popular participation in elections and extensive parliamentary experience, a politically mature middle class, with demands and expectations that would force politics into a new shape for their gratification, did not develop. There was not enough time for this adjustment; rather, politicians came to be regarded as corrupt, parasitic, somehow un-Japanese, and "politician" took on a pejorative ring in prewar Japan. Essential power remained entrenched in a small elite, civilian and military, with the latter having direct access to the Emperor and able to use him to sanction its objectives without reference to the wishes of the popularly elected Diet. Only six years after universal male suf-

[4] Maruyama, *loc. cit.*

frage was granted in 1925, the Japanese Army went on the march in Manchuria. From that time on the shibboleths of ultranationalism might be doubted or even ridiculed or scorned, but the choice before every Japanese was conformity or peril. In fact nearly everyone conformed; those who did not openly collaborate at least passively assented to the destructive course of militarism.

Post-War Readjustments

The ideology of ultranationalism had one fatal flaw: it did not work. With total defeat a deep distrust of all symbols that had brought nothing but misery was fixed in people's minds. Simultaneously Japanese society was flooded by social and political reforms. The reforming agent was a victorious foreign power, and the Meiji leaders must have turned over in their graves. Nevertheless the Occupation stimulated and gave legitimacy to many tendencies that had existed earlier but had been suppressed. Japanese life was torn open, and the air was let into it as never before.

The mythology of State Shintō was discredited and divorced from public support. The Emperor, who had been the theoretical zenith of all loyalties, was reduced to the role of constitutional monarch or "symbol" of the state. The empire was dismantled; the nativistic ideology, with its divine mission, its amuletic words and slogans, faded away in the reality of the war-devastated present. The top of the loyalty pyramid, so carefully erected by prewar leaders, was cut off, and the people, stripped for a time of pretensions, concerned themselves with feeding and clothing themselves and subsided into loyalty to local objects— the family, the firm, and that most local of all objects, the self. Social intercourse continued to be characterized by hierarchy, submission of the individual to group authority. The old instinct that the social whole has a greater validity than the mere sum of its parts remained strong. Selfishness still was seen as a cardinal vice. But consensus could no longer be mustered on the values and attitudes that should tie the society together, and concerning the ideology that should express those values and attitudes there was far less certainty than before. The Emperor was still revered, especially by the older generation which grew up before the war, but his unifying, rallying efficacy had been lost, and nothing, no new charismatic apparatus or device, was found to take his place. The police, the military, the flag, the national anthem, all were detracted from and lost face. Instead, abhorrence of war and of the repressive aspects of the prewar period were deeply implanted in the postwar temper. The new dream of the people became an unreasoning dream of peace.

"Democracy" was the new order of the day, and why not? It had worked, it had won the war, and besides, it gave plain advantages to the individual which many Japanese were quick to perceive. A whole new framework of legal freedoms became available in the postwar Constitution. Political power centered in the popularly elected Diet, to which the cabinet was made responsible. No longer could extraparliamentary bodies usurp state authority. Universal suffrage was proclaimed, farm tenancy was drastically reduced by reforms in the land tenure system, labor unions were encouraged to organize where before they had been fought, and the Occupation introduced new school courses and teaching methods to accustom future generations to the new democratic ideology. In all of this there was a certain naïveté. The very concept of popular sovereignty was unfamiliar to the Japanese, and the irony of its bestowal by a military regime was not missed. Americans moved in strange ways; but, though the new democracy was not yet an organic growth from within Japanese society, the Japanese had had experience in the operation of parties and parliamentary institutions for fifty years before the war. They had not formerly prevailed, but once parliamentarianism was established in law as well as in fact, once power and prestige flowed fully in that channel, there was hope that a new nationalism might grow from within these imported forms rather than later cast them off.

Changes in the social structure were accelerated after the war. Relationships between the sexes changed dramatically as women were released from legal bondage and gained legal equality with men in marriage and divorce; domestic courts were full of evidence of repression and upheaval within the family. In the enormous flux of the postwar period when practically everybody was on the move, the family itself often seemed to have lost its cohesive force. Its members were scattered. Desertion and abandonment of family responsibilities perplexed workers in welfare agencies. As more and more people from "elsewhere" moved to cities to live and work, ties with the village home and local temple grew somewhat more tenuous. The ramified family system, now legally abolished, began to give way, especially in cities, to the "nuclear" family of parents and their children. Within this smaller family, communication between the generations became difficult and sometimes quite impossible. Those who grew up during or just after the war repudiated the authority of their elders, and particularly in the cities joined a new generation which confused freedom with license. Exploding urban growth deepened the gap between social patterns in city and country areas. Vulgar mass media spread a nihilistic sexuality appalling to older people. This phenomenon is not solely Japanese, but the war left a chasm between young and old that cut across most of the vertical, hierarchical compartments of Japanese society. One saw this in the disorderliness of students, in changing attitudes toward birth control and the care of the aged, and in other contexts. The eclipse of older Confucian guides of conduct by a half-grasped "democracy" weakened social solidarity and created especially difficult problems.

For the first time Communists and Socialists campaigned and with full constitutional protection sat in the Japanese Diet. The former remained fundamentally subversive and illegitimate to most people; but the latter, for all their illiberality and leftist tendencies, represented a legitimate opposition. The labor movement became a medium of upward mobility for many Socialist leaders who in education and social origins were often quite unlike their Conservative rivals, and who represented a powerful new element on the political scene. On the far left, but still not Communists, were many middle-class intellectuals who had been corrupted or persecuted by the prewar authorities and had retreated, or had been pushed, into Marxist-influenced theories of a peculiarly antiquated variety. Except for a brief period in 1947, this combination of politicians with experience in labor unions and embittered theoreticians with little or no emotional interest in parliamentary government was unable to come to power after the war, but it shared the broad center of politics with the dominant Conservatives. The Socialists constantly played on the fear of war and exploited public resentment of Japan's postwar weakness and its "subservience" to America. Without positive domestic programs of their own, they agitated the peace neurosis that spread over the country and advanced their own style of patriotism in the form of an essentially escapist "neutralism" that sought to dissolve the cruel realities of the Cold War in peace pacts and defenseless "coexistence." By 1960 such appeals had raised the Socialist vote to nearly 35 per cent of the electorate, subjecting the Conservatives to constant harassment and facing them with the possible eventual loss of power.

In this greatly changed atmosphere, the main burden of reintegrating Japanese nationhood and directing the people toward new national goals rests today on Japan's Conservative leaders. The first fruits of modern nationalism were appallingly bitter. Now the leaders face the challenge of creating a new nationalism that will not seek merely to suppress the disorderly present but will somehow incorporate it in a new *Japanese* synthesis, which will itself be modified by all future occasions.

Who are the members of this conservative elite? Japan has been governed by civilian politicians since the end of World War II. The military bureaucracy was dispersed and the old titled aristocracy declassed. But defeat was not accompanied by social revolution. The Allied Occupation chose to govern through the existing bureaucracy rather than to demobilize it. Major war criminals were removed and punished and purges of thousands of government officials and business leaders permitted some new faces and firms to emerge, but for most of its victims the effect of the purge was temporary. By 1950 the meaning of Japan for the American national interest had changed, and directives that originally had been written to purge rightists were being used to extirpate leftists. Many persons who had been purged were "depurged" and re-entered high position, even including the prime ministership.

Nor was the basic structure of the Japanese economy radically changed, though such change was at first attempted by the Occupation. The holding companies through which a few families had controlled large *zaibatsu* empires were abolished. However, their place as capital suppliers was to a large extent filled by commercial banking houses associated with each of the few largest industrial combinations. The forced sale of shares dispersed ownership among more persons than before, but since the end of the Occupation anti-monopoly laws have been weakened and cross-investment and cartelization permitted and even officially encouraged. The degree of economic concentration has not yet reached prewar levels for a variety of reasons; but although the relative weight of heavy and light industry in total production has changed, the basic structure persists: behind a comparatively few large modern firms stands a multitude of small, dependent enterprises where wages, productivity, and working conditions are relatively low. Between October 1959 and October 1960 Mitsui Bussan, the largest trading company in the country, handled approximately 10 per cent of Japan's total foreign trade. This proportion was about half of that handled by Mitsui before the war, but recovery of its prewar position appears to be merely a matter of time.

Power now is shared by more people than ever before, but despite the greater mobility of postwar society, the economic and social origins of today's civilian elite show a strong continuity with prewar times. The men who run the Conservative party are the contemporary embodiments of that complex fusion of commercial and bureaucratic experience, half public and half private, that in the past led the mass of the Japanese people to serve Japan's interest as well as the interests of a few leaders. Many of them have retired into party politics, because that is where power now resides. But their past experience lies primarily in commercial management or the government bureaucracy. The historic union of politicians with top businessmen is symbolized in such bodies as the Federation of Economic Organizations (*Keidanren*), which is a major source of funds for the Conservative party at election time and consequently exerts a powerful influence on national policies.

These men are capable technicians and managers. They know how to import and export; how to produce, distribute, and sell goods, from ships to toys; how to organize a banking system and a taxation system; how to encourage savings and use accumulated savings in productive ways; how to promote consumption or restrain it; how to deliver mail and run trains on time. They are adept at taking foreign techniques and adapting them to what they believe are their own needs, and they are stubborn about deciding these needs for themselves. They are forever talking about "catching up" with the West and meeting the "challenge" of the industrialized countries. They are a vigorous lot, accustomed to power but unable, for the most part, to share experience; they have a rich vein of humor and humanity, but want somewhat the means of communicating these qualities to other peoples.

Although not without personalities of their own, the members of today's conservative elite form a group in which the individual is relatively submerged. Charisma is still lacking in Japanese politics. Men may be known among their fellows for special qualities of industriousness, stubbornness, loyalty, or equivocation, and leaders of various factions may vigorously oppose one another, but in most ways they are highly alike. The great majority graduated from one of the very few universities with top prestige that traditionally supply new members of the elite. Their backgrounds are remarkably similar, and they tend to solidify their positions by marrying within their own ranks.

Look, for example, at the cabinet of Prime Minister Hayato Ikeda as it stood in late November 1960. The Prime Minister, 60, son of a wealthy rice-wine brewer, graduated from Kyoto Imperial University, one of the very top schools, and spent his entire prewar career as a tax bureaucrat in the Finance Ministry. After the war he was elected to Parliament and became Finance Minister in an earlier postwar cabinet.

The Foreign Minister, Zentarō Kosaka, 48, was the son of the president of a chemical company. He graduated from the Tokyo University of Commerce and worked in the Mitsubishi Bank, while also taking an interest in his father's firm. Before the war he was elected to the lower house of Parliament from the same constituency from which his father had been appointed to the upper house. His wife comes from a famous Buddhist family; her aunt was the younger sister of the present Emperor's mother.

The Minister of International Trade and Industry, Mitsujirō Ishii, 71, was a prewar police bureaucrat and son-in-law of a famous industrialist. His son married into a large tire-manufacturing company. The Education Minister, Masuo Araki, 59, a Kyoto Imperial University graduate, was in the War Supply Ministry under General Tōjō and had a long career in the bureaucracy. Mikio Mizuta, 55, the Finance Minister, another Kyoto University man, is a well-to-do businessman with interests in steel, oil, and lumber. The Minister of Transportation was a former bureaucrat and graduate of Tokyo Imperial University. The Director of the Economic Planning Agency was a graduate of Tokyo University and a former Finance Ministry official; his wife was the eldest daughter of an admiral in the prewar navy. And so on.

All of these men grew up before the war. One or two were elected to the parliament then, but most came into politics only after the war. Almost without exception, however, their fathers were from the same social stratum—most were either businessmen or government officials.

In building a new, more positive nationalism to supplant the passion for peace which swept Japan in the postwar period, these men and their colleagues have at their disposal many of the same marked attributes of nationality which the Meiji leaders so successfully mobilized. Despite defeat, despite churning social turmoil and the collapse of the official ideology, the people's sense of their nationality has remained unimpaired. If nationalism means only a patriotic pride in Japanese-ness, then it belongs abundantly to young and old, city and country, conservative and socialist alike. Fifteen years of massive contact and a multiplicity of personal relationships between Japanese and foreigners since the war have not significantly reduced Japan's ignorance of other cultures. Racial integrity remains immensely strong, as is shown by the contempt felt for those who prostituted themselves in one way or another to the Occupation, and the continuing prejudice against the mixed-blood children of Occupation times. Linguistic integrity also is strong. Hundreds of foreign words are continually being imported into the Japanese language, but their pronunciation is so tortured within the narrow phonetic prison of the language that they are wholly altered and fail to give to Japanese the cosmopolitan character that it might otherwise have.

Nationalism in the basic sense of nationality is often expressed in other ways. Japanese politicians have stopped talking about a mystical *kokutai*, or national polity, but they have not lost their conviction that Japan should be a *taikoku*, or great country. Because Japan is far ahead of the rest of Asia industrially, Conservatives and Socialists alike are apt to condescend to other Asians, even as they seek to restore confidence in Japan's intentions overseas. Most Japanese citizens are only vaguely aware of the United Nations, but every time the Japanese delegate there makes a speech it is front page news. The same is true for every Japanese who climbs a Himalayan peak or endures an Antarctic winter for the greater glory of Japan and science. Japanese Olympic athletes who fail to win are deplored for their lack of nationalist spirit. Whatever shape Japanese nationalism takes, it will reflect a strong racial and cultural dignity.

In the region of implicit social values and the ideology of the new nationalism, however, Conservative leaders face tremendous problems. Their whole world has changed, as well as Japan's position in it. As politicians they represent a dubious tradition that failed once before; as former officials, some of them prominent participants in the imperialist era, they are subject now to the openly expressed suspicions and hatred of all those who fear a return of the past. Because the electorate still is predominantly Conservative, they have the votes to win elections; but their every attempt to express a new nationalist integration is checked by the skittish public mood, challenged from within the country by rival political forces who claim to be the true apostles of nationalism, and qualified from without by conditions over which Conservative leaders have little or no control. Even within the government, unity on goals is often lacking, as contending factions respond to competing pressures of individuals and groups. Caught between the Cold War and the heat of Socialist fury, the response of the Conservative elite to the changed era in which they live has been ambiguous, frustrated, and often intolerant.

Since the end of the Occupation in 1952, successive Conservative governments have attempted to reverse the reformist trend and restore some sense of values more fitting to "Japanese conditions." But what those "conditions" are remains a matter for disagreement among the Japanese people. In general it may be said that in those fields of national life in which the social righteousness of the people as a whole was most flagrantly offended by Occupation reforms, or where they were personally inconvenienced, the government has had the least difficulty in modifying the changes. Strikes in public transport and other government services, for example, have supported arguments that labor's rights should be somewhat curtailed; likewise, the radical political activities of schools teachers' unions and the disorderly demonstrations by radical student organizations have repelled most adult Japanese and helped the government to abolish elected school boards and revise curricula and teaching methods. Nevertheless, the postwar framework of labor legislation has not been basically altered, and the re-introduction of courses in "moral education" has alarmed most parents much less than the Marxist orientation of the Japan Teachers Union.

The postwar Constitution, with its explicit civil rights and protections, has been the central object of attack by the government, which has criticized it as an alien document, imposed by outside force on the Japanese people. For several years commissions have sat to consider specific revisions, and many rumors have circulated concerning Conservative intentions. In addition to recommended amendments to the rearmament clause, some government leaders have asserted, publicly or privately, that the Emperor should be restored from "symbol" to "head" of the State, that women should be deprived of the right to vote and of legal equality with men, that primogeniture should be legally restored, that Shintō shrines, which were turned into private religious corporations after the war, should be returned to state subsidy and administration; and so on. But opinion polls indicate that a majority of the people opposes constitutional revision. Even within the government opinions are mixed on many of the points raised for discussion. For example, what is to be the role of the Imperial Family? In many eyes the present Emperor remains a dubious figure, associated with an era of misery and defeat. His son, the Crown Prince, is as yet undamaged, and projects a quite different public image. The Crown Prince's attractive wife is clearly a national asset, and she is being exploited as a symbol of traditional Japanese elegance in the eyes of the outside world. But it is too early to tell what role the Crown Prince and Princess will assume in Japanese national goals in the future. At home they are popular with the somewhat mechanical popularity of Hollywood stars. Marxist intellectuals would apparently dispense with them; on the other hand, they may, like the British sovereign, in time provide a warm focus of affection and loyalty which is hardly provided by the Emperor today.

In any event the Constitution has not been revised, perhaps primarily because the votes to revise it have been lacking. But the opposition Socialists have shrewdly appointed themselves the guardians of the Constitution, and the present prime minister, Mr. Ikeda, has publicly stated that he would not attempt to revise it even if he had the necessary two-thirds majority of both houses of the Diet. A majority of the people would also have to approve revision in a referendum and, in Ikeda's words, until the people have reached a consensus favoring revision the government will have to wait and try to educate them to what is desirable. But evidently such a consensus is not near. While the Constitution remains, the rights and protections afforded by it to the individual cannot be arbitrarily withdrawn, but must be considered and dealt with by any government that expects to remain in power. In other words, short of a change in the form of government itself, nationalist goals may not be summarily imposed from above any longer, but must be designed to appeal to a far from voiceless public.

In other ways the Conservative elite today operates under heavy constraints of a sort unfamiliar to prewar governments. Since the end of the Occupation, Japan has been bound closely to the United States by treaties and agreements for the maintenance of military bases on Japanese soil, and Japan's economic position has depended heavily on America. One-third of all exports are sold in the United States, and about the same proportion of imports originates there. Special dollar earnings from American defense procurements have been mainly responsible for the favorable balance of payments in recent years. These facts are known and resented by a proud people who yearn for "independence" and are always ready to accuse their leaders of toadying to a foreign power. When in addition the opposition party raucously agitates the popular desire for peace, the Conservative leaders' shallow habit of toleration may break down entirely.

Several times in the last few years this situation has occurred, creating crises in Japanese political life and impeding the growth of a new consensus on national goals. In 1955 the Conservative government of Prime Minister Hatoyama attempted to gerrymander the electoral district system to give the Conservative Party the two-thirds Diet majority it needs to revise the Constitution. This move provoked loud and bitter press attacks and finally had to be suspended. A more serious incident occurred in late 1958, when the government of Prime Minister Kishi undertook to revise police legislation to increase powers of arrest and search. The fears of a wide sector of the urban public were immediately aroused, not only by the contents of the proposed legislation but also by the dubious methods which the government used to try to force it through the Diet. Within the government party itself the leadership was sharply divided on methods, and in the end the legislation had to be withdrawn.

The most spectacular example to date of the constraint and frustration under which Japanese Conservative leaders operate was the crisis over the new security treaty with the United States that excited the country during the spring and summer of 1960. In this episode the fear of war and the desire for peace and independence that lie diffused beneath the surface of Japanese life were brought up powerfully on an issue involving Japan's foreign relations.

The presence of American troops on their soil under the terms of the Mutual Security Treaty of 1951 had long been viewed with misgivings by most Japanese. But although the treaty was "unequal" in their minds, it had been "forced" upon their government, and there was no evidence of a popular disposition to seek a new treaty for which Japan would have to take the initiative. This, however, is precisely what Prime Minister Kishi attempted to do. Ignoring the escapist popular mood, he opened negotiations for a new treaty which would put a time-limit on American bases and otherwise give Japan a more equal voice. His objective was a legitimately nationalist one: to add glory to his regime by obtaining concessions from the United States. But in his impatience with the opposition's sterile boycott tactics Kishi resorted to some very dubious parliamentary maneuvers to drive the new treaty through the Diet. His behavior confirmed the suspicions of many voters that he wished to bring back the authoritarian past, and gave credence to Socialist appeals for abrogation of the treaty and "protection of Japanese democracy" through a neutralist foreign policy. Large numbers of the urban electorate were rudely reminded of the unpalatable reality of Japan's position in the Cold War and found themselves emotionally with the Socialists. Instead of policies that would enhance Japan's independence and glue together some of the jagged edges of Japanese society, Kishi offered only old-fashioned arrogance that exacerbated differences and invited the return of prewar-type political violence of the rightist as well as the leftist variety.

These episodes are cited as evidence that the urban press and a wide segment of the educated city classes are forces that must be heard as never before in Japanese political life. In this arena, nationalism of the right vies with "peace nationalism" of the left. And here the challenge to Conservative leaders is immense, for the society is changing with such speed that they are being expected to respond in a few years with attitudes that required centuries to evolve in the West. Since new unifying social ideals are still lacking, it is not surprising that some of the Conservative elite have tended to fall back on their demonstrated electoral majority and seek comfort in familiar paternalistic attitudes.

Further evidence of the frustration of Conservative leaders may be found in the issue of Japanese rearmament. Before the war Japan made its way up in an imperialistic age by building a modern armed force and deliberately drawing on ancient martial traditions to give it inner strength. Arms were an inevitable concomitant of nationalism in the struggle to be as strong as the West. In defeat, in the moment of deepest disillusionment with all things military, the constitutional right of the people to wage war was unrealistically denied. The right of self-defense itself was left equivocal, resting on a quibbling interpretation of Article Nine of the new Constitution. The Occupation suggested that Japan might well become an Asian Switzerland, but neglected to explain that Swiss neutrality did not preclude relatively strong armed forces. The Japanese Constitution was written with the awful record of Japanese militarism fresh in mind. Hardly had it been ratified, however, when the change in the world situation made perpetual Japanese disarmament seem a naive and dangerous dream in the Western view. But the common people of Japan did not respond with the same speed to the communist threat to themselves that was so obvious elsewhere. Their memory of Japanese militarism was vivid, their knowledge of communist imperialism largely abstract. They were, therefore, opposed in large numbers to the revision of the Constitution to permit open rearmament.

For this reason the government has had to seize upon the right of self-defense, and has named the new military "self-defense" forces. At present Japan possesses a ground self-defense force, or army, of about 170,000 men, a navy of some 40,000 men with assorted vessels of destroyer size or smaller, and a small air force with a few jet aircraft. These forces are under civilian control and their strength and the quality and variety of their weapons are slowly growing. But only about 10 per cent of the national budget is being put into defense, and the efforts of Conservative leaders to increase pride in military forces and dissipate the distrust of the public toward the military have not been very productive. Certain shifts of opinion are noticeable. Self-defense as an "inalienable" right has been more widely accepted, and the degree of contempt shown for military in uniform has diminished. However, there still is a notable lack of enthusiasm for the idea of rearmament. Pacifism is a pervasive atmosphere; moreover, the conviction that it is futile to rearm when nuclear destruction in another war will be inevitable is very widely encountered and is used by the opposition to embarrass the government before the voters. The Socialists more or less cynically proclaim that when they come to power they will turn the army into a sort of civilian conservation corps, and government circles have been less successful in exposing the futility of these claims than in publicizing other programs in the economic sphere aimed at improving living standards and raising national income. Some government leaders themselves would like to dream that Japan can preserve its national integrity through some kind of disarmed neutrality. The official position of the government, however, continues to be that such status will be possible only if and when there is an international armed force to protect it. Since none of the Conservative leaders believes that such a day is near, rearmament remains an essential ingredient in any new synthesis of conservative Japanese nationalism. But until the tension between leaders and people on this issue is resolved—not only by approval of the leaders in elections but also by popular trust in what they are up to—the development of a new nationalist consensus will be retarded.

Problems of the Present

The energy and the special talents of Japan's Conservative leaders are reflected in the physical resurrection of the country since 1945. Obviously the Japanese have not lost their habit of hard work or their skill at adapting imported technology to their own needs. Production indices and living standards have far surpassed prewar levels. In rural areas, where nearly half the people still live, the general level of peasant livelihood with its chemical fertilizers, washing machines, television sets, and power-driven farm machinery is far above traditional Asian standards. In the ugly cities that spread like invading growths over the surrounding lands and waters, constantly increasing thousands live pressed together in a smoky rush of making, buying, and selling. Preliminary figures for the 1960 census show a population fall since 1955 in twenty-six mainly rural prefectures. For the first time in modern history new rural births are failing to replace migrants as fast as or faster than they move to cities. This change is phenomenal and is being officially encouraged by programs of birth control and higher levels of investment to raise productivity and provide more city jobs.

Everywhere are manifestations of the new mass society with its mass culture, half-emerged from the dark cocoon of past habits and attitudes, now swept by new fads, now tantalized by new and old delinquencies. The craze for new things and techniques fills the day and distracts attention from the deeper questions of national being and becoming that are not answered, but are only made harder to answer, by successive doses of imported change. Consensus on nearly everything except the accumulation of money has been greatly weakened. Despite the material comeback of the country, many persons who think at all about such things believe that all is not right, that Japan is not as it should be. For all the prosperity and progress, the meaning of Japan in the world has more than ever been attenuated and dispersed into the general modern uncertainty.

In confronting the problems of their new mass society since

the war, Japan's Conservative leaders have shown that they still yearn for the social conformities and order of an earlier period. Their impatience with minority opinion has often shown through the thin surface of parliamentary tolerance. They have been sorely provoked by the opposition's unruly tactics, and their political and social vision has not been equal to their technological ingenuity. Even as it struggles to be modern, the Conservative imagination is entangled in dreams and clichés of the past. With all the assets of cultural nationalism at their disposal, Conservative leaders have not yet been able to provide a new set of vivid, unifying goals for the Japanese people to believe in and work toward together. On the contrary, the great scars opened in Japanese society by defeat and kept open by the long-drawn-out Cold War have not been closed, but remain deep and wounding today.

As long as power rests in the elected parties in the broad center of politics, Conservatives and Socialists will to some extent force change upon each other, and Japanese nationalism will have the opportunity to fulfill itself within the framework of parliamentary institutions. The Japanese will adapt these institutions to their own needs and put their own peculiar stamp upon them, as they have upon everything else alien they have touched. But today's politicians have no desire to cashier themselves. On the contrary, the longer the parliament is the effective center of power, the more the interests of individuals, parties, and pressure groups are bound up with its perpetuation. The Conservative Party may be a haven for retired bureaucrats, but most of its money comes from businessmen, who exercise more political influence than they did before the war. The Socialists may likewise be controlled by leftist labor unions, but some Socialist politicians continue to argue that the base of the party's support must be broadened in order to reach parliamentary power. With a free press and a system of free elections such as Japan is fortunate enough to have, Conservatives must react to Socialist proposals, not—whatever the constraints they feel—by sending down repressive ordinances, but by presenting an image of themselves that is ever more modern. Failure to do so can mean loss of power. Today "progressive conservatism" means more than ever before in such fields as social security, public welfare, and labor relations. Advances in these and other areas may be slow and grudging, but they are not imaginary.

The corollary to moderation and a more stable parliamentary government at home would be the peaceful expression of nationalism abroad through trade and technological assistance to less developed countries in Asia, Africa, and other areas. If a Socialist government should come to power, Japan's orientation would undoubtedly shift away from the free world toward a more "neutral" position. The country would then face the danger—which it now insufficiently realizes—of absorption into the communist bloc. However, in Socialist as well as Conservative visions of the future, Japan is seen as a leader, not a follower, in Asia. As an Asian country with great industrial experience, Japan is in a position to transmit to other countries technology imported from the West and adapted to the needs of an Asian environment. Many obstacles now prevent such a development from reaching full scale; but if Japan's leaders of whichever party could see economic cooperation as a means of raising the purchasing power and living standards of whole peoples, and not just as a means of filling Japanese pockets, there might be reduced the painful myopia of many Japanese who do not know, or wish to know, how well off they are in today's world and who continue to talk in self-pitying terms of "poor Japan."

On the negative side of the picture, xenophobia combined with obsessional pacifism is vigorously exploited by all who want to see parliamentary government fail, or who merely hope to gain from turbulence and disorder. The repressions of the prewar period have been made into an unspeakable bugbear with which to frighten the people. The wild storms of the summer of 1960 against Prime Minister Kishi and the U.S. security treaty blew up from this sick center of fear—fear of war and fear of the return of the ugly past—in which highly excitable groups of students, unionists, professors, and plain townspeople of all sorts who had no implacable ideological hatred of one another were incited by a few activists who played on fear for their own purposes.

In recent months there have been some very disturbing signs. Leftist violence, in which Socialists took a leading part, has produced a rightist reaction, and rightist extremist groups are more noticeable than at any time since the end of the war. Ties between Conservative politicians, businessmen, and ultranationalist groups are obscure but are known to exist, at least on the level of individual contact. On the other hand the radical leftist student organization, *Zengakuren*, represents the way of pure darkness. Most of its followers may be sentimental boys who are led by their emotions, but its young ringleaders have the same fanatical, elite mentality as the young army officers of the 1930s. They are just as sure as the officers were then that the farmers and the other "little people" who vote for the Conservatives do not know what they are doing and need "guidance." (Fortunately, the farmers have been thriving since the war and regard the radical students as rather foolish.) Though one extreme masks itself in communism, "Trotskyism," or plain anarchism, and the other mumbles in an archaic accent about the Emperor and the noble race, both point back to a closed Japanese past and both imply a reversal of the trend toward openness of the last fifteen years.

The Japanese are still buying time for their Western-modeled institutions to develop a Japanese meaning and become a binding faith. For this result economic prosperity alone is not enough, but without prosperity there is no hope. War or depression would very likely wipe out most if not all of the advances that have been made toward a more liberal parliamentarianism and replace them with some variety of rightist ultranationalism or with communism. The Cold War climate is unkind to any constructive growth. But given time and favorable economic conditions, Japanese politics may develop more tolerance, and fringe groups that today can capture attention through fortuitous issues of the Cold War may become less significant. As far as the Japanese people as a whole are concerned, the long drift is toward more freedom and opportunity. Most people want to keep their imported institutions with their imported technology and go on to new advances. They do not want to go back into the darkness of either left or right. Except for the Communists and the fanatical right—both of them now small in number—there is little irreconcilable ideological hostility within the Japanese in their attitudes toward one another. But neither do they want to serve as the bloody arena for anyone else's hostilities.

Conclusions

K. H. SILVERT

This book, true to its theme as well as its authors, was conceived and written with passion as well as discipline. Now that the creative cycle has moved toward its close, discipline and passion must combine anew to provide the impulse for a fresh set of intuitions, hypotheses, and investigations. In order to demonstrate that this cycle is not a circle—that we have made some advance from the point of departure—the concluding analysis must frankly assess the real usefulness of the theory against the data the selection of which it governed and the analysis of which it conditioned. This conclusion must also attempt to demonstrate the conceptual efficiency and the predictive value of the research. And lastly, if truly fruitful, the study should suggest further inquiries. These three sets of ethical and logical requirements are the subjects of this epilogue.

The Theory and the Cases

The twelve countries here considered were not pre-selected in order to fit the idea of nationalism proposed in this book. The dozen examples have been employed because American Universities Field Staff associates happen to be specialists in those countries, as well as in neighboring ones in the respective regions. There is, then, no deliberately built-in bias resulting from having constructed a theory to fit the cases. We do not have, of course, a random sample of underdeveloped lands. But beyond the fact of their "underdevelopedness," there was no pre-established relation between the eclectic choices of these particular cases and the nature of the theory we set out to test.

The questions we put to our areas led to varying success in finding answers. Naturally, the less national a country, the fewer social circumstances could this or any other theory of nationalism explain. As simple as this statement may sound, it is the primary test of the validity of the relationship between cases and theory. Consider what would have come of the suppositions behind this study if our basic notion of the key position of the socially decisive, impersonal, secular political marketplace were found to organize the entire gamut of political systems from Afghanistan to Bolivia. Our theory would have been encompassing the universe, when it was designed instead to distinguish only one kind of political development. On the other hand, the fact that the cases did indeed roughly order themselves according to level of national integration in correlation with the general degree of industrial, ideological, and social development offers us at least partial confirmation of the thesis that the developmental process is a total social occurrence intimately involved with the emergence of the nation-state.

It will be remembered that in the introduction we presumed differing relationships between ideologies and social values as the process of national integration proceeded. In the cases of Afghanistan, Bolivia, and Saudi Arabia, we found what we expected—that the formal ideologies of nationalism impregnated at most only very small elite groups, with some spread into cosmopolitan elements. Bolivia, however, suggests an important amendment to the theoretical predictions in providing evidence that a change welling up from an agrarian populace can propel the general growth of national identification and prod the national elite into action. The existence of a relatively thin layer of attitudinally national persons in the less developed lands was most sharply pointed up by the leadership and ideological crises described in the Philippines and Indonesia, both cases confirming the initial supposition that the ideologies of nationalism can be most disturbingly shrill in the absence of genuinely cohesive national values. As we moved through these five countries into an examination of more sophisticated and intricately interdependent social situations, the tool of national analysis clearly permitted us to examine ever larger groups of persons and to deal more meaningfully with broader and more complex problems. And when we finally treated Argentina, Israel, and Japan, we found that their problems in the achievement of full national integration suggest close parallels with either the immediate past or the difficult present of some of the nations we consider as unequivocally Western, such as France and Italy.

We also conclude that this approach was useful in lacing the country studies together as well as in organizing the data within each country. Comparison, of course, involves the construction of a theoretically composed independent measure against which the chosen examples may be placed. Our use of an ideal-type definition of national integration permitted us to order the cases comparatively by determining which were "more national" and "less national," and to examine in a broad fashion the relationship between the quality and extent of national values in given social groups and the general level of development of the countries studied. But because this approach concerns itself only with the positive existence of a particular social fact in given contexts, we are not prepared by this analysis to say with any categorical certainty what the non-existence of nationalism may signify in any affirmative sense. That is to say, we can label what fits inside the theory, but not what falls outside it. Our cases show clearly enough that the non-existence of national values is related to the absence or the near-absence of significant industrial development, for example, but not what the socially cohesive elements or the type of economic organization may be in such situations. It is in this positive but limited sense, then, that we see the theory as applied to the cases as having been useful in the ordering of materials and in methodical intercultural comparison.

Stages, Process, and the Theory

There is some danger in arraying our examples from least developed and least national to most developed and most national,

for it may be assumed that we are employing an implicitly unilin-
eal developmental notion in contradiction to the specific disclaimers to this effect advanced in the introduction. Despite the
organization of this volume, we continue *not* to agree that "to see
the process of development as a line along which the nations of
the world are spaced, in their various stages of development, is
to see both the process of and the policy for development with
considerably enhanced clarity."[1] To arrange our examples as we
did is not to imply that Argentina, for instance, is simply farther
along the same road as the one Bolivia "must" travel. We have
here concerned ourselves with the development of certain social
relationships; our evidence allows us to say only that the presumed connection between development and the nation holds
throughout all the studies, *but not that there is a fixed progression of stages for developing these relationships.* Indeed, the
country studies specifically support the opposite hypothesis advanced in the introduction—that the growth of the social elements and relationships involved in total development must
follow very different roads from country to country. To repeat
an example, the caste inhibitions to national integration in India
are qualitatively different from the stratification problems of
Argentina, and thus differing accommodations of the elements
involved in the modernization process will take place. The
similarity between the two is their common need for some set of
primary national loyalties, but certainly how that end will be
reached will be very different. Social predictions and resulting
developmental policy must then differ substantially between the
two countries in their pursuit of the same functional goal.

In recapitulation, it will be recalled that our explicit manner
of building the framework for organizing the social relationships
of developmental change was through the establishment of
given levels of generalization. Our first presumption and primary
reason for undertaking this research was that there is something
universal about the state of being developed, some set of relationships which must be found everywhere. The economic aspects
of modern production, industrial urbanization, and complex
occupational and class structures are commonly recognized
earmarks of development everywhere; we have sustained

[1] John Kenneth Galbraith, *Economic Development in Perspective*, Cambridge: 1962, p. 14.

throughout this work that the so far universal political component has been what we have defined as a widespread value of national identification expressed through the governmental institutions of the nation-state. Indeed we are tempted to add that the nation-state and its accompanying values are the primary elements in self-sustaining developmental patterns.

At a second level of generality, we have assumed that the developmental process in emergent lands will be affected by the particular state of the world marketplaces of technology and ideology at any given time. In a very broad but not universal sense, then, we see sweeping general historical facts which influence modernizing nations differently as the developed world itself changes and as intercommunications play among the partially developed. And at the third and most specific level, we have the particular conditions of each society itself. Taken as a whole, the total modernization process of each land will naturally be unique, as will be the patterns of relationships among the various elements which constitute the state of being developed. But certain fundamental elements within the relationships, and the necessity for accommodation to them by all other factors, will be universal. The array of possible relationships will also be finite and subject to the usual laws of probability.

To talk of developmental stages without this perspective is to imply similarity without indicating the limits of variability or the manner of adjustment of dissimilarities. On the other hand, to assume some common elements in a process of adjustment within unique sets of relationships is to posit a functional convergence toward a certain general social "condition," arrived at by following many different paths. This view also permits recognition that there will be not a single equal society at the end of the process, but a family of societies sharing certain common values, institutions, and procedures within the bounds of cultural diversity. This minimum complexity would seem to be necessary to adjust the unique to the universal for the purpose of imposing some conceptual order upon the development process without stripping the individual cases of their stubbornly special natures. The obvious and profound differences among the existing nation-states of the world are thus also accommodated by our theoretical views.

To sustain as we have that the modernization process is both multifaceted and not narrowly determined is not to answer another possible objection to this kind of study, which may still be faulted for presuming some Grand Design, even if it be a complicated one. Once again, we have attempted to escape this charge and this responsibility by stating that we have been working at the level of intermediate theory. We have not been seeking ultimate causation, but we have been trying to go beyond a string-of-beads examination of individual and unrelated cases. We are under no logical necessity to state that societies *must* undergo modernization in fulfilment of some kind of social teleology; it is sufficient for us to observe that such a tendency seems to be under way in one or another fashion in all the areas studied, and to attempt to find verification of the existence and functions of the elements we presume to be common within their unique relationships.

Some Further Questions

We do not have to delve into the root, metaphysical dynamics of the human condition to find fascinating areas of possible causation whose further exploration is most tempting. Much has already been said of "the explosion of Western civilization" and "the revolution of rising expectations"; many anthropologists have worked on the patterns of culture spread; the "demonstration effect" has become a popular phrase; and thousands of assistance programs are testimonials to the conviction that modernization can be imposed, directed, and taught. The more classical literature of the past several centuries also took into account the influence of European enterprise on the "colored" world as expressed through missionaries, explorers, slavers, military men, colonialists, and business entrepreneurs, a thread of morality weaving through the materials in the debate over the white man's burden. It would be gratuitous of us to venture many suggestions in a field already being well worked by the scholarly community.

Still, there is one nagging question concerning the reaction to Western stimuli which recurs throughout our country studies—the very fact of the overwhelming attractiveness of nationalism to developing persons in emergent countries. Just why are aspirations toward Western development so powerful as to promise in the long run ineluctably to override traditional patterns of life, no matter what or how tenacious they may be? A simple answer often advanced is that the desire for more worldly goods is enough to move mountains and cultures out of the way. But the "feel" of the country studies here presented suggests a much greater richness of motivation. The complex national mystiques, the dedicated leaders and sacrificing followers as well as the cynical leaders and blind followers, the innumerable detours and dead ends into which emergent lands steer themselves in their processes of change all indicate the Byzantine complication of the desires and anticipated returns and rationales of the developing peoples. Any simplistic "bellyist" notion of human motivation is not really demonstrable, and worse, it tends to scrub away the full human messiness of the behavior which, taken whole, may indeed lead us to some objectively governed insights.

There appears to be something in modern life of such powerful appeal to certain broad and profoundly human desires as eventually to be able to level all opposition. Of course, it would be flying in the face of all avowed ideologies of the past and present leaders of development to deny that a major part of the motivation is most emphatically economic. We can suggest a broadening of the concept of "wealth," however, into a more inclusive frame. Study after study of the newly arrived slum-dwellers in the world's exploding cities[2] give us information concerning the feeling of greater well-being enjoyed by most migrants from the poverty of the farm to the slums of the city. These depressed new urbanites become consumers of city streets, plazas, show windows, the parked cars of others, and the company of their closely packed fellows. Liberated from the shackles of stifling family ties and the boredom of empty space, at least for a while they feel themselves richer and freer and altogether more human. Maybe it is that some people of the underdeveloped world have been given or have partaken of sufficient conceptual matter of the West to be able to look out at the modern world as village folk

[2] See, for example, many of the supporting studies in Philip M. Hauser, ed., *Urbanization in Latin America*, New York: 1961, a UNESCO publication.

look to the modernizing cities of their own countries, seeing variety, a wealth of new symbols, excitement, broader human interaction, greater choice for themselves and their children. Certainly these projections are occurring. We do not know whether it is "inevitable" in "human nature" to yearn toward the possibility of greater individual unfolding based on a wider spectrum of social communication and participation, but surely it seems that the choices being made today are all in that direction. It is the imposing strength of that yearning we need to explain.

The suburban mother of intellectual pretensions deplores the television tube as the impoverishing traducer of her children. The professional worrier about "mass culture," too, often loses himself in a rural romanticism which leads him to the conclusion that "his" natives would be better off staying with their animism, say, than becoming involved with the crassness of modern values. But the "natives," once budged and introduced to the television tube, find it just as irresistible to attempt some adjustment to the artifacts of modernism as do modern men. What we venture to ask is whether there is really any long-range choice at all in the bare fact of the acceptance of closer ties with the rest of humanity and the resultant potentially richer individualism which modern life promises. Of course, we all know too the risks of this century: total war, total authoritarianism, cultural enslavement, and such other niceties of our new technological might. At least a partial answer to the question of whether the possible benefits of full development are of such fundamental appeal that these risks will be run willy-nilly may be found by exploring the quality and intensity of the expectations and aspirations of the emergent world. Is the search in the emergent lands—or anywhere—merely for material riches, or is it also for human richness? The evidence we have advanced clearly indicates that part at least of the consciously expressed motivation for change in the developing world is tied to the latter. The universality of the relationship taken for granted among development, the nation, freedom, and human dignity cannot be lightly dismissed as a mere cynical manipulation of value symbols, ingenuousness, or error. Western theorists of development also postulated such a constellation of relations with their explications of natural law, the secular marketplace, the pleasure-pain calculus, social Darwinism, and the inevitability of Progress.

A great river of Western intellectual history is thus being joined by many freshets, all sustaining that nations and freedom and economic and emotional satisfactions grow together. Is there anything in the materials we have gathered to indicate that there might indeed be a functional link between freedom and development? In the introduction we specifically stated the relationship in limited form, holding nationalism to be a necessary but insufficient condition for democracy. If we consider the question of freedom of choice, however, instead of the more formal and strictly defined matter of democracy, we may approach the means of finding a mechanism for answering the question. Development may proceed with widely varying degrees of authoritarianism. The *quality* of the process to an important extent, however, may well be a function of the degree of rationality and freedom of choice involved in making those decisions appropriate to the relevant social conditions. Afghanis, for example, must make choices concerning the relationship between a small, tightly knit group at the top and their own tribally divided body social as well as pressing foreign interests. The Japanese, on the other hand, must make decisions concerning mass matters, involving millions of citizens aspiring to full participation and divided one from another in class, not caste or tribal categories. Each society will have to make decisions of a qualitatively different nature in terms of the deciders themselves, the type of consensus, the overt power available, and the social expectations involved in the decisions. Can it be assumed, however, that if the end desired is modernization, then better judgments and more reliable predictions will follow if pragmatic techniques are used within a context of sufficient freedom for the derivation of as rational a set of decisions and reactions as possible?

In other words, the hypothesis we are advancing is that the degree of freedom required to make the most rational decisions needed at the level of development of the country concerned may be a functional requisite for *self-sustaining* development. Authoritarian techniques of development have their capabilities, of course; they can be used to build pyramids and factories, force savings and mobilize labor. We suggest, however, that it may

be that when the course of the change nears contemporary
modernism, then gratuitously unfree procedures cause break-
downs, being conducive to neither rational public decisions nor to
the generation of the attitudes and values necessary for the chain
reactions of the modern, empirical society. This line of reasoning
linking freedom with efficiency and continuity is not a novel
concept among philosophers of science.

> The existing practice of scientific life embodies the claim
> that freedom is an efficient form of organization. . . . The
> co-ordinative principle of science . . . consists in the adjust-
> ment of each scientist's activities to the results hitherto
> achieved by others. In adjusting himself to the others each
> scientist acts independently, yet by virtue of these several
> adjustments scientists keep extending together with a
> maximum efficiency the achievements of science as a
> whole. . . .[3]

The scientific community, of course, is not society. But at
least in certain respects the semi-empirical and semi-pragmatic
practices that define modernism follow these precepts. The
citizen of the nation-state is expected to adjust his public actions
to those of his fellows in a system of broad mutual interdependence. It is neither illogical nor romantic to presume that
the more voluntary the association, the greater the degree of
anticipatory and reactive individual self-adjustment one should
expect, and thus the better able the society will be to integrate
change. Liberty to be rational and to inform oneself and to have
social confidence, equality before the laws, and the fraternity of
the enlarged national community remain primary guides to the
social and political requisites of development.

Viewed in this light, the crises of development apparent in
the more nearly national of our case studies are also crises of
freedom. The Israeli Establishment is grappling with desires for
greater participation on the part of ethnically very disparate
groups; the Argentines are being torn between the values of
freedom and of authoritarianism within an already highly industrialized and urbanized setting; and the Japanese are at-

[3] Michael Polanyi, *The Logic of Liberty: Reflections and Rejoinder*,
Chicago: 1951, pp. 34-5.

tempting the adjustment of a conservative leadership to the aspirations attendant on the rapid emergence of a mass society. Decisions for that freedom which will allow ever greater rationality and self-adjustment may also well be the most efficient developmental choices which can be made.

The expectant peoples of the underdeveloped lands are reaching out for what they see as the rewards of the already developed world. The political mechanism they have chosen is nationalism. They can fall into the irrationalities of xenophobia, the cruelties of wanton personalistic rule, or the attractions of mechanistic "managerial" totalitarianisms. Or they can treat the social nation as the larger community within which the individual can confidently enrich himself and others, a larger world which can feed vitality both to the smaller community and the growing life of global interdependence. The developed peoples should distill their own experience of the nation-state so that the useful aspects may be taught to the emergent peoples. We will be rewarded with a new richness of human diversity and the cultural converse of brothers. Let us not forget that new nations, unlike baby tigers, need not repeat the history of their kind as they grow.

Appendix

A set of definitions, propositions, and hypotheses on nationalism was prepared to serve as a common theoretical starting place both for this book and for an empirical study of social development in four Latin American countries undertaken by K. H. Silvert and Frank Bonilla. The following statement was employed to indicate the total dimensions of the subject as we have defined it, thus permitting each individual contributor to know better how his particular area of theoretical emphasis meshed into the entire study. This outline also served the more obvious purpose of ensuring that terminology would be understood and employed similarly by all the authors.

Definitions, Propositions, and Hypotheses Concerning Modernism, Class, and National Integration

Definitions

A national society is one in which the state is the social institution in which ultimate individual and group loyalty is invested.

Nationality as a formal concept refers to the legal relationships (a) between a citizen and the state (citizenship, passports, legally imposed ethnic and religious discrimination, etc.); and (b) among states internationally (juridical questions of sovereignty, irredentist claims, etc.).

Nationality as a symbolic concept is that stock of patriotic symbols surrounding matters of cultural generality; e.g., language, dress, food habits, physical surroundings, the flag, the anthem, and so on.

Nationalism as a social value is that norm defining loyalty as being due (a) to fellow citizens; and (b) to the state, the latter holding the institutional position of being the mediating and enforcing agency in the event of the "disloyalty" of individuals or groups.

Nationalistic ideologies are those explicit bodies of political thought concerning the manner in which loyalty should be organized, toward what ends, and with what means.

Class, Modernism, and Change

Propositions

1. All societies with more than a minimum degree of articulation of function have a class structure.
2. Classes are defined in terms of the clustering of powers in groups whose manipulative ability, life chances, life style, and potential are substantially different.
3. All class structures imply a division of community of interest and hence conflict of one or another sort.
4. All societies having class structures also have integrating values to contain the play of class and other group interests.
5. A degree of social complexity including widespread ownership, a market economy, manufactures, and so forth implies sufficient complication of interest and spread of power to involve the forcing apart of traditional, bi-class feudal structures and the interpolation of a "middle class."
6. The integrating value of a multi-class industrial society is nationalism.

Hypothesis A. The consensus of nationalistic loyalty ensures systematic continuity within the more highly complex and organized society by submitting the class to the national interest. This submission includes elite groups, the best known form of such inclusiveness being expressed in the universality of the rule of law.

Hypothesis B. In the early phases of European industrialization, occupational specialization and the degree of economic productivity accompanying the transformation to national organization resulted in the nationalized citizens being restricted almost wholly to middle and upper classes. A higher level of technology and consequently a higher order of specialization and productivity imply "massification," and hence the immediate possibilities for including all social classes within the nation. (This hypothesis is necessary in order to explain historical differences in the development of nationalism as between, say, Great Britain and the former Belgian Congo.)

Hypothesis C. The epoch, then, in which the transformation to national integration occurs is of crucial importance, for the influence of contemporary ideologies of mass politics on mimetic and importing groups within the countries in transition tends to cause them to accept ideologies of nationalism embracing all classes without regard to the level of economic development past the minimum point necessary to maintain the mimetic groups in the first place. Nationalistic ideologies in such settings will anticipate the fact of national integration as such in word and often in attempted action.

Hypothesis D. In complex, developed, and mature societies (a) the nature of class tends to change as mobility becomes routinized; and (b) class boundaries tend to blur as the nature of economic power changes to include greater emphasis upon the consuming function.

Hypothesis E. In complex, developed, and mature societies the push toward high orders of complexity and international interdependence contributes to changing loyalty identifications. In consequence the symbols of nationality and ideologies must also change.

Proposition derived from Hypotheses B, C, and D above.

7. Nationalism in contemporary underdeveloped areas develops in manners organically different from the classical British and American patterns.

Hypothesis F. The symbols of nationality and the ideologies of nationalism are transmitted to the transitional societies concerned through cosmopolitan groups before the social, political, and economic structures are sufficiently articulated to give immediate functional meaning to these symbols and ideologies. (The process of transculturation may also occur through the presence of foreign companies, colonialism, religious proselytizing and so forth.)

Hypothesis G. The rate of change in contemporary underdeveloped areas is vastly accelerated over the industrialization of eighteenth and nineteenth century Western nations. Traditional and "modern" customs and usages thus overlap strongly in the present situation, and clash is amplified.

Hypothesis H. The inherent complexity of the new economic techniques, and the global nature of modern ideology lead to the necessity for mass recruitment into the new social, political, and occupational groups.

Hypothesis I. The introduction of mass media of communications—which reduces the importance of simple literacy to the integration process—propels the "revolution of expectations" and makes possible the accelerated recruitment to the national sphere.

Hypothesis J. The rapidity of change precipitates crises of leadership—the old leaders are recalcitrant and the new ones often inept and unprepared.

Hypothesis K. In the early phases of transition we should find:
   1. Nationality slogans and ideologies confined to the upper class and rudimentary middle classes, but with little real feeling of loyalty identification, for there is as yet nothing to which to be loyal.
   2. Revolutionary politics or a crudely tutelary government.

3. Charisma of great importance in the legitimation of leadership.

4. Very broad ideological alliances—all those in the innovating camp opposed to all those aligned against it.

5. Significant masses of persons untouched by the process.

6. Strong desires for upward mobility among the members of the small middle groups.

7. Great dependency upon foreign example.

8. Strongly anti-imperialist ideologies.

Hypothesis L. In the intermediate stages of transition we should find:

1. Loyalty values of strength primarily in the middle group as well as in certain sectors of the upper (especially the "new" upper), and in the upper part of the lower group.

2. Nationalistic slogans and symbols very widely spread through schools and other media of communications.

3. Strong ideological divisions following usual right, left, and center divisions.

4. Parties caught between interest and ideological status.

5. Strong urges throughout middle and lower groups for increased levels and varieties of consumption.

6. Populist parties of importance.

7. The trade union movement in its beginning, social security an issue.

8. Strong moves towards egalitarianism of all sorts.

9. Strong rivalry among institutions: church-state, family-state, economy-state. The particular circumstances will dictate what set of such clashes may be occurring and in what terms.

10. Strong mobility urges in upper part of lower group; middle group beginning to resist.

11. Classes very strongly differentiated by external manifestations as well as in social function.

12. The patterns of economic power quite complex.

13. Federal-unitary clashes.

14. A sense of dedication among many persons involved in politics, and the predominance of youth, with charisma declining in importance.

15. Less dependence on foreign example, continued strong anti-imperialist sentiment.

Hypothesis M. In the last stages of transition we should find:

1. Classes fully differentiated along lines of economic, social, and political power.

2. Mobility paths clearly defined and institutionalized.

3. Loyalty values well-nigh universal and very functional.

4. A continued difference in the strength of reactions to national symbols, strongest in lower middle and upper lower groups in direct correlation with mobility urges.

5. Mobility pressure strongest in lower middle and upper lower groups, as above.

6. Ideological division stylized and simplified.

7. Traditional values submerged, some surviving pathetically as the raw material for national symbols.

8. The state unequivocally triumphant over other institutions in relative strength in the resolution of disputes.

9. The economy very highly articulated along ownership and control lines.

10. Secularism, pragmatism, and rationalism widespread in routine manners.

11. Government centralized in power, centralized or decentralized in function.

12. Decreased dependence on foreign ideas and technicians, reduced heat of anti-imperialism, greater economic dependence on foreign nations.

13. Parties professionalized, importance of charisma contained, interest group structure ramified.

14. Ideological differences blurred internally, ideological differences with other nations accentuated.

NATIONALISM AND THE POLITY

Propositions

1. The willingness to adopt and function within nationalistic loyalty values defines the political actors in a national state.

2. The organizational fact which flows from this adoption of a

shared value implies the creation of a special kind of political power. This change produces a special order of *consent* and *consensus*. The greater magnitude of social power flowing from this relationship (a) enlarges the potentialities of the state and (b) at the same time broadens the capacity of the governed at least potentially to set outside limits to governmental action. This statement may be put in another fashion: government gains power because the rate of anticipated obedience is much higher in nationally integrated societies than in other historical predecessor states. Thus governmental authority rests in greater measure than in other antecedent systems upon legitimacy and responsiveness to broader social groups.

Hypothesis N. One may expect to see the following generalized desires vis-à-vis governments in national systems, whether democratic or authoritarian in nature:

1. Widespread desires for participation in the governmental policy-making function.

2. Widespread desires for access to the fruits of governmental policy; e.g., governmental services, public education, even influence peddling.

3. Widespread desires for an even impact of the costs of government; e.g., taxation, military service, etc.

4. Widespread desires for the equal application of the law, impersonality, state action as a neutral mediator of conflicting interests in the name of the nationality.

5. Widespread desires for access to channels of political communication.

Hypothesis O. To the extent to which national government is effectively supported by national organization, there should be a high level of acceptance of law; to the extent to which this support is viable, the government should be faced with a relatively low order of necessity for overt force, unless directed against castes and expelled elements.

Hypothesis P. When national integration is incomplete because of (for example) war, strong institutional inhibitions, the influence of traditional cultural elements, depression, or the like, the existing national identification can be employed for the very purpose of deepening division. *Incomplete transition toward*

*national integration may as well serve irrationality and vicious-
ness as rationality and humaneness.*

NATIONALISM AND THE ECONOMY

Propositions

1. National loyalties are necessary to any economy sufficiently differentiated and specialized so that confidence and prediction become indispensable. Although industrial societies obviously carry this requirement to a high intensity and even into the international scene, the necessity also exists wherever ownership is widespread and a free market economy exists (such as the smallholder economy of Costa Rica).

2. The minimum legal role of government concerns the guarantee of contracts, in which control of the future and confidence are buttressed by legal enforcement.

3. The maximum role of government may be that of entrepreneur, as in Soviet Russia. *The basic function holds*: to guarantee into the future the risks of specialization and interdependence.

Hypothesis Q. Some of the relevant earmarks of economic activity within a national context at the level of production are:

1. Acceptance of a higher degree of specialization by labor and entrepreneur.

2. Acceptance of the necessity for longer periods of schooling.

3. A "free" labor market—free in the sense that it is removed from the family context, paid in money, with impersonal standards of selection, and that it involves an element of choice in mobility, education, specialization, capital investment, etc.

Hypothesis R. Some of the relevant earmarks of economic activity within a national context at the level of consumption are:

1. A drive for higher levels of consumption.

2. A drive for more egalitarian distribution.

3. A drive for more varied styles of consumption.

4. A drive for right to work and a living wage, with the state guaranteeing minimum levels.

(*Note*: For the following divisions, no propositions or hypotheses will be advanced, for the foregoing cover the field. Below are offered merely detailed research areas for each subject, as reminders.)

NATIONALISM AND THE FAMILY

Relevant Areas:
1. The general economic shift and its effect on life styles.
2. The work of women in paid occupations outside the home.
3. The shift to impersonalism as it serves to attack the integrity of the family and restricts its extension.
4. Mobility-education equation as it breaks down family tradition.

NATIONALISM AND EDUCATION

1. Equal access to educational opportunities.
2. The school as creator, transmitter, and preserver of national values.
3. The school as creator, transmitter, and preserver of class values.
4. The school as supplier of trained persons for the economy.
5. The school as a socializing surrogate for the family.
6. The school as integrating agency for migrants both from without the country and from farm to city.
7. The school as creator and transmitter of consumption standards.
8. The school in its civic function—training for citizenship in a narrow sense, and so forth.

NATIONALISM AND RELATIONS AMONG STATES

1. Sovereignty.
2. Self-determination of peoples.
3. Boundaries.
4. The functions of the military.
5. Xenophobia.
6. The search for approval.
7. The twisting of domestic institutions when they face outward: the church and warfare, overseas business investments, etc.

JUSTIFICATION: THE UTILITY OF NATIONALISM IN DOMESTIC STUDIES

1. Nationalism describes tension areas involved in change:
    a. Caste vs. national integration.
    b. Class vs. national integration.
    c. Institutions vs. national integration and accommodation.
    d. National value identification vs. universalism.
    e. National value identification vs. localism and regionalism.

2. Nationalism, viewed as a value equatable with class, is thus at the same level of generalization as class, both having to do with primary categorical distinctions in the analysis of societies.

3. The concept can be studied through all standard research methods, for it may be examined at the level of individual psychology as well as that of institutional analysis: it relates individuals to each other, individuals to groups, individuals to class, and individuals to nation.

4. Nationalism is a necessary but insufficient condition for a wide array of other phenomena. It is an organizing concept of a high and complex order of generality.

JUSTIFICATION: THE UTILITY OF NATIONALISM FOR COMPARATIVE SOCIAL RESEARCH

1. Because national integration will not be found in village cultures, feudal or "traditional" organization, or at a tribal level, it is useful only negatively in differentiating these societies.

2. Nationalism in its fullest sense (as defined above) is most useful as an indicator of necessarily concomitant social factors in those societies in process of transition into national integration and organization.

3. Once national integration has been achieved and class lines change their nature because of the partially equalizing effects of social integration, the nature of nationalism also undergoes a partial shift with a weakening of ideological and symbolic factors.

PARADIGM

Purpose

1. To keep clear the various dimensions of nationalistic phenomena defined as relevant within the theoretical framework.

2. To keep clear the methodological distinctions required among the various kinds of data on the basis of which judgments will be made about the presence, absence, or intensity of these phenomena.

3. To allow us a fairly exhaustive cataloguing of the substantive and topical areas it seems necessary to cover in order to trace the many relationships posited in the theoretical framework.

Design: The three theoretically derived categories (Nationality, National Identification, and Nationalistic Ideology) are further specified along three dimensions: first, the *cognitive elements* or statements of reality and descriptions of the social environment; second, the *evaluative elements* or statements about what *should* be and the scale of preferences; and third, the *affective elements* or statements indicative of quality and intensity of emotion.

Content

The nine-cell matrix of the paradigm may be tentatively filled as follows:

NATIONALITY:

Cognitive: Descriptions of the chief external marks of national identification, with special emphasis on the symbolic affirmations of national unity and individual solidarity with the nation. Some ideas of class differences in the perception of national symbols should emerge, as well as notions of differential access to them.
Evaluative: Judgments or choices regarding which symbols or marks of national identification should be honored.
Affective: Indications of the intensity of feeling aroused by or associated with such national symbols.

(*Note*: According to the theory, responsiveness to this kind of national symbol does not by itself constitute a basis for national integration. A quite elaborate symbolic apparatus of nationality that is widely recognized and has considerable emotional potency can exist without producing nationalism as an institutionalized and integrating social value.)

NATIONAL IDENTIFICATION:

Cognitive: Essential fact sheet data to locate the individual in his various institutional roles as well as his view of what each of these worlds (economic, political, religious particularly) is like, especially in terms of the power structure within each world and the individual's own place in this power hierarchy.

Evaluative: The focus here is on the presence or absence in each institutional sphere of the various values we assume to be associated with the presence of nationalism. It is hoped we can be direct and selective. (The sets of values are listed in the theoretical statement.)

Affective: The degree of attachment to this loyalty; the degree of sacrifice the individual is willing to make in accordance with it; the strength of feeling concerning anticipated rewards.

(*Note*: The fundamental aim is to classify respondents on the degree to which they hold loyalty to the nation above personal and group interests, and to find out enough about how this value is accommodated within the framework of demands from other institutional loyalties so that inferences may be drawn about the effects of nationalism on behavior in the economic, political, religious, and family spheres.)

NATIONALISTIC IDEOLOGY:

Cognitive: Beliefs about the main obstacles to the realization of national objectives, about causes of lack of internal unity, about who are the enemies of national development. Ideology is by definition heavily evaluative and affective, but because it is also *express* belief, the cognitive cell can be well filled with objective understandings of the varying alternatives offered by the ideologies in currency.

Evaluative: The basis for the defense of nationalistic values against those seen as challengers and underminers of the nation. Choice of possible solutions open to the nation.

Affective: Emotional commitment or involvement in the systematic defense of nation, however defined, and ideology.

An Introductory Bibliography

The following sources are suggested for beginners in each of the countries and areas covered. We have not necessarily listed what we consider the "best" general books available, but rather those which can most effectively lead the reader into some greater richness of comprehension of the geographical and conceptual areas we have been discussing in this book. Articles were included only when the individual contributor to this bibliography considered citation of them necessary to fill a gap left by the book materials. Wherever possible, we have also restricted ourselves to sources in English. It is plain that there cannot be many works published on nationalism as we have defined it in the cultures we have considered; the books listed here may assist the reader to some greater independent vigor in his questioning of the application of our ideas to our areas.

For the next bibliographical step which the curious may wish to take, see *A Select Bibliography: Asia, Africa, Eastern Europe, Latin America*, New York: American Universities Field Staff, 1960, as well as the Supplement 1961.

AFGHANISTAN

Sir Olaf Caroe, *The Pathans: 550 B.C.–A.D. 1957*, New York: St. Martin's Press, 1958.

Primarily history, including much legend accepted as fact, this book also has good ethnographic material scattered throughout, concerning principally the Pathans on the Pakistan side of the Durand Line. The political nonalignment of tribes is emphasized.

Louis Dupree, "Religion, Technology and Islam," in L. P. Vidyarthi, ed., *Aspects of Religion in Indian Society*, Meerut: Kedar Nath Ram Nath, 1961.

Sir W. Kerr Fraser-Tytler, *Afghanistan: A Study of Political Developments in Central Asia*, 2nd ed., London: Oxford University Press, 1953.
Written by a British diplomat with many years of experience in India and Afghanistan, this work ably presents the British point of view while demonstrating a sympathy for the Afghan position. Although some interesting ethnic material is included, the emphasis remains upon the events of the nineteenth and twentieth centuries.

Dilip Kumar Ghosh, *England and Afghanistan: A Phase in Their Relations*, Calcutta: The World Press Private, Ltd., 1960.
An excellent analysis of British activities in Afghanistan in the nineteenth century is presented here by an Indian historian who had access to Lord Lytton's papers.

Laurence Lockhart, *The Fall of the Safavi Dynasty and the Afghan Occupation of Persia*, New York: Cambridge University Press, 1958.
This is a first-rate study of the Irano-Afghan area in the eighteenth century.

Sayyid Qasim Rishtiya, *Afghanistan Qorun-nazdeh (Afghanistan in the 19th Century)*, Kabul: The Government Press, 1957.
In Persian, but soon to be out in an English edition, this study of Afghan relations with European countries is from the Afghan viewpoint of an Afghan scholar.

Sovremennyy Afghanistan, Moscow: Publishing House of Eastern Literature, 1960.
Written in Russian, this critical analysis of modern Afghan social, economic, and political institutions has been commented on in detail in English in *Central Asian Review*, Vol. 9, No. 2,

1961, pp. 206-219, a journal published by the Central Asian Research Centre. Each chapter in the book is written by a recognized Soviet expert.

Sir Percy M. Sykes, *A History of Afghanistan*, 2 vols., London: Macmillan, 1940.
The author's British bias often shows through in this general survey of Afghan history from early times to 1935.

Donald N. Wilber, ed., *Afghanistan*, New Haven: Human Relations Area Files, 1956; Second Edition, 1962.
This book is the best readily available source in English.

T. Cuyler Young, ed., *Current Problems in Afghanistan*, Princeton: The Princeton University Conference, 1961.
The volume contains a series of articles by various experts on such problems as education, development, and "Pushtunistan."

ARGENTINA

George I. Blanksten, *Perón's Argentina*, Chicago: University of Chicago Press, 1953.
There is no better treatment of the profound social and political reasons for the emergence of Peronism than this most useful book which, incidentally, almost precisely predicted the patterns of the Peronist defeat of 1955. The work remains helpful in explaining contemporary Argentina.

Miron Burgin, *The Economic Aspects of Argentine Federalism, 1820-1852*, Cambridge: Harvard University Press, 1946.
This classical treatment is mentioned here to reveal the striking profundity of Argentina's growth after 1870, as well as to provide the economic framework for understanding certain behavior patterns which still persist in modified form in the more traditional of Argentina's provinces.

John J. Johnson, *Political Change in Latin America: The Emergence of the Middle Sectors*, Stanford: Stanford University Press, 1958.
This book is widely recognized as one of the most important of the recent synthetic statements on Latin American political

change. Argentina is a particularly appropriate example of the influence of the emergence of middle-class politics on national development.

John J. Kennedy, *Catholicism, Nationalism, and Democracy in Argentina*, Notre Dame: The University of Notre Dame Press, 1958.

This serious and scholarly work may seek too diligently to excuse Church support of Peronism, but the author's arguments are well-organized and he brings to light valuable information of utility to a general understanding of Argentina.

Ricardo Levene, *A History of Argentina*, tr. and ed. by William S. Robertson, Chapel Hill: University of North Carolina Press, 1937.

Levene, one of Argentina's most prolific recent historians, presents a standard political history which stops immediately after the beginning of the emergence of modern Argentina. The background offered is invaluable and otherwise not easily available in English.

Carl C. Taylor, *Rural Life in Argentina*, Baton Rouge: Louisiana State University Press, 1948.

No bibliography concerning the land of wheat and meat would be complete without some work on the soil. Although Taylor's book is only by inference significant for a study of nationalism, its inclusion here is justified by the author's good analyses of the life of those persons in rural areas of Argentina who are increasingly agitating on the national scene.

Arthur P. Whitaker, *The United States and Argentina*, Cambridge: Harvard University Press, 1954.

Whitaker's work, a neat, clean and altogether admirable little volume with much historical material on the emergence of national Argentina, should be read by those who would satisfy themselves with but one book.

THE ARAB WORLD

J. M. Ahmed, *The Intellectual Origins of Egyptian Nationalism*, London: Oxford University Press, 1960.

Beginning at the turn of the century, Mr. Ahmed traces the growth of the Egyptian nationalist movement to the point in recent decades where it began to merge with the Pan-Arab movement.

George Antonius, *The Arab Awakening*, London: Hamish
    Hamilton, 1937 (U.S. edition: Philadelphia: Lippincott,
    1939).
This is the classical introduction to the development of Arab nationalism beginning in the nincteenth century and going through World War I. It is unusually valuable for its description of the beginnings of the movement in the nineteenth century, but has the drawback of focusing almost exclusively on the Levant States and, as is perhaps inevitable from the hand of a Christian Arab, of somewhat overemphasizing minority participation in the movement.

Morroe Berger, *The Arab World Today*, Garden City: Double-
    day & Co., 1962.
The modest title conceals a perceptive study divided into three sections, dealing respectively with history, social institutions, and social change. Chapters 7, 8, and 9, which describe social groups, the social basis of political institutions, and national and international ideologies, are particularly useful for understanding the bases of Arab nationalism.

Jacques Berque, *Le Maghreb entre deux guerres*, Paris:
    Editions du Seuil, 1962.
——————, *Les Arabes d'hier à demain*, Paris: Editions du Seuil,
    1960.
The leading French sociologist of Arab studies has sketched an equally incisive but more subjective and subtly Gallic account of the area than Morroe Berger's. In both works, Berque is primarily concerned with the breakup of traditional society and the way in which Western techniques are absorbed, modified, and rejected. *Les Arabes d'hier à demain* treats only the Middle Eastern Arab states and is contemporary, while the other volume is confined to the North African Arab countries and, as its title indicates, concentrates on the period 1918-1939 when North

African society was undergoing something of the transformation the Middle East had experienced a generation earlier.

Sir Hamilton Gibb, *Mohammedanism*, London: Oxford University Press, 1949.

———, *Modern Trends in Islam*, Chicago: University of Chicago Press, 1947.

No one should overlook *Mohammedanism*, the author's basic work, now available as a paperback in the United States (New York: Mentor Press, 1955). But more to the immediate point of the interlocking struggle of ideas between religion and nationalism is *Modern Trends in Islam*, a small volume which is a permanent classic of the greatest importance.

Khalid Muhammad Khalid, *From Here We Start*, tr. by Ismail R. el Faruqi, Washington: American Council of Learned Societies, 1953.

The most telling personal statement from the pen of a modern Arab nationalist comes in this work. The author can be considered in many ways as the intellectual father of the Egyptian revolution of 1952. His controversial call, made in this book in 1950, for a thoroughly reformed society in which Islam is separate from a lay, socialist state has had enormous influence in shaping Nasserian Egypt.

Roger Le Tourneau, *Evolution politique de l'Afrique du Nord musulmane*, Paris: Armand Colin, 1962.

The author presents a detailed, straightforward account of the nationalist movements in Tunisia, Algeria, and Morocco from 1920 to 1961.

Hazem Zaki Nuseibeh, *The Ideas of Arab Nationalism*, Ithaca: Cornell University Press, 1956.

Nuseibeh, who espouses no single nationalist school, presents a synthesis and sympathetic analysis of all the currents in Arab nationalism. He has occupied several ministerial posts in the Jordanian Government and is generally regarded as a moderate. The appendix, a statement on "Approaches to the Study of Nationalism," is the most objective utterance on this subject yet put in print by any important Arab political or literary figure.

Wilfred Cantwell Smith, *Islam in Modern History*, Princeton: Princeton University Press, 1957.

This recent study of high quality is valuable for its survey of the entire Islamic world, and to students of Arab nationalism the chapter, "The Arabs: Islamic Crisis," will provide a very critical but not unfair exposition of modern Arab thought and reactions to current problems.

BOLIVIA

Charles W. Arnade, *The Emergence of the Republic of Bolivia*, Gainesville: University of Florida Press, 1957.
An able study of Bolivia's transformation from colonial rule to independent statehood, helpful in understanding the country's lack of nationalism during the nineteenth century.

Robert J. Alexander, *The Bolivian National Revolution*, New Brunswick: Rutgers, 1958.
An account of developments, including some symptoms of nationalism, in Bolivia since 1952 by an author outspokenly sympathetic to the Nationalist Revolutionary Movement Party and government.

Harold Osborne, *Bolivia: A Land Divided*, London: Royal Institute of International Affairs, 1955.
An excellent short presentation of people and problems forming the background of the 1952 nationalistic revolution. Unfortunately it does not include an account of events after the revolution.

Alberto Ostría Gutiérrez, *The Tragedy of Bolivia: A People Crucified*, tr. by Eithne Golden, New York: Devin-Adair, 1958.
A literary indictment of the Nationalistic Revolutionary Movement by a man whose firsthand experience is the basis for his antagonism.

BRAZIL

Fernando de Azevedo, *Brazilian Culture: An Introduction to the Study of Culture in Brazil*, tr. by William R. Crawford, New York: Macmillan & Co., 1950.
An encyclopedic and cultural compendium, this book traces the

evolution of Brazilian institutions and national character. Though some of the sociological and psychological generalizations drawn are dubious, the work provides a wide-ranging survey of Brazilian life and history. The volume is profusely illustrated and includes extensive bibliographies.

Euclides da Cunha, *Rebellion in the Backlands*, tr. by Samuel Putnam, Chicago: University of Chicago Press, 1944.
A dramatic account of a religious uprising in Brazil's perennially troubled Northeast at the turn of the century, this work is not only a landmark in Brazilian literature, but its first two chapters contain an intensive analysis of ecological and racial factors in Brazilian development. Though seriously challenged by later advances in theory and research, da Cunha's absorbing study is a classic of its kind.

Lloyd A. Free, *Some International Implications of the Political Psychology of Brazilians*, Princeton: Institute for International Social Research, 1961.
Free reports on a 1960 survey of rural, urban, and legislative opinion on a wide range of political issues, many of which touch directly on problems of economic development and nationalist ideology.

Celso Furtado, "Brazil," in Adamantios Pepelasis, Leon Mears, and Irma Adelman, *Economic Development*, New York: Harper & Bros., 1961.
This chapter contains a brief historical and analytical summary of Brazilian economic development by a major participant in Brazilian economic planning who also has contributed importantly to the elaboration of Brazil's ideology for national development.

Ernest Hambloch, *His Majesty the President*, London: Methuen & Co., Ltd., 1935.
This volume is an engaging documentation of the argument that Brazilian political ills flow from the constitutionally imposed tyranny of the executive power over the other arms of government.

Karl Lowenstein, *Brazil Under Vargas*, New York: Macmillan & Co., 1942.

The social and political transformation of Brazil begun during the early years of Getulio Vargas' domination of the country is carefully examined in this study.

Jânio Quadros, "Brazil's New Foreign Policy," *Foreign Affairs*, October 1961, pp. 19-27.
Quadros presents for an American audience a detailed exposition and justification of the independent line in foreign policy initiated in the seven months of 1961 during which he held his presidential office.

INDIA

Maulana Abul Kalam Azad, *India Wins Freedom*, New York: Longmans, Green, 1960.
As ranking leader of the Nationalist Muslim faction opposed to the Muslim League demand for creation of the separate Muslim state of Pakistan, Maulana Azad was unusually well situated to observe the events surrounding partition. The publication of his memoirs was a major political *cause célèbre* in India and Pakistan and has been the focus of other post mortems concerning the last days of the Raj.

Michael Brecher, *Nehru: A Political Biography*, New York: Oxford University Press, 1959.
This is an objective and readable narrative of modern Indian political history. Although the life of Nehru provides the basic framework for this study, Professor Brecher writes with a broad perspective on the evolution of the nationalist movement and handles with special effect the partition of the Indian subcontinent in 1947.

Selig S. Harrison, *India: The Most Dangerous Decades*, Princeton: Princeton University Press, 1960.
In a lucid and comprehensive analysis of the rise of the social and political forces threatening the integrity of Indian nationalism, Mr. Harrison emphasizes the trend to intellectual regionalization along the lines of the ten major linguistic territories of India. He also assesses the effect of divisive factors on economic

development as well as on the structure of parliamentary democracy.

Jawaharlal Nehru, *Toward Freedom*, New York: John Day, 1941.
The autobiography of Nehru not only provides a view of his life and thought up to 1935 but remains the most significant statement of the nationalist rationale to come out of the Freedom Movement.

―――, *The Unity of India*, London: Lindsay Drummond, 1948.
The central contribution of Nehru as the champion of political unity in an historically fragmented society emerges in this collection of his writings from the interval (1937-1940) between his two terms of imprisonment.

Edmond Taylor, *Richer By Asia*, Boston: Houghton Mifflin, 1947.
This penetrating first-person account of the author's wartime encounter with India highlights the psychological dimensions of intergroup conflict in South Asia. Part III ("The City of Dreadful Night") is of special contemporary interest.

Barbara Ward, *India and the West*, New York: W. W. Norton, 1960.
In a lucid statement of economic challenge and opportunity in India, Miss Ward includes a hopeful measure of the challenge and a plea for a greatly stepped-up Western program of economic assistance. The social and political tensions are minimized, and she presents the view that parliamentary institutions can be maintained during the period of transition to sustained economic growth.

Marshall Windmiller and Gene Overstreet, *Communism in India*, Berkeley: University of California Press, 1959.
Windmiller and Overstreet have written a definitive historical analysis of the Indian Communist Party.

Maurice Zinkin, *Development for Free Asia*, Fairlawn, N. J.: Basic Books, 1956.
This study by an experienced British observer generalizes beyond the confines of India but bases its illustrations on the

Indian example. It places the development plans of the Indian Government in a social and political perspective and discusses with insight the inhibitions on planning in a society committed to equality.

Planning Commission, Government of India, *The New India*, New York: Macmillan Company, 1958.
An officially sponsored summary and description of the Indian Second Five-Year Plan, this volume has enduring relevance to the study of successive Indian plans.

INDONESIA

Herbert Feith, *The Wilopo Cabinet, 1952-53: A Turning Point in Post-Revolutionary Indonesia*, Ithaca, N. Y.: Cornell University Modern Indonesian Project, Southeast Asia Program, 1958.
Feith studies the period and the circumstances just preceding the Indonesian government's overt swing to extreme nationalism.

Willard A. Hanna, *Bung Karno's Indonesia*, rev., New York: American Universities Field Staff, 1961.
This series of twenty-five status reports on Indonesia covers the years 1959 and 1960, a period of grim prospects.

Benjamin Higgins, *Indonesia's Economic Stabilization and Development*, New York: Institute of Pacific Relations, 1957.
This analysis of Indonesia's problems of national economic development deals with the period prior to 1957, a year of swiftly compounded difficulties.

George McT. Kahin, *Nationalism and Revolution in Indonesia*, Ithaca, N. Y.: Cornell University Press, 1952.
Written during a period when the promise seemed brightest, Kahin's work is the standard history of Indonesian nationalism.

Soedjatmoko, "The Role of Political Parties in Indonesia," in *Nationalism and Progress in Free Asia*, Phillip W. Thayer, ed., Baltimore: Johns Hopkins Press, 1956.
A leading Indonesian political commentator analyzes distinctive features of national political activity.

President Sukarno, *Toward Freedom and the Dignity of Man,
A Collection of Five Speeches*, Government of Indonesia:
Department of Foreign Affairs, 1961.
President Sukarno's statements present the new nationalist
ideology.

ISRAEL

David Ben-Gurion, *Rebirth and Destiny of Israel*, New York:
Philosophical Library, 1954.
The explanation of purpose and hope made by the country's
first and virtually continuous Prime Minister.

Marver H. Bernstein, *The Politics of Israel*, Princeton: The
Princeton University Press, 1957.
Although no longer up to date, this book admirably covers the
first decade of internal political development.

Richard Crossman, *A Nation Reborn*, London: Hamish Hamilton, 1960.
A statement (actually three lectures) of the British point of
view toward the leaders of Israel during its inception. On the
whole, its position is pro-Israeli, but Crossman deals fairly with
those who opposed the formation of the state.

Ben Halpern, *The Idea of the Jewish State*, Cambridge:
Harvard University Press, 1961.
Halpern presents a useful and readable study of the political
development of Zionism, tracing its early themes through the
first years of the State of Israel.

Arthur Hertzberg, ed., *The Zionist Idea*, Garden City: Doubleday & Co., 1959.
This volume is a compilation of writings by the nineteenth
century intellectual leaders of Zionism whose combined thought
provided the religious and political arguments that motivated the
movement in the 1890s.

Walter Z. Laquer, ed., *The Middle East in Transition*, New
York: Praeger, 1958.
This is one of several general texts attempting to describe the
tensions of the contemporary Middle East within a framework

of either Western defense, socio-economic transition, or political history; as a symposium, the book is particularly useful.

Alfred M. Lilienthal, *What Price Israel?* Chicago: Henry
  Regnery, 1954.
The position opposed to Israel taken by many "assimilationist" Jews and supported organizationally by the American Council for Judaism is presented by Lilienthal in a shrill, journalistic effort.

James Parkes, *A History of Palestine*, New York: Oxford University Press, 1949.
As standard history books go, this one is not only orthodox but has the advantage of approaching modern times with virtually no bias. Dr. Parkes, an Anglican clergyman and a careful historian, is a noted student of Jewish (and particularly anti-Semitic) affairs. Also worth-while is his short *A History of the Jewish People*, London: Weidenfeld and Nicolson, 1962, which places the emergence of Israel within the context of European history and philosophical development.

Alex Rubner, *The Economy of Israel*, New York: Praeger,
  1959.
Written by an Israeli economics editor and observer, this realistic study reveals the special financial and economic mechanics of the developing state; it is of considerable practical value.

The government printer (Jerusalem, Israel) publishes an *Annual Yearbook* and an *Annual Statistical Abstract*, and the Israel Office of Information in New York publishes a useful annual compendium of information known as *Facts About Israel*.

JAPAN

R. P. Dore, *City Life in Japan*, Berkeley: University of California Press, 1958.
Dore, a British sociologist, presents a case study of life in an area of Tokyo; it is by far the best work of its kind.

———, *Land Reform in Japan*, London and New York: Oxford University Press, 1959.
The author draws upon prolonged experience in Japanese vil-

lages to analyze the social and political realities of life in the most complete work on the American-sponsored land reform of the late forties.

Nobutaka Ike, *Japanese Politics, An Introductory Survey*, New York, Alfred Knopf, 1957.
This is the most lucid, readable and discerning work on the subject to appear since World War II.

Donald Keene, *Living Japan*, Garden City: Doubleday, 1959.
Keene, well-known translator and teacher of Japanese literature, writes interestingly on literature, art, religion, politics, economic problems, and other aspects of contemporary Japan.

I. I. Morris, *Nationalism and the Right Wing in Japan; A Study of Post-War Trends*, London and New York: Oxford University Press, 1960.
In a careful study of nationalist sentiment since 1945, Morris presents detailed material on new right wing organizations and their ties with business, politicians, and the military.

Lawrence Olson, *Dimensions of Japan*, New York: American Universities Field Staff, Inc., 1963.
This is a collection of reports, originally published in separate form, on many aspects of political, economic, and social life in Japan since 1955.

Thomas C. Smith, *The Agrarian Origins of Modern Japan*, Stanford: Stanford University Press, 1959.
This work is an original inquiry into the structure and functioning of Japan's peasant society before 1868 and helps to explain more fully the nation's modern industrial success.

SAUDI ARABIA

Charles Montagu Doughty, *Travels in Arabia Deserta*, an abridgement by Edward Garnett, Garden City: Doubleday, 1955.
First published by Cambridge University Press in 1888, this work has been re-edited and reprinted many times. It has justly been described by T. E. Lawrence as a "bible of its kind . . .

the first and indispensable work upon the Arabs of the desert . . . one of the great prose works of our literature."

Roy Lebkicher, George Rentz, and Max Steineke, *The Arabia of Ibn Saud*, New York: Moore, 1952.
This is a well-done introductory survey of the history, geography and culture of Saudi Arabia, including excellent maps and charts.

George A. Lipsky and Others, *Saudi Arabia, Its People, Its Society, Its Culture*, New Haven: Human Relations Area Files, 1959.
This volume is another useful contribution of the HRAF books-by-committee program.

H. St. John Bridger Philby, *Sa'udi Arabia*, New York: Praeger, 1955.
This thoroughgoing historical survey of the House of Saud from its beginnings some two centuries ago up until the death of "the great king" Ibn Saud in 1953 is by the dean of the chroniclers of Arabia.

Richard Harlakenden Sanger, *The Arabian Peninsula*, Ithaca: Cornell University Press, 1954.
A U.S. Foreign Service officer presents here a bland but readable introductory survey.

K. S. Twitchell, with the collaboration of Edward J. Jurji and B. Bayly Winder, *Saudi Arabia, With an Account of the Development of Its Natural Resources*, Princeton: Princeton University Press, 1958.
In this study socio-economic development in Saudi Arabia is discussed by a perceptive American engineer who helped to accelerate the process.

REPUBLIC OF SOUTH AFRICA

Gwendolen M. Carter, *The Politics of Inequality: South Africa Since 1948*, London: Thames and Hudson, 1958.

Cornelius William de Kiewiet, *A History of South Africa, Social and Economic*, Oxford: Clarendon, 1941.

What emerges from much sifting and cogitation is a brilliant study of the new society of the Cape, frontier days, the Boer War, the poor whites and the poor blacks, and the great depression.

———, *The Anatomy of South African Misery*, London and New York: Oxford, 1956.
A critical, compassionate, and concise examination of the racial problem by an American historian respected by all sides in South Africa.

Daniel Wilhelmus Kruger, *The Age of the Generals: A Short Political History of the Union of South Africa*, Johannesburg: Dagbreek Book Store, 1958.

Albert John Luthuli, *Let My People Go*, London: Collins, 1962. Nobel Laureate Luthuli's presidency of the African National Congress has covered a critical period of South African politics. This is his short autobiography with annexes.

Phillip Mayer, *Townsmen or Tribesmen: Urbanization in a Divided Society*, Cape Town: Oxford, 1961.
The rural "red blanket" in contact with and in transition to the urban "school society" of the Xhosa-speaking peoples is the subject of this anthropological study.

Edwin S. Munger, *African Field Reports Annotation: 1952-1961*, Cape Town: C. Struik, 1961.
Both Afrikaner and African nationalism are discussed in this series of many reports.

Michael Roberts and A. E. G. Trollip, *The South African Opposition, 1939-1945*, New York: Longmans, Green, 1947.
Choppily written but unique, this is an account of Nationalist Afrikaner groups during World War II.

Edward Roux, *Time Longer Than Rope*, London: Gollancz, 1948.
A history of the black man's struggle for freedom in South Africa.

F. A. Van Jarrsveld, *The Awakening of Afrikaner Nationalism, 1868-1881*, Cape Town: Oxford, 1961.

Van Jaarsveld describes the earliest consciousness of "nation" before the political drive really became significant.

Eric Anderson Walker, *A History of South Africa*, 2nd ed., New York: Longmans, Green, 1941.
The most comprehensive one-volume history, Walker's work is professionally better than either Theal's eleven-volume or Cory's five-volume histories not included in this bibliography. The 1957 revision is not recommended; the added sections do not sustain the level of earlier scholarship.

SOUTHEAST ASIA

Claude A. Buss, *The Arc of Crisis*, Garden City: Doubleday, 1961.
This is a well-written survey of contemporary Asia. It affords the reader an up-to-date estimate of the political setting in which the forces of nationalism are at work and examines some of the consequences of this process for the future of these often newly independent nations.

Raul S. Manglapus, *Faith in the Filipino; The Ripening Revolution*, Manila: Regal, 1961.
This collection of articles and speeches by one of the ablest of the new generation of Filipino leaders offers vivid glimpses of the ideas that motivate them. The book reveals the determination of this group to make the values of Christianity and democracy that have come from the West applicable to the heritage and the needs of their society today. The aim is to overcome the tendency of the nationalism that fostered independence to become ingrown and to make it instead a vehicle for progress. As a newly elected and unusually articulate Senator, Raul Manglapus now has an opportunity to help translate these thoughts into reality.

Lucian W. Pye, *Politics, Personality and Nation Building; Burma's Search for Identity*, New Haven: Yale University Press, 1962.
This work from the Center for International Studies, Massachusetts Institute of Technology, offers revealing insights into

the motivations that shape national decisions in one of Asia's most troubled new nations where World War II has left a heritage of destruction and disorder. The book also indicates some of the difficult problems involved in harmonizing Western parliamentary forms with Burma's different values and traditions.

G. William Skinner, *Chinese Society in Thailand*, Ithaca, New York: Cornell University Press, 1957.

The overseas Chinese are a critical factor in the equation of nationalism. This study of their role in Thailand affords insights regarding their effect upon the economy and the Thai power structure. It indicates why the financial success of this energetic, competent minority can foster the opportunity for militant nationalist leaders to make appeals readily understood by their fellow citizens. And in the background looms the ever-present question of the relationship of the overseas Chinese to their ancestral homeland which dominated the scene long before the Western colonial powers arrived.

The Authors

E. A. BAYNE, author of the chapter on Israel, is a writer and political observer who for nearly 20 years has been closely associated with economic and social development in Africa, Asia, and Europe. Before joining the American Universities Field Staff he lived and worked in these areas as an official attached to American or international projects. Since becoming an AUFS Associate in 1953, he has reported at first hand on the affairs of Italy, Iran, and Israel; more recently he has visited and written about the Horn of Africa. Early in his career he was a newspaperman and editor, and at one time was a Fellow of the Rockefeller Foundation. Later he served as personal economic adviser to the prime ministers of Iran and Nationalist China, as a consultant to the Department of State, and as a director of the American economic aid program to what were then Europe's overseas colonial territories. He was for a period with the International Bank for Reconstruction and Development as loan officer for the Middle East and Africa.

FRANK BONILLA, who wrote the chapter on Brazil, has for many years concentrated on communications research in Latin America. A graduate of the College of the City of New York, he earned the M.A. in sociology from New York University and the Ph.D. in the same field from Harvard. He has held a John Hay Whitney Opportunity Fellowship and a Doherty Foundation Fellowship for advanced study in Latin America. As Director of Communications Research for International Research Associates, Inc., from 1950 to 1960 Dr. Bonilla planned large-scale opinion and attitude surveys in many Latin American countries as well as India, Singapore-Malaya, and Japan. On leave from INRA, he worked at the M.I.T. Center for International Studies and at the Bureau of Applied Social Research at Columbia University. Before his appointment as an AUFS Associate in 1961, he assisted Dr. K. H. Silvert in directing a study of the relationship of education to social and economic development in Latin America. In 1963 he became Associate Professor of Political Science at the Massachusetts Institute of Technology.

LOUIS DUPREE, who wrote the chapter on Afghanistan, has specialized in the Indo-European language areas of the Middle East and Central Asia, with emphasis on Afghanistan and Iran. He received the M.A. and Ph.D. in anthropology from Harvard University. He has made two field trips to Afghanistan for the American Museum of Natural History, of which he has been elected a Research Associate, and one to Iran for the University of Pennsylvania. A former Associate Professor of Middle Eastern Studies at the Air University, he was, at the time of his appointment to the AUFS in 1959, Associate Professor of Anthropology at Pennsylvania State University. His published works include four monographs and over 50 articles and reviews in the allied fields of anthropology, archaeology, geography, geology, and zoology. Recently he has been based in Afghanistan to observe developments there, with particular attention to Afghanistan's relationships with the United States, the U.S.S.R., and Pakistan.

CHARLES F. GALLAGHER, who contributed the chapter on the Arab world, has been studying Arab society since 1951. Concentrating at first on Morocco, Tunisia, and Algeria, he has recently been concerned also with developments in the Arab countries of the Middle East. Mr. Gallagher's academic studies were interrupted by World War II. During the war he was trained in Japanese, saw service as an officer in the U.S. Navy, and afterward was Cultural Property Adviser to the Supreme Commander for the Allied Powers in Japan. Returning to academic life, he received his degree from Harvard University *summa cum laude*. He then devoted two years in Paris and three in North Africa to a program of study and research on the Arab and Islamic world, facilitated by Fulbright and Ford fellowships. He joined the AUFS in 1956. A member of the Council on Foreign Relations, he has published articles in Foreign Affairs, the

Middle East Forum, the Virginia Quarterly Review, and other journals.

WILLARD A. HANNA, author of the chapter on Indonesia, is at present on AUFS assignment in Southeast Asia. He has maintained an interest in the Far East since he first went to China in 1932 as a teacher. After four years there he returned to the United States and completed his work for a doctorate in English literature at the University of Michigan. During World War II he served with the U.S. Navy, reaching the rank of Lieutenant Commander. Under Navy auspices he took Japanese language training and earned an M.A. in international administration at Columbia University, and later was Chief of the Military Government Office of Education and Cultural Affairs on Okinawa. In 1946 he entered the U.S. Foreign Service and was Chief Public Affairs Officer in Manila, Djakarta and Tokyo before joining the AUFS in 1954. His published writings include fiction, magazine articles, and a collection of AUFS Reports, *Bung Karno's Indonesia*.

SELIG S. HARRISON, who wrote the chapter on India, has observed South Asian affairs as a journalist and scholar since his assignment in 1951 as Associated Press correspondent covering India, Pakistan, Afghanistan, Ceylon and Nepal. On his return in 1954 he studied Indian civilization at Harvard on a Nieman Fellowship as part of his preparation for a book analyzing problems of national consolidation, *India: The Most Dangerous Decades* (Princeton, 1960). His articles on political developments in South Asia and issues of United States policy have appeared in *Foreign Affairs*, *The American Political Science Review*, *The New Republic*, of which he was an editor from 1956 to 1962, and *The Washington Post*, of which he is currently New Delhi correspondent. In "Case History of a Mistake" and other studies he has advocated an integrated regional policy approach by the United States in South Asia. He edited *India and the United States* (Macmillan, 1960) and contributed to *Leadership and Political Institutions in India* (Princeton, 1960).

EDWIN S. MUNGER, who wrote the chapter on South Africa, has specialized in the affairs of sub-Saharan Africa since 1946 and has written extensively on political, economic and social developments there. He has repeatedly visited every sub-Saharan country and major island and has devoted extended periods to research in Liberia (1947); Uganda (1949), on a Fulbright grant; and Ghana (1951) and Southern Rhodesia (1953), as a Fellow of the Institute of Current World Affairs. He has given special attention to the study of South Africa, having spent some time in that country each year since 1949. He received the Ph.D. in geography from the University of Chicago in 1951 and until 1961 taught a course on Africa there during his periods in the United States. From 1957 to 1961 he was chairman of the Ford Foundation-supported African Universities Program, which gave assistance to emergent institutions on the continent. An Associate of the American Universities Field Staff from 1951 to 1961, Dr. Munger wrote more than one hundred Reports for the AUFS, many of them collected in an 800-page volume (*African Field Reports Annotation: 1952-1961*, Cape Town, C. Struik, 1961). His published work also includes articles in *Foreign Affairs*, the *Encyclopaedia Britannica Atlas*, and numerous journals here and abroad. In 1961 he joined the California Institute of Technology as Professor of Geography and in 1962 became co-director of a three-year Caltech study of economic development in southern Africa.

RICHARD H. NOLTE, author of the chapter on Saudi Arabia, is a student of Islamic law and society, well acquainted with Middle Eastern affairs through study and long periods of residence in the area. He holds a master's degree in international relations from Yale, and with a Rhodes Scholarship continued his studies at Oxford (1947-50) in the Faculty of Oriental Studies, taking his degree with Class I honors. Under the sponsorship of the Institute of Current World Affairs, he made field trips to the Middle East in 1948 and 1950, and lived in Lebanon and Egypt from the spring of 1951 to the fall of 1952. As an AUFS Associate he lived in the area again during the summer of 1954 and in 1956-57, observing and reporting on cultural, social, economic, and political affairs. Mr. Nolte served with the

Rockefeller Foundation as Assistant Director in the Humanities during 1958 and 1959, a position he left to become Executive Director of the Institute of Current World Affairs.

LAWRENCE OLSON, who contributed the chapter on Japan, received his Ph.D. from Harvard University and has taught at the University of Wisconsin and Vassar College. Originally in the field of literature, he focused his interest on the Far East following his experience in the Japanese language program at Boulder, Colorado, and service as a translator with the U.S. Navy for three years during World War II. Subsequently, he held several government posts, including that of Cultural Attaché at the American Embassy in the Philippines, and then returned to Harvard to complete work for the Ph.D. in Japanese history and language. He was a fellow of the Harvard-Yenching Institute and the Ford Foundation Foreign Area Training Program. Since January 1955 he has been reporting on developments in Japan for the AUFS. Among his other writings are poems and criticism which have appeared in numerous magazines, and a volume of poetry, published in 1947.

RICHARD W. PATCH, author of the chapter on Bolivia, is an anthropologist who has made the affairs of Latin America the subject of his research and writing for more than a decade. A former Fellow of the Institute of Current World Affairs, he took his undergraduate work at Deep Springs, California, and at Cornell University, from which he also received the Ph.D. in 1956. He joined the AUFS in 1957 after a year at Tulane University as Visiting Assistant Professor of Anthropology. His return to Latin America in 1960 was his sixth field trip to the Andean area. In 1951-52 he studied industrialization and migration patterns in rural Peru; the next year he engaged in an ethnography of a highland Peruvian Indian community; in 1954-55 he studied Bolivian agrarian reform; in 1956 and again in 1957-59 he surveyed social and economic trends in Peru and Bolivia; in 1960-62 he resumed his study there with attention to urban-rural social interaction and to resettlement trends. He directed a study of colonization for the Bolivian government and

US/AID and was a member of the Inter-American Development Bank Mission for Rural Development to Bolivia.

ALBERT RAVENHOLT, who wrote the chapter on the Philippines, has specialized in the Far East since the beginning of World War II, when he served as a correspondent in China, Burma, India, Indochina, and the Philippines. In 1946, as a Fellow of the Institute of Current World Affairs, he spent a year at Harvard University in advanced study of Far Eastern history and affairs. In 1948 he returned to China and for more than two years observed the changes in Chinese society as the Communists solidified their control of the mainland. His work during that period also took him to Formosa, Hong Kong, and the Philippines. He became associated with the AUFS when it was founded in 1951, and through frequent extended visits to Asia has kept in close touch with political, economic, and social trends as they have developed in the postwar years. Now based in Manila, he writes about Philippine affairs and travels to Hong Kong, Formosa, and countries of Southeast Asia to report on significant developments.

K. H. SILVERT, the general editor and the author of the chapter on Argentina, has combined an interest in political science and in Latin America since his undergraduate days at the University of Pennsylvania, which also awarded him the Ph.D. in 1948. His first major research in Latin America was in Chile during 1947-48, when he held a Penfield Traveling Scholarship. He became closely identified with Central American affairs when he was on the faculty of Tulane University. An intensive study of Guatemalan society, with emphasis on political structure, made during these field trips provided the basis for his two-volume work, *A Study in Government: Guatemala*. After becoming an AUFS Associate in 1955 he revisited Central America under AUFS auspices, in 1956-58 reporting on affairs in Argentina, Chile, and Uruguay, and in 1960-61 directing a major study of the role of education in social and economic development in Latin America. This study was made possible by a grant to the AUFS from the Carnegie Corporation of New York. In addition to his AUFS duties, Mr. Silvert has also served as Professor of Government at Dartmouth College since 1962.

Index

A NOTE ON THE TYPE

The text of this book is set in Monticello, a Linotype revival of the original Binny & Ronaldson Roman No. 1, cut by Archibald Binny and cast in 1796 by that Philadelphia type foundry. The face was named Monticello in honor of its use in the monumental fifty-volume *Papers of Thomas Jefferson*, published by Princeton University Press. Monticello is a transitional type design, embodying certain features of Bulmer and Baskerville, but it is a distinguished face in its own right.